Dynamic Econometric Modeling brings together presentations of some of the fundamental new research that has begun to appear in the areas of dynamic structural modeling, nonlinear structural modeling, time series modeling, nonparametric inference, and chaotic attractor inference. These areas of research have in common a movement away from the use of static structural models in econometrics.

The contents of this volume comprise the proceedings of the third conference in a series entitled *International Symposia in Economic Theory and Econometrics*. This conference was held in 1986 at the IC² (Innovation, Creativity and Capital) Institute at the University of Texas at Austin. The symposia in this series are sponsored by the IC² Institute and the RGK Foundation.

This volume, edited by Professors William A. Barnett, Ernst R. Berndt, and Halbert White, consists of four parts: Part I examines dynamic structural modeling; Part II, linear time series modeling; Part III, chaotic attractor modeling; and Part IV, applications of these models.

Dynamic econometric modeling

International Symposia in Economic Theory and Econometrics

Editor
William A. Barnett, *University of Texas at Austin and Duke University*

Other books in the series
William A. Barnett and Kenneth J. Singleton *New approaches to monetary economics*

Dynamic econometric modeling

Proceedings of the Third International Symposium in Economic Theory and Econometrics

Edited by

WILLIAM A. BARNETT
University of Texas at Austin and Duke University

ERNST R. BERNDT
Massachusetts Institute of Technology

HALBERT WHITE
University of California at San Digeo

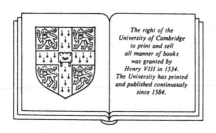

The right of the
University of Cambridge
to print and sell
all manner of books
was granted by
Henry VIII in 1534.
The University has printed
and published continuously
since 1584.

CAMBRIDGE UNIVERSITY PRESS

Cambridge
New York   Port Chester   Melbourne   Sydney

CAMBRIDGE UNIVERSITY PRESS
Cambridge, New York, Melbourne, Madrid, Cape Town, Singapore, São Paulo

Cambridge University Press
The Edinburgh Building, Cambridge CB2 2RU, UK

Published in the United States of America by Cambridge University Press, New York

www.cambridge.org
Information on this title: www.cambridge.org/9780521333955

First published 1988
Reprinted 1989
This digitally printed first paperback version 2005

A catalogue record for this publication is available from the British Library

Library of Congress Cataloguing in Publication data
International Symposium in Economic Theory and Econometrics (3rd: 1986: Austin, Tex.)
Dynamic econometric modeling / proceedings of the Third International Symposium in Economic
Theory and Econometrics; edited by William A. Barnett, Ernst R. Berndt, Halbert White.
p. cm.—(International symposia in economic theory and econometrics)
ISBN 0-521-33395-4
1. Econometric models—Congresses.   I. Barnett, William A.
II. Berndt, Ernst R.   III. White, Halbert.   IV. Title.   V. Series.
HB141.157   1986
330'.028-dc19   87-33958

ISBN-13 978-0-521-33395-5 hardback
ISBN-10 0-521-33395-4 hardback

ISBN-13 978-0-521-02340-5 paperback
ISBN-10 0-521-02340-8 paperback

Contents

Editors' introduction

The contents of this volume comprise the proceedings of a conference held at the IC² Institute at the University of Texas at Austin on May 22–3, 1986.[1] The conference was entitled "Dynamic Econometric Modeling," and was organized to bring together presentations of some of the fundamental new research that has begun to appear in the areas of dynamic structural modeling, time series modeling, nonparametric inference, and chaotic attractor inference. These areas of research have in common a movement away from the use of static linear structural models in econometrics.

The conference that produced this proceedings volume is the third in a new conference series, called *International Symposia in Economic Theory and Econometrics*.[2] The proceedings series is under the general editorship of William A. Barnett. Individual volumes in the series will often have co-editors, and the series has a permanent Board of Advisory Editors. The symposia in the series are sponsored by the IC² Institute at the University of Texas at Austin and are cosponsored by the RGK Foundation.

This third conference also was cosponsored by the Federal Reserve Bank of Dallas and by the Department of Economics, Department of Finance, Graduate School of Business, and Center for Statistical Sciences at the University of Texas at Austin. The first conference in the series was co-organized by William A. Barnett and Ronald Gallant, who also co-edited the proceedings volume. It appeared as the volume 30, October/November 1985 edition of the *Journal of Econometrics*. The topic was "New Approaches to Modelling, Specification Selection, and Econometric Inference."

---

[1] IC² stands for Innovation, Creativity, and Capital.

[2] The title of the series recently was changed from *Austin Symposia in Economics* as a result of the increasingly international nature of the symposia in the series.

Beginning with the second symposium in the series, the proceedings of the symposia appear as volumes in this Cambridge University Press monograph series. The co-organizers of the second symposium and co-editors of its proceedings volume were William A. Barnett and Kenneth J. Singleton. The topic was new approaches to monetary economics. The co-organizers of the third symposium, which produced the current proceedings volume, were William A. Barnett and Ernst R. Berndt; and the coeditors of this proceedings volume are William A. Barnett, Ernst R. Berndt, and Halbert White.

The co-organizers of the fourth symposium, held on May 28–9, 1987 and entitled "Economic Complexity: Chaos, Sunspots, Bubbles, and Non-linearity," are William A. Barnett, John Geweke, and Karl Shell, who are also the coeditors of the proceedings volume. The fifth symposium in the series, on nonparametric and seminonparametric methods, currently is being organized for May 1988 by William A. Barnett, James Powell, George Tauchen, and Jean-François Richard. The sixth symposium will be held at CORE in Belgium and is being organized by William A. Barnett, Jean-François Richard, and Claude D'Aspremont. The topic is general equilibrium theory and applications.

The intention of the volumes in the proceedings series is to provide refereed journal-quality collections of research papers of unusual importance in areas of highly visible current activity within the economics profession. Because of the refereeing requirements associated with the editing of the proceedings, the volumes in the series will not necessarily contain all of the papers presented at the corresponding symposia.

William A. Barnett
*University of Texas at Austin and
Duke University*

Ernst R. Berndt
Massachusetts Institute of Technology

Halbert White
University of California at San Diego

Contributors

Andrew B. Abel
The Wharton School
University of Pennsylvania and
 National Bureau of Economic
 Research

Dennis J. Aigner
Department of Economics
University of Southern California

William A. Barnett
Department of Economics
University of Texas at Austin and
 Duke University

Charles Bates
Department of Political Economy
Johns Hopkins University

Ernst R. Berndt
Sloan School of Management
Massachusetts Institute of Technology

Olivier J. Blanchard
Department of Economics
Massachusetts Institute of Technology

W. A. Brock
Department of Economics
University of Wisconsin

Ping Chen
Department of Economics
University of Texas at Austin

W. D. Dechert
Department of Economics
Rice University

W. Erwin Diewert
Department of Economics
University of British Columbia

Ian Domowitz
Department of Economics
Northwestern University

John Geweke
Department of Economics
Duke University

Damayanti Ghosh
Department of Economics
University of Southern California

Lars Peter Hansen
Department of Economics
University of Chicago

Alberto Holly
Département d'économétrie et
 d'économie politique
Université de Lausanne

Nicholas M. Kiefer
Department of Economics
Cornell University

Agustín Maravall
Servicio de Estudios
Banco de España

Dale T. Mortensen
Department of Economics
Northwestern University

Lars Muus
Department of Economics
Northwestern University

Contributors

George R. Neumann
Department of Economics
University of Iowa

Yaw Nyarko
Department of Economics
Brown University

Lawrence Ostensoe
Department of Economics
University of British Columbia

Georg Michael Rockinger
Département d'économétrie et
    d'économie politique
Université de Lausanne

Peter E. Rossi
Graduate School of Business
University of Chicago

Friedrich Schneider
Department of Economics
University of Linz

Halbert White
Department of Economics
University of California
    at San Diego

Adonis John Yatchew
Department of Economics
University of Toronto

PART I

Dynamic structural modeling

CHAPTER 1

Efficient instrumental variables estimation of systems of implicit heterogeneous nonlinear dynamic equations with nonspherical errors

Charles Bates and Halbert White

1   Introduction

First used by the zoologist Sewall Wright (1925), the method of instrumental variables (IVs) was initially given a formal development by Reiersøl (1941, 1945) and Geary (1949). It is now one of the most useful and widely applied estimation methods of modern econometrics. Major contributions to the early development of this method in econometrics are those of Theil (1953), Basmann (1957), and Sargan (1958) for systems of linear simultaneous equations with independent identically distributed (i.i.d.) errors. A major concern of this development was to make efficient use of the available instrumental variables by finding instrumental variables estimators that have minimal asymptotic variance.

This concern is also evident in the subsequent work of Zellner and Theil (1962), Brundy and Jorgenson (1974), and Sargan (1964), who consider contemporaneous correlation in linear systems; Sargan (1959), Amemiya (1966), Fair (1970), Hansen and Sargent (1982), and Hayashi and Sims (1983), who consider specific forms of serial correlation for errors of linear equations or systems of equations; and Amemiya (1983), Bowden and Turkington (1985), and White (1984, Chapter 7), who consider specific forms of heteroscedasticity. For systems of linear equations White (1984, Chapter 4; 1986) considers general forms of nonsphericality in an instrumental variables context. Investigation of the properties of instrumental variables estimators in nonlinear contexts was undertaken in seminal work

The authors are grateful to William Barnett, Lars Hansen, Alberto Holly, Whitney Newey, Kenneth Singleton, and the participants of the Austin Symposium in Economic Theory and Econometrics for helpful comments. Errors remain the authors' responsibility. Research support for White was provided by NSF grant SES-8510637.

3

by Amemiya (1974, 1977) for single equations and for systems of nonlinear equations with contemporaneous correlation. Further important contributions are those of Barnett (1976), Gallant (1977), Gallant and Jorgenson (1979), and Burguete, Gallant, and Souza (1982). Research initiated by Hansen (1982) has recently culminated in a general and elegant theory of efficient instrumental variables estimation for systems of nonlinear dynamic equations with errors exhibiting general forms of conditional nonsphericality (Hansen 1985).

Hansen's results exploit techniques of Gordin (1969) for approximating stationary ergodic sequences with sums of martingale difference sequences and thus apply directly to models relating stationary ergodic processes. Recent work of Eichenbaum and Hansen (1986) extends Hansen's results to allow for the inclusion of deterministic trends. However, Hansen's approach does not readily lend itself to situations involving heterogeneous time series. Because nonexplosive economic time series cannot be guaranteed to be stationary, it is useful to investigate whether results similar to Hansen's hold for heterogeneous time series. We obtain such results here using the method of Bates and White (1987) to obtain the efficient estimator in an appropriate class of instrumental variables estimators. In the general case of heterogeneous time series processes, one can follow the approach of Gallant and White (in press), who obtain results for IV estimators in the context of near-epoch-dependent functions of mixing processes. The near epoch dependence approach provides an approximation procedure for heterogeneous processes analogous to the martingale difference approximation procedure of Gordin (1969) and Hansen (1985) for stationary ergodic sequences. Our results are formulated so as to allow sample-based transformation procedures. Proofs of results are given in the appendix. We illustrate the content of our results with several simple examples.

2   Nonlinear instrumental variables estimators

In this section we consider a class of nonlinear instrumental variables (NLIV) estimators for the parameters of a system of implicit nonlinear dynamic equations with possibly nonspherical errors. We provide conditions ensuring that the NLIV estimators form a regular consistent asymptotically normal indexed (RCANI) class (Bates and White 1987). We then find the efficient NLIV estimator using Corollary 2.11 of Bates and White.

We first provide definitions that make it possible to specify precisely the models of interest to us. We specify the properties of the exogenous variables and errors determining the dependent variables of interest in the following way.

Definition 2.1. Let $(\Omega, \mathfrak{F})$ be a measurable space, and let $e_{nt} \colon \Omega \to I\!\!R^p$ and $X_{nt} \colon \Omega \to I\!\!R^q$ be functions measurable with respect to $\mathfrak{F}$, $t = 1, \ldots, n$, $n = 1, 2, \ldots$.

We say that $\{(X_{nt}, e_{nt})\}$ *admits a family* $\mathcal{P}$ *of probability measures generating instrumental variable candidates and removable nonsphericalities* if and only if there exists a nonempty collection $\mathcal{P}$ of probability measures P on $(\Omega, \mathfrak{F})$ satisfying the following conditions:

(i) For $t = 1, \ldots, n$, $n = 1, 2, \ldots$, there exists $W_{nt} \colon \Omega \to I\!\!R^{w_{nt}}$, $w_{nt} \in I\!\!N$, measurable-$\mathfrak{F}$ such that with $\mathcal{G}_{nt} \equiv \sigma(W_{nt}) \subset \mathfrak{F}$

$$E(e_{nt} \mid \mathcal{G}_{nt}) = 0 \text{ a.s.-}P$$

and $e_{nth}e_{n\tau g}$ is not measurable-$\mathcal{G}_{nt\tau} \equiv \mathcal{G}_{nt} \vee \mathcal{G}_{n\tau}$ for all $h, g = 1, \ldots, p$; and for any $\tilde{\mathcal{G}}_{nt} \supset \mathcal{G}_{nt}$, $\tilde{\mathcal{G}}_{nt} \subset \mathfrak{F}$, either

$$P[E(e_{nt} \mid \tilde{\mathcal{G}}_{nt}) \neq 0] > 0$$

or $e_{nth}e_{n\tau g}$ is measurable-$\tilde{\mathcal{G}}_{nt\tau} \equiv \tilde{\mathcal{G}}_{nt} \vee \tilde{\mathcal{G}}_{n\tau}$ for some n, t, τ, h, g.

(ii) There exists a matrix function $B_n \colon \Omega \to I\!\!R^{pn \times pn}$ measurable-$\mathfrak{F}$ and nonsingular a.s.-P, $n = 1, 2, \ldots$, such that with $B_n \equiv [b_{nt\tau}]$, $B_n^{-1} \equiv [b_n^{t\tau}]$, $b_{nt\tau} \colon \Omega \to I\!\!R^{p \times p}$ and $b_n^{t\tau} \colon \Omega \to I\!\!R^{p \times p}$ are measurable-$\mathcal{G}_{nt}$, $\tau = 1, \ldots, n$, $n = 1, 2, \ldots$, and with $e_n^* \equiv B_n e_n$, where e_n is the $np \times 1$ vector

$$e_n' = (e_{n11}, \ldots, e_{n1p}, \ldots, e_{nth}, \ldots, e_{nn1}, \ldots, e_{nnp}),$$

there exists $W_{nt}^* \colon \Omega \to I\!\!R^{w_{nt}^*}$, $w_{nt}^* \in I\!\!N$, measurable-$\mathfrak{F}$ such that with $\mathcal{G}_{nt}^* \equiv \sigma(W_{nt}^*)$

$$E(e_{nt}^* \mid \mathcal{G}_{nt}^*) = 0 \text{ a.s.-}P$$

and $e_{nth}^* e_{n\tau g}^*$ is not measurable-$\mathcal{G}_{nt\tau}^* \equiv \mathcal{G}_{nt}^* \vee \mathcal{G}_{n\tau}^*$ for all $h, g = 1, \ldots, p$; and for any $\tilde{\mathcal{G}}_{nt}^* \supset \mathcal{G}_{nt}^*$, $\tilde{\mathcal{G}}_{nt}^* \subset \mathfrak{F}$, either

$$P[E(e_{nt}^* \mid \tilde{\mathcal{G}}_{nt}^*) \neq 0] > 0$$

or $e_{nth}^* e_{n\tau g}^*$ is measurable-$\tilde{\mathcal{G}}_{nt\tau}^* \equiv \tilde{\mathcal{G}}_{nt}^* \vee \tilde{\mathcal{G}}_{n\tau}^*$ for some n, t, τ, h, g. Further,

$$\mathcal{G}_{nt} = \bigwedge_{\{1 \leq \tau \leq n, 1 \leq g \leq p \colon P[b_n^{\tau tgh} \neq 0] > 0\}} \mathcal{G}_{n\tau}^*, \quad h = 1, \ldots, p,$$

and

$$E(e_{nt}^* e_{n\tau}^{*\prime} \mid \mathcal{G}_{nt\tau}^*) = \Sigma_{nt}^* 1[t = \tau] \text{ a.s.-}P,$$

where Σ_{nt}^* is nonsingular a.s.-P and $P[E(e_{nt}^* e_{n\tau}^{*\prime} \mid \tilde{\mathcal{G}}_{nt\tau}^*) \neq \Sigma_{nt}^*] > 0$ for $\tilde{\mathcal{G}}_{nt}^* \subset \mathcal{G}_{nt}^*$ for some n, t. $\qquad \square$

Heuristically, the errors e_{nt} admit instrumental variables candidates W_{nt}, that is, $E(e_{nt} \mid W_{nt}) = 0$, and also possess possible nonsphericalities in that $E(e_{nt} e_{n\tau}' \mid W_{nt}, W_{n\tau}) \neq I_p 1[t \neq \tau]$ with positive probability. These nonsphericalities may include autocorrelation, heteroscedasticity, and/or contemporaneous correlation. At this point, the available number of instrumental variables candidates is not critical. Although there may well be available strictly exogenous random variables $\{X_{nt}\}$ that can serve as instrumental variables in the presence of serially correlated errors, the constant unity [which generates the trivial information set $(\Omega, \varnothing)$] is always available.

The transformation B_n "removes" correlation between the errors in such a way that the elements e_{nt}^* of the transformed errors $e_n^* = B_n e_n$ share a common set of instrumental variables candidates W_{nt}^* and exhibit only possible heteroscedasticity and/or contemporaneous correlation conditional on this set of instrumental variables candidates. The instrumental variables candidates W_{nt}^* may contain more information than W_{nt}. Thus, one may be able to use predetermined rather than only strictly exogenous variables as instrumental variables candidates after a suitable transformation.

In particular contexts (recursive systems of structural equations or panel observations in which dynamics are important), a different set of instrumental variables candidates may be available for each observation. In such cases, the analogous results obtain after an additional transformation, yielding the complete set of instrumental variables candidates W_{nth}^{**}. Alternatively, analogous results obtain by first removing serial correlation (across t) and then applying the theory given here with observations reindexed so that $p = 1$. We do not treat this case explicitly because of the unwieldy notation required.

In contrast to the case for the untransformed errors, the information content of the instrumental variables candidates with respect to the transformed errors turns out to be important, as indicated in what follows.

We now specify how the dependent variables Y_{nt} are generated.

Definition 2.2. Let Θ be a compact subset of $\mathbb{R}^k$, $k \in \mathbb{N}$, and let F_{nt}: $\mathbb{R}^{tp} \times \mathbb{R}^{nq} \times \Theta \to \mathbb{R}^p$ define the sequence Y_{nt}: $\Theta \to \mathbb{R}^p$, $t = 1, \ldots, n$, uniquely by the implicit relation

$$e_{nt} = F_{nt}(Y_n^t(\theta), X_n^n, \theta), \quad t = 1, \ldots, n, \; n = 1, 2, \ldots,$$

with $X_n^n \equiv (X_{n1}, \ldots, X_{nn})$ and $Y_n^t \equiv (Y_{n1}, \ldots, Y_{nt})$, where F_{nt} is such that there exists G_{nt}: $\mathbb{R}^{tp} \times \mathbb{R}^{nq} \times \Theta \to \mathbb{R}^p$ for which

$$Y_{nt}(\theta) = G_{nt}(e_n^t, X_n^n, \theta), \quad t = 1, \ldots, n, \; n = 1, 2, \ldots,$$

where for each θ in Θ, $G_{nt}(\cdot, \cdot, \theta)$ is measurable-$\mathcal{B}$ $(\mathbb{R}^{tp} \times \mathbb{R}^{nq})$.

Then we say that $\{F_{nt}, X_{nt}, e_{nt}\}$ *implicitly determines* $\{Y_{nt}\}$. $\square$

This is a fairly standard system of nonlinear implicit simultaneous equations, except for the dependence of all the functions on n. Note that dynamics are allowed by letting all lags of Y_{nt} appear in F_{nt}. Further dynamics are allowed by letting e_{nt} be autocorrelated. The "strictly exogenous" variables X_{nt} are allowed to enter at all lags and leads, although it is not necessary to have all of these. The index t appearing on G_{nt} and F_{nt} allows given initial values to enter the determination of Y_{nt}, and also allows for the heterogeneity introduced by regime changes.

The model of interest is obtained by letting the underlying probability measure and parameters of interest range over the relevant values.

Definition 2.3. Let $(\Omega, \mathfrak{F})$ be a measurable space and let $\Theta \subseteq \mathbb{R}^k$, $k \in \mathbb{N}$, as in the preceding. Let $\mathcal{P}$ be a family of probability measures on $(\Omega, \mathfrak{F})$.

We say that $(\mathcal{P} \times \Theta)$ *induces a regular probability model* $\mathcal{Q} = \{\mathcal{Q}_n\}$ *for* $\{Y_{nt}\}$ *with instrumental variable candidates and removable nonsphericalities* if and only if $\{Y_{nt}\}$ is determined implicitly by $\{F_{nt}, X_{nt}, e_{nt}\}$ and $\{X_{nt}, e_{nt}\}$ admits the family $\mathcal{P}$ generating instrumental variable candidates and removable nonsphericalities, where for each element (P^o, θ^o) of $\mathcal{P} \times \text{int } \Theta$:

(i) $\epsilon_{nt}^o(\cdot) \equiv F_{nt}(Y_n^t(\theta^o), X_n^n, \cdot)$ is continuously differentiable on Θ a.s.- P^o, $t = 1, \ldots, n$, $n = 1, 2, \ldots$;

(ii) there exist measurable functions $Z_{nth}: \Omega \to \mathbb{R}^k$, $h = 1, \ldots, p$, $t = 1, \ldots, n$, $n = 1, 2, \ldots$, such that the rows $\ddot{Z}_{nth}$ of $\ddot{Z}_n \equiv B_n'^{-1} Z_n$ (where Z_n has rows Z_{nth}) are measurable-$\mathcal{G}_{nt}^*$ and for which

(a) $Z_n' \epsilon_n^o(\theta) - \bar{\psi}_n^o(\theta) \to^{P^o} 0$ uniformly on Θ, where $\bar{\psi}_n^o(\theta) \equiv E^o(Z_n' \epsilon_n^o(\theta)/n)$ is $O(1)$,
(b) $V_n^{o-1/2} n^{-1/2} Z_n' e_n \sim^{A^o} N(0, I_k)$, where $V_n^o \equiv \text{var}^o[n^{-1/2} Z_n' e_n]$ is $O(1)$ and uniformly positive definite, and
(c) $Z_n' \nabla \epsilon_n^o(\theta) - \nabla \bar{\psi}_n^o(\theta) \to^{P^o} 0$ uniformly on Θ, where $\nabla \bar{\psi}_n^o(\theta) \equiv E^o(Z_n' \nabla \epsilon_n^o(\theta)/n)$ is $O(1)$;

(iii) for Z_n as in (ii)

(a) $\bar{\psi}_n^o(\theta)$ satisfies the generalized rank condition at θ^o;
(b) $\nabla \bar{\psi}_n^o(\theta^o)$ is nonsingular uniformly in n.

The probability model $\mathcal{Q}_n$ is the set of all probability measures for $\{Y_n^n(\theta), X_n^n\}$ on $(\mathbb{R}^{pn} \times \mathbb{R}^{qn}, \mathbb{B}(\mathbb{R}^{pn} \times \mathbb{R}^{qn}))$ induced by letting P range over $\mathcal{P}$ and θ over int Θ. The parameters of interest are defined by the mapping $\mathfrak{J}: \mathfrak{M} \to \text{int } \Theta$, where $\mathfrak{M}$ is the space of sequences of probability measures $\mathcal{Q}_n$ on $(\mathbb{R}^{pn} \times \mathbb{R}^{qn}, \mathbb{B}(\mathbb{R}^{pn} \times \mathbb{R}^{qn}))$ for which $\mathfrak{J}(\{\mathcal{Q}_n\}) = \theta$ for any sequence $\{Q_n\}$ such that Q_n is induced by a given $\theta \in \Theta$ for any element P in $\mathcal{P}$. □

In this definition, the notations E^o, var^o, and $\sim^{A^o}$ refer to expectation, variance, and convergence in distribution, respectively, under P^o. The "regularity" imposed in this definition is a set of conditions ensuring that there exists a consistent, asymptotically normal NLIV estimator

$$\hat{\theta}_{n,\text{NLIV}} \equiv \text{argmin } \epsilon_n(\theta)' Z_n V_n^- Z_n' \epsilon_n(\theta),$$

where $\epsilon_n(\theta) \equiv [F_{nt}(Y_n^t, X_n^n, \theta)]$ and V_n^- is a generalized inverse for V_n (e.g., the Moore–Penrose inverse) provided that V_n has the property that $V_n - V_n^o \to^{P^o} 0$ for all (P^o, θ^o) in $\mathcal{P} \times \text{int } \Theta$.

This NLIV estimator is easily recognized as a particular form of the generalized method of moments (GMM) estimator (Hansen 1982), arrived at by focusing on moment conditions $E^o(Z_n' e_n) = 0$ and by explicitly using V_n^- in forming the objective function defining the estimator. Use of V_n^- yields a minimum χ^2 estimator, which is known to give the efficient estimator for a given choice of instruments (Hansen 1982; White 1982; Bates and White 1987). These restrictions allow us to focus attention directly on choosing the instruments.

The instruments of interest are specified in condition 2.3(ii) as satisfying particular measurability requirements. To indicate the possibilities allowed by this condition, we give the following result.

Proposition 2.4. *Let $Z_n = A_n S_n$, where A_n is an $np \times np$ matrix with $A_n \equiv [a_{nt\tau}]$, $a_{nt\tau} \equiv [a_{nt\tau hg}]$, such that $a_{nt\tau hg}$ is measurable-$\mathcal{G}_{n\tau}$, h, $g = 1, \ldots, p$, $t = 1, \ldots, n$, and S_n is an $np \times k$ matrix with typical row S_{nth}.*

Suppose either that $A_n = B_n'$ and S_{nth} is measurable-$\mathcal{G}_{nt}^*$ or that S_{nth} is measurable-$\mathcal{G}_{nt}$ and $C_n \equiv B_n'^{-1} A_n$ is such that $P[c_{nt\tau hg} \neq 0] > 0$ if and only if $P[b_n^{\tau tgh} \neq 0] > 0$, where

$$C_n \equiv [c_{nt\tau}], \qquad c_{nt\tau} \equiv [c_{nt\tau hg}], \qquad c_{nt\tau hg} = \sum_{\lambda=1}^{n} \sum_{\gamma=1}^{p} b_n^{\lambda t \gamma h} a_{n\lambda\tau\gamma g}.$$

Then $\ddot{Z}_n = B_n'^{-1} Z_n$ has rows $\ddot{Z}_{nth}$ that are measurable-$\mathcal{G}_{nt}^*$, $h = 1, \ldots, p$, $t = 1, \ldots, n$, $n = 1, 2, \ldots$. □

This proposition establishes that instruments satisfying 2.3(ii) may be formed either as specific linear combinations of functions of the instrumental variables candidates compatible with the transformed errors $e_n^* = B_n e_n$ ($A_n = B_n'$, S_{nth} measurable-$\mathcal{G}_{nt}^*$) or as linear combinations of functions of the instrumental variables candidates compatible with the untransformed errors. A key restriction in this latter case is that C_n must have zeros in the same locations as B_n'. In particular, if B_n is lower triangular, C_n must be upper triangular. This is guaranteed if A_n is upper triangular.

Primitive conditions ensuring the convergences in condition 2.3(ii.a–c) will differ from case to case depending on the behavior of the specific stochastic processes involved. The following result uses definitions and results of Gallant and White (in press) to give primitive conditions ensuring 2.3(ii.a–c) in the general context of dependent heterogeneous double arrays.

Proposition 2.5. *Let $\mathcal{P}$ and Θ be as previously given, let $\{F_{nt}, X_{nt}, e_{nt}\}$ implicitly determine $\{Y_{nt}\}$, and let $V_t: \Omega \to \mathbb{R}^v$, $v \in \mathbb{N}$, be measurable-$\mathcal{F}$, $t = 1, \dots$. Suppose condition 2.4(i) holds and that for all P^o in $\mathcal{P}$ $\{V_t\}$ is a mixing process with either ϕ_m of size $-r/(r-1)$ or α_m of size $-2r/(r-2)$, $r > 2$. If for each (P^o, θ^o) in $\mathcal{P} \times \mathrm{int}\,\Theta$ the elements of $Z_{nth}' \epsilon_{nth}(\theta)$ and of $Z_{nth}' \nabla \epsilon_{nth}^o(\theta)$ are*

(a) *r-dominated on Θ with respect to P^o uniformly in $t = 1, \dots, n$, $n = 1, 2, \dots, r > 2$ for $h = 1, \dots, p$;*
(b) *Lipschitz-L_1 a.s.-P^o;*
(c) *near-epoch-dependent-P^o on $\{V_t\}$ of size -1 uniformly on $(\Theta, |\cdot|)$; and*
(d) *$V_n^o \equiv \mathrm{var}^o(n^{-1/2} Z_n' e_n)$ is $O(1)$ and uniformly positive definite,*

then conditions 2.3(ii.a–c) hold. $\qquad\square$

In less general settings, one may be able to state weaker moment and/or smoothness conditions ensuring 2.3(ii.a–c).

Conditions 2.3(iii.a, b) are fundamental identification conditions for θ^o [see Bates and White (1985) for the generalized rank conditions] ensuring that there are "enough" instrumental variables.

In general, there will exist more than one consistent asymptotically normal NLIV estimator. We consider the following class of all such NLIV estimators.

Definition 2.6. Let $(\mathcal{P} \times \Theta)$ induce a regular probability model $\mathcal{Q}$ for $\{Y_{nt}\}$ with instrumental variables candidates and removable nonsphericalities.

Let Γ_n be the set of all functions $\hat{Z}_n: \Omega \to \mathbb{R}^{pn \times k}$ measurable-$\mathcal{F}$, $n = 1, 2, \dots$, and denote a typical element of Γ_n as $\gamma_n = \hat{Z}_n$.

The class of regular NLIV estimators $\mathcal{E}_{\mathrm{NLIV}}(\Gamma, \mathcal{Q}, \mathfrak{Z})$ is the set of all sequences $\hat{\theta}_{\mathrm{NLIV}} = \{\hat{\theta}_n(\gamma_n, \cdot): \Omega \to \mathbb{R}^k\}$ such that

$$\hat{\theta}_n(\gamma_n, \cdot) \equiv \mathrm{argmin}_\Theta\, \epsilon_n(\theta)' \hat{Z}_n \hat{V}_n(\gamma_n)^- \hat{Z}_n' \epsilon_n(\theta)$$

for $\gamma \equiv \{\gamma_n\} \in \Gamma \subseteq \Gamma^\infty \equiv \times_{n=1}^\infty \Gamma_n$, where Γ is the set of all sequences γ in Γ^∞ such that for all (P^o, θ^o) in $\mathcal{P} \times \text{int } \Theta$

(i) $n^{-1}(\hat{Z}_n'\epsilon_n^o(\theta) - Z_n'\epsilon_n^o(\theta)) \to^{P^o} 0$ uniformly on Θ;

(ii) $n^{-1}(\hat{Z}_n'\nabla\epsilon_n^o(\theta) - Z_n'\nabla\epsilon_n^o(\theta)) \to^{P^o} 0$ uniformly on Θ;

(iii) $n^{-1/2}(\hat{Z}_n'e_n - Z_n'e_n) \to^{P^o} 0$; and

(iv) $\hat{V}_n(\gamma_n)^- - V_n^{o-1} \to^{P^o} 0$,

where $\{Z_n : \Omega \to \mathbb{R}^{pn \times k}\}$ is a sequence satisfying conditions 2.3(ii) and 2.3(iii) and $\hat{V}_n(\gamma_n) : \Omega \to \mathbb{R}^{k \times k}$ is measurable-$\mathcal{F}$ for each $\gamma_n \in \Gamma_n$, $n = 1, 2, \dots$. $\square$

The convergence conditions 2.6(i)–(iv) permit sample-based procedures in which feasible NLIV estimators are constructed in several stages. A typical situation occurs when parametric models for the conditional covariance structure of e_n are posited and estimated, as in the method of three-stage least squares or as in the heteroscedastic error model of White (1980), in which variances differ across cross-sectional groups. Unknown parameters may also be embedded in the expression for the desired instruments, as in the binary endogenous variable example of White (1986). The present conditions allow for their estimation in a prior stage as well.

Although parametric models are often useful in prior stages, it may be possible to use nonparametric techniques in arriving at $\hat{Z}_n$, as in Newey (1986) and Robinson (1987). Given the usual stage of ignorance in economics, such techniques might be very useful indeed. Conditions 2.6(i)–(iv) permit the use of appropriately regular nonparametric methods in constructing instruments.

Essentially, these conditions ensure that $\hat{Z}_n$ functions in a manner asymptotically equivalent to non-sample-based instruments Z_n, constructed in a manner compatible with the conditions of Definition 2.3. Note that a given sequence $\{Z_n\}$ is associated with a particular element γ of Γ, although we usually leave this dependence implicit for notational convenience.

The conditions of Definition 2.6 ensure that the class of NLIV estimators is a regular consistent asymptotically normal indexed (RCANI) class, as defined by Bates and White (1987, Definition 2.3). This is formally stated as follows.

Theorem 2.7.   *The class of regular NLIV estimators* $\mathcal{E}_{\text{NLIV}}(\Gamma, \mathcal{Q}, \mathcal{I})$ *is a RCANI class, with*

$$C_n^o(\gamma)^{-1/2}(\hat{\theta}_n(\gamma_n, \cdot) - \theta^o) \overset{A^o}{\sim} N(0, I_k),$$

where

$$C_n^o(\gamma) \equiv \nabla \tilde{\psi}_n^o(\gamma)'^{-1} V_n^o(\gamma) \nabla \tilde{\psi}_n^o(\gamma)^{-1},$$

$$\nabla \tilde{\psi}_n^o(\gamma) \equiv E^o(Z_n(\gamma)' \nabla \epsilon_n^o(\theta^o)/n). \qquad \square$$

Bates and White (1987) define the asymptotically efficient estimator in a RCANI class as one having a maximal concentration property (their Definition 2.7) and show that this is equivalent to having the smallest asymptotic covariance matrix (their Theorem 2.8) in the usual sense. Theorem 2.9 and Corollary 2.11 of Bates and White (1987) make it possible to find the efficient estimator in a RCANI class. In the present case we have the following result.

Theorem 2.8. *Suppose that* $\hat{\theta}_{\mathrm{NLIV}}^* \in \mathcal{E}_{\mathrm{NLIV}}(\Gamma, \mathcal{Q}, \mathcal{J})$, *where* $\hat{\theta}_{\mathrm{NLIV}}^* = \{\hat{\theta}_n^*\}$,

$$\hat{\theta}_n^* \equiv \mathrm{argmin}_{\Theta} \, \epsilon_n(\theta)' \hat{Z}_n^* \hat{V}_n^{*-} \hat{Z}_n^{*\prime} \epsilon_n(\theta)$$

with $\hat{Z}_n^*$ *such that conditions 2.6(i)–(iv) hold with* $Z_n^* \equiv [Z_{nt}^*]$ *given by*

$$Z_{nt}^* = \sum_{\tau=1}^{n} b_{n\tau t} \Sigma_{n\tau}^{*-1} E^o(\nabla \epsilon_{n\tau}^*(\theta^o) \,|\, \mathcal{G}_{n\tau}^*),$$

where $\nabla \epsilon_n^*(\theta^o) \equiv [\nabla \epsilon_{nt}^*(\theta^o)] = B_n \nabla \epsilon_n^o(\theta^o)$.
Then $\hat{\theta}_{\mathrm{NLIV}}^*$ *is the efficient NLIV estimator. In particular,*

$$\mathrm{avar}^o \, \hat{\theta}_{\mathrm{NLIV}}^* = E^o(\nabla \epsilon_n^o(\theta^o)' \Omega_n^{-1} \nabla \epsilon_n^o(\theta^o)/n)^{-1},$$

where $\Omega_n \equiv B_n^{-1} \Sigma_n^* B_n'^{-1}$. $\qquad \square$

The formula for $\mathrm{avar}^o \, \hat{\theta}_{\mathrm{NLIV}}^*$ gives an asymptotic variance bound identical to that found by Hansen (1985). Whereas Hansen's result applies to stationary ergodic processes, the present results apply to heterogeneous and/or dependent sequences. Note the clear similarity to the formula for the variance of the GLS estimator [replace $\nabla \epsilon_n^o(\theta^o)$ with X].

An efficient estimator that is not necessarily feasible obtains by setting $\hat{Z}_n^* = Z_n^*$, $\hat{V}_n^* = V_n^o$. Leaving feasibility aside for the moment, we see that in the context of Proposition 2.4, the best choice for A_n is B_n', which removes correlations in e_n, and the best choice for $S_{n\tau}$ is $\Sigma_{n\tau}^{*-1} E^o(\nabla \epsilon_{n\tau}^*(\theta^o) \,|\, \mathcal{G}_{n\tau}^*)$, which is measurable-$\mathcal{G}_{n\tau}^*$, as required. Note that $\Sigma_{n\tau}^{*-1}$ is acting to remove heteroscedasticity and/or contemporaneous correlation conditional on the instrumental variables candidates for the transformed series e_n^*.

A useful feature of the present result is that it specifies (an equivalence class of) feasible estimators that may achieve the efficiency bound. We see how this is possible in the next section.

Note that the result does not guarantee that the efficient estimator exists in the class of NLIV estimators. However, in specific contexts it is usually straightforward to construct regularity conditions that will ensure the existence of the efficient estimator.

3   Examples

To illustrate the content of Theorem 2.8, we briefly discuss some simple examples: a probit model with latent errors exhibiting serial correlation, an ARCH(1) model, and an ARMA(1, 1) model with conditional heteroscedasticity. To keep things simple, we do not discuss detailed regularity conditions. We content ourselves with examining the form of the efficient estimator should it exist and considering how one might obtain feasible efficient estimators.

First, consider a latent scalar variable Y_t^* generated as

$$Y_t^* = X_t \beta_o + v_t,$$

$$v_t = \sum_{\tau=1}^p \alpha_\tau v_{t-\tau} + \eta_t, \quad t = 1, 2, \ldots,$$

where $\{\eta_t\}$ is i.i.d. $N(0, 1)$ and X_t is independent of η_τ for all $t, \tau = 1, 2, \ldots$. We do not observe Y_t^*. Instead we observe $Y_t = 1[Y_t^* > 0]$. This model is similar to those considered by Gourieroux, Monfort, and Trognon (1985) (GMT) and more recently by Poirier and Ruud (1987).

For this model, maximum-likelihood estimation is intractable, but it is known that probit estimation of β_o ignoring serial correlation is consistent (GMT). Poirier and Rudd (1987) propose an interesting class of quasi-maximum-likelihood estimators (QMLE's) with improved efficiency for this model. Using Theorem 2.8, we can derive an optimal NLIV estimator analogous to the QMLE of Poirier and Ruud.

In the present case $\theta = \beta$ and $e_t = \epsilon_t(\beta_o)$, with

$$\epsilon_t(\theta) = Y_t - \Phi(X_t \beta),$$

where Φ is the unit normal cumulative distribution function (c.d.f.). Because $\{X_t\}$ is strictly exogenous, the instrumental variables candidates generate the information set $\mathcal{G} = \sigma(\ldots, X_{t-1}, X_t, X_{t+1}, \ldots)$. To find an appropriate transformation B_n, we consider $\Sigma_n \equiv [\sigma_{t\tau}]$, where

$$\sigma_{t\tau} = E(e_t e_\tau \mid \mathcal{G})$$
$$= \Psi(X_t \beta_o, X_\tau \beta_o; \rho_{t-\tau}) - \Phi(X_t \beta_o) \Phi(X_\tau \beta_o),$$

with $\Psi(\cdot, \cdot; \rho)$ representing the bivariate normal c.d.f. with correlation coefficient ρ. Here $\rho_\tau \equiv E(v_t v_{t-\tau})$.

It can be readily verified that letting B_n be a Choleski factorization of Σ_n^{-1} (i.e., $B_n' B_n = \Sigma_n^{-1}$) gives transformed errors $e_n^* = B_n e_n$ satisfying the conditions of Definition 2.1 with $\mathcal{G}_{nt}^* = \mathcal{G}$. (A larger information set is available, essentially containing past values of e_{nt}^*; however, the conditional covariances of e_{nt}^* are not affected by this information – this is the relevance of the last condition of Definition 2.1.) With this choice for B_n, we have

$$E(e_{nt}^* e_{n\tau}^{*\prime} \mid \mathcal{G}) = 1[t = \tau].$$

Now $\nabla\epsilon_t(\theta) = -X_t \phi(X_t \beta)$, so that $E(\nabla\epsilon_t(\theta_o) \mid \mathcal{G}) = -X_t \phi(X_t \beta_o)$, where ϕ is the unit normal density function. Letting $S_n = [-X_t \phi(X_t \beta_o)]$, it follows from Theorem 2.8 that the optimal instruments are of the form

$$Z_n^* = \Sigma_n^{-1} S_n,$$

so that an efficient NLIV estimator is

$$\hat{\theta}_n^* = \operatorname{argmin}_\Theta \epsilon_n(\theta)' \Sigma_n^{-1} S_n [E(S_n' \Sigma_n^{-1} S_n)]^{-1} S_n' \Sigma_n^{-1} \epsilon_n(\theta).$$

This is readily interpreted as a nonlinear generalized least-squares (GLS) estimator, with asymptotic variance $[E(S_n' \Sigma_n^{-1} S_n)/n]^{-1}$.

As is typically the case, this estimator is not feasible. It appears, however, that replacing β_o and the elements of Σ_n^{-1} with consistent estimates does provide the basis for an efficient feasible estimator. As mentioned at the outset, we do not verify the sufficient regularity conditions for this here but only consider how consistent estimates may be obtained.

We have already noted that a consistent estimate for β_o is available (ordinary probit). To construct a consistent estimator of $\Sigma_n = [\sigma_{t\tau}]$, one may obtain consistent estimates of $\sigma_{t\tau}$ using the feasible nonlinear regressions

$$Y_t Y_{t-\tau} = \Psi(X_t \hat{\beta}_n, X_{t-\tau} \hat{\beta}_n; \rho_\tau) + u_{nt}, \quad \tau = 1, \ldots, p,$$

where ρ_τ is estimated by grid search or other methods (see GMT), $\tau = 1, \ldots, p$. The Yule–Walker equations are then used to solve for estimates $\hat{\alpha}_\tau$. These then imply estimates for ρ_τ, $\tau > p$. For the case $p = 1$, this gives an estimator asymptotically equivalent to that of the example given by Poirier and Ruud (1987).

Now consider an ARCH (Engle 1982) data-generating process

$$Y_t = X_t \beta_o + u_t,$$

$$E(u_t \mid \mathcal{F}^{t-1}) = 0, \qquad E(u_t^2 \mid \mathcal{F}^{t-1}) \equiv h_t = \gamma_o + \delta_o u_{t-1}^2,$$

$$E(u_t^3 \mid \mathcal{F}^{t-1}) = 0, \qquad E(u_t^4 \mid \mathcal{F}^{t-1}) = \alpha_o h_t^2,$$

where $\mathcal{F}^{t-1} = \sigma(\ldots, X_{t-1}, Y_{t-1}, X_t)$. This formulation is a slight extension of those of Engle (1982) and Bollerslev (1985), who postulate specific conditional distributions for the error process $\{u_t\}$. Here we specify only the conditional moments up to order 4. When the conditional distributions are normal, $\alpha_o = 3$. Bollerslev (1985) considers conditional t_v distributions (degrees of freedom $= v$). For this case $\alpha_o = 3(v-2)/(v-4)$.

The residuals of the relevant model can be written as

$$\epsilon_{t1}(\theta) = Y_t - X_t\beta,$$

$$\epsilon_{t2}(\theta) = (Y_t - X_t\beta)^2 - \gamma - \delta(Y_{t-1} - X_{t-1}\beta)^2,$$

where now $\theta = (\beta, \gamma, \delta)$ and $e_t \equiv (\epsilon_{t1}(\theta_o), \epsilon_{t2}(\theta_o))'$. Construction of the model by stacking models of different conditional moments is similar to an approach proposed by MaCurdy (1982). Given the assumptions on u_t, the instrumental variables candidates generate the information set $\mathcal{F}^{t-1} = \sigma(\ldots, X_{t-1}, Y_{t-1}, X_t)$. Because

$$E(\epsilon_t(\theta_o)\epsilon_\tau(\theta_o) \mid \mathcal{F}^{t-1}) = 0, \quad \tau < t,$$

under the assumptions on u_t, we choose $\mathcal{G}_{nt}^* = \mathcal{F}^{t-1}$, with $B_n = I_n$. To obtain the optimal instrumental variables, we require

$$\Sigma_{nt}^* = E(\epsilon_t(\theta_o)\epsilon_t(\theta_o)' \mid \mathcal{F}^{t-1})$$

and

$$E(\nabla\epsilon_t(\theta_o) \mid \mathcal{F}^{t-1}).$$

It is readily verified that

$$E(\epsilon_{t1}(\theta_o)^2 \mid \mathcal{F}^{t-1}) = E(u_t^2 \mid \mathcal{F}^{t-1}) = h_t,$$

$$E(\epsilon_{t1}(\theta_o)\epsilon_{t2}(\theta_o) \mid \mathcal{F}^{t-1}) = E(u_t(u_t^2 - h_t) \mid \mathcal{F}^{t-1}) = 0,$$

$$E(\epsilon_{t2}(\theta_o)^2 \mid \mathcal{F}^{t-1}) = E([u_t^2 - h_t]^2 \mid \mathcal{F}^{t-1}) = (\alpha_o - 1)h_t^2,$$

so that

$$\Sigma_{nt}^* = \begin{bmatrix} h_t & 0 \\ 0 & (\alpha_o - 1)h_t^2 \end{bmatrix}.$$

Because

$$\nabla\epsilon_{t1}(\theta) = [-X_t, 0, 0],$$

$$\nabla\epsilon_{t2}(\theta) = [-2X_t(Y_t - X_t\beta) + 2\delta X_{t-1}(Y_{t-1} - X_{t-1}\beta), 1, -(Y_{t-1} - X_{t-1}\beta)^2],$$

we have

$$E(\nabla\epsilon_{t1}(\theta_o) \mid \mathcal{F}^{t-1}) = [-X_t, 0, 0],$$

$$E(\nabla\epsilon_{t2}(\theta_o) \mid \mathcal{F}^{t-1}) = [2\delta_o X_{t-1}u_{t-1}, 1, -u_{t-1}^2].$$

This implies that the optimal instrumental variables are of the form

$$Z^*_{nt1} = [-X_t h_t^{-1}, 0, 0],$$
$$Z^*_{nt2} = [2\delta_o X_{t-1} u_{t-1} h_t^{-2}(\alpha_o - 1)^{-1}, h_t^{-2}(\alpha_o - 1)^{-1}, -u_{t-1}^2 h_t^{-2}(\alpha_o - 1)^{-1}].$$

Because these optimal instrumental variables contain the unknown paramaters α_o, β_o, γ_o, and δ_o, the associated estimator is not feasible. However, it appears that a feasible efficient estimator can be obtained by replacing these unknown parameters with consistent estimates. A consistent estimate of β_o is given by the ordinary least-squares (OLS) estimator $\hat{\beta} = (X'X)^{-1}X'Y$. Forming $\hat{u}_t = Y_t - X_t \hat{\beta}$, consistent estimates $\hat{\gamma}$ and $\hat{\delta}$ for γ_o and δ_o can be obtained by regressing $\hat{u}_t^2$ on $\hat{u}_{t-1}^2$ and a constant. Finally, a consistent estimate of α_o can be obtained as the average of $\hat{u}_t^4/\hat{h}_t^2$, where $\hat{h}_t = \hat{\gamma} + \hat{\delta}\hat{u}_{t-1}^2$.

Finally, consider the case in which $\{Y_t\}$ is generated by an ARMA(1,1) process with conditional heteroscedasticity, so that

$$Y_t = \rho_o Y_{t-1} + e_t, \qquad e_t = \eta_t - \alpha_o \eta_{t-1},$$
$$E(\eta_t \mid \mathcal{F}^{t-1}) = 0, \qquad E(\eta_t^2 \mid \mathcal{F}^{t-1}) = h_t, \quad t = 1, 2, \dots,$$

where $\mathcal{F}^{t-1} = (Y_o, \eta_o, \dots, \eta_{t-1})$. For simplicity, we assume that h_t is known. When it is of known form up to some unknown parameters, analysis similar to that for the ARCH model is relevant.

If we consider a model with residuals of the form

$$\epsilon_t(\theta) = Y_t - \rho Y_{t-1},$$

where now $\theta = \rho$, we have

$$E(\epsilon_t(\theta_o) \mid \mathcal{F}^{t-\tau}) = E(e_t \mid \mathcal{F}^{t-\tau}) = 0 \quad \text{for all } \tau \geq 2.$$

However, the information sets $\mathcal{F}^{t-\tau}$ are not suitable as choices for $\mathcal{G}_{nt}$ because they create difficulties in finding the transformation B_n. A choice for $\mathcal{G}_{nt}$ that creates no such difficulties is $\mathcal{G}_{nt} = (\Omega, \varnothing)$, the trivial σ-field. For this choice we have $E(e_t \mid \mathcal{G}_{nt}) = E(e_t) = 0$ and for $t \geq 2$

$$E(e_t^2 \mid \mathcal{G}_{nt}) = E(e_t^2) = 1 + \alpha_o^2,$$
$$E(e_t e_{t-1} \mid \mathcal{G}_{nt}) = E(e_t e_{t-1}) = -\alpha_o,$$
$$E(e_t e_{t-\tau} \mid \mathcal{G}_{nt}) = E(e_t e_{t-\tau}) = 0, \quad \tau \geq 2.$$

A choice for B_n that "removes" this autocorrelation in e_t is the lower triangular matrix

$$B_n = \begin{bmatrix} 1 & 0 & \cdots & & & 0 \\ \alpha_o & 1 & 0 & \cdots & & 0 \\ \alpha_o^2 & \alpha_o & 1 & 0 & \cdots & 0 \\ \vdots & & & & & \vdots \\ \alpha_o^{n-1} & \alpha_o^{n-2} & \cdots & & & 1 \end{bmatrix},$$

provided for convenience that $e_1 = \eta_1$ [so that $E(e_1^2) = 1$]. This can be ensured by suitable choice of starting value Y_o. For simplicity, we assume this can be appropriately chosen. Note that because the elements of B_n and B_n^{-1} are constants, they are all appropriately measurable.

It is readily verified that with $e_n^* = B_n e_n$, $e_{nt}^* = \eta_t$. Now we see that the instrumental variables candidates G_{nt}^* generate the σ-field $\mathcal{F}^{t-1} = \sigma(Y_o, \eta_o, ..., \eta_{t-1})$, illustrating the way in which the transformation B_n may augment the available instrumental variable candidates. Because $\mathcal{F}^{t-1} = \sigma(\eta_o, Y_o, ..., Y_{t-1})$ also, the transformation B_n now allows all predetermined variables to be used as instrumental variable candidates.

Because $\nabla \epsilon_t(\theta) = -Y_{t-1}$, we have $\nabla \epsilon_t^*(\theta_o) = -\sum_{\tau=1}^t \alpha_o^{\tau-1} Y_{t-\tau}$, which implies that

$$E(\nabla \epsilon_t^*(\theta_o) \mid \mathcal{F}^{t-1}) = -\sum_{\tau=1}^t \alpha_o^{\tau-1} Y_{t-\tau}.$$

Because $\Sigma_{nt}^* = h_t$ so that $\Sigma_n^* = \text{diag}[h_1, ..., h_n]$, we have

$$Z_{nt}^* = \sum_{\tau=1}^n b_{n\tau t} h_t^{-1} E(\nabla \epsilon_t^*(\theta_o) \mid \mathcal{F}^{t-1})$$

or

$$-Z_n^* = B_n' \Sigma_n^{*-1} B_n Y_{-1} = \Omega_n^{-1} Y_{-1},$$

where $Y_{-1} = (Y_o, ..., Y_{n-1})$ and $\Omega_n^{-1} \equiv B_n' \Sigma_n^{*-1} B_n$.

Not surprisingly, this implies that the optimal instrumental variables estimator is of the form

$$\hat{\rho} = (Y_{-1}' \Omega_n^{-1} Y_{-1})^{-1} Y_{-1}' \Omega_n^{-1} Y,$$

which is just the GLS estimator. The interesting feature of this result is the form of Ω_n. When conditional heteroscedasticity is absent, we have the usual GLS estimator in the presence of MA(1) errors. Otherwise, Ω_n properly incorporates the conditional heteroscedasticity.

Although this estimator attains the minimum asymptotic variance bound, $E(Y_{-1}' \Omega_n^{-1} Y_{-1}/n)^{-1}$, it is not feasible unless α_o and h_t are known. If α_o is known and h_t can be consistently estimated, it appears that an asymptotically equivalent feasible estimator can be constructed in a manner analogous to the previous case. However, when α_o is unknown, it appears that condition 2.7(iii) will fail unless an efficient estimator of α_o is used in constructing the feasible estimator. In this case, it is more appropriate to estimate α_o and ρ_o jointly using a model such as that having residuals

$$\epsilon_t(\theta) = \sum_{\tau=1}^{t-1} \alpha^\tau (Y_{t-\tau} - \rho Y_{t-\tau-1}).$$

This model gives $\epsilon_t(\theta_o) = \eta_t$ directly. The optimal instrumental variables estimator in this case can be verified to be a generalized nonlinear least-squares estimator.

Although the NLIV estimators discussed here typically involve non-linear optimization, it is useful to remark that asymptotically equivalent efficient estimators can in general be obtained in a manner analogous to the method of Le Cam (1956). This involves taking one step of a Newton–Raphson iteration for the efficient estimator from a $\sqrt{n}$-consistent estimator for the parameters of interest, such as those forming the basis for the feasible estimator. If such an estimator is denoted $\hat{\theta}_n$ (the first step estimator), an asymptotically efficient two-step estimator is

$$\hat{\theta}_n^* = \hat{\theta}_n - (\hat{Z}_n^{*\prime} \, \nabla \hat{\epsilon}_n)^{-1} \hat{Z}_n^{*\prime} \hat{\epsilon}_n,$$

where $\nabla \hat{\epsilon}_n \equiv \nabla \epsilon_n(\hat{\theta}_n)$, $\hat{\epsilon}_n \equiv \epsilon_n(\hat{\theta}_n)$, similar to the estimators considered by Newey (1986).

4   Summary and concluding remarks

We provide results that allow determination of efficiency bounds for NLIV estimators in contexts allowing for implicit heterogeneous nonlinear dynamic equations with nonspherical errors. The bounds are obtained as the asymptotic covariance matrices of specific NLIV estimators. These results therefore extend those of Hansen (1985) to situations other than that of stationary ergodic processes. We also provide conditions that allow construction of feasible efficient NLIV estimators.

Several examples illustrate the content of our main result. Our examples are superficial in that they do not set out rigorous conditions under which the natural feasible estimators will have the desired efficiency properties. Nevertheless, these examples suggest some interesting and potentially useful estimators and illustrate how the efficient estimator is to be constructed.

One feature of our results that is not exploited in any of our examples is the possible dependence of the processes of interest on the sample size n. This feature appears useful for studying the behavior of NLIV estimators under sequences of local alternatives. This is an appropriate area for further research.

Another interesting area for investigation is the possible use of non-parametric techniques for constructing feasible versions of optimal instruments. Nonparametric estimation of the relevant conditional expectations would allow construction of efficient estimators in the presence of non-sphericalities of unknown form and for situations in which the reduced forms for particular endogenous variables are also of unknown form. Work in this direction has already been undertaken by Newey (1986) and Robinson (1987). Theorem 2.7 provides a general framework in which such results may possibly be embedded.

Mathematical appendix

All symbols and notation are as given in the text.

Proof of Proposition 2.4:   By construction,

$$Z_n = A_n S_n.$$

If $A_n = B'_n$,

$$\ddot{Z}_n = B_n'^{-1} B'_n S_n = S_n.$$

Because S_n has rows S_{nth} measurable-$\mathcal{G}_{nt}^*$, it follows trivially that $\ddot{Z}_{nth} = S_{nth}$ is measurable-$\mathcal{G}_{nt}^*$.

Now suppose that $A_n \neq B'_n$. Then

$$\ddot{Z}_n = B_n'^{-1} A_n S_n = C_n S_n,$$

so that

$$\ddot{Z}_{nth} = \sum_{\tau=1}^{n} \sum_{g=1}^{p} c_{nt\tau hg} S_{n\tau g}.$$

Because

$$c_{nt\tau hg} \equiv \sum_{\lambda=1}^{n} \sum_{\gamma=1}^{p} b_n^{\lambda t \gamma h} a_{n\lambda\tau\gamma g},$$

the measurability assumptions on $b^{\lambda t \gamma h}$ and $a_{n\lambda\tau\gamma g}$ ensure that $c_{nt\tau hg}$ is measurable with respect to

$$\mathcal{G}_{n\tau} \vee_{\{1 \leq \lambda \leq n, 1 \leq \gamma \leq p: P[b_n^{\lambda t \gamma h} \neq 0] > 0\}} \mathcal{G}_{n\lambda}.$$

Now $S_{n\tau g}$ is measurable-$\mathcal{G}_{n\tau}$ by assumption, so that $\ddot{Z}_{nth}$ is measurable with respect to

$$\mathcal{H}_{nt} \equiv \vee_{\{1 \leq \tau \leq n, 1 \leq g \leq p: P[c_{nt\tau hg} \neq 0] > 0\}} (\mathcal{G}_{n\tau} \vee_{\{1 \leq \lambda \leq n, 1 \leq \gamma \leq p: P[b_n^{\lambda t \gamma h} \neq 0] > 0\}} \mathcal{G}_{n\lambda})$$

$$= \vee_{\{1 \leq \tau \leq n, 1 \leq g \leq p: P[b_n^{\tau t g h} \neq 0] > 0\}} \mathcal{G}_{n\tau},$$

given that $P[c_{nt\tau hg} \neq 0] > 0$ if and only if $P[b_n^{\tau t g h} \neq 0] > 0$.

By condition 2.1(ii) we have that

$$\mathcal{G}_{n\tau} = \wedge_{\{1 \leq \lambda \leq n, 1 \leq \gamma \leq p: P[b_n^{\lambda t \gamma h} \neq 0] > 0\}} \mathcal{G}_{n\lambda}^*.$$

It follows that whenever $P[b_n^{\lambda t \gamma h} \neq 0] > 0$, $\mathcal{G}_{n\tau} \subset \mathcal{G}_{nt}^*$.

Because $\mathcal{H}_{nt}$ is the smallest σ-field containing the union of σ-fields $\mathcal{G}_{n\tau}$ each of which is contained in $\mathcal{G}_{nt}^*$, it follows that $\mathcal{H}_{nt} \subset \mathcal{G}_{nt}^*$. Thus, $\ddot{Z}_{nth}$ is measurable-$\mathcal{G}_{nt}^*$.   □

Proof of Proposition 2.5:   Given the conditions of the proposition, it follows from an analogue of Theorem 3.18 of Gallant and White (in press) for uniform weak convergence of sums of doubly indexed arrays of near-epoch-dependent parametric functions of mixing processes that

$$Z_n'\epsilon_n^o(\theta) - \bar{\psi}_n^o(\theta) \xrightarrow{P_o} 0 \quad \text{and} \quad Z_n'\nabla\epsilon_n^o(\theta) - \nabla\bar{\psi}_n^o(\theta) \xrightarrow{P_o} 0$$

uniformly on Θ, establishing conditions 2.3(ii.a) and 2.3(ii.c). The asymptotic normality condition 2.3(ii.b) follows under the conditions given by Wooldridge's (1986) central limit theorem for near-epoch-dependent functions of mixing processes. $\qquad\square$

Proof of Theorem 2.7: We verify the conditions of Definition 2.3 of Bates and White (1987). This requires the existence of $\{d_n^o: \Gamma \times \Omega \to I\!R^k\}$ for every (P^o, θ^o) in $\mathcal{P} \times \text{int } \Theta$ such that

$$n^{1/2}(\hat{\theta}_n(\gamma_n, \cdot) - \theta^o) - n^{1/2}d_n^o(\gamma, \cdot) \xrightarrow{P_o} 0,$$

$\{C_n^o(\gamma) \equiv \text{var}^o n^{1/2}d_n^o(\gamma, \cdot)\}$ is $O(1)$, $n^{1/2}d_n^o(\gamma, \cdot) \to^{d^o} N(0, C_n^o(\gamma))$, and the existence of $\{\hat{C}_n: \Gamma \times \Omega \to I\!R^{k \times k}\}$ such that $\hat{C}_n(\gamma_n, \cdot) - C_n^o(\gamma) \to^{P_o} 0$, where $\{C_n^o(\gamma)\}$ is uniformly positive definite, for every γ in Γ.

Fix (P^o, θ^o) in $\mathcal{P} \times \text{int } \Theta$ and γ in Γ. First we establish that $\hat{\theta}_n$ is consistent for θ^o. (We drop the dependence of $\hat{\theta}_n$ on γ_n for notational convenience.) Condition 2.3(ii.a) ensures that

$$n^{-1}Z_n'\epsilon_n^o(\theta) - E^o(n^{-1}Z_n'\epsilon_n^o(\theta)) \xrightarrow{P_o} 0$$

uniformly on Θ. Condition 2.6(i) ensures that

$$n^{-1}\hat{Z}_n'\epsilon_n^o(\theta) - n^{-1}Z_n'\epsilon_n^o(\theta) \xrightarrow{P_o} 0$$

uniformly on Θ, so that

$$n^{-1}\hat{Z}_n'\epsilon_n^o(\theta) - E^o(n^{-1}Z_n'\epsilon_n^o(\theta)) \xrightarrow{P_o} 0$$

uniformly on Θ. Condition 2.6(iv) ensures that $\hat{V}_n(\gamma_n)^- - V_n^{o-1} \to^{P_o} 0$, which implies that

$$n^{-2}\epsilon_n^o(\theta)'\hat{Z}_n\hat{V}_n(\gamma_n)^-\hat{Z}_n'\epsilon_n^o(\theta) - n^{-2}E^o(\epsilon_n^o(\theta)'Z_n)V_n^{o-1}E^o(Z_n'\epsilon_n^o(\theta)) \xrightarrow{P_o} 0$$

uniformly on Θ by Lemma 2.4 of Bates and White (1985) and the multivariate analog of Theorem 2.4.4 of Lukacs (1975) (the subsequence theorem). Condition 2.3(iii.a) and the condition on V_n^o ensure that θ^o is the identifiably unique minimizer of

$$n^{-2}E^o(\epsilon_n^o(\theta)'Z_n)V_n^{o-1}E^o(Z_n'\epsilon_n^o(\theta))$$

by Theorem 4.5 of Bates and White (1985). It follows from Theorem 3.14 of White (1987) that $\hat{\theta}_n \to^{P_o} \theta^o$.

To find the function d_n^o, we verify the conditions of Theorem 6.8 of White (1987). In the present application, White's ℓ_n corresponds to $\hat{Z}_n'\epsilon_n^o(\theta)/n$. This satisfies the required measurability and differentiability conditions by 2.3(i) and the measurability of $\hat{Z}_n$. Next we must verify that

$n^{-1/2}\hat{Z}'_n\epsilon^o_n(\hat{\theta}_n)\to^{P^o}0$. As just established, $\hat{\theta}_n\to^{P^o}\theta^o$, whereas $\hat{V}^-_n-V^{o-1}_n\to^{P^o}$ 0 by assumption, and $n^{-1}\nabla\epsilon^o_n(\hat{\theta}_n)'\hat{Z}_n-E^o(n^{-1}\nabla\epsilon^o_n(\theta^o)'Z_n)\to^{P^o}0$ follows given that $n^{-1}\nabla\epsilon^o_n(\theta)'\hat{Z}_n-n^{-1}\nabla\epsilon^o_n(\theta)'Z_n\to^{P^o}0$ uniformly on Θ [condition 2.6(ii)] and conditions 2.3(i) and (ii.c), together with $\hat{\theta}_n(\gamma_n,\cdot)\to^{P^o}\theta^o$, by Corollary 3.8 of White (1987). Given any subsequence $\{n'\}$, it follows that there exists a further subsequence $\{n''\}$ such that $\hat{\theta}_{n''}\to\theta^o$, $\hat{V}^-_{n''}-\hat{V}^{o-1}_{n''}\to 0$ and $n''^{-1}\nabla\epsilon^o_{n''}(\hat{\theta}_{n''})'\hat{Z}_{n''}-E^o(n''^{-1}\nabla\epsilon^o_{n''}(\theta^o)'Z_{n''})\to 0$ a.s.-P^o. This implies that for all n'' sufficiently large $\hat{\theta}_{n''}$ is interior to Θ (given interiority of θ^o) and $\hat{V}_{n''}$ and $n''^{-1}\nabla\epsilon^o_{n''}(\hat{\theta}_{n''})'\hat{Z}_{n''}$ are nonsingular a.s.-P^o. Because $\hat{\theta}_{n''}=$ argmin $n''^{-2}\epsilon^o_{n''}(\theta)'\hat{Z}_{n''}\hat{V}^-_{n''}\hat{Z}'_{n''}\epsilon^o_{n''}(\theta)$, it follows by interiority and differentiability that $\hat{\theta}_{n''}$ satisfies the first-order condition

$$n''^{-2}\nabla\epsilon^o_{n''}(\hat{\theta}_{n''})'\hat{Z}_{n''}\hat{V}^{-1}_{n''}\hat{Z}'_{n''}\epsilon^o_{n''}(\hat{\theta}_{n''})=0$$

for all n'' sufficiently large a.s.-P^o. Because $n''^{-1}\nabla\epsilon^o_{n''}(\hat{\theta}_{n''})'\hat{Z}_{n''}$ and $\hat{V}^{-1}_{n''}$ are nonsingular for almost all (a.a.) n'' a.s.-P^o, it follows that

$$n''^{-1/2}\hat{Z}'_{n''}\epsilon^o_{n''}(\hat{\theta}_{n''})=0 \text{ a.a. } n'' \text{ a.s.-}P^o.$$

Because this holds for arbitrary subsequences $\{n'\}$, it follows that

$$n^{-1/2}\hat{Z}'_n\epsilon^o_n(\hat{\theta}_n)\overset{P^o}{\to}0$$

by the subsequence theorem, as desired.

Next we require that

$$V^{o-1/2}_n n^{-1/2}\hat{Z}'_n e_n\overset{A^o}{\approx}N(0,I_k).$$

Now

$$V^{o-1/2}_n(n^{-1/2}\hat{Z}'_n e_n-n^{-1/2}Z'_n e_n)\overset{P^o}{\to}0$$

because $V^{o-1/2}_n$ is $O(1)$ given 2.3(iii.c) and the term in parentheses is $o_{P^o}(1)$ given 2.6(iii). Thus, it suffices that

$$V^{o-1/2}_n n^{-1/2}Z'_n e_n\overset{A^o}{\approx}N(0,I_k),$$

which is condition 2.3(ii.b).

Finally, we require that $n^{-1}\hat{Z}'_n\nabla\epsilon^o_n(\theta)-E^o(n^{-1}Z'_n\nabla\epsilon^o_n(\theta))\to^{P^o}0$ uniformly on Θ, but this holds, as already argued. Furthermore, conditions 2.3(ii) and (iii) ensure that $E^o(n^{-1}Z'_n\nabla\epsilon^o_n(\theta^o))$ is $O(1)$ and uniformly nonsingular. It now follows from Theorem 6.8 of White (1987) that

$$\sqrt{n}(\hat{\theta}_n(\gamma_n,\cdot)-\theta^o)-\sqrt{n}d^o_n(\gamma,\cdot)\overset{P^o}{\to}0,$$

where

$$d^o_n(\gamma,\cdot)\equiv E^o(n^{-1}\nabla\epsilon^o_n(\theta^o)'Z_n)^{-1}n^{-1}\hat{Z}'_n\epsilon^o_n(\theta^o).$$

Because $E^o(n^{-1}\nabla\epsilon^o_n(\theta^o)'Z_n)^{-1}$ is $O(1)$ and

$$n^{-1/2}\hat{Z}'_n\epsilon^o_n(\theta^o)-n^{-1/2}Z'_n\epsilon^o_n(\theta^o)\to^{P^o}0,$$

we have

$$\sqrt{n}(\hat{\theta}_n(\gamma_n,\cdot)-\theta^o)-\sqrt{n}d^o_n(\gamma,\cdot)\to^{P^o}0,$$

where $d_n^o(\gamma, \cdot) = E^o(n^{-1}\nabla\epsilon_n^o(\theta^o)'Z_n)^{-1}n^{-1}Z_n'\epsilon_n^o(\theta^o)$, as desired. Furthermore,

$$C_n^o(\gamma) \equiv \text{var}^o\, n^{1/2}d_n^o(\gamma, \cdot) = E^o(n^{-1}\nabla\epsilon_n^o(\theta^o)'Z_n)^{-1}V_n^o E^o(n^{-1}Z_n'\nabla\epsilon_n^o(\theta^o))^{-1}$$

is $O(1)$ and uniformly positive definite given 2.3(iii.b) and (ii.b). The asymptotic normality of $V_n^{o-1/2}n^{-1/2}Z_n'\epsilon_n^o(\theta^o)$ ensures that

$$n^{1/2}d_n^o(\gamma, \cdot) \overset{A^o}{\sim} N(0, C_n^o(\gamma)).$$

Because (P^o, θ^o) and γ are arbitrary, it follows that $\mathcal{E}_{\text{NLIV}}(\Gamma, \mathcal{Q}, \mathfrak{I})$ is a CANI class by Definition 2.3 of Bates and White (1987).

To show that it is RCANI, we require the existence of $\hat{C}_n(\gamma_n)$ such that $\hat{C}_n(\gamma_n, \cdot) - C_n^o(\gamma) \to^{P^o} 0$. For this, take

$$\hat{C}_n = (\nabla\epsilon_n^o(\hat{\theta}_n)'\hat{Z}_n/n)^- \hat{V}_n(\hat{Z}_n'\nabla\epsilon_n^o(\hat{\theta}_n)/n)^-.$$

Because $\hat{V}_n^- - V_n^{o-1} \to^{P^o} 0$ and $n^{-1}\hat{Z}_n'\nabla\epsilon_n^o(\hat{\theta}_n) - E(n^{-1}\hat{Z}_n'\nabla\epsilon_n^o(\theta^o)) \to^{P^o} 0$, given any subsequence $\{n'\}$, there exists a further subsequence $\{n''\}$ such that $\hat{V}_{n''}^- - V_{n''}^{o-1} \to 0$, $n''^{-1}\hat{Z}_{n''}'\nabla\epsilon_{n''}^o(\hat{\theta}_{n''}) - E(n''^{-1}Z_{n''}'\nabla\epsilon_{n''}^o(\theta^o)) \to 0$ a.s.-P^o, and for all n'' sufficiently large $\hat{V}_{n''}^-$ and $n''^{-1}\hat{Z}_{n''}'\nabla\epsilon_{n''}^o(\hat{\theta}_{n''})$ are nonsingular given 2.3(ii.b) and (iii.b). This implies that

$$\hat{C}_{n''}(\gamma_{n''}, \cdot) - C_{n''}^o(\gamma) \to 0 \text{ a.s.-}P^0.$$

As $\{n'\}$ is arbitrary, it follows that

$$\hat{C}_n(\gamma_n, \cdot) - C_n^o(\gamma) \overset{P^o}{\to} 0,$$

as required. Because this holds for arbitrary (P^o, θ^o) and γ, it follows that $\mathcal{E}_{\text{NLIV}}(\Gamma, \mathcal{Q}, \mathfrak{I})$ is a RCANI class. $\qquad\square$

Proof of Theorem 2.8: We verify the conditions of Corollary 2.11 of Bates and White (1987). Given the results of Theorem 2.7, the asymptotically efficient RCANI estimator is such that

$$E^o(n^{-1}\nabla\epsilon_n^o(\theta^o)'Z_n) = \text{cov}^o[n^{-1/2}Z_n^{*'}e_n, n^{-1/2}Z_n'e_n]$$

for all (P^o, θ^o) in $\mathcal{P} \times \text{int}\,\Theta$ and all γ in Γ. Now

$$\begin{aligned}
\text{cov}^o[n^{-1/2}Z_n^{*'}e_n, n^{-1/2}Z_n'e_n] &= E^o(Z_n^{*'}e_n e_n' Z_n/n) \\
&= E^o(Z_n^{*'}B_n^{-1}B_n e_n e_n' B_n' B_n'^{-1}Z_n/n) \\
&= E^o(Z_n^{*'}B_n^{-1}e_n^* e_n^{*'} B_n'^{-1}Z_n/n) \\
&= E(\ddot{Z}_n^{*'}e_n^* e_n^{*'}\ddot{Z}_n/n),
\end{aligned}$$

where $\ddot{Z}_n^* \equiv B_n'^{-1}Z_n^*$, $\ddot{Z}_n \equiv B_n'^{-1}Z_n$, and $e_n^* = B_n e_n$, as in Definition 2.1. By condition 2.3(ii), we have that $\ddot{Z}_n^*$ and $\ddot{Z}_n$ have rows $\ddot{Z}_{nth}^*$ and $\ddot{Z}_{nth}$ that are measurable-$\mathcal{G}_{nt}^*$. It follows that

$$\begin{aligned}
E^o(\ddot{Z}_n^{*'}e_n^* e_n^{*'}\ddot{Z}_n/n) &= E^o(\ddot{Z}_n^{*'}\Sigma_n^*\ddot{Z}_n/n) \\
&= n^{-1}\sum_{t=1}^{n} E^o(\ddot{Z}_{nt}^{*'}\Sigma_{nt}^*\ddot{Z}_{nt}),
\end{aligned}$$

where $\Sigma_n^* = [\Sigma_{nt\tau}^*]$, $\Sigma_{nt\tau}^* \equiv E(e_{nt}^* e_{n\tau}^* \mid \mathcal{G}_{nt\tau}^*)$. By the conditions of Definition 2.1, $\Sigma_{nt\tau}^* = 0$ if $t \neq \tau$, justifying the preceding summation.

Now consider $E^o(n^{-1} \nabla \epsilon_n^o(\theta^o)' Z_n)$. Letting $\nabla \epsilon_n^*(\theta^o) = B_n \nabla \epsilon_n^o(\theta^o)$, we have

$$E^o(n^{-1} \nabla \epsilon_n^o(\theta^o)' Z_n) = E^o(n^{-1} \nabla \epsilon_n^o(\theta^o)' B_n' B_n'^{-1} Z_n)$$

$$= E^o(n^{-1} \nabla \epsilon_n^*(\theta^o)' \ddot{Z}_n)$$

$$= n^{-1} \sum_{t=1}^{n} E^o(\nabla \epsilon_{nt}^*(\theta^o)' \ddot{Z}_{nt}).$$

If the equality $E^o(n^{-1} \nabla \epsilon_n^o(\theta^o)' Z_n) = \mathrm{cov}^o[n^{-1/2} Z_n^{*'} e_n, n^{-1/2} Z_n' e_n]$ is to hold for $n = 1, 2, \dots$, it follows that

$$E^o(\ddot{Z}_{nt}^{*'} \Sigma_{nt}^* \ddot{Z}_{nt}) = E^o(\nabla \epsilon_{nt}^*(\theta^o)' \ddot{Z}_{nt}), \quad t = 1, \dots, n.$$

For this, it clearly suffices that

$$E^o(\ddot{Z}_{nt}^{*'} \Sigma_{nt}^* \mid \mathcal{G}_{nt}^*) = E^o(\nabla \epsilon_{nt}^*(\theta^o)' \mid \mathcal{G}_{nt}^*).$$

Because $\ddot{Z}_{nt}^*$ and Σ_{nt}^* are measurable-$\mathcal{G}_{nt}^*$ and Σ_{nt}^* is nonsingular a.s.-P^o, it follows that

$$\ddot{Z}_{nt}^* = \Sigma_{nt}^{*-1} E^o(\nabla \epsilon_{nt}^*(\theta^o) \mid \mathcal{G}_{nt}^*)$$

or, because $Z_n^* = B_n' \ddot{Z}_n^*$,

$$Z_{nt}^* = \sum_{\tau=1}^{n} b_{n\tau t} \Sigma_{n\tau}^{*-1} E^o(\nabla \epsilon_{n\tau}^*(\theta^o) \mid \mathcal{G}_{n\tau}^*).$$

Thus, the conditions of Corollary 2.11 of Bates and White (1987) hold, and the efficiency of $\hat{\theta}_{\mathrm{NLIV}}^*$ is established.

The formula for $\mathrm{avar}^o \, \hat{\theta}_{\mathrm{NLIV}}^*$ follows straightforwardly from Theorem 2.7. In the present case we have $\nabla \bar{\psi}_n^o(\gamma^*) = V_n^o(\gamma^*)$, so that

$$\mathrm{avar}^o \, \hat{\theta}_{\mathrm{NLIV}}^* = \nabla \bar{\psi}_n^o(\gamma^*)^{-1}$$

$$= E(\nabla \epsilon_n^o(\theta^o)' Z_n^*)^{-1}$$

$$= E(\nabla \epsilon_n^o(\theta^o)' B_n' \ddot{Z}_n)^{-1}$$

$$= E(\nabla \epsilon_n^o(\theta^o)' B_n' \Sigma_n^{*-1} B_n \nabla \epsilon_n^o(\theta^o))^{-1},$$

and the result follows by definition of Ω_n. $\qquad\qquad\square$

REFERENCES

Amemiya, T. 1966. "Specification Analysis in the Estimation of Parameters of a Simultaneous Equation Model with Autocorrelated Residuals." *Econometrica* 34: 283–306.

1974. "The Non-linear Two-Stage Least Squares Estimator." *Journal of Econometrics* 2: 105-10.

1977. "The Maximum Likelihood and the Non-linear Three-Stage Least Squares Estimator in the General Non-linear Simultaneous Equation Model." *Econometrica* 45: 955-68.

1983. "Partially Generalized Least Squares and Two-Stage Least Squares Estimators." *Journal of Econometrics* 23: 275-84.

Barnett, W. A. 1976. "Maximum Likelihood and Iterated Aitken Estimation of Nonlinear Systems of Equations." *Journal of the American Statistical Association* 71: 354-60.

Basmann, R. L. 1957. "A Generalized Classical Method of Linear Estimation of Coefficients in a Structural Equation." *Econometrica* 25: 77-83.

Bates, C. E. and H. White. 1985. "A Unified Theory of Consistent Estimation for Parametric Models." *Econometric Theory* 1: 151-78.

1987. "Efficient Estimation of Parametric Models." Department of Economics Discussion Paper 87-3, University of California, San Diego.

Bollerslev, T. 1985. "A Conditionally Heteroskedastic Time-Series Model for Security Prices and Rates of Return Data." Department of Economics Discussion Paper 85-32, University of California, San Diego.

Bowden, R. J. and D. A. Turkington. 1985. *Instrumental Variables.* Cambridge: Cambridge University Press.

Brundy, J. M. and D. W. Jorgenson. 1974. "Consistent and Efficient Estimation of Systems of Simultaneous Equations by Means of Instrumental Variables." In *Frontiers in Econometrics,* P. Zarembka, Ed. New York: Academic, pp. 215-44.

Burguete, J., A. Gallant, and G. Souza. 1982. "On the Unification of the Asymptotic Theory of Nonlinear Econometric Models." *Econometric Reviews* 1: 151-212.

Eichenbaum, M. and L. Hansen. 1986. "Estimating Models with Intertemporal Substitution using Aggregate Time Series Data." Carnegie Mellon Graduate School of Industrial Administration.

Engle, R. F. 1982. "Autoregressive Conditional Heteroskedasticity with Estimates of the Variance of U.K. Inflation." *Econometrica* 50: 394-419.

Fair, R. 1970. "The Estimation of Simultaneous Equation Models with Lagged Endogenous Variables and First Order Serially Correlated Errors." *Econometrica* 38: 507-16.

Gallant, A. R. 1977. "Three Stage Least Squares Estimation for a System of Simultaneous, Nonlinear, Implicit Equations." *Journal of Econometrics* 5: 71-88.

Gallant, A. R. and D. W. Jorgenson. 1979. "Statistical Inference for a System of Simultaneous Nonlinear Implicit Equations in the Context of Instrumental Variables Estimation." *Journal of Econometrics* 11: 275-302.

Gallant, A. R. and H. White. In press. *A Unified Theory of Estimation and Inference for Nonlinear Dynamic Models.* Oxford: Basil Blackwell.

Geary, R. C. 1949. "Determination of Linear Relations between Systematic Parts of Variables with Errors in Observation, the Variances of Which Are Unknown." *Econometrica* 17: 30-59.

Gordin, M. I. 1969. "The Central Limit Theorem for Stationary Processes." *Soviet Mathematics Doklady* 10: 1174-6.

Gourieroux, C., A. Monfort, and A. Trognon. 1985. "A General Approach to Serial Correlation." *Econometric Theory* 1: 315-40.

Hansen, L. 1982. "Large Sample Properties of Generalized Method of Moments Estimators." *Econometrica* 50: 1029-54.

1985. "A Method for Calculating Bounds on the Asymptotic Covariance Matrices of Generalized Methods of Moments Estimators." *Journal of Econometrics* 30: 203-38.

Hansen, L. and T. Sargent. 1982. "Instrumental Variables Procedures for Estimating Linear Rational Expectations Models." *Journal of Monetary Economics* 9: 263-96.

Hayashi, K. and C. Sims. 1983. "Nearly Efficient Estimation of Time Series Models with Predetermined but Not Exogenous Instruments." *Econometrica* 51: 783-98.

Le Cam, L. 1956. "On the Asymptotic Theory of Estimation and Testing Hypotheses." In *Proceedings of the Third Berkeley Symposium on Mathematical Statistics and Probability,* Vol. 2, J. Neyman, Ed. Berkeley: University of California Press, pp. 129-56.

Lukacs, E. 1975. *Stochastic Convergence.* New York: Academic.

MaCurdy, T. 1982. "Using Information on the Moments of Disturbances to Increase the Efficiency of Estimation." Stanford University mimeo.

Newey, W. 1986. "Efficient Estimation of Models with Conditional Moment Restrictions." Princeton University, Department of Economics mimeo.

Poirier, D. J. and P. A. Ruud. 1987. "Probit with Dependent Observations." University of California Berkeley Department of Economics Working Paper 8734.

Reiersøl, O. 1941. "Confluence Analysis by Means of Lag Moments and Other Methods of Confluence Analysis." *Econometrica* 9: 1-24.

1945. "Confluence Analysis by Means of Instrumental Sets of Variables." *Arkiv for Mathematik, Astronomi och Fysic* 32A.

Robinson, P. M. 1987. "Asymptotically Efficient Estimation in the Presence of Heteroskedasticity of Unknown Form." *Econometrica* 55: 875-92.

Sargan, J. D. 1958. "The Estimation of Economic Relationships Using Instrumental Variables." *Econometrica* 26: 393-415.

1959. "The Estimation of Relationships with Autocorrelated Residuals by Means of Instrumental Variables." *Journal of the Royal Statistical Society, Series B* 21: 91-105.

1964. "Three Stage Least Squares and Full Information Maximum Likelihood Estimates." *Econometrica* 32: 77-81.

Theil, H. 1953. *Estimation and Simultaneous Correlation in Complete Equation Systems.* The Hague: Central Planbureau.

White, H. 1980. "Nonlinear Regression on Cross-Section Data." *Econometrica* 48: 721-46.

1982. "Instrumental Variables Regression with Independent Observations." *Econometrica* 50: 483-500.

1984. *Asymptotic Theory for Econometricians.* New York: Academic.

1986. "Instrumental Variables Analogs of Generalized Least Squares Estimators." In *Advances in Statistical Computing and Statistical Analysis,* Vol. 1, R. Mariano, Ed. London: JAI Press, pp. 173-227.

1987. "Estimation, Inference and Specification Analysis." Department of Economics manuscript, University of California, San Diego.

Wooldridge, J. 1986. "Asymptotic Properties of Econometric Estimators." Department of Economics Ph.D. Dissertation, University of California, San Diego.

Wright, S. 1925. *Corn and Hog Correlations.* Washington: U.S. Department of Agriculture Bulletin 1300.

Zellner, A. and H. Theil. 1962. "Three Stage Least Squares: Simultaneous Estimation of Simultaneous Equations." *Econometrica* 30: 54–78.

CHAPTER 2

Envelope consistent functional separability

Ernst R. Berndt

1   Introduction

For some time now, it has been known that homothetic functional separability, the consistency of sequential optimization, the existence of input price or quantity aggregates, and the equality of certain substitution elasticities involve similar, if not identical, restrictions on the underlying production or utility function.[1] Because functional separability has such important implications, therefore, separability restrictions have been the focus of a variety of empirical studies.[2]

The empirical and theoretical literature on functional separability in production or cost functions to date has been almost exclusively presented in the context of cases in which all inputs or commodities are hypothesized to adjust instantaneously to their long-run or full equilibrium levels.[3] By contrast, in recent work on factor demand models it has become increasingly common to assume instead that in the short run certain inputs (such as capital plant and equipment) are fixed but that in the long run these quasi-fixed inputs are variable.[4]

The helpful comments of William Barnett, Angus Deaton, W. Erwin Diewert, Melvyn Fuss, and Robin Sickles are gratefully acknowledged, as is the research support from the National Science Foundation.

[1] See, e.g., Berndt and Christensen (1973a) and Blackorby, Primont, and Russell (1975).

[2] Among such empirical studies are Berndt and Christensen (1973b, 1974), Berndt and Wood (1975, 1979), Denny and May (1978), and Denny and Pinto (1978).

[3] A very recent exception is the paper by Hazilla and Kopp (1986).

[4] There is a related literature in consumer demand theory that deals with the effects of rationing; see, e.g., Deaton and Muellbauer (1980), especially Sections 4.3, 5.1, and 12.4. Although theoretical issues of intertemporal separability on utility functions are discussed, the related empirical literature on tests for separability is virtually nil. It might also be noted that this literature does not consider types of separability in which both fixed and variable goods are separable from other goods, a separability form that in this chapter turns out to be of particular interest.

At least since the work of Viner (1931), it has been known that the firm's long-run average total-cost (LRATC) curve can be constructed as the envelope of tangencies with short-run average total-cost (SRATC) curves. In this chapter attention is focused on the following issues: If functional separability holds on the LRATC function, what restrictions are implied on the SRATC function? Similarly, what does functional separability on the SRATC function imply for the corresponding LRATC function? In brief, the envelope consistency of functional separability restrictions is examined in the context of cost functions.[5]

The chapter proceeds as follows. In Section 2 the envelope condition relating SRATC and LRATC functions is presented, and in Section 3 the notion of functional separability is briefly reviewed. Then in Section 4 necessary and sufficient conditions are presented for envelope consistency between a functionally separable-constrained LRATC function and its SRATC curve. These general restrictions are interpreted in Section 5 in the context of a specific functional form, the translog short-run, or restricted-cost, function. A number of important findings emerge, among the most important being that if separability involves a fixed input being separable from variable or fixed inputs, the implied restrictions on the translog form are in most cases more stringent than if variable inputs are separable from fixed or other variable inputs. Finally, in Section 6 concluding remarks are presented, as are suggestions for further research.

2   Envelope consistency

Assume there exists a twice-differentiable production function $Y = f(X) = f(X_1, X_2, ..., X_m)$ relating the flow of output Y to the flows of m inputs, $X_1, X_2, ..., X_m$; let f be homogeneous of degree 1 in X. Assume further that the inputs X can be partitioned into two mutually exclusive and exhaustive subsets, $X = \{V; F\}$, where $V = \{V_1, V_2, ..., V_N\}$ is a $1 \times N$ vector of variable inputs; $F = \{F_1, F_2, ..., F_J\}$ is a $1 \times J$ vector of quasi-fixed inputs, fixed in the short run but variable in the long run; and $m = N + J$. Denote the $1 \times N$ vector of exogenous input prices corresponding to V as $w = \{w_1, w_2, ..., w_N\}$ and the $1 \times J$ exogenous ex ante service price or user cost vector corresponding to F as $u = \{u_1, u_2, ..., u_J\}$. With Y, w, and F given, the variable or restricted unit cost function dual to f can be written as

$$\text{AVC} \equiv \text{VC}/Y = G(w; F/Y), \tag{1}$$

where $\text{VC} \equiv w'V$ is the inner product of w and V.

---

[5] It is worth noting that Lau (1978, pp. 166-9) has established separability equivalences between production functions and normalized restricted profit functions.

Define the shadow values or ex post service prices r as the reduction in variable costs attainable given an increase in F, that is,

$$r \equiv \frac{\partial G(w; F/Y)}{\partial F} < 0, \tag{2}$$

where the $1 \times J$ vector $r = \{r_1, r_2, \ldots, r_J\}$. In full or long-run equilibrium where SRATC curves are tangent to the LRATC curve, shadow and ex ante service prices are equal, that is, $r = -u$.

Given Y, w, and u, one can solve for the optimal F – denoted F^* – as that level of F at which $r = -u$. This implies that

$$F^*/Y = g(w; u). \tag{3}$$

Average variable costs at the SRATC–LRATC tangency point are obtained by substituting (3) into (1), yielding

$$\text{AVC} \equiv \text{VC}/Y = G[w; g(w; u)], \tag{4}$$

and average *total* costs at this same tangency point can therefore be written as

$$\text{AVC} \equiv (\text{VC} + u'F)/Y = G[w; g(w; u)] + u'g(w; u) = H(w; u). \tag{5}$$

Note also that with the LRATC function H, according to Shephard's lemma, cost-minimizing or optimal-input demands can be derived simply by differentiating $H(w; u)$ with respect to input prices, that is,

$$H_w \equiv \frac{\partial H(w; u)}{\partial w} = \frac{V}{Y}, \qquad H_u \equiv \frac{\partial H(w; u)}{\partial u} = \frac{F^*}{Y}. \tag{6}$$

3   Functional separability: a brief review

We now briefly review the notion of functional separability. Consider an alternative partition of the m inputs, one in which inputs are partitioned into t mutually exclusive and exhaustive subsets, a partition we call T. Following Sono (1945), Leontief (1947), Goldman and Uzawa (1964), and Strotz (1969), the production function f is said to be weakly separable with respect to the partition T if the marginal rate of substitution (MRS, the ratio of marginal products) for any two inputs X_i and X_j from any subset N_s, $s = 1, 2, \ldots, t$, is independent of the quantities of inputs outside of N_s, that is,

$$\frac{\partial (f_i/f_j)}{\partial X_k} = 0, \quad \text{for all } i, j \in N_s \text{ and } k \notin N_s, \tag{7}$$

where f_i are derivatives of f with respect to X_i, $i = 1, 2, \ldots, m$. Further, the production function f is said to be strongly separable with respect to the partition T if the MRS between any two inputs from subsets N_s and N_t does not depend on quantities of inputs outside of N_s and N_t, that is,

$$\frac{\partial(f_i/f_j)}{\partial X_k} = 0, \quad \text{for all } i \in N_s, \ j \in N_t, \ k \notin N_s \cup N_t. \tag{8}$$

Each of these separability restrictions on the production function can be written alternatively as

$$f_i f_{jk} - f_j f_{ik} = 0, \tag{9}$$

and, as has been shown by Berndt and Christensen (1973a), each is equivalent to certain equality restrictions on the Allen partial elasticities of substitution. More specifically, inputs i and j separable from k are equivalent to

$$\sigma_{ik} = \sigma_{jk}, \tag{10}$$

where the i, j, k subscripts follow either weak [(7)] or strong [(8)] separability.

Finally, as shown by Shephard (1970, pp. 143–6), the homothetic production function f is weakly (strongly) separable with respect to the partition T in input quantities if and only if the dual homothetic LRATC function H is weakly (strongly) separable in input prices according to the same partition. Denote first and second partial derivatives of the LRATC function H [see (5)] with respect to prices of inputs i and inputs i and j as H_i and H_{ij}, respectively. It follows therefore that (9) holds if and only if it is also the case that

$$H_i H_{jk} - H_j H_{ik} = 0. \tag{11}$$

Obviously, when there are more than three inputs, for separability to hold, the i, j, k relationships in (9) and (11) must hold simultaneously; that is, i, j, and k must exhaust all inputs, as stated in (7) and (8).

To simplify notation, the following convention is now adopted: Inputs i and j separable from input k is written as $\{(i, j), k\}$ separability, ℓ is a variable input if $\ell \in V$, and ℓ is a fixed input if $\ell \in F$.

4 Envelope consistent functional separability: a general treatment

The question now addressed is, what do the separability restrictions (11) on the long-run or envelope average total-cost function $H(w; u)$ imply in terms of restrictions on the short-run average variable-cost function $G(w; F/Y)$ and on the optimal fixed-factor intensity function $g(w; u)$, noting that by (3) and (6),

$$g(w; u) = H_u(w; u)? \tag{12}$$

Similarly, if separability restrictions were imposed on the short-run average variable-cost function G in (4), what would this imply in terms of restrictions on g in (3) and therefore on H in (5)?

There are six cases of $\{(i,j),k\}$ separability to be considered:

$$
\begin{aligned}
&\text{Case 1:} \quad i,j,k \in V, \\
&\text{Case 2:} \quad i,j,k \in F, \\
&\text{Case 3:} \quad i,j \in V, \ k \in F, \\
&\text{Case 4:} \quad i,j \in F, \ k \in V, \\
&\text{Case 5:} \quad i,k \in V, j \in F, \\
&\text{Case 6:} \quad i \in V, \ j,k \in F.
\end{aligned}
\tag{13}
$$

Note that if capital is a fixed input and if all other inputs are variable, the very common value-added separability condition is encompassed in case 5 (or, perhaps, in case 6). Furthermore, in principle, separability could be weak, strong, approximate, global, weakly recursive, or strongly recursive.[6]

It will be useful to begin by noting several relationships and introducing further notation. These relationships will prove particularly helpful for evaluating the various cases of (11). For $i \in V$,

$$
H_i = G_i[w; g(w;u)] + G_g[w; g(w;u)] \cdot g_i(w;u) + u'g_i(w;u),
$$

where G_g is $1 \times J$ and g_i is $J \times 1$. But since by the envelope condition $G_g = r = -u$, the second and third terms on the right side of H_i cancel, leaving

$$
H_i = G_i[w; g(w;u)], \quad i \in V.
\tag{14}
$$

Further, for $i,k \in V$,

$$
H_{ik} = G_{ik} + G_{ig}g_k,
\tag{15}
$$

where G_{ik} is a scalar, G_{ig} is a $1 \times J$ vector, and g_k is a $J \times 1$ vector. Finally, for $i \in V$ and $k \in F$,

$$
H_{ik} = G_{ig}g_k.
\tag{16}
$$

If, however, $i \in F$,

$$
H_i = g^i(w; v),
\tag{17}
$$

a scalar, where the i superscript denotes the ith fixed input. Further, for $i \in F$ and $k \in V$,

$$
H_{ik} = g_k^i,
\tag{18}
$$

a scalar, whereas for $i,k \in F$, it is also the case that

[6] A useful summary of these various types of separability is found in Blackorby et al. (1975).

$$H_{ik} = g_k^i. \tag{19}$$

We now consider each of the six cases. For case 1 where $i, j, k \in V$, substitution of (14)–(16) into (11) yields, for $\{(i,j), k\}$ separability,

$$(G_i G_{jk} - G_j G_{ik}) + (G_i G_{jg} - G_j G_{ig}) \cdot g_k = 0. \tag{20}$$

Hence, when i, j, and k are each variable inputs, $\{(i,j), k\}$ separability on the long-run function H implies restrictions not only on the variable-input portion of the short-run variable-cost function G [the first part of (20)], but also on the vector of optimal fixed-factor intensity functions g [the second part of (20)].

Now consider the opposite extreme situation, denoted case 2, where i, j, and k are each fixed inputs. Substituting (17)–(19) into (11) gives

$$g^i g_k^j - g^j g_k^i = 0. \tag{21}$$

Thus, in this case of $\{(i,j), k\}$ separability involving only fixed inputs, the separability restrictions on H involve constraints only on the derivatives of the optimal fixed-factor intensity functions g.

Case 3 is our first situation of four mixed cases, in which now $i, j \in V$ but $k \in F$. Here we substitute (14) and (16) into (11), obtaining

$$(G_i G_{jg} - G_j G_{ig}) \cdot g_k = 0. \tag{22}$$

Notice that in this mixed variable–fixed input separability specification, the restrictions imposed involve constraints both on G and g and are equivalent (with subscripts referring to different inputs, however) to those in the second half of case 1 [see (20)].

In case 4, $i, j \in F$ but $k \in V$ – fixed inputs are separable from a variable input. Here we substitute (17) and (18) into (11) and thereby obtain

$$g^i g_k^j - g^j g_k^i = 0, \tag{23}$$

which is the same as in the all-fixed input case 2, except here the k subscript refers to a variable input. Note, however, that $\{(i,j), k\}$ separability here implies restrictions only on the optimal fixed-factor intensity functions g^i and g^j.

In case 5, $i, k \in V$ but $j \in F$ – a mix of variable and fixed inputs is separable from a variable input. We therefore substitute (14), (15), (17), and (18) into (11), rearrange, and derive, for $\{(i,j), k\}$ separability,

$$G_i g_k^j - g^j G_{ik} - g^j G_{ig} g_k = 0. \tag{24}$$

As can be seen, since (24) involves a number of terms, this type of separability may be particularly restrictive.

Finally, in case 6 a mix of variable and fixed inputs is separable from a fixed input; that is, $i \in V$ but $j, k \in F$. Substituting (14), (16), (17), and (19) into (11) results in, for $\{(i,j), k\}$ separability,

$$G_i g_k^j - g^j G_{ig} g_k = 0. \tag{25}$$

Notice that in (25) there appears to be one less term in the constraint than in case 5 (see (24)]; however, since G_{ig} and g_k are $1 \times J$ and $J \times 1$ vectors, condition (25) is rather severe.

Until now we have only considered implications of separability on the long-run cost function for restrictions on the short-run variable-cost function G and on the optimal fixed-factor intensity functions g. We now ask the symmetrical question, what do separability restrictions on the short-run or variable-cost function imply for the long-run or envelope cost function? In answering this, it is useful to note that separability was originally defined on the production function f – see (7)–(9). These separability conditions were therefore assumed to be global in the sense that they hold for any possible input combinations. In particular, as long as the input combination is technically efficient and therefore on the production function frontier, the global separability conditions must hold. This implies that if the production function is separable, this separability must be reflected in each and every variable-cost function. Moreover, if global separability is tested using information from the short-run variable-cost function, this necessarily implies corresponding separability on the production function and the long-run or envelope cost function.

But how might global separability be inferred using information from the short-run variable-cost function? Recall that in Section 2 the notion of shadow costs was developed – see (2). Following Berndt and Fuss (1986), define the shadow average total-cost (SHATC) function as the average variable-cost function plus the average "fixed"-cost function, where fixed inputs are evaluated at their shadow ($-r$) rather than ex ante (u) transactions prices, that is,

$$\text{SHATC} \equiv (\text{VC} - r'F)/Y = G(w; F/Y) - r'F/Y$$
$$= G[w; g(w; r)] - r'g(w; r) = S(w; r). \tag{26}$$

Note that, by construction, the F/Y values are optimal given shadow prices r. Treating these shadow prices as fixed, one could then test for global separability conditions on the shadow average-cost function,

$$S_i S_{jk} - S_j S_{ik} = 0, \tag{27}$$

where the i, j, k subscripts would now refer to alternative combinations of variable input prices and shadow prices. Clearly, if separability restrictions held for all $-r$, they would also hold for all u; alternatively, if they hold evaluated at all possible F/Y, they also hold evaluated at all possible F^*/Y. Hence, $\{(i, j), k\}$ separability of the shadow average total-cost function S is equivalent to the same separability on the long-run or envelope cost function H and on the production function f.

Before concluding this discussion of envelope consistent functional separability, it is useful also to consider a less restrictive form of separability, called *weak approximate separability* by Denny and Fuss (1977). With weak approximate separability, the restrictions of separability are imposed only at one data point and not at all data points; in the Denny-Fuss environment based on a translog cost function, the approximation point chosen was the expansion point at which the translog could be considered a second-order Taylor series approximation to an arbitrary cost function.

In the present context, approximate separability of a shadow average-cost function would have implications for approximate separability of the envelope or long-run cost function (and vice versa) if and only if the point of approximation coincided with the point of tangency between the SHATC and the LRATC curves. Note, however, that since this tangency point depends in general on the particular combination of input prices, the approximation will be exact only at the tangency of one particular SHATC curve with one corresponding LRATC curve; more specifically, it is generally not possible based on a single point of approximation to draw out the locus of tangency points with various SHATC and LRATC curves. As a result, in general, it is not possible to infer approximate separability of the LRATC function based on approximate separability of the SHATC function. Analogous arguments hold for the impossibility, in general, of inferring approximate separability features of the short-run restricted-cost function based on approximate separability of the long-run or envelope function.

5   Envelope consistent functional separability: the translog function

In the previous section the envelope consistency of functional separability was discussed in a rather general context, with reference only to a neo-classical production function with constant returns to scale. The various types of separability restrictions in the context of a particular functional form are now presented, namely, the translog restricted or variable-cost function.[7]

In order to keep notation manageable, the six different cases of separability presented in the previous section will be considered in the context of a four-input restricted translog cost function, where input i will hereafter be denoted with a subscript 1, j with a subscript 2, and k with a sub-

---

[7] For early applications of the translog variable-cost function, see Atkinson and Halvorsen (1976) and Brown and Christensen (1981).

script 3, and the fourth input will be assumed to be a variable input. Note that since case 2 separability involves three inputs, the four-input function is the minimal complex case available.

The translog variable-cost function can be written as

$$\ln \frac{VC}{Y} = \alpha_0 + \sum_{i=1}^{N} \alpha_i \ln w_i + \sum_{j=1}^{J} \beta_j \ln \frac{F_j}{Y} + 0.5 \sum_{i=1}^{N} \sum_{j=1}^{N} \gamma_{ij} \ln w_i \ln w_j$$

$$+ 0.5 \sum_{i=1}^{J} \sum_{j=1}^{J} \delta_{ij} \ln F_i \ln F_j + \sum_{i=1}^{N} \sum_{j=1}^{J} \rho_{ij} \ln w_i \ln \frac{F_j}{Y}$$

$$+ \sum_{j=1}^{J} \pi_j [\ln Y \ln F_j - 0.5(\ln Y)^2], \tag{28}$$

where $\gamma_{ij} = \gamma_{ji}$, $\delta_{ij} = \delta_{ji}$, and linear homogeneity in prices, given F_j/Y, implies the restrictions

$$\sum_{i=1}^{N} \alpha_i = 1, \qquad \sum_{i=1}^{N} \gamma_{ij} = \sum_{j=1}^{N} \gamma_{ij} = \sum_{i=1}^{N} \rho_{ij} = 0, \quad j = 1, ..., J. \tag{29}$$

Further, constant returns to scale on the underlying production function implies the additional restrictions that

$$\pi_j + \sum_{i=1}^{J} \delta_{ij} = 0, \quad j = 1, ..., J. \tag{30}$$

In order to save space, we do not present here the various separability-related derivatives corresponding with the translog restricted- or variable-cost function; the interested reader is instead referred to Brown and Christensen (1981, pp. 211–14, 220) and to Berndt and Hesse (1986).

In order for $\{(1, 2), 3, 4\}$ separability to obtain, it is necessary and sufficient that the $\{(1, 2), 3\}$ and the $\{(1, 2), 4\}$ separability restrictions hold simultaneously. With the translog form, as noted already by Berndt and Christensen (1973b, 1974), the global separability restrictions can be imposed either as linear or as nonlinear restrictions on the translog parameters; further, these linear and nonlinear restrictions form separate, nonnested branches of the unrestricted translog. Finally, we also compute weak approximate separability restrictions for the translog, which, following Denny and Fuss (1977), impose separability at only a single data point.

We begin with case 1, which provides a base or standard case in that all inputs are assumed to be variable. In this alternative the linear restrictions for $\{(1, 2), 3, 4\}$ separability turn out to be

$$\gamma_{13} = \gamma_{23} = \gamma_{14} = \gamma_{24} = 0, \tag{31}$$

whereas those for nonlinear separability are

$$\frac{\alpha_1}{\alpha_2} = \frac{\gamma_{13}}{\gamma_{23}} = \frac{\gamma_{14}}{\gamma_{24}} = \frac{\gamma_{11}}{\gamma_{12}} \Rightarrow \frac{\gamma_{12}}{\gamma_{22}}. \tag{32}$$

The corresponding restrictions for weak approximate separability (WAS) are a subset of the nonlinear restrictions (32), in particular, the first two equalities.

Case 2 is the opposite polar extreme case, in which inputs 1, 2, and 3 are fixed and only 4 is variable. In such a case the restricted-cost function reduces to an input requirement function and thus is extremely restricted. This alternative is not pursued, therefore, because even a slightly less constrained case (case 6) will be shown to be very highly restrictive.

Case 3 represents an alternative in which inputs 1, 2, and 4 are variable and only 3 is fixed. In the context of a production function with capital (K), labor (L), energy (E), and nonenergy intermediate materials (M) inputs, an example might be $\{(E,M),K,L\}$ separability in which the energy and nonenergy intermediate material inputs E and M are assumed to be separable from the fixed input K and the variable input L; that is, an (M^*,K,L) specification is being tested, where M^* is an aggregate of E and M. For this type of separability to hold on the translog function globally, the four necessary and sufficient linear separability restrictions are

$$\gamma_{14} = \gamma_{24} = \rho_{31} = \rho_{32} = 0, \tag{33}$$

whereas the three global nonlinear separability restrictions turn out to be

$$\frac{\alpha_1}{\alpha_2} = \frac{\rho_{31}}{\rho_{32}} = \frac{\gamma_{11}}{\gamma_{12}} = \frac{\gamma_{12}}{\gamma_{22}} \Rightarrow = \frac{\gamma_{14}}{\gamma_{24}}. \tag{34}$$

As in case 1, WAS again involves only two nonlinear restrictions; here they are

$$\frac{\alpha_1}{\alpha_2} = \frac{\rho_{31}}{\rho_{32}} = \frac{\gamma_{14}}{\gamma_{24}}. \tag{35}$$

Note that in case 3, the number of restrictions corresponding with linear, nonlinear, and WAS is the same as in case 1; this is also shown in Table 1.

Case 4 is the first alternative in which fixed inputs are included in the separable set; in particular, inputs 1 and 2 are fixed and 3 and 4 are variable in the $\{(1,2),3,4\}$ specification. An example of this might be a function in which two fixed inputs, producers' durable equipment and nonresidential structures, are specified to be separable from labor and an all-materials input, where the latter two inputs are variable. The necessary and sufficient linear restrictions for such a type of separability again number 4,

Table 1. *Summary of {(1,2), 3, 4} separability restrictions on translog form*

Case	Number of free parameters	V	F	General form of restrictions	Number of restrictions Linear	Nonlinear	WAS
1	9	1234		$(G_i G_{jk} - G_j G_{ik}) + (G_i G_{jg} - G_j G_{ig})\cdot g_k = 0$	4	3	2
3	9	124	3	$(G_i G_{jg} - G_j G_{ig})\cdot g_k = 0$	4	3	2
4	9	34	12	$(g^i g_k^j - g^j g_k^i) = 0$	4	3	3
5	9	134	2	$(G_i g_k^j - g^j G_{ik} - g^j G_{ig} g_k) = 0$	5	3	3
6	9	14	23	$(G_i g_k^j - g^j G_{ig} g_k) = 0$	6	6*	5

Note: 6* refers to six linear restrictions; the six nonlinear restrictions are mutually inconsistent unless zero linear restrictions are imposed.

$$\rho_{14} = \rho_{24} = \delta_{11} + \delta_{12} = \delta_{12} + \delta_{22} = 0 \Rightarrow \pi_1 = \pi_2 = 0, \tag{36}$$

whereas the corresponding three independent nonlinear restrictions have the form

$$\frac{\beta_1}{\beta_2} = \frac{\delta_{11}}{\delta_{12}} = \frac{\delta_{12}}{\delta_{22}} = \frac{\rho_{13}}{\rho_{23}} \Rightarrow = \frac{\rho_{14}}{\rho_{24}}. \tag{37}$$

An interesting result that emerges in this case, however, is that the WAS conditions coincide with those for nonlinear separability [(37)]; this implies that testing for WAS in case 4 is equivalent to testing for global non-linear separability.

Case 5 represents an alternative in which a mix of a variable (input 1) and fixed (2) inputs are specified to be separable from two variable inputs (3 and 4). One example of this, suggested by the findings of Berndt and Wood (1975, 1979), is that the fixed-input capital (input 2) and variable energy (input 1) are specified to be separable in the long run from the labor and nonenergy intermediate materials inputs, that is, $\{(K, E), L, M\}$ separability. A somewhat surprising result here is that the necessary and sufficient linear restrictions for this type of separability are more severe than in cases 1, 3, and 4; in particular, the five independent linear parameter restrictions turn out to be

$$\rho_{21} = \rho_{23} = \pi_2 = \gamma_{11} = \gamma_{13} = 0 \Rightarrow \rho_{24} = \gamma_{14} = 0. \tag{38}$$

For nonlinear separability, however, the number of required independent restrictions is only 3, as in cases 1, 3, and 4:

$$\frac{\alpha_1}{\beta_2} = \frac{\gamma_{11}}{\rho_{21}} = \frac{\gamma_{13}}{\rho_{23}} = \frac{\rho_{23}}{\pi_2} \Rightarrow = \frac{\gamma_{14}}{\rho_{24}}. \tag{39}$$

Moreover, as in case 4, in this case 5 the conditions for local WAS separability coincide with those for global nonlinear separability (39), implying that for $\{(1,2), 3, 4\}$ separability, testing for WAS is tantamount to testing for global separability. Both the nonlinear and the WAS separability restrictions number less than those required for linear separability; see Table 1.

Finally, in case 6 there are two fixed inputs (2 and 3) and two variable inputs (1 and 4). An example of this alternative might be the case in which capital and labor were each considered to be fixed, whereas energy and nonenergy materials were variable, and in which E and K were separable from L and M, that is, $\{(E, K), L, M\}$ separability. Not surprisingly, given the results of case 5, it turns out that this case is extremely restrictive. In particular, the number of required independent linear restrictions is 6,

$$\rho_{21} = \rho_{31} = \pi_2 = \pi_3 = \gamma_{14} = \delta_{22} = 0 \Rightarrow \gamma_{11} = \gamma_{44} = \rho_{24} = \rho_{34} = \delta_{23} = \delta_{33} = 0.$$

For reasons similar to those described in Berndt and Christensen (1973b), the corresponding six nonlinear separability restrictions are mutually inconsistent and can only hold if linear separability restrictions are instead imposed. Finally, for WAS the corresponding restrictions reduce to the translog attempting to approximate a four-input constant-elasticity-of-substitution (CES) function, implying that the number of restrictions is 5 and the number of remaining free parameters is 4 (three intercept terms plus a single substitution elasticity parameter).

6   Concluding remarks and suggestions for further research

This chapter has examined the following issue: What do separability restrictions on a long-run total-cost function (where all inputs are variable) imply in terms of constraints on the corresponding short-run or restricted-cost function (where some inputs are fixed) and vice versa? Using the Wong–Viner envelope relationship, I have derived the conditions for envelope consistent functional separability. If separability on the underlying production function is specified to be global (which is typically the case), separability restrictions on long-run total-cost and short-run shadow cost functions are equivalent; if, however, the separability is only local (e.g., at one data point or at a point of expansion in a Taylor series framework), inference regarding separability between short-run and long-run cost functions can be valid in general only if the point of expansion coincides with the point at which the approximation is exact. Hence, unless separability is specified to be approximate, complete inference concerning separability of the short-run function can be obtained from the long-run function and vice versa.

With this in mind, separability restrictions for six types of separability were derived for the translog restricted- or variable-cost function, where the six alternatives correspond with varying mixes of fixed and variable inputs. Several important findings emerged. First, whenever the separable input bundle contained a fixed input, the WAS restrictions were more severe than in the case of a model with only variable inputs. Second, in several cases involving a separable input bundle containing one or two fixed inputs, the conditions for nonlinear separability coincided with those for WAS, implying that global inference could be obtained using appropriate WAS constraints. Finally, when the separable input bundle involved a fixed input and a variable input, the conditions for linear separability were considerably more restrictive and in particular involved a greater number of parameter restrictions than in a corresponding model with only variable inputs. One implication of these findings is, therefore, that with the translog function the presence of fixed inputs can increase the severity of separability restrictions, particularly if the separable input bundle involves a mix of fixed and variable inputs.[8]

These findings suggest a number of issues meriting further research. First, for the translog form the substitution elasticity restrictions corresponding with each of the six separability types should be derived and interpreted. Second, corresponding separability restrictions should be examined for functional forms other than the translog, such as the generalized Leontief, generalized Box–Cox,[9] and other flexible functional forms recently proposed in the literature. Finally, since separability restrictions involving fixed inputs appear to be rather severe, it may be useful for empirical research to examine empirical possibilities of even weaker forms of separability, such as the weakly recursive specifications discussed by Blackorby, Primont, and Russell (1975).

REFERENCES

Atkinson, S. E. and R. Halvorsen. 1976. "Interfuel Substitution in Steam Electric Power Generation." *Journal of Political Economy* 84(5): 959–78.

Berndt, E. R. and L. R. Christensen. 1973a. "The Internal Structure of Functional Relationships: Separability, Substitution and Aggregation." *Review of Economic Studies* 40(3): 403–10.

1973b. "The Translog Function and the Substitution of Equipment, Structures and Labor in U.S. Manufacturing, 1929–1968." *Journal of Econometrics* 1(1): 81–113.

1974. "Testing for the Existence of a Consistent Aggregate Index of Labor Inputs." *American Economic Review* 64(3): 391–404.

Berndt, E. R. and M. A. Fuss. 1986. "Productivity Measurement with Adjustments for Variations in Capacity Utilization and Other Forms of Temporary Equilibrium." *Journal of Econometrics* 33(1/2): 7–29.

Berndt, E. R. and D. M. Hesse. 1986. "Measuring and Assessing Capacity Utilization in the Manufacturing Sectors of Nine OECD Countries." *European Economic Review* 30: 961–89.

Berndt, E. R. and M. S. Khaled. 1979. "Parametric Productivity Measurement and Choice Among Flexible Functional Forms." *Journal of Political Economy* 87(6): 1220–45.

Berndt, E. R. and D. O. Wood. 1975. "Technology, Prices and the Derived Demand for Energy." *Review of Economics and Statistics* 52(3): 259–68.

1979. "Engineering and Econometric Interpretations of Energy-Capital Complementarity." *American Economic Review* 69(3): 342–54.

Blackorby, C., D. Primont, and R. Russell. 1975. "Budgeting, Decentralization and Aggregation." *Annals of Economic and Social Measurement* 4(1): 23–44.

[8] The empirical findings of Pindyck and Rotemberg (1983), where labor is treated as fixed and then is disaggregated into production and nonproduction workers, require particularly careful interpretation in this context.

[9] See Berndt and Khaled (1979) for a discussion of the generalized Box–Cox and its various special cases.

Brown, R. S. and L. R. Christensen. 1981. "Estimating Elasticities of Substitution in a Model of Partial Static Equilibrium: An Application to U.S. Agriculture, 1947–1974." In *Modeling and Measuring Natural Resource Substitution,* E. R. Berndt and B. C. Field, Eds. Cambridge, MA: MIT Press, pp. 209–29.

Deaton, A. and J. Muellbauer. 1980. *Economics and Consumer Behavior.* Cambridge: Cambridge University Press.

Denny, M. G. S. and M. A. Fuss. 1977. "The Use of Approximation Analysis to Test for Separability and the Existence of Consistent Aggregates." *American Economic Review* 67(3): 404–18.

Denny, M. G. S. and J. D. May. 1978. "Homotheticity and Real Value-Added in Canadian Manufacturing." In *Production Economics: A Dual Approach to Theory and Applications,* Vol. 2, M. Fuss and D. McFadden, Eds. Amsterdam: North-Holland, pp. 53–70.

Denny, M. G. S. and C. Pinto. 1978. "An Aggregate Model with Multi-Product Technologies." In *Production Economics: A Dual Approach to Theory and Applications,* Vol. 2, M. Fuss and D. McFadden, Eds. Amsterdam: North-Holland, pp. 249–67.

Goldman, S. M. and H. Uzawa. 1964. "A Note on Separability in Demand Analysis." *Econometrica* 32: 387–98.

Hazilla, M. and R. J. Kopp. 1986. "Testing for Separable Functional Structure Using Temporary Equilibrium Models." *Journal of Econometrics* 33(1/2): 119–42.

Lau, L. J. 1978. "Applications of Profit Functions." In *Production Economics: A Dual Approach to Theory and Applications,* Vol. 1, M. Fuss and D. McFadden, Eds. Amsterdam: North-Holland, pp. 133–216.

Leontief, W. W. 1947. "Introduction to a Theory of the Internal Structure of Functional Relationships." *Econometrica* 15: 361–73.

Pindyck, R. S. and J. J. Rotemberg. 1983. "Dynamic Factor Demands, Energy Use, and the Effects of Energy Price Shocks." *American Economic Review* 73(5): 1066–79.

Shephard, R. W. 1970. *The Theory of Cost and Production Functions.* Princeton: Princeton University Press.

Sono, M. 1945. "The Effect of Price Changes on the Demand and Supply of Separable Goods." In Japanese, *Kokumin Keisai Zasshi* 74: 1–51. Translated into English, *International Economic Review* 2(2): 239–71, 1961.

Strotz, R. H. 1969. "The Utility Tree: A Correction and Further Appraisal." *Econometrica* 27: 482–8.

Viner, J. 1931. "Cost Curves and Supply Curves." *Zeitschrift fur Nationalokonomie* III: 23–46. Reprinted in American Economic Association. *Readings in Price Theory.* Homewood, IL: Irwin, 1952, pp. 198–238.

CHAPTER 3

Flexible functional forms for profit functions and global curvature conditions

W. Erwin Diewert and Lawrence Ostensoe

1   Introduction

In empirical applications using flexible functional forms,[1] it often tran-
spires that the estimated functional form does not satisfy the theoretically
appropriate curvature properties. In this chapter, a functional form is
proposed for a *restricted profit function*[2] that has the property that the
appropriate curvature conditions can be imposed globally in a manner
that does not destroy the flexibility of the functional form. Our proposed
functional form is based on the work of Fuss (1977), Diewert and Wales
(1987), and Diewert (1986).

A brief outline of the chapter follows. In Section 2, we define a new
functional form for a restricted profit function that is flexible for a constant-returns-to-scale technology. Moreover, the theoretically appropriate
curvature conditions can be imposed globally without destroying the flexibility of the functional form. In Section 3, we define a functional form
that is flexible for a nonconstant-returns-to-scale technology. Section 4
concludes.

Research support from the National Science Foundation, Grant SES-8420937, is gratefully
acknowledged. The research reported here is part of the National Bureau of Economic Research's research program in productivity. Any opinions expressed are those of the authors
and not those of the National Bureau of Economic Research. The authors are indebted to
A. Deaton and M. Fuss for helpful comments.

[1] A functional form is flexible if it can approximate an arbitrary twice continuously differentiable function to the second order at a point. For an analysis and comparison of alternative formal definitions of the flexibility property, see the Appendix in Barnett (1983).

[2] This is the term used by McFadden (1966). The concept is due to Samuelson (1953). Gorman (1968) uses the term *gross profit function,* whereas Diewert (1973, 1974) uses the term
variable profit function.

2   Normalized quadratic profit function

Let $p \equiv [p_1, \ldots, p_N] \gg 0_N$ denote a vector of positive prices for variable outputs and inputs that the producer faces in a period.[3] Suppose that the producer's technology can be summarized by a (static) production function f, where $x_1 = f(x_2, \ldots, x_N, z)$, $x \equiv [x_1, x_2, \ldots, x_N]$ is a vector of variable outputs and inputs, and $z \equiv [z_1, \ldots, z_M]$ is a nonnegaive capital stock vector. Then the producer's *restricted profit function* π is defined as the solution to the following variable profit maximization problem:

$$\pi(p, z) \equiv \max_{x_1, \ldots, x_N} \left\{ \sum_{i=1}^{N} p_i x_i : x_1 = f(x_2, \ldots, x_N, z) \right\}. \tag{1}$$

We now make the following sign convention: If x_1 is an output (input), then $x_i > 0$ (< 0). Thus, $\pi(p, z)$ is the maximum net revenue the producer can obtain if he or she faces the price vector p for variable goods and has the vector z of effective capital services.

Under various assumptions on the technology, $\pi(p, z)$ will satisfy various regularity conditions.[4] However, $\pi(p, z)$ must be linearly homogeneous and convex in p for each z.

Consider the following functional form for π:

$$\pi(p, z) \equiv \tfrac{1}{2}\alpha^T z p^T A p p_1^{-1} + \tfrac{1}{2}\beta^T p z^T B z z_1^{-1} + p^T C z, \tag{2}$$

where $\alpha > 0_M$ and $\beta > 0_N$ are prespecified parameter vectors; $A \equiv [a_{ij}] = A^T$ with $a_{1i} = a_{i1} = 0$ for $i = 1, \ldots, N$; $B \equiv [b_{ij}] = B$ with $b_{1j} = b_{j1} = 0$ for $j = 1, \ldots, M$ and $C \equiv [c_{ij}]$. Thus, A and B are symmetric matrices of parameters that have first rows and columns equal to vectors of zeros and C is a (nonsymmetric) matrix of parameters of size $N \times M$. Note that the *normalized quadratic profit function* π defined by (2) is linearly homogenous in p and z separably. This means that the underlying dual technology is subject to constant returns to scale; see Diewert (1973, 1974). In order for $\pi(p, z)$ to be a convex function of p for each fixed z, it is necessary and sufficient that the A matrix be positive semidefinite; see Diewert and Wales (1987). Finally, note that there are $N(N-1)/2 + M(M-1)/2 + NM$ free parameters in the A, B, and C matrices. This turns out to be the minimal number that is required for a profit function to be flexible when the underlying technology is subject to constant returns to scale, as shown in what follows.

As mentioned above, $\pi(p, z)$ must be linearly homogeneous in p for fixed z. In the case of a twice continuously differentiable π, Euler's theo-

---

[3] Notation: $p \gg 0_N$ means each component of p is positive; $p > 0_N$ means $p \geq 0_N$ but $p \neq 0_N$, and $p^T x \equiv \sum_{i=1}^{N} p_i x_i$ is the inner product of the vectors p and x.

[4] See Gorman (1968), McFadden (1966), and Diewert (1973, 1974).

rem on homogeneous functions implies the following $1 + N + M$ restrictions on the first and second derivatives of π:[5]

$$\pi(p, z) = p^T \nabla_p \pi(p, z), \tag{3}$$

$$0_N = \nabla_{pp}^2 \pi(p, z)p, \tag{4}$$

$$\nabla_z \pi(p, z) = \nabla_{zp}^2 \pi(p, z)p, \tag{5}$$

where

$$\nabla_p \pi(p, z) \equiv [\partial \pi(p, z)/\partial p_1, \ldots, \partial \pi(p, z)/\partial p_N]^T$$

is the vector of first-order partial derivatives of π with respect to the components of p, $\nabla_{zp}^2 \pi(p, z)$ is the $M \times N$ matrix of second-order partial derivatives of π with respect to the components of p and z, and so on.

In the case of a constant-returns-to-scale technology $\pi(p, z)$ will also be linearly homogeneous in z for each fixed p. In the twice-differentiable case, this implies the following restrictions on the derivatives of π:

$$\pi(p, z) = z^T \nabla_z \pi(p, z), \tag{6}$$

$$0_M = \nabla_{zz}^2 \pi(p, z)z, \tag{7}$$

$$\nabla_p \pi(p, z) = \nabla_{pz}^2 \pi(p, z)z. \tag{8}$$

However, not all of the restrictions (3)–(8) are independent. Premultiplying both sides of (5) by z^T and using (6), we deduce that

$$z^T \nabla_{zp} \pi(p, z)p = \pi(p, z). \tag{9}$$

Premultiplying both sides of equation (8) by p^T and using equation (3), we deduce that

$$p^T \nabla_{pz} \pi(p, z)z = \pi(p, z). \tag{10}$$

By the symmetry of the second-order partial derivatives of π, we have

$$[\nabla_{pz} \pi(p, z)]^T = \nabla_{zp}^2 \pi(p, z), \tag{11}$$

and thus (9) is equivalent to (10). Hence, only $1 + 2N + 2M$ of restrictions (3)–(8) are independent.

A flexible functional form π for a function of $N + M$ variables with no linear homogeneity restrictions must have $1 + N + M + N(N+1)/2 + M(M+1)/2 + NM$ independent parameters. However, if $\pi(p, z)$ is linearly homogeneous in both p and z separately, then we may reduce the preceding number of parameters by $1 + 2N + 2M$, and so we need only have $N(N-1)/2 + M(M-1)/2 + NM$ independent parameters, which is exactly the number π defined by equation (2) has.

[5] See Diewert (1974, pp. 143–6).

Theorem 1. *The normalized quadratic profit function π defined by equation (2) is a flexible functional form in the class of profit functions that are consistent with a constant-return-to-scale technology; that is, for any $p^* \gg 0_N$ and $z^* \gg 0_M$, we may choose A, B, and C satisfying the restrictions listed following equation (2) for any $\alpha > 0_M$ and $\beta > 0_N$, so that the following equations are satisfied for any twice continuously differentiable profit function π^* that is consistent with a constant-returns-to-scale technology:*

$$\pi(p^*, z^*) = \pi^*(p^*, z^*), \tag{12}$$

$$\nabla_p \pi(p^*, z^*) = \nabla_p \pi^*(p^*, z^*), \tag{13}$$

$$\nabla_z \pi(p^*, z^*) = \nabla_z \pi^*(p^*, z^*), \tag{14}$$

$$\nabla_{pp}^2 \pi(p^*, z^*) = \nabla_{pp}^2 \pi^*(p, z^*), \tag{15}$$

$$\nabla_{zz}^2 \pi(p^*, z^*) = \nabla_{zz}^2 \pi^*(p^*, z^*), \tag{16}$$

$$\nabla_{pz}^2 \pi(p^*, z^*) = \nabla_{pz}^2 \pi^*(p^*, z^*). \tag{17}$$

Proof: Let $\pi^*(p, z)$ be an arbitrary twice continuously differentiable function at p^*, z^* that is linearly homogeneous in p, z separately. Then π^* will also satisfy restrictions (3)–(8) at (p^*, z^*). In view of these restrictions, all of the equations (12)–(17) will be satisfied if we can satisfy the last $N-1$ by $N-1$ equations in (15), the last $M-1$ by $M-1$ equations in (16), and the NM equations in (17). Differentiating (2) yields the following equations:

$$\frac{\partial^2 \pi(p, z)}{\partial p_i \, \partial p_j} = a_{ij} p_1^{-1} \alpha^T z, \quad i, j = 2, 3, \dots, N; \tag{18}$$

$$\frac{\partial^2 \pi(p, z)}{\partial z_i \, \partial z_j} = b_{ij} z_1^{-1} \beta^T p, \quad i, j = 2, 3, \dots, M; \tag{19}$$

$$\frac{\partial^2 \pi(p, z)}{\partial p_i \, \partial z_j} = c_{ij} + \sum_{n=2}^{N} a_{in} p_n p_1^{-1} \alpha_j + \sum_{m=2}^{M} b_{jm} z_m z_1^{-1} \beta_1,$$
$$i = 2, 3, \dots, N, \quad j = 2, 3, \dots, M; \tag{20}$$

$$\frac{\partial^2 \pi(p, z)}{\partial p_1 \, \partial z_1} = c_{11} - \frac{1}{2} \sum_{n=2}^{N} \sum_{k=2}^{M} a_{nk} p_n p_k p_1^{-2} \alpha_1$$
$$- \frac{1}{2} \sum_{m=2}^{N} \sum_{j=2}^{M} b_{mj} z_m z_j z_1^{-2} \beta_1; \tag{21}$$

$$\frac{\partial^2 \pi(p, z)}{\partial p_1 \, \partial z_m} = c_{1m} - \frac{1}{2} \sum_{n=2}^{N} \sum_{k=2}^{N} a_{nk} p_n p_k p_1^{-2} \alpha_m$$
$$+ \sum_{j=2}^{M} b_{mj} z_j z_1^{-1} \beta_1, \quad m = 2, 3, \dots, M; \tag{22}$$

$$\frac{\partial^2 \pi(p,z)}{\partial p_n \, \partial z_1} = c_{n1} + \sum_{k=2}^{N} a_{nk} p_k p_1^{-1} \alpha_1 - \frac{1}{2} \sum_{m=2}^{M} \sum_{k=2}^{M} b_{mk} z_m z_j z_1^{-2} \beta_n,$$

$$n = 2, 3, \dots, N. \quad (23)$$

Substitute equations (18) evaluated at p^*, z^* into equations (15) and solve for the a_{ij} parameters. This determines the nonzero parameters in the symmetric A matrix. Similarly, use equations (19) and (16) to determine the nonzero b_{ij} parameters in the symmetric B matrix. Now substitute equations (20)–(23) into (17) and determine the C matrix.   Q.E.D.

The producer's system of short-run net supply functions $x(p,z)$, may be obtained by differentiating the profit function defined by (2) with respect to the components of the price vector p (Hotelling's lemma):

$$x(p,z) = \nabla_p \pi(p,z). \quad (24)$$

Suppose that the producer faces the vector of rental prices $w \gg 0_M$ for the capital stock components. Then the producer will want to choose the capital vector z that solves the following profit maximization problem:

$$\max_z \{ \pi(p,z) - w^T z : z \ge 0_M \}. \quad (25)$$

The first-order necessary conditions for an interior solution for (25) are

$$w = \nabla_z \pi(p,z). \quad (26)$$

In the case of a constant-returns-to-scale technology, the solution to (25) need not be unique. In the zero-profits case, there will be a solution ray; nevertheless, each positive z solution should satisfy (26).

The second-order necessary conditions for (25) require that $\nabla^2_{zz} \pi(p,z)$ be negative semidefinite. Necessary and sufficient conditions for this condition are that the matrix B be negative semidefinite.

Equations (24) and (26) are linear in the components of the A, B, and C matrices. Hence, linear regression techniques may be used to estimate the unknown parameters in (2).[6] All of the parameters can be identified using only equations (24) or (26). Indeed, the profit equation itself, (2), is linear in the unknown parameters so it too could be used to estimate the unknown parameters.[7]

In order for $\pi(p,z)$ to be convex in p, it is necessary and sufficient that the matrix A be positive semidefinite. If the estimated A matrix is not

---

[6] Kohli (1978) used simple transformations of these equations to estimate a translog variable profit function.

[7] However, equation (2) is not independent of equations (24) or (26), and so if (24) and/or (26) are estimated, (2) should not be added as an estimating equation. Moreover, if the data satisfy $p^t \cdot x^t = w^t \cdot z^t$ for each period t, then one of the equations in (24) and (26) must be dropped.

positive semidefinite, the investigator may wish to impose this curvature property. This can be done without destroying the flexibility of the functional form using a technique explained in Diewert and Wales (1987): Use the technique due originally to Wiley, Schmidt, and Bramble (1973, p. 318) and replace A by say EE^T, where E is a lower triangular matrix that in addition has zero elements in its first column. This will ensure the global convexity of $\pi(p, z)$ in p. Similarly, if the investigator uses equations (26), then the B matrix must be negative semidefinite. If the estimated B matrix is not negative semidefinite, then this property may be imposed in a flexible manner by replacing B by, say, $-FF^T$, where F is a lower triangular matrix with zeros in its first column. If this is done, the resulting $\pi(p, z)$ will be globally concave in z for each fixed p, and the dual technology set will be convex.[8]

3   Nonconstant-returns-to-scale technologies

There is a very simple method that may be used to generalize the functional form defined by equation (2) to cover the case of a nonconstant-returns-to-scale technology: Add an additional (artificial) capital variable, z_{M+1}, say, to the z vector and set z_{M+1} equal to a constant (say, 1) for every observation. If we do this, then the reader can verify that the following terms will be added to the right side of (2):

$$\beta^T p b^T z z_1^{-1} + \tfrac{1}{2}\beta^T p b_0 z_1^{-1} + p^T c, \tag{27}$$

where b_0, $b^T \equiv [0, b_2, \ldots, b_M]$, and $c^T \equiv [c_1, \ldots, c_N]$ are $M + N$ additional new parameters that must be estimated, and β is the old vector of predetermined parameters. Note that b_1 is set equal to zero so that the first row of the augmented B matrix continues to be a row of zeros.

Our functional form defined by (2) [plus the additional terms in (27)] differs from the biquadratic restricted profit function defined by Diewert (1986, pp. 89–96), although it is closely related. The main advantage of the present functional form is that a flexible constant-returns-to-scale case is imbedded as a special case of the general functional form defined by (2) and (27). The following $M + N$ linear restrictions on the parameters of (27) are necessary and sufficient for the constant-returns-to-scale property:

$$b_0 = 0, \qquad b_2 = 0, \ldots, b_M = 0, \qquad c_1 = 0, \ldots, c_N = 0. \tag{28}$$

If it is deemed desirable to impose global concavity on the profit function $\pi(p, z)$ with respect to $z \equiv [z_1, \ldots, z_M]^T$, we need only replace the augmented B matrix,

---

[8] See Diewert (1973).

$$\begin{bmatrix} B_T & b \\ b & b_0 \end{bmatrix}$$

by $-GG^T$, where G is an $(M+1) \times (M+1)$ lower triangular matrix with zeros in its first column.

We leave to the reader the task of deriving the appropriate estimating equations (24) and (26), but we note that these equations are linear in the unknown parameters (provided that A and B are not replaced by products of triangular matrices).

4   Conclusion

We conclude this chapter by noting the relationship of our normalized quadratic restricted profit function in the constant-returns-to-scale case defined by (2) to the *Fuss quadratic normalized restricted profit function*[9] defined as follows:

$$\pi(p, z) \equiv p_1 z_1 \left[a_0 + \tilde{a}^T \frac{\tilde{p}}{p_1} + \tilde{b}^T \frac{\tilde{z}}{z_1} + \frac{1}{2} \left(\frac{\tilde{p}}{p_1} \right)^T A \frac{\tilde{p}}{p_1} \right.$$
$$\left. + \frac{1}{2} \left(\frac{\tilde{z}}{z_1} \right)^T B \frac{\tilde{z}}{z_1} + \frac{\tilde{p}}{p_1^T} C \frac{\tilde{z}}{z_1} \right], \tag{29}$$

where $\tilde{p} \equiv (p_2, \ldots, p_N)^T$, $\tilde{z} \equiv (z_2, \ldots, z_M)^T$, a_0 is a scalar parameter, $\tilde{a} \equiv (a_2, \ldots, a_N)^T$ is an $(N-1)$-dimensional vector of parameters, $b \equiv (b_2, \ldots, b_M)^T$ is an $(M-1)$-dimensional vector of parameters, $A = A^T$ is an $(N-1) \times (N-1)$ symmetric matrix of parameters, $B = B^T$ is an $(M-1) \times (M-1)$ symmetric matrix of parameters, and C is an $(N-1) \times (M-1)$ matrix of unknown parameters. Thus, there are $1 + (N-1) + (M-1) + \frac{1}{2}N(N-1) + \frac{1}{2}M(M-1) + (N-1)(M-1)$ unknown parameters in the Fuss functional form, which is just the minimal number required for the flexibility property in the constant-returns-to-scale case. In fact, the π defined by (29) is a flexible functional form for a restricted profit function in the class of constant-returns-to-scale technologies; that is, it is straightforward to prove a version of Theorem 1 using (29) instead of (2).

Using Hotelling's lemma (24), the last $N-1$ variable net supply functions, $x(p, z) \equiv [x_2(p, z), \ldots, x_N(p, z)]^T$, divided by z_1 are

$$\tilde{x}(p, z)/z_1 = \tilde{a} + A(\tilde{p}/p_1) + C(\tilde{z}/z_1). \tag{30}$$

---

[9] This functional form was originally defined by Fuss (1977). The corresponding restricted cost function (which is the negative of a restricted profit function) has been used by Denny, Fuss, and Waverman (1981, p. 237) and Morrison and Berndt (1981).

Using the last $M-1$ equations in (26) and dividing by p_1, we obtain the following $M-1$ equations, where $\tilde{w}(p, z) \equiv [w_2(p, z), \ldots, w_M(p, z)]$:

$$\tilde{w}(p, z)/p_1 = \tilde{b} + B(\tilde{z}/z_1) + C(\tilde{p}/p_1). \tag{31}$$

Dividing both sides of (29) by $p_1 z_1$ and appending errors to the resulting equation and equations (30) and (31) leads to a nice system of estimating equations that is linear in the unknown parameters.

It can readily be verified that $\nabla^2_{\tilde{p}\tilde{p}} \pi(p, z) = Az_1/p_1$. Hence, if $z_1 \geq 0$ and $p_1 > 0$, $\pi(p, z)$ will be *globally convex* in p if and only if A is a positive semidefinite matrix. Hence, if necessary, we can impose global convexity by replacing A by EE^T, where E is lower triangular. Similarly, $\nabla^2_{\tilde{z}\tilde{z}} \pi(p, z) = Bp_1/z_1$. Hence, $\pi(p, z)$ will be globally concave in z if and only if B is a negative semidefinite matrix. As usual, if necessary, we may impose the negative semidefiniteness property on B by replacing B by $-FF^T$, where F is lower triangular.

Thus, in the case of a constant-returns-to-scale technology (and the data have been constructed so that the value of outputs equals the value of inputs), we might conclude that the Fuss functional form defined by (29) is preferable to (2) since it is not necessary to specify the parameter vectors α and β and, moreover, the estimating equations (30) and (31) have a very simple structure. However, appearances can be deceiving: It can be verified that (29) is a special case of (2) (set α and β equal to unit vectors with a 1 in the first component). Thus, we should perhaps call our functional form (2) the *generalized Fuss restricted profit function*.

REFERENCES

Barnett, W. A. 1983. "New Indices of Money Supply and the Flexible Laurent Demand System." *Journal of Business and Economic Statistics* 1: 7–23.
Denny, M., M. Fuss, and L. Waverman. 1981. "Substitution Possibilities for Energy: Evidence from U.S. and Canadian Manufacturing Industries." In *Modeling and Measuring Natural Resource Substitution*, E. R. Berndt and B. C. Field, Eds. Cambridge, MA: MIT Press, pp. 230–58.
Diewert, W. E. 1973. "Functional Forms for Profit and Transformation Functions." *Journal of Economic Theory* 6: 284–316.
    1974. "Applications of Duality Theory." In *Frontiers of Quantitative Economics*, Vol. II, M. D. Intriligator and D. A. Kendrick, Eds. Amsterdam: North-Holland, pp. 106–71.
    1986. *The Measurement of the Economic Benefits of Infrastructure Services*. Lecture Notes in Economics and Mathematical Systems 278. Berlin: Springer-Verlag.
Diewert, W. E. and T. J. Wales. 1987. "Flexible Functional Forms and Global Curvature Conditions." *Econometrica* 55: 43–68.
Fuss, M. A. 1977. "Dynamic Factor Demand Systems with Explicit Costs of Adjustment." In *Dynamic Models of the Industrial Demand for Energy*,

E. R. Berndt, M. Fuss, and L. Waverman, Eds. Palo Alto, CA: Electric Power Research Institute.

Gorman, W. M. 1968. "Measuring the Quantities of Fixed Factors." In *Value, Capital and Growth: Papers in Honour of Sir John Hicks,* J. N. Wolfe, Ed. Chicago: Aldine.

Kohli, U. J. R. 1978. "A Gross National Product Function and the Derived Demand for Imports and Supply of Exports." *Canadian Journal of Economics* 11: 167–82.

McFadden, D. 1966. "Cost, Revenue and Profit Functions: A Cursory Review." Working Paper 86, IBER, University of California, Berkeley.

Morrison, C. J. and E. R. Berndt. 1981. "Short-Run Labor Productivity in a Dynamic Model." *Journal of Econometrics* 16: 339–65.

Samuelson, P. A. 1953. "Prices of Factors and Goods in General Equilibrium." *Review of Economic Studies* 21: 1–20.

Wiley, D. E., W. H. Schmidt, and W. J. Bramble. 1973. "Studies of a Class of Covariance Structure Models." *Journal of the American Statistical Association* 68: 317–23.

CHAPTER 4

Likelihood inference in the nonlinear regression model with explosive linear dynamics

Ian Domowitz and Lars Muus

1   Introduction

The rapid growth of dynamic economic theory has contributed to the increasing use of nonlinear regression in applied time series econometrics. The interest in tractable theories of estimation and hypothesis testing for such nonlinear time series models has grown accordingly. The body of theory relevant to parametric structures that has emerged over the past few years is quite elegant and virtually complete in some respects.

Standard limiting results, such as the asymptotic normality of an estimator or the chi-squared distribution of a test statistic for testing restrictions, rely on trade-offs between moment assumptions and assumptions regarding the dependence of the stochastic process being considered. In particular, most current theories that allow deviations from stationarity assumptions rely on dependence concepts stronger than the ergodic property appropriate for stationary structures.[1] Stationarity and/or such restrictions on the dependence properties of the involved stochastic processes are notoriously hard to verify in nonlinear models.

The problem addressed in this chapter rests on a potentially more serious consideration than difficulties in the verification of assumptions. Recent investigations of the stochastic properties of decision variables arising from various classes of dynamic models reveal that the stochastic processes describing such decision variables can indeed fail to have the

This work was supported by the National Science Foundation. We are grateful to Bill Barnett, Soren Johansen, Nick Kiefer, Dale Mortensen, Peter Phillips, Gene Savin, and two anonymous referees for helpful comments and suggestions.

[1] See Crowder (1976) for a thorough analysis of the maximum-likelihood estimator based on dependent observations. The role of dependence conditions is discussed in Domowitz (1985).

53

ergodic property. Theoretical results obtained by Chamberlain and Wilson (1984) for a wide class of intertemporal consumption plans indicate this. Empirical examples illustrating explosiveness in models of consumption include the work of Hall (1978) and Daly and Hadjimatheou (1981). Estimates indicating explosiveness in fixed investment processes are contained in Blanchard (1981). This analysis and the investigation of decision rules arising from models of interrelated factor demand in Domowitz and Muus (1984) and Muus and Lederman (1986) stress the possibility of explosiveness in the decision variables. Majumdar, Mitra, and Nyarko (1986) demonstrate that decision variables from well-defined stochastic dynamic programming problems relating to economic growth can have an arbitrarily large number of ergodic classes associated with them.

In this chapter, we begin the analysis of maximum-likelihood inference in the dynamic nonlinear regression model when the ergodic assumption fails. To our knowledge, this chapter presents the first attempt at such an exercise, and we consider only a special case, namely, a model in which the nonergodic dynamics (here, explosive) enter linearly and are separable with respect to a nonlinear response function of exogenous variables and parameters. Although such a structure may appear artificial, it represents a common class of decision rules arising from stochastic dynamic programming problems. Forward-looking partial adjustment models with rational expectations and convex costs of adjustment fall into this class, for example.

Conditions are provided under which the maximum-likelihood estimator (MLE) of the model parameters converges to a variance mixture of normally distributed random variables. Another way of stating this is to characterize the limiting distribution as multivariate normal but one in which the variance is a nondegenerate random variable. The distribution of the variance structure is derived under conditions stated in the next sections. Generality of such auxiliary assumptions is occasionally sacrificed in order to obtain the sharpest possible results with a minimum of extraneous detail.

Such distributional results would be utterly useless to the practitioner without corresponding results for standard test statistics. We define a class of conditional inference procedures in which the variable conditioned upon is the limiting information matrix itself. We can then show that standard test statistics for testing nonlinear restrictions remain chi-squared distributed under the null hypothesis. Performance under the alternative presents some rather difficult problems outside the scope of this chapter, however. The results presented here complement the unconditional analysis of tests of linear restrictions in Domowitz and Muus (1987). As such, we move closer to a satisfactory theory of hypothesis testing, when the ergodic assumption fails.

2   The basic framework

Asymptotic theory underlying the standard analysis of maximum-likelihood procedures in parametric models is based on the concept of locally asymptotically normal (LAN) families of distributions.[2] Under certain regularity conditions, which include assumptions implying the ergodicity of the relevant stochastic processes, the score vector tends in law to a normally distributed random variable, and the variance of this distribution is nonstochastic and finite. In statistical models based on nonergodic processes, the asymptotic distribution of the MLE need not be normal and may, in general, have infinite variance.[3] More precisely, however, the limiting distribution is characterized by a variance that is a nondegenerate random variable, as pointed out by Basawa and Scott (1983).[4] In this section we shall state easily interpretable conditions under which the MLE has such a distribution in a general setting; in the subsequent discussion of the general framework we shall apply the modified framework formulated by Domowitz and Muus (1987), since this provides the basic asymptotic results based on conditions less general than those stated by Basawa and Scott (1983) but more familiar to the econometrician.

Let $(\Omega, \mathfrak{F}, P)$ be a probability space, and let (y_t) be a stochastic process with a joint density $f_T(y_1, \ldots, y_T; \theta)$ with respect to some σ-finite measure, where $\theta \in \Theta \subseteq \mathfrak{R}^k$, and let $\ell_T(\theta) = \log f_T(y_1, \ldots, y_T; \theta)$ be the log-likelihood function based on the T observations $y_1, \ldots, y_T$. We shall impose the following standard regularity conditions facilitating the analysis of the limiting behavior of the MLE.

Assumption 2.1. $\Theta \subseteq \mathfrak{R}^k$ is compact.

Assumption 2.2.   The function $\ell_T: \Theta \rightarrow \mathfrak{R}^k$ is twice continuously differentiable on int Θ almost surely.

Assumption 2.3. $E[(\partial \ell_T / \partial \theta_i)^2] < \infty$ for all T, $i = 1, \ldots, k$.

Let $\nabla \ell_T(\theta)$ be the score vector, and let $I_T(\theta)$ be the negative of the matrix of second-order derivatives of ℓ_T with respect to θ; that is,

$$I_T(\theta) = -\left[\frac{\partial^2 \ell_T}{\partial \theta_i \, \partial \theta_j} \right]_{i,j=1,\ldots,k}. \tag{2.1}$$

Let $D_T(\theta)$ be the nonstochastic diagonal matrix given by

---

[2] See LeCam (1960) for a rigorous treatment.

[3] See, e.g., the work of White (1958), Anderson (1959), and Rao (1961) on pure autoregressive models.

[4] Such a result is implicit in the analysis of Anderson (1959) and Rao (1961).

$$D_T(\theta) = \text{diag}\left\{E\left[\left(\frac{\partial \ell_T}{\partial \theta_i}\right)^2\right]\right\}_{i=1,\ldots,k}. \tag{2.2}$$

Finally, let

$$\nabla \ell_T^*(\theta) = D_T(\theta)^{-1/2} \nabla \ell_T(\theta) \tag{2.3}$$

be the "normalized" score vector, and let

$$I_T^*(\theta) = D_T(\theta)^{-1/2} I_T(\theta) D_T(\theta)^{-1/2} \tag{2.4}$$

be the "normalized" observed Fisher information matrix. As shown in Basawa and Scott (1983) and Domowitz and Muus (1987), the normalizations introduced in the preceding are crucial in order to obtain useful asymptotic results.[5] The normalizing factor chosen cannot guarantee the convergence of a quantity such as $I_T^*(\theta)$ to a constant, although the weights may grow at an exponential rate, as the following additional assumptions suggest.

Assumption 2.4. $D_T(\theta)^{-1/2} \to 0$ *for* $T \to \infty$, *uniformly in* $\theta \in \Theta$.

Assumption 2.5.   *There exists a* $k \times k$ *random matrix* $I^*(\theta)$ *that is almost surely (a.s.) finite and positive semi-definite such that*

$$I_T^*(\theta) \to a.s. \ I^*(\theta) \quad \text{for } T \to \infty$$

uniformly in $\theta \in \Theta$.

Assumption 2.4 is a consistency requirement that must be fulfilled in any application of interest. Assumption 2.5 is the crucial condition. It essentially defines the mixing distribution of the limiting distribution of the MLE. A nonstochastic limiting matrix $I^*(\theta)$ is a defining characteristic of analysis for ergodic processes. On the basis of these assumptions the following results hold.

Proposition 2.1.   *For* $\theta \in \text{int } \Theta$,

$$\nabla \ell_T^*(\theta) \to^d I^*(\theta)^{1/2} Z \quad \text{for } T \to \infty,$$

where $Z \sim N_k(0, I_k)$, *where the random vector* Z *is independent of* $I^*(\theta)$.

Proposition 2.2

(i)   *There exists almost surely a sequence* (θ_T) *such that* $\ell_T(\theta_T) = \max_{\theta \in \Theta} \ell_T(\theta)$.

(ii) $\theta_T \to a.s. \ \theta$ *for* $T \to \infty$.

---

[5] More general weighting matrices are considered in Domowitz and Muus (1987).

(iii) *For $\theta \in \text{int } \Theta$ and $I^*(\theta)$ a.s. positive definite,*

$$D_T(\theta)^{1/2}(\theta_T - \theta) \to^d I^*(\theta)^{-1/2} Z \quad \text{for } T \to \infty,$$

where $Z \sim N_k(0, I_k)$ and the random vector Z is independent of $I^*(\theta)$.

Assumptions 2.1–2.5 ensure the existence, consistency, and "asymptotic normality" of the MLE. The basic difficulty in calculating the limiting distribution of the estimator lies in computing the distribution of the limiting matrix $I^*(\theta)$ followed by the calculation of the resulting mixture distribution. This would be required in any unconditional inference procedure, such as finding the usual standard errors for coefficients.

3 Dynamic nonlinear regression model

Consider the nonlinear dynamic regression model given by

$$y_t = \alpha_1 y_{t-1} + \alpha_2 y_{t-2} + \cdots + \alpha_p y_{t-p} + f(x_t, \beta_0) + \epsilon_t, \quad t = 1, \ldots, T, \quad (3.1)$$

where $y_0, y_{-1}, \ldots, y_{-p+1}$ are arbitrary constants, $\alpha_p \neq 0$, x_t is a vector of nonstochastic regressors, and (ϵ_t) is a Gaussian white-noise process (i.e., $\epsilon_t \sim N(0, \sigma^2)$, $\sigma^2 > 0$). The unknown parameters are $\alpha = [\alpha_1 \cdots \alpha_p]'$, $\beta = [\beta_1 \cdots \beta_k]'$, and σ^2.

Let $\rho_1, \ldots, \rho_p$ be the p roots of the characteristic equation

$$\rho^p - \alpha_1 \rho^{p-1} - \cdots - \alpha_p = 0. \quad (3.2)$$

Without loss of generality, let ρ_1 be a root such that

$$|\rho_1| = \max\{|\rho_1|, \ldots, |\rho_p|\}.$$

We shall make the following assumption, ensuring that the stochastic process (3.1) is explosive and hence nonergodic.

Assumption 3.1

(i) *The root ρ_1 is unique, and $|\rho_1| > 1$.*
(ii) *The roots of (3.2) are distinct.[6]*

We do not rule out the existence of other roots with the modulus in excess of unity. Furthermore, the present framework allows for unit roots as soon as one root has a modulus in excess of unity. Notice that ρ_1 is real, since complex roots will occur in conjugate pairs.

---

[6] At the expense of considerable complexity, the analysis can easily be extended to include roots with multiplicity greater than 1; only expression (3.3) will change, without invalidating the proof presented in Section 4.

In our subsequent analysis we shall use the following factorization of the process (3.1), generalizing the expression of Mann and Wald (1943, p. 178).

Lemma 3.1.   *The stochastic process* (y_t) *defined by* (3.1) *can be written as*

$$y_t = \sum_{j=1}^{p} \omega_j \rho_j^t + \sum_{j=1}^{p} \lambda_j \sum_{i=1}^{t} \rho_j^{t-1}[f(x_i, \beta_0) + \epsilon_i], \tag{3.3}$$

where

$$\sum_{j=1}^{p} \omega_j \rho_j^t = y_t, \quad t = 0, -1, \dots, -p+1, \tag{3.4}$$

and

$$\sum_{j=1}^{p} \lambda_j \rho_j^t = \delta_t, \quad t = 0, -1, \dots, -p+1, \tag{3.5}$$

where $\delta_t = 1$ *for* $t = 0$ *and* $\delta_t = 0$ *for* $t = -1, \dots, -p+1$.

A proof of Lemma 3.1 is provided in the next section. Notice, in particular, that

$$\sum_{j=1}^{p} \lambda_j = 1. \tag{3.6}$$

For the first-order process (i.e., $p = 1$)

$$y_t = \alpha y_{t-1} + f(x_t, \beta_0) + \epsilon_t, \tag{3.7}$$

we get $\omega_1 = y_0$ and $\lambda_1 = 1$, and we obtain the familiar expression

$$y_t = \alpha^t y_0 + \sum_{i=1}^{t} \alpha^{t-i}[f(x_i, \beta_0) + \epsilon_i]. \tag{3.8}$$

Let (z_t) be the stochastic process defined by

$$z_t = y_t - \mu_t, \tag{3.9}$$

where $\mu_t = E[y_t]$. From Lemma 3.1 we then get the expressions

$$z_t = \lambda_1 \sum_{i=1}^{t} \rho_1^{t-i}\epsilon_i + \cdots + \lambda_p \sum_{i=1}^{t} \rho_p^{t-1}\epsilon_i \tag{3.10}$$

and

$$\mu_t = \omega_1 \rho_1^t + \cdots + \omega_p \rho_p^t + \lambda_1 \sum_{i=1}^{t} \rho_1^{t-i}f(x_i, \beta_0)$$

$$+ \cdots + \lambda_p \sum_{i=1}^{t} \rho_p^{t-i}f(x_i, \beta_0). \tag{3.11}$$

In order to find the limiting distribution of the MLE and associated asymptotic test statistics, we shall impose the following regularity conditions on the gradient of the regression function

$$\nabla f(x_t, \beta) = [\partial f(x_t, \beta)/\partial \beta_i]_{i=1,\dots,k}.$$

For notational convenience, we denote $\partial f(x_t, \beta)/\partial \beta_i$ as ∇f_{it} and ∇f_t as $[\nabla f_{1t} \cdots \nabla f_{kt}]'$, suppressing the argument β when no confusion results.

Assumption 3.2. *The parameter vector* $[\alpha \ \beta \ \sigma^2]'$ *lies in the interior of a compact subset* Θ *of* $\Re^s$, *where* $s = p + k + 1$.

Assumption 3.3. *The function* $f(x_t, \cdot): \Theta \to \Re$ *is twice continuously differentiable on* int Θ.

Assumption 3.4

(i) $f(x_t, \beta)$ *and* ∇f_{it} *are* $o(\gamma^t)$ *uniformly in* β *for all* $|\gamma| > 1$, $i = 1, \dots, k$.

(ii) $\sum_{t=1}^{T} \nabla f_{it} \nabla f_{jt} / (\sum_{t=1}^{T} \nabla f_{it}^2)^{1/2} (\sum_{t=1}^{T} \nabla f_{jt}^2)^{1/2} \to q_{ij} < \infty$, *for* $T \to \infty$, *uniformly in* β, *where the* $k \times k$ *matrix* $Q = [q_{ij}]_{i,j=1,\dots,k}$ *is positive definite.*

(iii) $\sup_{1 \le t \le T} \nabla f_{it}^2 / \sum_{s=1}^{T} \nabla f_{is}^2 \to 0$, *for* $T \to \infty$, *uniformly in* β, $i = 1, \dots, k$.

Assumption 3.5

$$\lim_{T \to \infty} \frac{1}{T} \sum_{t=1}^{T} [f(x_t, \beta_0) - f(x_t, \beta)]^2 \ne 0 \quad \text{if } \beta \ne \beta_0.$$

Assumptions 3.2 and 3.3 are quite standard, pertaining to continuity requirements allowing a Taylor series expansion. Assumption 3.5 corresponds to the identification requirement in Amemiya (1983, equation 2.12).

Assumption 3.4 is slightly unusual in its present form but has obvious antecedents in the literature. When $f(x_t, \beta)$ is a linear function, such requirements are sometimes referred to as Grenander conditions. The assumption rules out exponential growth in the regression function gradients while allowing polynomial growth. Thus, polynomial time trends are allowed within the present framework. If the denominator in Assumption 3.4(ii) is replaced by T, the requirement is precisely that of Amemiya (1983, condition 2.20). We have chosen different normalizing constants, while Assumption 3.4(ii) ensures that no term dominates the relevant partial sums. Sufficient conditions for Assumption 3.4 are easily found, particularly if time trends in the gradients are ruled out in favor of, say, logistic growth.[7]

The log-likelihood function (apart from a constant) corresponding to the dynamic regression model (3.1) is given by

$$\ell_T(\alpha, \beta, \sigma^2) = -\frac{T}{2} \log \sigma^2$$

$$- \frac{1}{2\sigma^2} \sum_{t=1}^{T} [y_t - \alpha_1 y_{t-1} - \cdots - \alpha_p y_{t-p} - f(x_t, \beta)]^2. \quad (3.12)$$

By differentiation we obtain the $(p+k+1) \times 1$ score vector

$$\nabla \ell_T(\alpha, \beta, \sigma^2) = \begin{bmatrix} \frac{1}{\sigma^2} \sum_{t=1}^{T} \epsilon_t y_{t-1} \\ \vdots \\ \frac{1}{\sigma^2} \sum_{t=1}^{T} \epsilon_t y_{t-p} \\ \frac{1}{\sigma^2} \sum_{t=1}^{T} \epsilon_t \nabla f_t \\ -\frac{T}{2\sigma^2} + \frac{1}{2\sigma^4} \sum_{t=1}^{T} \epsilon_t^2 \end{bmatrix}, \quad (3.13)$$

from which we can obtain the well-known MLE by solving the likelihood equations $\nabla \ell_T(\alpha, \beta, \sigma^2) = 0$.

Using the nonstochastic diagonal weighting matrix $D_T(\alpha, \beta, \sigma^2)$ given by

$$D_T(\alpha, \beta, \sigma^2) = \operatorname{diag}\left\{ \sigma^{-2} \sum_{t=1}^{T} E[y_{t-1}^2], \ldots, \sigma^{-2} \sum_{t=1}^{T} E[y_{t-p}^2], \right.$$

$$\left. \sigma^{-2} \sum_{t=1}^{T} \nabla f_{1t}^2, \ldots, \sigma^{-2} \sum_{t=1}^{T} \nabla f_{kt}^2, \frac{T}{2\sigma^4} \right\}, \quad (3.14)$$

we obtain the normalized observed Fisher information matrix $I_T^*(\alpha, \beta, \sigma^2)$ given by

$$I_T^*(\alpha, \beta, \sigma^2) = \begin{bmatrix} A_T^* & B_T^* & C_T^* \\ & Q_T^* & F_T^* \\ & & G_T^* \end{bmatrix}, \quad (3.15)$$

---

[7] Boundedness of the gradients, combined with the convergence of the empirical distribution function of the (x_t) sequence, is discussed by Jennrich (1969). The role of domination conditions is brought out in Jennrich (1969) and White (1980). An overview of such conditions is contained in Barnett (1981, Chapter 4). Given that a variety of options exists, we follow Amemiya (1983, p. 339) in suggesting that the best procedure is to leave (3.4) as it is and allow direct verification for special cases.

where

$$A_T^*(i,j) = \sum_{t=1}^{T} y_{t-i} y_{t-j} \bigg/ \left(\sum_{t=1}^{T} E[y_{t-i}^2] \right)^{1/2} \left(\sum_{t=1}^{T} E[y_{t-j}^2] \right)^{1/2},$$

$$A_T^* = \begin{bmatrix} A_T^*(1,1) & \cdots & A_T^*(1,p) \\ \vdots & & \vdots \\ A_T^*(p,1) & \cdots & A_T^*(p,p) \end{bmatrix},$$

$$B_T^*(i,j) = \sum_{t=1}^{T} y_{t-i} \nabla f_{jt} \bigg/ \left(\sum_{t=1}^{T} E[y_{t-i}^2] \right)^{1/2} \left(\sum_{t=1}^{T} \nabla f_{jt}^2 \right)^{1/2},$$

$$B_T^* = \begin{bmatrix} B_T^*(1,1) & \cdots & B_T^*(1,k) \\ \vdots & & \vdots \\ B_T^*(p,1) & \cdots & B_T^*(p,k) \end{bmatrix},$$

$$C_T^*(i) = \left(\frac{2}{T\sigma^2} \right)^{1/2} \sum_{t=1}^{T} y_{t-i} \epsilon_t \bigg/ \left(\sum_{t=1}^{T} E[y_{t-i}^2] \right)^{1/2},$$

$$C_T^* = \begin{bmatrix} C_T^*(1) \\ \vdots \\ C_T^*(p) \end{bmatrix},$$

$$Q_T^*(i,j) = \sum_{t=1}^{T} \nabla f_{it} \nabla f_{jt} \bigg/ \left(\sum_{t=1}^{T} \nabla f_{it}^2 \right)^{1/2} \left(\sum_{t=1}^{T} \nabla f_{jt}^2 \right)^{1/2},$$

$$Q_T^* = \begin{bmatrix} Q_T^*(1,1) & \cdots & Q_T^*(1,k) \\ \vdots & & \vdots \\ Q_T^*(k,1) & \cdots & Q_T^*(k,k) \end{bmatrix},$$

$$F_T^*(i) = \left(\frac{2}{T\sigma^2} \right)^{1/2} \sum_{t=1}^{T} \nabla f_{it} \epsilon_t \bigg/ \left(\sum_{t=1}^{T} \nabla f_{it}^2 \right)^{1/2},$$

$$F_T^* = \begin{bmatrix} F_T^*(1) \\ \vdots \\ F_T^*(k) \end{bmatrix},$$

$$G_T^* = \frac{2}{T\sigma^2} \sum_{t=1}^{T} \epsilon_t^2 - 1.$$

Let

$$c = \lim \rho_1^{-t} \mu_t \tag{3.16}$$

(this limit exists, cf. Lemma 4.3), and let

$$\phi = \lambda_1 \sigma (\rho^2 - 1)^{-1/2}. \tag{3.17}$$

Furthermore, let the $p \times p$ matrix Ω be given by

$$\Omega = [\rho_1^{2-i-j}]_{i,j=1,\dots,p}. \tag{3.18}$$

Notice that the rank of Ω is 1. Finally, let

$$\eta_1 = \phi(\phi^2 + c^2)^{-1/2} \tag{3.19}$$

and

$$\eta_2 = c(\phi^2 + c^2)^{-1/2}. \tag{3.20}$$

Thus, $\eta_1^2 + \eta_2^2 = 1$.

The convergence of $I_T^*(\alpha, \beta, \sigma^2)$ is established by considering the limiting properties of each individual element. A proof is given in the next section.

Theorem 3.1. *Under Assumptions* 3.1–3.5

$$I_T^*(\alpha, \beta, \sigma^2) \to a.s.\ I^*(\alpha, \beta, \sigma^2) \quad for\ T \to \infty,$$

where

$$I^*(\alpha, \beta, \sigma^2) = \begin{bmatrix} V\Omega & 0 & 0 \\ & Q & 0 \\ & & 1 \end{bmatrix},$$

where V is a random variable that can be expressed as

$$V = (\eta_1 W + \eta_2)^2,$$

where $W \sim N(0,1)$.

With Assumptions 3.1–3.5 the remaining conditions of Section 2 are easily satisfied, yielding the result

$$\nabla \ell_T^*(\theta_0) \to^d I^*(\theta_0)^{1/2} Z \quad for\ T \to \infty \tag{3.21}$$

and the consistency of $(\hat\theta_T)$ for θ_0, where $\theta_0 = [\alpha_0' \beta_0' \sigma^2]'$, $\hat\theta_T = [\alpha_T' \beta_T' \sigma_T^2]$, is the MLE of θ_0, and $Z \sim N_s(0, I_s)$. Further, it follows that the (normalized) MLE of β is asymptotically normal, given the block diagonality of $I^*(\theta)$.

The information of the MLE of α is, however, singular. The problem lies in the choice of normalization matrix $D(\theta)$. We have effectively normalized with respect to two stochastic orders of convergence, one in powers of t and one at an exponential rate depending on the largest root of the characteristic equation. Let $Z_t' = (y_{t-1}, \dots, y_{t-p})$. If, as in Sims, Stock, and Watson (1987), we could find a linear transformation S, such that the rows of S select combinations of Z that are of different orders in probability, we would have

$$y_t = \tilde{Z}'_t \gamma + f(x_t, \beta) + \epsilon_t,$$

where $\tilde{Z}' = Z'S$ and $\gamma = S^{-1}\alpha$. In such a case, we could simply apply the present analysis to the transformed equation directly, exploiting the fact that the underlying α's are linear in γ. In the Sims, Stock, and Watson (1987) analysis of unit roots, this is, indeed, the case, but a suitable linear transformation may be hard to find here. Resolution of this issue deserves further research. As things stand now, the hypothesis-testing results of the next section are directly applicable to the β vector and, with minor modification with respect to the use of generalized inverses, are applicable generally.

A number of special cases have appeared in the literature. Basawa and Koul (1979) and Basawa and Brockwell (1984) have considered the pure autoregressive process with no regressors. In this case,

$$I^*(\alpha, \sigma^2) = \begin{bmatrix} W^2 \Omega & 0 \\ 0 & 1 \end{bmatrix}, \tag{3.22}$$

where $W \sim N(0, 1)$, since $\eta_2 = 0$. In the case of a pure first-order autoregressive process, the matrix Ω reduces to 1, yielding

$$I^*(\alpha, \sigma^2) = \begin{bmatrix} W^2 & 0 \\ 0 & 1 \end{bmatrix}. \tag{3.23}$$

In this case we obtain the well-known result of Anderson (1959):

$$\left(\sum_{t=1}^{T} E[y_{t-1}^2] \right)^{1/2} (\alpha_T - \alpha)$$

is asymptotically Cauchy distributed.

The major complication in conducting unconditional inference based on the limiting Fisher information matrix of Theorem 3.2 is the computation of the involved scale mixture of normals [cf. Proposition 2.2(iii)]. The distribution of the mixing random variable $V = (\eta_1 W + \eta_2)^2$ depends on the normality assumption given our technique of proof. The density of V is given by

$$f(v) = (2\eta_1 \sqrt{2\pi v})^{-1} \{ \exp[-(\sqrt{v} - \eta_2)^2 / 2\eta_1^2] $$
$$+ \exp[-(\sqrt{v} + \eta_2)^2 / 2\eta_1^2] \}, \tag{3.24}$$

from which it is obvious that all moments exist. The low-order moments of the density in terms of η_1 are given in Domowitz and Muus (1987).

4   Proofs of Lemma 3.1 and Theorem 3.1

In this section proofs for Lemma 3.1 and Theorem 3.1 are presented. The convergence of the normalized Fisher information matrix $I_T^*(\alpha, \beta, \sigma^2)$

is established by considering in turn each element of the matrix. In this respect, frequent use is made of the expression (3.3) contained in Lemma 3.1.

Proof of Lemma 3.1:   Let $u_t = f(x_t, \beta_0) + \epsilon_t$. Then the model (3.1) can be written as the nonhomogeneous pth-order linear difference equation

$$y_t = \alpha_1 y_{t-1} + \cdots + \alpha_p y_{t-p} + u_t. \tag{4.1}$$

Obviously, y_t is a linear combination of $u_1, \ldots, u_t$:

$$y_t = \zeta_0(t) + \zeta_1(t) u_1 + \cdots + \zeta_t(t) u_t. \tag{4.2}$$

Inserting (4.2) into (4.1) yields, for $t > p$,

$$\begin{aligned}
\zeta_0(t) &+ \zeta_1(t) u_1 + \cdots + \zeta_t(t) u_t \\
&= \alpha_1 [\zeta_0(t-1) + \zeta_1(t-1) u_1 + \cdots + \zeta_{t-1}(t-1) u_{t-1}] \\
&+ \\
&\vdots \\
&+ \alpha_p [\zeta_0(t-p) + \zeta_1(t-p) u_1 + \cdots + \zeta_{t-p}(t-p) u_{t-p}] \\
&+ u_t.
\end{aligned} \tag{4.3}$$

Upon equating coefficients, we thus see that the functions $\zeta_0, \zeta_1, \ldots, \zeta_t$ satisfy the homogeneous difference equation

$$\zeta_j(t) = \alpha_1 \zeta_j(t-1) + \cdots + \alpha_p \zeta_j(t-p), \quad j = 0, 1, \ldots, k. \tag{4.4}$$

Thus, the solution to (4.4) is

$$\zeta_j(t) = A_{j1} \rho_1^t + \cdots + A_{jp} \rho_p^t, \quad j = 0, 1, \ldots, k, \tag{4.5}$$

where $A_{j1}, \ldots, A_{jp}$ are arbitrary constants to be determined from initial conditions. Let $A_{jk}^* = A_{jk} \rho_k^j$. Initial conditions then yield

$$\sum_{k=1}^{p} A_{jk}^* \rho_k^t = \delta_t, \quad j = 1, \ldots, k, \; t = 0, -1, \ldots, -p+1, \tag{4.6}$$

where $\delta_t = 1$ for $t = 0$, and $\delta_t = 0$ for $t = -1, \ldots, -p+1$. We thus see that $A_{jk}^* = \lambda_k$, $j = 1, \ldots, k$. For $j = 0$ we obtain the initial conditions

$$\sum_{k=1}^{p} \omega_k \rho_k^t = y_t, \quad t = 0, -1, \ldots, -p+1, \tag{4.7}$$

where $\omega_k = A_{0k}^*$. Inserting into (4.5) and (4.2) then yields the result stated in Lemma 3.1.   Q.E.D.

The following result states the convergence of most terms of the normalized Fisher information matrix.

Lemma 4.1. *Under Assumptions* 3.1–3.5,

   (i) $Q_T^*(i,j) \to q_{ij}$ *for* $T \to \infty$,
   (ii) $G_T^* \to a.s.\ 1$ *for* $T \to \infty$,
   (iii) $F_T^*(i) \to a.s.\ 0$ *for* $T \to \infty$, *and*
   (iv) $C_T^*(i) \to a.s.\ 0$ *for* $T \to \infty$.

Proof: The proof of (i) follows immediately from Assumption 3.2(ii). The proof of (ii) follows from Kolmogorov's strong law of large numbers since $G_T^* = (2/T)\chi^2(T) - 1$. The proof of (iii) follows immediately since $F_T^*(i) \sim N(0, 2/T)$. The proof of (iv) follows from Kolmogorov's law of large numbers since $E[C_T^*(i)] = 0$ and $\mathrm{Var}[C_T^*(i)] = 2/T$.   Q.E.D.

What remains to be shown is thus the convergence of the elements $A_T^*(i,j)$ and $B_T^*(i,j)$. Through a sequence of lemmas, we first establish the convergence of the elements $A_T^*(i,j)$.

Consider the stochastic process (W_t) defined by

$$W_t = \rho_1^{-t} z_t = \lambda_1 \xi_{1t} + \cdots + \lambda_p \xi_{pt}, \tag{4.8}$$

where

$$\xi_{jt} = \rho_1^{-t} \sum_{i=1}^{t} \rho_j^{t-i} \epsilon_i, \quad j = 1, \ldots, p. \tag{4.9}$$

Obviously, $E[\xi_{jt}] = 0$, $j = 1, \ldots, p$, $t = 1, 2, \ldots$.

Lemma 4.2

$$W_t \to a.s.\ \phi W \quad \text{for } t \to \infty,$$

where $W \sim N(0,1)$, and $\phi = \lambda_1 \sigma (\rho_1^2 - 1)^{-1/2}$.

Proof: For $j \geq 2$ we have

$$E[\xi_{jt}^2] = \rho_1^{-2t} \sum_{i=1}^{t} \rho_j^{2(t-i)} \sigma^2.$$

Hence,

$$\sum_{t=1}^{\infty} E[\xi_{jt}^2] = \sigma^2 \sum_{t=1}^{\infty} \rho_1^{-2t} \sum_{i=1}^{t} \rho_j^{2(t-1)} < \infty,$$

since $|\rho_j/\rho_1| < 1$. Hence, for $j \geq 2$, $\xi_{jt} \to a.s.\ 0$ for $t \to \infty$. Now, the stochastic process (ξ_{1t}) forms an L_2 martingale, since

$$E[\xi_{1t} \mid F_{t-1}] = \xi_{1,t-1},$$

where $F_t = \sigma(\{y_0, y_1, \ldots, y_t\})$. Since

$$E[\xi_{1t}^2] = \sigma^2 \sum_{i=1}^{t} \rho_1^{-2i},$$

we have

$$\sup_t E[\xi_{1t}^2] = \sigma^2 \sum_{i=1}^{\infty} \rho_1^{-2i} = \sigma^2(\rho_1^2-1)^{-1}.$$

By the martingale convergence theorem (cf. Hall and Heyde 1980, p. 18), it follows that there exists a random variable ξ_1 such that $\xi_{1t} \to$ a.s. ξ_1 for $t \to \infty$. Since, by normality, $\xi_{1t} \sim N(0, \sigma^2 \sum_{i=1}^{t} \rho_1^{-2i})$, it follows that $\xi_1 \sim N(0, \sigma^2(\rho_1^2-1)^{-1})$. The lemma then follows immediately.   Q.E.D.

Let the sequence (b_t) be defined as

$$b_t = \rho_1^{-t} \mu_t. \tag{4.10}$$

Lemma 4.3. $\lim_{t \to \infty} b_t$ exists.

Proof: Using expression (3.12) yields

$$b_t = \lambda_1 \sum_{i=1}^{t} \rho_1^{-i} f(x_i, \beta_0) + \cdots + \lambda_p \sum_{i=1}^{t} \left(\frac{\rho_p}{\rho_1}\right)^t \rho_p^{-i} f(x_i, \beta_0)$$

$$+ \omega_1 + \omega_2 \left(\frac{\rho_2}{\rho_1}\right)^t + \cdots + \omega_p \left(\frac{\rho_p}{\rho_1}\right)^t.$$

Since $|\rho_j/\rho_1| < 1$ for $j > 1$, convrgence then follows from Assumption 3.4(i).   Q.E.D.

In view of Lemma 4.3, let

$$c = \lim_{t \to \infty} b_t. \tag{4.11}$$

Lemma 4.4

$$\rho_1^{-2T} \sum_{t=i}^{T} y_{t-i}^2 \to a.s. \; \rho_1^{2-2i}(\rho_1^2-1)(\phi W + c)^2 \quad for \; T \to \infty.$$

Proof: We have

$$\rho_1^{-2T} \sum_{t=i}^{T} y_{t-i}^2 = \rho_1^{-2T} \sum_{t=i}^{T} (z_{t-i} + \mu_{t-i})^2$$

$$= \rho_1^{-2i} \sum_{t=i}^{T} \rho_1^{-2(T-t)}(W_{t-i} + b_{t-i})^2$$

$$= \rho_1^{-2i} \sum_{k=1}^{\infty} \rho_1^{-2k}(W_{T-k-i} + b_{T-k-i})^2 \mathbf{1}_{[0,T-1]}(k)$$

$$\to \text{a.s. } \rho_1^{-2i}(\phi W + c)^2 \sum_{k=0}^{\infty} \rho_1^{-2k}$$

$$= \rho_1^{2-2i}(\rho_1^2 - 1)(\phi W + c)^2, \quad \text{for } T \to \infty,$$

by dominated convergence, since (i) $\lim_{T \to \infty} b_{T-k-i} = c$, (ii) $\sum_{k=0}^{\infty} \rho_1^{-2k} < \infty$, and (iii) there exists $K(\omega)$ such that $|W_t(\omega)| < K(\omega)$ for almost all realizations of ω; cf. Lemma 4.1. Q.E.D.

Lemma 4.5

$$\rho_1^{-2T} E \left[\sum_{t=i}^{T} y_{t-i}^2 \right]^{1/2} E \left[\sum_{t=j}^{T} y_{t-j}^2 \right]^{1/2} \to \rho_1^{2-i-j}(\rho_1^2 - 1)(\phi^2 + c^2) \quad \text{for } T \to \infty.$$

Proof: For $i = j$ we obtain, from Lemma 4.3, by dominated convergence,

$$\rho_1^{-2T} E \left[\sum_{t=1}^{T} y_{t-i}^2 \right] = E \left[\sum_{t=i}^{T} \rho_1^{-2T} y_{t-i}^2 \right]$$

$$\to \rho_1^{2-2i}(\rho_1^2 - 1)(\phi^2 + c^2) \quad \text{for } T \to \infty,$$

from which the result follows. Q.E.D.

The convergence of the elements $A_T^*(i, j)$, where $i \neq j$, is somewhat more difficult to establish, as is evident in the proof of the next lemma.

Lemma 4.6. *For $i > j$,*

$$\rho_1^{-2T} \sum_{t=i}^{T} y_{t-i} y_{t-j} \to \text{a.s. } \rho_1^{2-2i}(\rho_1^2 - 1)(\phi W + c)^2 \quad \text{for } T \to \infty.$$

Proof: For $i > j$,

$$\rho_1^{-2T} \sum_{t=i}^{T} y_{t-i} y_{t-j} = \rho_1^{-2T} \sum_{t=i}^{T} (z_{t-i} + \mu_{t-i})(z_{t-j} + \mu_{t-j})$$

$$= \rho_1^{-2T} \sum_{t=i}^{T} z_{t-i} z_{t-j} + \rho_1^{-2T} \sum_{t=i}^{T} z_{t-i} \mu_{t-j}$$

$$+ \rho_1^{-2T} \sum_{t=i}^{T} z_{t-j} \mu_{t-i} + \rho_1^{-2T} \sum_{t=i}^{T} \mu_{t-i} \mu_{t-j}.$$

We shall analyze each of these four terms separately. We have

$$\rho_1^{-2T} \sum_{t=i}^{T} \mu_{t-i} \mu_{t-j} = \rho_1^{-i-j} \sum_{t=i}^{T} \rho_1^{-2(T-t)} b_{t-i} b_{t-j}$$

$$= \rho_1^{-i-j} \sum_{k=0}^{T-i} \rho_1^{-2k} b_{T-k-i} b_{T-k-j} =$$

$$= \rho_1^{-i-j} \sum_{k=0}^{\infty} \rho_1^{-2k} b_{T-k-i} b_{T-k-j} \mathbf{1}_{[0,T-i]}(k)$$

$$\to \rho_1^{2-i-j}(\rho_1^2-1)c^2 \quad \text{for } T\to\infty,$$

by dominated convergence and Lemma 4.3. We have

$$\rho_1^{-2T} \sum_{t=i}^{T} z_{t-i}\mu_{t-j} = \rho_1^{-i-j} \sum_{t=i}^{T} \rho_1^{-2(T-t)} W_{t-i} b_{t-j}$$

$$= \rho_1^{-i-j} \sum_{k=0}^{T-i} \rho_1^{-2k} W_{T-k-i} b_{T-k-j}$$

$$= \rho_1^{-i-j} \sum_{k=0}^{\infty} \rho_1^{-2k} W_{T-k-i} b_{T-k-j} \mathbf{1}_{[0,T-i]}(k)$$

$$\to \text{a.s. } \rho_1^{2-i-j}(\rho_1^2-1)\phi Wc \quad \text{for } T\to\infty,$$

by Lemma 4.2 and dominated convergence. Similarly,

$$\rho_1^{-2T} \sum_{t=i}^{\infty} \mu_{t-i} z_{t-j} \to \text{a.s. } \rho_1^{2-i-j}(\rho_1^2-1)\phi Wc \quad \text{for } T\to\infty.$$

Finally,

$$\rho_1^{-2T} \sum_{t=i}^{T} z_{t-i} z_{t-j} = \rho_1^{-i-j} \sum_{t=i}^{T} \rho_1^{-2(T-t)} W_{t-i} W_{t-j}$$

$$= \rho_1^{-i-j} \sum_{m=1}^{p} \sum_{k=1}^{p} \sum_{t=i}^{T} \rho_1^{-2(T-t)} \lambda_k \lambda_m \xi_{k,t-i} \xi_{m,t-j}.$$

For $m=k=1$ we obtain (cf. Lemma 4.2)

$$\rho_1^{-i-j} \sum_{t=i}^{T} \rho_1^{-2(T-t)} \lambda_1^2 \xi_{1,t-i} \xi_{1,t-j} \to \text{a.s. } \rho_1^{2-i-j}\phi^2 W^2 \quad \text{for } T\to\infty$$

whereas for $m\neq1$ or $k\neq1$, we trivially have

$$\rho_1^{-i-j} \sum_{t=i}^{T} \rho_1^{-2(T-t)} \lambda_k \lambda_m \xi_{k,t-i} \xi_{m,t-j} \to \text{a.s. } 0 \quad \text{for } T\to\infty.$$

Combining the preceding results yields the result stated in the lemma.

Q.E.D.

Combining Lemmas 4.4–4.6 thus yields the following result regarding the convergence of the term $A_T^*(i,j)$.

Proposition 4.7

$$A_T^*(i,j) \to \text{a.s. } \rho_1^{2-i-j}(\phi W+c)^2/(\phi^2+c^2) \quad \textit{for } T\to\infty.$$

Defining

$$\eta_1 = \phi(\phi^2 + c^2)^{-1/2} \tag{4.12}$$

and

$$\eta_2 = c(\phi^2 + c^2)^{-1/2}, \tag{4.13}$$

we have

$$A_T^*(i, j) \to a.s. \ \rho_1^{2-i-j} V, \tag{4.14}$$

where

$$V = (\eta_1 W + \eta_2)^2 \tag{4.15}$$

and $\eta_1^2 + \eta_2^2 = 1$.

Finally, we shall establish the convergence of the element $B_T^*(i, j)$.

Lemma 4.8

$$\left(\sum_{t=1}^{T} \nabla f_{it}^2 \right)^{-1/2} \rho_1^{-T} \left(\sum_{t=1}^{T} \nabla f_{it}^2 \right) \left(\sum_{t=1}^{T} E[y_{t-j}^2] \right)^{1/2}$$
$$\to \rho_1^{2-i-j} (\rho_1^2 - 1)(\phi^2 + c^2) \quad for \ T \to \infty.$$

Proof: The proof follows immediately from Lemma 4.5.　　　Q.E.D.

Lemma 4.9

$$\left(\sum_{t=1}^{T} \nabla f_{it}^2 \right)^{-1/2} \rho_1^{-T} \sum_{t=1}^{T} \nabla f_{it} y_{t-j} \to a.s. \ 0 \quad for \ T \to \infty.$$

Proof: We have

$$\left(\sum_{t=1}^{T} \nabla f_{it}^2 \right)^{-1/2} \rho_1^{-T} \sum_{t=1}^{T} \nabla f_{it} y_{t-j}$$
$$= \sum_{t=1}^{\infty} \left[\nabla f_{it}^2 \left(\sum_{t=1}^{T} \nabla f_{it}^2 \right)^{-1} \right]^{1/2} \rho_1^{-T} y_{t-j} \mathbf{1}_{[1, T-j]}(t)$$
$$\to a.s. \ 0 \quad for \ T \to \infty,$$

by dominated convergence in conjunction with Assumption 3.2(iii).

　　　　　　　　　　　　　　　　　　　　　　　　Q.E.D.

Combining Lemmas 4.8 and 4.9, we obtain the following result.

Proposition 4.10. $B_T^*(i, j) \to a.s. \ 0 \ for \ T \to \infty$.

Collecting the results of Lemma 4.1, Proposition 4.7, and Proposition 4.10 establishes the result stated in Theorem 3.1.

5   Conditional inference

The practical consequence of the results obtained in the last section is to complicate unconditional inference in some respects by requiring an explicit calculation of the distribution of $I^*(\theta)^{1/2}Z$ and $I^*(\theta)^{-1/2}Z$. A potentially attractive alternative is inference conditional on $I^*(\theta)$. For cases in which this option is possible, such conditional analysis returns us to conventional asymptotic theory, and standard hypothesis testing results under the null will remain valid. In the present case, the distribution of W does not depend on the parameter vector $[\alpha'\beta'\sigma^2]'$. Hence, W is an ancillary statistic upon which we may condition. Using the general results of Domowitz and Muus (1987), we then obtain

$$\nabla \ell_T^*(\theta) \to^d I^{*1/2}Z \quad \text{for } T \to \infty \tag{5.1}$$

and

$$I_T^*(\theta) \to^d I^* \quad \text{for } T \to \infty \tag{5.2}$$

under P^*, where P^* is the conditional probability under P given $I^*(\theta) = I^*$.

The treatment of a test of nonlinear restrictions conditional on $I^*(\theta)$ is then no different from the analysis in the usual case. Let $g: \Re^p \to \Re^q$, $q \le p$, and consider the null hypothesis $H_0: g(\theta) = 0$ against the alternative $H_1: g(\theta) \ne 0$, where $\theta = [\alpha'\beta'\sigma^2]'$. Assuming that the null hypothesis considered is "smooth" [i.e., the function $g: \Re^p \to \Re^q$ is continuously differentiable and its Jacobian $G(\theta)$ has rank q], the asymptotic equivalence of the Wald, likelihood ratio, and Lagrange multiplier statistics is established for unconditional analysis in Domowitz and Muus (1987). In a conditional analysis, the preceding remarks imply that the Wald test statistic

$$W_T = g(\theta_T)'[G(\theta_T)D_T(\theta_T)^{-1/2}I_T^*(\theta_T)^{-1}D_T(\theta_T)^{-1/2}G(\theta_T)']^{-1}g(\theta_T)$$

is asymptotically central chi-squared distributed with q degrees of freedom. This result justifies standard econometric practice should the ergodic assumption fail in the class of models considered in this chapter.

6   Conclusion

We have established conditions under which the normalized information matrix converges to a nondegenerate random variable in the context of a nonlinear regression model with linear nonergodic dynamics. Further, we have characterized the distribution of the limiting information, opening up the possibility of conducting unconditional inference in the present framework. This analysis will allow investigation of potential efficiency losses due to the type of conditioning discussed here as well as losses associated with estimators other than the MLE. At this time, however, the appropriate efficiency concept is not obvious due to the nonnormality of the asymptotic distribution of the estimator.

REFERENCES

Amemiya, T. 1983. "Nonlinear Regression Models." In *Handbook of Econometrics, Vol. I,* Z. Griliches and M. Intriligator, Eds. Amsterdam: North-Holland.

Anderson, T. W. 1959. "On Asymptotic Distributions of Estimates of Parameters of Stochastic Difference Equations." *Annals of Mathematical Statistics* 30: 676–87.

Barnett, W. 1981. *Consumer Demand and Labor Supply.* Amsterdam: North-Holland.

Basawa, I. V. and P. J. Brockwell. 1984. "Asymptotic Conditional Inference for Regular Nonergodic Models with an Application to Autoregressive Processes." *Annals of Statistics* 12: 161–71.

Basawa, I. V. and H. L. Koul. 1979. "Asymptotic Tests of Composite Hypotheses for Non-Ergodic Type Stochastic Processes." *Stochastic Processes and Their Applications* 9: 291–305.

Basawa, I. V. and D. J. Scott. 1983. *Asymptotic Optimal Inference for Non-Ergodic Models.* New York: Springer-Verlag.

Blanchard, O. J. 1981. "What is Left of the Multiplier Accelerator?" *American Economic Review* 71: 150–4.

Chamberlain, G. and C. Wilson. 1984. "Optimal Intertemporal Consumption Under Uncertainty." Working Paper No. 8422, Social Systems Research Institute, University of Wisconsin, Madison.

Crowder, M. J. 1976. "Maximum Likelihood Estimation for Dependent Observations." *Journal of the Royal Statistical Society, Series A* 139: 45–53.

Daly, V. and G. Hadjimatheou. 1981. "Stochastic Implications of the Life Cycle–Permanent Income Hypothesis: Evidence for the U.K. Economy." *Journal of Political Economy* 89: 596–9.

Domowitz, I. 1985. "New Directions in Non-Linear Estimation with Dependent Observations." *Canadian Journal of Economics* 19: 1–27.

Domowitz, I. and L. T. Muus. 1984. "Decision Rules Originating from Stochastic Dynamic Programs: A General Framework for Empirical Analysis." In *Proceedings of the 1984 International Congress on Technology and Technology Exchange.* Pittsburgh, PA: International Technology Institute.

1987. "Some Aspects of Inference in Nonergodic Econometric Models." Unpublished manuscript, Northwestern University.

Hall, P. and C. C. Heyde. 1980. *Martingale Limit Theory and its Applications.* New York: Academic.

Hall, R. E. 1978. "Stochastic Implications of the Life Cycle–Permanent Income Hypothesis: Theory and Evidence." *Journal of Political Economy* 86: 971–87.

Jennrich, R. I. 1969. "Asymptotic Properties of Non-Linear Least Squares Estimators." *Annals of Mathematical Statistics* 40: 633–43.

LeCam, L. 1960. "Locally Asymptotically Normal Families of Distributions." *University of California Publications in Probability and Statistics* 3: 27–98.

Majumdar, M., T. Mitra, and Y. Nyarko. 1986. "Dynamic Optimization Under Uncertainty: Non-Convex Feasible Set." Unpublished manuscript, Cornell University.

Mann, H. B. and A. Wald. 1943. "On the Statistical Treatment of Linear Stochastic Difference Equations." *Econometrica* 11: 173–220.

Muus, L. T. and E. Lederman. 1986. "Tax Incentives and Factor Demand in Post War U.S. Manufacturing Industries." Unpublished manuscript, Cornell University.

Rao, M. M. 1961. "Consistency and Limit Distributions of Estimators of Parameters in Explosive Stochastic Difference Equations." *Annals of Mathematical Statistics* 32: 195–218.

Sims, C. A., J. H. Stock, and M. W. Watson. 1987. "Inference in Linear Time Series Models With Some Unit Roots." Working Paper E-87-6, The Hoover Institution, Stanford University.

White, H. 1980. "Nonlinear Regression on Cross-Section Data." *Econometrica* 48: 721–46.

White, J. S. 1958. "The Limiting Distribution of the Serial Correlation Coefficient in the Explosive Case." *Annals of Mathematical Statistics* 29: 1188–97.

CHAPTER 5

Exact inference in models with autoregressive conditional heteroscedasticity

John Geweke

1   Introduction

Virtually without exception, inference in dynamic econometric models of
aggregate economic time series data is based on the asymptotic sampling-
theoretic distribution of estimators, often maximum-likelihood estimators. There is no population for which sets of observations of aggregate
economic time series can be drawn repeatedly, as may be the case with
longitudinal or panel data. Sampling-theoretic results for independent
populations have been extended to inference from a single realization of
a time series, but the length of periods for which parametric models of
economic time series may reasonably be regarded as stable usually limit
attention to modest departures from the linear model. There is no way to
incorporate carefully the inequality restrictions that often emerge from
economic theory. Improvements on asymptotic theory, especially for
highly nonlinear estimators, are arduous theoretical tasks whose occasional completion seems to have had little effect on the way applied work
is carried out.

This situation and recent drastic reductions in computing costs suggest
that alternatives to this standard approach to inference for economic time
series be contemplated. This chapter explores a formal numerical Bayesian approach with diffuse priors, relying on cheap computing to disregard

Financial support for this work was provided by National Science Foundation Grants
SES8318778 and SES8605867, the Pew Foundation, and the Symposium. Data acquisition
was facilitated by the editorial office of *Journal of Money, Credit and Banking*. The chapter
has benefited from the comments of two anonymous referees. A technical appendix providing FORTRAN code and data is available from the author, as is a disk with the same
information.

the analytical intractability of useful priors and functions of the parameters of interest. The ability to select diffuse priors arbitrarily means that inequality restrictions can be imposed, and the power to choose functions of interest for their bearing on empirical questions means that issues relegated to equivocal discussions can be treated formally. This exploration takes place in the context of the linear model with autoregressive conditional heteroscedasticity (ARCH linear model, for short; Engle 1982, 1983) and an empirical application in which we undertake exact inference about time series that goes to the heart of the application but could never be attempted using a standard, asymptotic sampling-theoretic approach. The ARCH linear model is chosen because it is a rich nonlinear model that incorporates a very specific empirical phenomenon: the tendency of disturbances that are large in absolute value to be clustered together in aggregate economic time series. We believe that application of the methods described here further enriches that model.

In the next section a recapitulation of the ARCH model as set forth by Engle (1982) is presented; we indicate only the essentials of the model, and the reader is referred to the original paper for the derivations. Section 3 describes the numerical methods for inference with a diffuse prior, and employing an artificial data set uses these methods to learn more about the structure of the likelihood function. The power of this approach to address substantive questions in a direct and formal way is illustrated in Section 4, where the empirical application of Engle (1983) is considered again. There is a brief concluding section.

2   Linear model with autoregressive conditional heteroscedasticity

Let $\mathbf{x}_t: k \times 1$ and y_t be time series for which the distribution of y_t conditional on $\psi_{t-1} = \{\mathbf{x}_{t-s}, y_{t-s}, s \geq 1\}$ is

$$y_t \mid \psi_{t-1} \sim N(\mathbf{x}_t' \beta, h_t). \tag{1}$$

Defining $\epsilon_t = y_t - \mathbf{x}_t' \beta$, take

$$h_t = \alpha_0 + \sum_{j=1}^{p} \alpha_j \epsilon_{t-j}^2 = h\left(\epsilon_{t-1}, \ldots, \epsilon_{t-p}; \underset{q \times 1}{\gamma}\right).$$

The parameterization in terms of γ allows restrictions like $\alpha_0 = \gamma_0$ and $\alpha_j = \gamma_1(p+1-j)$, the linearly declining weights employed by Engle (1982, 1983). For equation (1) to be plausible, it is necessary that $\alpha_0 > 0$ and $\alpha_j \geq 0$ ($j = 1, \ldots, p$). For $\{\epsilon_t\}$ to be stationary, it is necessary and sufficient that the roots of $1 - \sum_{j=1}^{p} \alpha_j z^j$ all be outside the unit circle. (Subsequently, we refer to this as the stationarity condition.) If $\{\epsilon_t\}$ is stationary, its unconditional variance is $h \equiv \alpha_0/(1 - \sum_{j=1}^{p} \alpha_j)$ (Engle 1982, Theorem 2).

Given the sample $(\mathbf{x}_t, y_t;\ t = 1, \ldots, T)$, the log-likelihood function is (up to an additive constant)

$$\ell = -\frac{1}{2} \sum_{t=p+1}^{T} \log h_t - \frac{1}{2} \sum_{t=p+1}^{T} h_t^{-1} \epsilon_t^2. \tag{2}$$

Engle (1982) has shown that for large samples $\partial^2 \ell/\partial \boldsymbol{\beta} \, \partial \boldsymbol{\gamma}' \doteq 0$, and the maximum-likelihood estimates $\hat{\boldsymbol{\beta}}$ of $\boldsymbol{\beta}$ and $\hat{\boldsymbol{\gamma}}$ of $\boldsymbol{\gamma}$ are asymptotically independent. In using a gradient procedure to maximize (2), revision of the estimate $\boldsymbol{\beta}^{(i)}$ of $\boldsymbol{\beta}$ and the estimate $\boldsymbol{\gamma}^{(i)}$ of $\boldsymbol{\gamma}$ may therefore proceed separately at each step; the result will be asymptotically equivalent to maximum likelihood.

Following Engle (1982), in the case of $\boldsymbol{\gamma}$,

$$\frac{\partial \ell}{\partial \boldsymbol{\gamma}} = \frac{1}{2} \sum_{t=p+1}^{T} h_t^{-1} \frac{\partial h_t}{\partial \boldsymbol{\gamma}} (h_t^{-1} \epsilon_t^2 - 1),$$

$$\frac{\partial^2 \ell}{\partial \boldsymbol{\gamma} \, \partial \boldsymbol{\gamma}'} = -\frac{1}{2} \sum_{t=p+1}^{T} h_t^{-2} \frac{\partial h_t}{\partial \boldsymbol{\gamma}} \frac{\partial h_t}{\partial \boldsymbol{\gamma}'} (h_t^{-1} \epsilon_t^2)$$

$$+ \frac{1}{2} \sum_{t=p+1}^{T} (h_t^{-1} \epsilon_t^2 - 1) \frac{\partial}{\partial \boldsymbol{\gamma}'} \left\{ h_t^{-1} \frac{\partial h_t}{\partial \boldsymbol{\gamma}} \right\}.$$

This leads to the scoring algorithm

$$e_t^{(i)} \equiv y_t - \mathbf{x}_t' \boldsymbol{\beta}^{(i)},$$

$$\tilde{\mathbf{z}}_t^{(i)} \equiv (h_t^{(i)})^{-1} [\partial h_t^{(i)} \, \partial \boldsymbol{\gamma}^{(i)}], \tag{3}$$

$$f_t^{(i)} \equiv [(e_t^{(i)})^2 - h_t^{(i)}]/h_t^{(i)},$$

$$\boldsymbol{\gamma}^{(i+1)} = \boldsymbol{\gamma}^{(i)} + \left[\sum_{t=p+1}^{T} \tilde{\mathbf{z}}_t^{(i)} \tilde{\mathbf{z}}_t^{(i)\prime} \right]^{-1} \sum_{t=p+1}^{T} \tilde{\mathbf{z}}_t^{(i)} f_t^{(i)}. \tag{4}$$

Similarly, for $\boldsymbol{\beta}$ the scoring algorithm is

$$r_t \equiv \left[(h_t^{(i)})^{-1} + 2(e_t^{(i)})^2 \sum_{j=1}^{p} (\alpha_j^{(i)})^2 (h_{t+j}^{(i)})^{-2} \right]^{1/2},$$

$$s_t \equiv (h_t^{(i)})^{-1} - \sum_{j=1}^{p} (\alpha_j^{(i)})(h_{t+j}^{(i)})^{-2} [(e_{t+j}^{(i)})^2 - h_{t+j}],$$

$$\tilde{\mathbf{x}}_t^{(i)} = \mathbf{x}_t r_t^{(i)}, \qquad \tilde{e}_t^{(i)} = e_t s_t^{(i)}/r_t^{(i)},$$

$$\boldsymbol{\beta}^{(i+1)} = \boldsymbol{\beta}^{(i)} + \left[\sum_{t=p+1}^{T} \tilde{\mathbf{x}}_t^{(i)} \tilde{\mathbf{x}}_t^{(i)\prime} \right]^{-1} \sum_{t=p+1}^{T} \tilde{\mathbf{x}}_t^{(i)} \tilde{e}_t^{(i)}. \tag{5}$$

The asymptotic variance for $\hat{\gamma}$ is $2[\sum_{t=p+1}^{T} \mathbf{z}_t^{(i)} \mathbf{z}_t^{(i)'}]^{-1}$ and that for $\hat{\beta}$ is $[\sum_{t=p+1}^{T} \tilde{\mathbf{x}}_t^{(i)} \tilde{\mathbf{x}}_t^{(i)'}]^{-1}$.

Engle (1982) takes the summation in (2) from $t=1$ to $t=T$, and to compute the likelihood function, $h_t = h$, $t \le 0$. This "end effect" is, of course, inconsequential asymptotically but matters in samples typical of work in macroeconomics. In applying the scoring algorithm, we have found that a final computation of $\hat{\beta}$ using standard generalized least-squares formulas, the converged values

$$\hat{h}_t = h(\hat{e}_{t-1}, \dots, \hat{e}_{t-p}; \hat{\gamma})$$

and the sample $(\mathbf{x}_t, y_t; t = p+1, \dots, T)$ increase the value of the likelihood function; more important, for the use of $\hat{\gamma}$ and $\hat{\beta}$ described subsequently in this chapter, the value of $\hat{\beta}$ so calculated is much closer to the actual maximum of the likelihood function. This improvement takes place because (5) incorporates an asymptotic approximation to the true gradient in β, as Engle [1982, equation (22)] has noted.

3   Inference with diffuse prior

Classical inference in the ARCH linear model can proceed in a straightforward way. The scoring algorithm as outlined in Engle (1982) is ingeniously efficient, and this approach has been applied and extended in a number of empirical applications (Engle and Bollerslev 1986). There are two aspects of empirical work with the ARCH linear model that asymptotic classical theory is ill-equipped to handle. These aspects are the motivation for this chapter.

The first aspect is that the ARCH linear model imposes the strict inequality restrictions

$$\alpha_0 > 0, \qquad \alpha_j \ge 0 \quad (j=1,\dots,p).$$

As discussed at greater length in Geweke (1986), classical inference subject to inequality restrictions is unworkable. One may also wish to impose the restrictions that the roots of $1 - \sum_{j=1}^{p} \alpha_j z^j$ lie outside the unit circle, and this condition is even more awkward to incorporate in classical inference. With a sufficiently informative sample these difficulties would vanish. If the restrictions are satisfied with $\alpha_j > 0$ $(j=1,\dots,p)$, asymptotic theory applies; if they are violated, this fact will become clear; and borderline cases are difficult but in principle might be resolved using tools similar to those employed by Gourierioux, Holly, and Monfort (1982) – although for the ARCH linear model borderline cases seem a priori unlikely. Unfortunately, samples to which the ARCH linear model is likely to be applied are not sufficiently informative that asymptotic theory is very useful. One example is the application in Engle (1982) in which $T = 77$ and

$$h_t = \gamma_0 + \gamma_1 \sum_{j=1}^{4} \frac{5-j}{10} \epsilon_{t-j}^2;$$

the reported estimates are $\hat{\gamma}_0 = 14 \times 10^{-6}$ (asymptotic standard error, 8.5×10^{-6}) and $\hat{\gamma}_1 = 0.955$ (asymptotic standard error, 0.298). Given the restriction $\gamma_0 > 0$, $|\gamma_1| < 1$, it is inappropriate to proceed assuming normal distributions on the coefficients. We shall return to this issue in a fully articulated example subsequently in this section.

A second, awkward aspect of applications of the ARCH model is that the parameters of direct interest are often the conditional variances $\{h_t\}$ rather than the parameter vector γ or α. Close reading of the discussion of empirical findings with the ARCH linear model suggests that investigators are interested in the absolute size of the conditional variances as well as in the hypotheses that conditional variances in certain periods are greater than in certain other periods. One could methodically grind out asymptotic standard errors for the h_t, but in view of the problems in interpreting the asymptotic normal distribution of γ itself, these standard errors would be all but meaningless. The more relevant problem of comparing averages of conditional variances over different time periods is even more intractable. We present a solution of this problem using Bayesian methods and diffuse priors in the next section: The results are pleasantly surprising.

To develop the new approach, let $\theta' = (\beta', \gamma')$, and let $g(\theta)$ denote a known function of the unknown parameter vector θ whose value is of interest or an indicator function for an event of interest. Examples of such functions include

$$g(\theta) = \alpha_0 \left/ \left(1 - \sum_{j=1}^{p} \alpha_j\right) \right. \quad \text{(unconditional variance of } \epsilon_t\text{);}$$

$$g(\theta) = h_t = \alpha_0 + \sum_{j=1}^{p} \alpha_j \epsilon_{t-j}^2 \quad \text{(conditional variance of } \epsilon_t\text{);}$$

$$g(\theta) = (t_2 - t_1 + 1)^{-1} \sum_{t=t_1}^{t_2} h_t \quad \text{(average conditional variance over } [t_1, t_2]\text{);}$$

$$g(\theta) = \begin{cases} 1 & \text{if } h_s > h_t, \\ 0 & \text{otherwise,} \end{cases} \quad \text{(indicator function for } h_s > h_t\text{);}$$

$$g_i(\theta) = \begin{cases} 1 & \text{if } h_i > h_t \; \forall t \neq i, \\ 0 & \text{otherwise,} \end{cases} \quad \begin{array}{l}\text{(indicator functions for maximum} \\ \text{conditional variance).}\end{array}$$

Next, let $\pi(\theta)$ be proportional to a prior probability density function (p.d.f.) for θ. (The prior need not be proper; i.e., it need not have finite integral over the space for θ.) To introduce three diffuse priors employed subsequently, let $J(\theta)$ be an indicator function that is 1 if $\alpha_0 > 0$, $\alpha_j \geq 0$ $(j = 1, \ldots, p)$, and $K(\theta)$ be an indicator function that is 1 if the roots of $1 - \sum_{j=1}^{p} \alpha_j z^j$ are outside the unit circle. Then define

$$\text{Prior A:} \quad \pi(\theta) = \left[\left(1 - \sum_{j=1}^{p} \alpha_j \right) \Big/ \alpha_0 \right]^{1/2} J(\theta) K(\theta);$$

$$\text{Prior B:} \quad \pi(\theta) = J(\theta) K(\theta);$$

$$\text{Prior C:} \quad \pi(\theta) = J(\theta).$$

Note that prior A becomes the standard conjugate prior for the normal linear regression model when $\alpha_j = 0$ $(j = 1, \ldots, p)$. Finally, let $L(\theta) = \exp(\ell)$, with ℓ defined in (2); $L(\theta)$ is proportional to the likelihood function. Then

$$E[g(\theta)] = \int_{\mathbb{R}^{k+q}} g(\theta) \pi(\theta) L(\theta) \, d\theta \Big/ \int_{\mathbb{R}^{k+q}} \pi(\theta) L(\theta) \, d\theta \qquad (6)$$

so long as the integrals exist, which they typically will. If $g(\theta)$ is a function whose value is of interest, (6) provides the posterior mean of that function; if $g(\theta)$ is an indicator function for an event, (6) provides the posterior probability that the event is true.

Purely analytical evaluation of the integrals in (6) is a practical impossibility. Instead, we employ an adaptation of Monte Carlo integration methods described by Kloek and Van Dijk (1978) and Van Dijk and Kloek (1980, 1983) developed in detail in Geweke (1987); our motivation is similar to that of Monahan (1983), who also used numerical integration procedures to impose stationarity. The idea is to generate synthetic random variables $\{\theta_i\}$ whose probability density function $I(\cdot)$ (called an importance function) approximates the posterior density $\pi(\theta) L(\theta)$; evaluate the numerator and denominator of (6); record the running sum of the numerator and denominator correcting for the fact that the θ_i are drawn from the p.d.f. $I(\cdot)$. Let n denote the number of these evaluations, or replications, and define

$$\bar{g}_n = \left\{ \sum_{i=1}^{n} g(\theta_i) \pi(\theta_i) L(\theta_i) / I(\theta_i) \right\} \Big/ \left\{ \sum_{i=1}^{n} \pi(\theta_i) L(\theta_i) / I(\theta_i) \right\}. \qquad (7)$$

If the support of $I(\theta)$ includes the support of $\pi(\theta) L(\theta)$, the integrals in the numerator and denominator of (6) both exist, and the sequence of $\{\theta_i\}$

is independent and identically distributed (i.i.d.), $\bar{g}_n \rightarrow E[g(\theta)]$ almost surely (Geweke 1987, Theorem 1).

Achieving practical rates of convergence of $\bar{g}_n$ requires care in the choice of an importance function $I(\cdot)$. If, in addition to our other assumptions, $\mathrm{var}[g(\theta)] < \infty$ and $\pi(\theta)L(\theta)/I(\theta)$ is bounded above,

$$n^{1/2}(\bar{g}_n - E[g(\theta)]) \Rightarrow N(0, \sigma^2),$$

where $\sigma^2 = E\{[g(\theta) - E[g(\theta)]]^2 \pi(\theta)L(\theta)/I(\theta)\}/\int L(\theta)\pi(\theta)\,d\theta$ and $n\hat{\sigma}_n^2 \rightarrow \sigma^2$, with

$$\hat{\sigma}_n^2 \equiv \sum_{i=1}^{n} [g(\theta_1) - \bar{g}_n]^2 [\pi(\theta_i)L(\theta_i)/I(\theta_i)]^2 \bigg/ \left[\sum_{i=1}^{n} \pi(\theta_i)L(\theta_i)/I(\theta_i) \right]^2 \qquad (8)$$

(Geweke 1987, Theorem 3, Corollary 2). If these conditions are satisfied, standard errors for numerical accuracy computed using (8) provide a reliable indication of the approximation error inherent in the Monte Carlo integration. Subsequently, we shall refer to $\hat{\sigma}_n \equiv (\hat{\sigma}_n^2)^{1/2}$ as the "numerical standard error" of $\bar{g}_n$. In practice, more rapid rates of convergence are achieved the lower the bound on $\pi(\theta_i)L(\theta_i)/I(\theta_i) \int L(\theta)\pi(\theta)\,d\theta$ and the smaller the variance in $g(\theta)$.

The asymptotic distribution of maximum-likelihood estimators provides a paradigm for the choice of importance functions: If $I(\cdot)$ is the estimated asymptotic distribution of $\hat{\theta}$, then for reasonably large samples $L(\theta)/I(\theta)$ may not fluctuate much for θ in a large (say, six-standard-deviation) region about $\hat{\theta}$. Globally, the requirement that $L(\theta)/I(\theta)$ be bounded above is important, and multivariate t approximations to the normal are often sufficient to assure this. Examination of the tails of the likelihood function shows that the multivariate t importance sampling density should have no more than $T - p - k$ degrees of freedom for β and no more than $\frac{1}{2}(T-p) - q$ degrees of freedom for γ. For samples of the size used in the work reported here these corrections to the normal are minute. Indeed, to the extent the asymptotic theory is appropriate, we should expect $I(\cdot)$ so chosen to be a good importance function. Moreover, synthetic random sampling from the multivariate t is routine. If the asymptotic theory is poor – that is, the asymptotic distribution provides a poor approximation to the likelihood function – that fact will be revealed in large standard errors for numerical approximation and in large variations in the ratio $L(\theta)/I(\theta)$, as indicated in diagnostics such as

$$\omega = \max_{i=1,\dots,n} [\pi(\theta_i)L(\theta_i)/I(\theta_i)]^2 \bigg/ \sum_{j=1}^{n} [\pi(\theta_j)L(\theta_j)/I(\theta_j)]^2.$$

In this case a greater number of Monte Carlo iterations will be required;

Table 1. *Parameter estimates, with artificial data*

	β_1	β_2	γ_0	γ_1
Maximum likelihood				
Estimate	1.1111	0.9972	0.8934	0.2807
Asymptotic s.e.	0.1039	0.1468	0.2801	0.0443
Prior A				
Posterior mean	1.0929	0.9563	1.0751	0.2553
Numerical s.e.	0.0012	0.0018	0.0053	0.0007
Posterior s.d.	0.0924	0.1351	0.2885	0.0472
Prior B				
Posterior mean	1.0904	0.9570	1.0963	0.2431
Numerical s.e.	0.0013	0.0018	0.0054	0.0006
Posterior s.d.	0.0925	0.1358	0.2915	0.0456
Prior C				
Posterior mean	1.0970	0.9524	1.0116	0.2792
Numerical s.e.	0.0011	0.0016	0.0048	0.0008
Posterior s.d.	0.0918	0.1338	0.3014	0.0658

Note: Posterior means and standard deviations (s.d.) are based on 10,000 Monte Carlo replications; computation time 28:35.69 with a MicroVAX II.

by contrast, classical inference based on the asymptotic distribution may be entirely inappropriate.

To show how the method works in the ARCH linear model, an artificial sample of size 200 was generated:

$$y_t = \sum_{j=1}^{2} \beta_j x_{tj} + \epsilon_t, \qquad \beta_1 = \beta_2 = 1;$$

$$x_{t1} = 1, \qquad x_{t2} = \cos(2\pi t/200);$$

$$\epsilon_t \sim N(0, h_t), \qquad h_t = 1 + 0.5\epsilon_{t-1}^2 + 0.25\epsilon_{t-2}^2.$$

(By using an artificial sample, we concentrate on the technical features of the likelihood function, independent of specification error.) The parameterization of the ARCH process in estimation was

$$h_t = \gamma_0 + \gamma_1(2\epsilon_{t-1}^2 + \epsilon_{t-2}^2); \qquad \alpha_0 = \gamma_0, \quad \alpha_1 = 2\gamma_1, \quad \alpha_2 = \gamma_1.$$

Maximum-likelihood estimates of β and γ and their asymptotic standard errors (s.e.) were computed as described in Section 2, and these values are shown in rows 2 and 3 of Table 1.

Using the asymptotic distributions of β and γ as the importance function in Monte Carlo integration produces poor results. In particular, ω

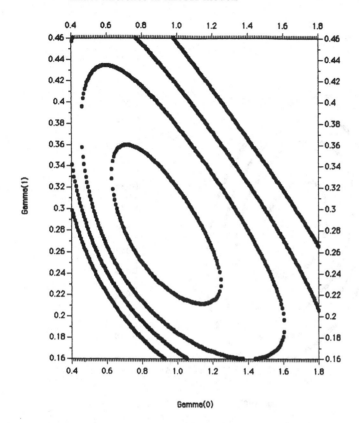

Figure 1. Likelihood function for artificial sample conditional on maximum-likelihood values of β_1 and β_2.

typically exceeds 0.3. This indicates that $L(\theta)/I(\theta)$ is quite large for certain θ relative to its value elsewhere: In some directions from $\hat{\theta}$ the likelihood function declines slowly whereas the asymptotic normal approximation to the likelihood function falls relatively rapidly. Systematic exploration of the likelihood function over β with γ fixed at $\hat{\gamma}$ suggests, not unsurprisingly, that the exact likelihood function for β conditional on $\gamma = \hat{\gamma}$ is very close to bivariate normal. The likelihood function for γ conditional on $\beta = \hat{\beta}$ is not well approximated by the multivariate t, as indicated in Figure 1, which shows iso-likelihood contours for the likelihood function, and in Figure 2, which shows iso-likelihood contours for the multivariate t approximation. In each case, the contours indicate levels below the maximum corresponding to the 0.5, 0.75, 0.975, and 0.995 critical points

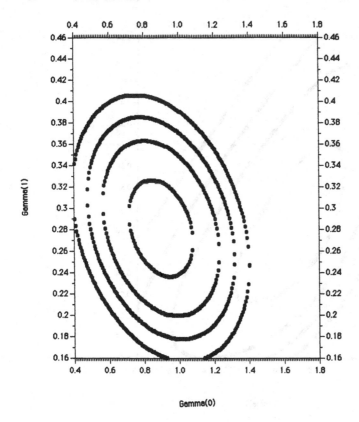

Figure 2. Asymptotic approximation to likelihood function for artificial sample conditional on maximum-likelihood values of β_1 and β_2.

of the $\chi^2(2)$ distribution. The contrast between Figures 1 and 2 and the fact that our artificial sample has many observations ($T = 200$) and few parameters ($k + q = 4$) relative to most applications suggest that asymptotic expansions in α are unreliable in the ARCH linear model even before taking into account nonnegativity and stability restrictions.

Three problems in using the multivariate t approximation as an importance function are apparent from Figures 1 and 2. Most important, the actual likelihood function is asymmetric and falls rather slowly as α_0 increases from $(\hat{\gamma}_0, \hat{\gamma}_1)$. Even allowing for this asymmetry, the approximation produces confidence regions that look too small. Finally, the northwest-to-southeast ridge in the actual likelihood function is convex, whereas that in the normal approximation is linear. We cope with the

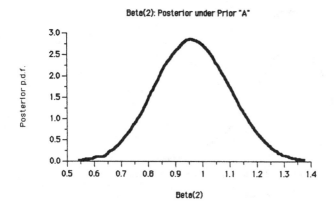

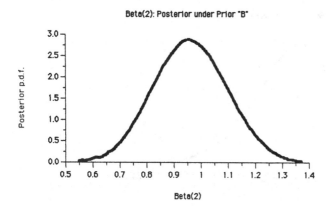

Figure 3. Exact posterior distributions for β_2.

first two of these problems by modifying the asymptotic normal approximation to produce a better importance function. Denote the asymptotic, multivariate approximation $t(\hat{\gamma}, V; \nu)$, and let $V = LL'$ be the Choleski decomposition of V with L lower triangular. (This decomposition is used in any event to generate the synthetic multivariate normal if the multivariate t approximation is used as the importance function.) Let $\mathbf{e}_i$ be a $q \times 1$ vector whose ith element is 1 and all other elements are 0. For each $i = 1, \ldots, q$, the log-likelihood function is evaluated at $\beta = \hat{\beta}$, $\gamma = \hat{\gamma} + \delta L \mathbf{e}_i$, $\delta = (0, 0.5, 1.0, \ldots, 6.0)$. If the likelihood function were really multivariate t, it would be the case that

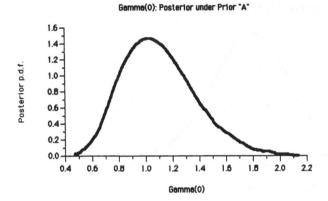

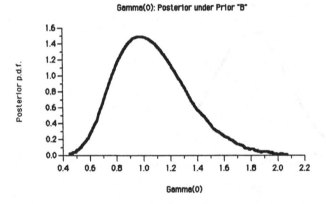

Figure 4. Exact posterior distributions for γ_0.

$$M(\delta) \equiv \log L(\hat{\beta}, \hat{\gamma})/\log L(\hat{\beta}, \gamma) = (1 + \nu^{-1}\delta^2)^{(\nu+k)/2}.$$

The multivariate t approximation is extended in the direction Le_i by scaling the ith row of L by $\max\{\nu^{-1/2}|\delta|[M(\delta)^{2/(\nu+k)} - 1]^{-1/2}\}$ for $\delta = 0, 0.5,$ $1.0, \ldots, 6.0$. This produces a new matrix L^* and a new variance matrix $V^* = L^*L^{*\prime}$. This process is repeated for each axis, for negative as well as positive values of δ, and for both β and γ. [Full details of this procedure are provided in Geweke (1987, Section 4).] Results using this procedure appear to be quite satisfactory. In the example here and the one in the next section, $\omega \approx 0.02$ when $N = 10,000$. Reported standard errors for numerical accuracy speak for themselves.

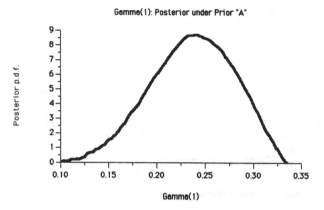

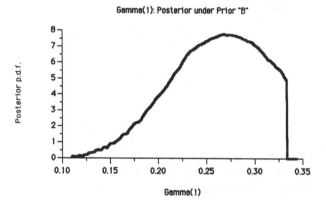

Figure 5. Exact posterior distributions of γ_1.

Point estimates and standard errors for parameters are given in Table 1. Exact (up to small numerical approximation error) Bayesian means and standard errors are given under prior A (unconditional variance of ϵ_t finite; prior proportional to inverse of unconditional standard of ϵ_t), prior B (unconditional variance of ϵ_t finite), and prior C [flat in the parameter space $\mathbb{R}^2 \times \mathbb{R}^{2+}$ for (β, γ)]. Point estimates for the β_j are similar under all the priors, with posterior standard errors only slightly smaller than the asymptotic standard errors. The posterior distributions for β_1 and β_2 are close to normal – those for β_2 under priors A and B are shown in Figure 3.

The situation with respect to γ is different. The posterior means and standard deviations under prior C reflect the rightward skew in the distri-

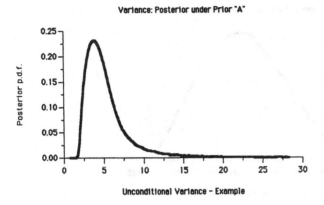

Variance: Posterior under Prior "A"

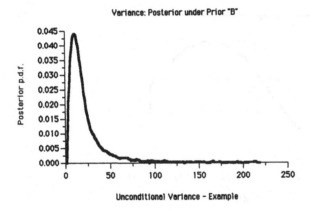

Variance: Posterior under Prior "B"

Figure 6. Exact posterior distributions for unconditional variance of ϵ_t in constructed example.

bution of γ_0 revealed in Figure 4, and the standard deviations under this prior relative to the asymptotic standard errors reflect the fact that the latter are too conservative. The restriction that the unconditional variance of ϵ_t not be explosive requires $\gamma_1 < \frac{1}{3}$, and in the presence of this restriction the maximum-likelihood estimate of γ_1 and its asymptotic standard error are difficult to interpret. In this situation exact Bayesian inference with the restriction imposed provides an interpretation of the likelihood function, but the result must be sensitive to the way the restriction is imposed. As one would anticipate, the posterior mean and standard deviation of γ_1 rise as one proceeds from priors A and B to prior C. The pos-

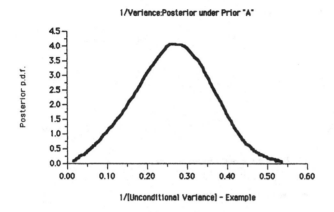

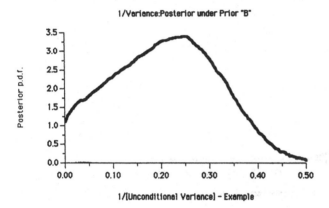

Figure 7. Exact posterior distributions for inverse of unconditional variance of ϵ_t in constructed example.

terior distribution of γ_0 is nonnormal under either prior A or prior B, as seen in Figure 4: The mean exceeds the mode, and there is a long upper tail on the distribution. The distribution of γ_1 is similar to that of a normal below its mode (Figure 5), but as $\gamma_1 \to \frac{1}{3}$, the distribution is sensitive to the choice of the prior in an obvious way. Under prior C, $P[\gamma_1 < \frac{1}{3}] = 0.8015$ (numerical s.e. 0.0046).

The posterior distribution of the unconditional variance

$$\sigma^2 = \gamma_0/(1 - 3\gamma_1)$$

may be computed under either prior A or B. It is evident that $E[\sigma^2]$ cannot exist under either prior because the posterior density of γ_1 is bounded

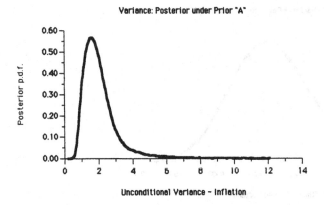

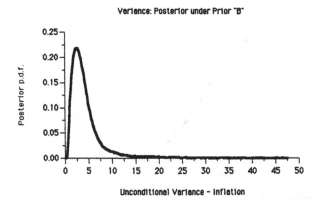

Figure 8. Exact posterior distributions for unconditional variance of ϵ_t in empirical example.

below in a neighborhood of $\gamma_1 = \frac{1}{3}$. This is reflected in very high posterior standard deviations and large numerical standard errors if it is attempted to approximate $E(\sigma^2)$ using (7): Under prior A the estimated posterior mean is 21.64, the posterior standard deviation is 485.0, and the numerical standard error is 6.510. Under prior B the estimated posterior mean is 6.364, the posterior standard deviation is 59.66, and the numerical standard error is 0.1240. This suggests that high numerical standard errors may indicate nonexistent $E[g(\theta)]$ in other, less transparent applications. There is no difficulty in applying (7) to estimate the posterior cumulative density function (c.d.f.) of σ^2, since only indicator functions are involved. The corresponding p.d.f.'s, shown in Figure 6, resemble neither normals

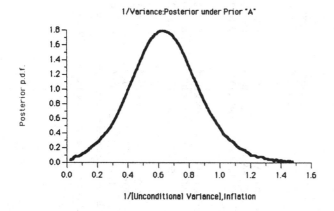

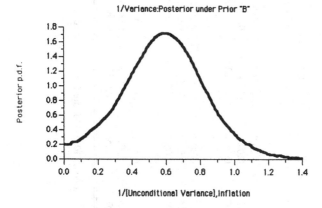

Figure 9. Exact posterior distributions for inverse of unconditional variance of ϵ_t in empirical example.

nor chi-squares. (The difference in scale under priors A and B is accounted for by the fact that the plotting routine chooses the domain to be the central 99 percent of the distribution plus an extension equal to 5 percent of the length of the domain on either end of the distribution.) The distribution of σ^{-2} is much more nearly symmetric, but distinctly nonnormal, under prior A (Figure 7); under prior B there is considerably more mass near zero, as expected.

This artificial example shows that with the proper importance function, exact inference in the ARCH linear model is feasible. The example here used 10,000 replications and required just under 30 min on a MicroVAX

Table 2. *Parameter estimates, postwar inflation model*

	β_1	β_2	β_3	β_4	β_5	β_6	γ_0	γ_1
Engle (1983)								
Estimate	2.0×10^{-5}	0.33	0.20	0.06	0.16	0.05	6.0×10^{-6}	0.56
Asymptotic s.e.	1.4×10^{-6}	0.08	0.08	0.02	0.05	0.06	2.2×10^{-6}	0.21
Maximum likelihood								
Estimate	4.706×10^{-5}	0.2217	0.1669	0.0822	0.1614	0.0081	5.773×10^{-6}	0.6002
Asymptotic s.e.	1.846×10^{-5}	0.0927	0.0883	0.0176	0.0463	0.0524	2.841×10^{-6}	0.2600
Prior A								
Posterior mean	4.548×10^{-5}	0.2129	0.2022	0.0763	0.1682	0.0100	5.951×10^{-6}	0.6324
Numerical s.e.	0.026×10^{-5}	0.0013	0.0013	0.0003	0.0006	0.0008	0.065×10^{-6}	0.0025
Posterior s.d.	1.851×10^{-5}	0.0897	0.0848	0.0183	0.0457	0.0546	2.091×10^{-6}	0.1472
Prior B								
Posterior mean	4.564×10^{-5}	0.2128	0.2019	0.0762	0.1675	0.0105	6.000×10^{-6}	0.6582
Numerical s.e.	0.027×10^{-5}	0.0014	0.0141	0.0003	0.0006	0.0008	0.075×10^{-6}	0.0030
Posterior s.d.	1.862×10^{-5}	0.0904	0.0854	0.0186	0.0457	0.0550	2.137×10^{-6}	0.1572
Prior C								
Posterior mean	4.605×10^{-5}	0.2121	0.2030	0.0758	0.1672	0.0112	5.781×10^{-6}	0.6915
Numerical s.e.	0.027×10^{-5}	0.0014	0.0014	0.0003	0.0006	0.0008	0.073×10^{-6}	0.0037
Posterior s.d.	1.865×10^{-5}	0.0907	0.0859	0.0188	0.0457	0.0549	2.245×10^{-6}	0.1954

Note: Posterior means and standard deviations are based on 10,000 Monte Carlo replications; computation time 7:07:11.35 with a MicroVAX for all tables and figures pertaining to this example.

Table 3. *Average conditional variance in three subperiods*

$H_1 = \dfrac{\sum_{49:4}^{54:2} h_t}{19}$	$H_2 = \dfrac{\sum_{56:2}^{71:2} h_t}{61}$	$H_3 = \dfrac{\sum_{73:2}^{79:4} h_t}{27}$
H_1	H_2	H_3

	H_1	H_2	H_3
Prior A			
Posterior mean	6.228	1.090	1.357
Numerical s.e.	0.019	0.005	0.005
Posterior s.d.	1.280	0.176	0.202
Prior B			
Posterior mean	6.464	1.115	1.395
Numerical s.e.	0.023	0.006	0.006
Posterior s.d.	1.373	0.180	0.220
Prior C			
Posterior mean	6.746	1.118	1.415
Numerical s.e.	0.030	0.005	0.005
Posterior s.d.	1.695	0.181	0.233

Note: All variances have been scaled by 10^5.

II. (For the figures, 100,000 replications were used to produce smooth posterior p.d.f.'s.) What exact inference reveals about the ARCH linear model itself is more disconcerting. The information contained in a sample of size 200 with no specification problems (the latter guaranteed by the artificial sample) reveals rather little about the variance process. The true generation process for the variances was not nearly unstable, but the posterior odds ratio for the hypothesis of stability against instability is only 4 with a flat prior. The dispersion of the unconditional variance, as indicated in Figures 6 and 7, is several times that which would result in a normal linear regression model with the same regressors and a disturbance with variance 4. These problems all pertain to the parameters of the model on which we have focused here to illustrate technical issues. In empirical work these parameters tend to be subordinate to other functions of interest. The following empirical example suggests that the ARCH linear model can be informative about these functions.

4 Conditional variance of U.S. inflation, 1951–79

An empirical application of the ARCH linear model is provided by Engle (1983), who employs a reduced-form equation for the gross domestic prod-

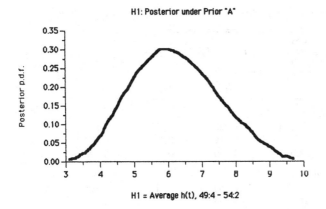

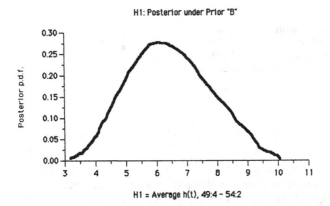

Figure 10. Exact posterior distributions for average conditional variance of inflation for quarter 4, 1949, to quarter 2, 1954.

uct (GDP) deflator (P_t) as a function of a constant, time trend (t), the import deflator (PM_t), wages (W_t), and money supply (M_t):

$$\log \frac{P_t}{P_{t-1}} = \beta_0 + \beta_1 t + \beta_2 \log \frac{P_{t-1}}{P_{t-2}} + \beta_3 \log \frac{P_{t-2}}{P_{t-3}}$$

$$+ \beta_4 \log \frac{PM_t}{PM_{t-1}} + \beta_5 \log \frac{W_t}{W_{t-1}} + \beta_6 \log \frac{M_t}{M_{t-1}} + \epsilon_t;$$

$$\epsilon_t \mid \psi_{t-1} \sim N(0, h_t), \qquad h_t = \gamma_0 + \gamma_1 \sum_{j=1}^{8} \frac{9-j}{36} \epsilon_{t-j}^2. \tag{9}$$

[The data are quarterly. They were obtained by the author through the editorial office of the *Journal of Money, Credit and Banking;* ordinary

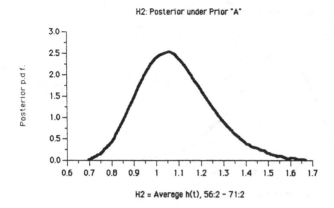

H2: Posterior under Prior "A"

H2 = Average h(t), 56:2 – 71:2

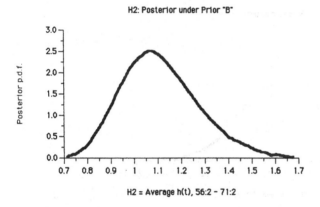

H2: Posterior under Prior "B"

H2 = Average h(t), 56:2 – 71:2

Figure 11. Exact posterior distributions for average conditional variance of inflation for quarter 2, 1956, to quarter 2, 1971.

least-squares regressions using these data are identical to those reported in Engle (1983).]

The purpose of the empirical work is to determine whether the conditional variance of inflation differed systematically over the three decades of the sample. Following Engle (1983), we focus here on the early period including the Korean War price controls plus the following four quarters (fourth quarter 1949 to second quarter 1954), the period between the Korean War controls and the Nixon freeze of 1971 (second quarter 1956 to second quarter 1971), and the period following the Nixon phased decontrol (second quarter 1973 to fourth quarter 1979). We also examine the conditional variance of inflation on a year-by-year basis and report means and standard deviations for the model's parameters.

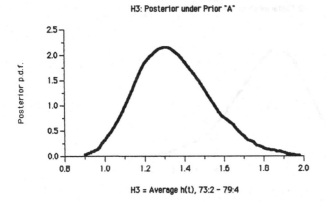

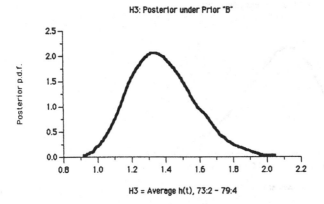

Figure 12. Exact posterior distributions for average conditional variance of inflation for quarter 2, 1973, to quarter 4, 1979.

The model [equation (9)] was estimated as described in Section 2. Posterior means of functions of interest were computed as described in Section 3 in connection with priors A, B, and C introduced there. Numerical integration was undertaken with 10,000 Monte Carlo replications requiring about 7 hr on the MicroVAX II. (The computation time was much increased by the evaluation of 5,300 functions of interest in each replication in order to produce the tables and graphs.) The maximum-likelihood estimates differ from those reported by Engle (see Table 2) because initial conditions are not handled in the same way, as discussed in Section 3.

The posterior means of the linear coefficients (the β_j) differ from the maximum-likelihood estimates by from 0.04 maximum-likelihood asymp-

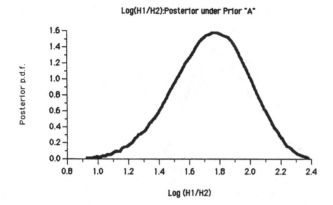

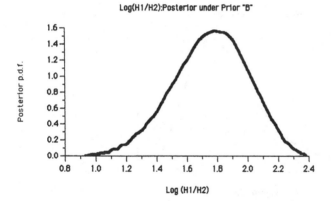

Figure 13. Exact posterior distribution for difference of logarithms of conditional variance of inflation for quarter 4, 1949, to quarter 2, 1954, and quarter 2, 1956, to quarter 2, 1971.

totic standard errors (β_6) to 0.42 asymptotic standard errors (β_3); given the numerical standard errors, not much of these differences can be ascribed to numerical approximation error. Differences among posterior means are always less than 0.03 times the standard deviation of the posterior, and these differences are generally less than the numerical precision of integration with 10,000 Monte Carlo replications. We conclude (for this example) that posterior means for the β_j are insensitive to choice of diffuse prior and clearly, but not greatly, differ from the maximum-likelihood estimates. The posterior mean of γ_1 differs systematically according to the prior employed in the way one would expect, increasing by

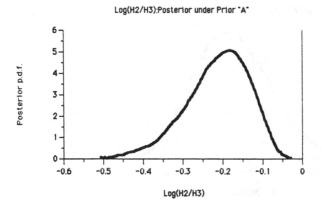

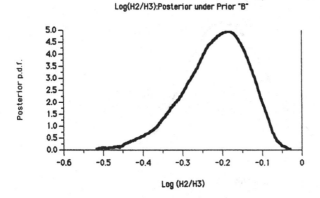

Figure 14. Exact posterior distribution for difference of logarithms of conditional variance of inflation for quarter 2, 1956, to quarter 2, 1971, and quarter 2, 1973, to quarter 4, 1979.

about 0.38 posterior standard deviations going from prior A to C. (Under prior C, $P[\gamma_1 > 1.0] = 0.067$.) Posterior distributions for the unconditional variance and the inverse of the unconditional variance – whose posterior means do not exist – are shown in Figures 8 and 9. The shapes of these distributions are similar to those of the corresponding distributions in the artificial example and are again considerably more diffuse than the posterior distribution of variance and inverse variance in the normal linear regression model with the same priors.

Substantive interest in this example is on the conditional variances $\{h_t\}$ rather than directly on the parameter vectors β and γ. Since $\{h_t\}$ is a se-

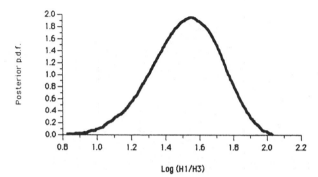

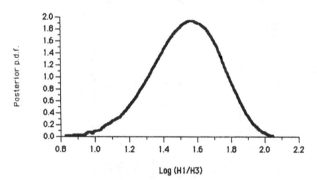

Figure 15. Exact posterior distribution for difference of logarithms of conditional variance of inflation for quarter 4, 1949, to quarter 2, 1954, and quarter 2, 1973, to quarter 4, 1979.

quence of known functions of β and γ, posterior means of functions of $\{h_t\}$ can be constructed by the methods described in Section 3. Bayesian inference about $\{h_t\}$ confronts the questions of interest about varying conditional heteroscedasticity formally and directly. Consider first the posterior means of averages of the h_t over the three periods of interest presented in Table 3. The posterior means differ systematically over priors, as one would expect, increasing by from 16 percent of the posterior standard deviation (H_2) to 38 percent of the posterior standard deviation (H_1) moving from prior A to C. Note that computation of standard deviations for the posteriors is routine, whereas the derivation of asymptotic

Table 4. Comparison of average conditional variances in three subperiods

$$H_1 = \frac{\sum_{49:4}^{54:2} h_t}{19} \qquad H_2 = \frac{\sum_{56:2}^{71:2} h_t}{61} \qquad H_3 = \frac{\sum_{73:2}^{79:4} h_t}{27}$$

Event	Posterior probability under prior A		Posterior probability under prior B		Posterior probability under prior C	
	Probability	Numerical s.e.	Probability	Numerical s.e.	Probability	Numerical s.e.
$H_1 \geq H_2 \geq H_3$	0.0001	0.0001	0.0001	0.0001	0.0001	0.0001
$H_1 \geq H_3 > H_2$	0.9999	0.0001	0.9999	0.0001	0.9999	0.0001
$H_1/H_2 > 2$	0.9999	0.0001	0.9999	0.0001	0.9999	0.0001
$2 > H_1/H_2 > 1$	0.0001	0.0001	0.0001	0.0001	0.0001	0.0001
$2 > H_2/H_3 > 1$	0.0001	0.0001	0.0001	0.0001	0.0001	0.0001
$1 > H_2/H_3 > 0.5$	0.9996	0.0002	0.9984	0.0013	0.9978	0.0014
$0.5 > H_2/H_3$	0.0003	0.0002	0.0015	0.0013	0.0021	0.0013
$H_1/H_3 > 2$	0.9997	0.0002	0.9997	0.0001	0.9997	0.0001
$2 > H_1/H_3 > 1$	0.0003	0.0002	0.0003	0.0001	0.0003	0.0001

standard errors based on maximum-likelihood estimates would be awkward, the computations involved, and the results of dubious reliability. Posterior distributions for the H_j are provided in Figures 10–12 (in which all variances have been scaled by 10^5).

Of greater interest are systematic differences between H_1, H_2, and H_3. The events of interest chosen for inference were the six possible orderings among H_1, H_2, and H_3 and pairwise comparisons among the H_j, differentiating between differences by a factor of more than 2 and differences by a factor of less than 2. Technically, the choice of events of interest amounts to setting up the appropriate indicator functions as discussed in Section 3 and involves only development of a trivial subroutine executed once during each Monte Carlo replication. The nonzero posterior probabilities are given in Table 4. It is virtually certain that $H_1 \geq H_3 > H_2$, H_1 exceeds each of H_2 and H_3 by a factor of more than 2, and H_3 exceeds H_2 by a factor of less than 2. This conclusion is insensitive to the choice of diffuse prior A, B, or C. The posterior distributions of the $\log(H_j/H_k)$ are presented in Figures 13–15; these distributions also indicate nearly total insensitivity to choice of diffuse prior.

Average annual conditional variance (scaled by 10^5) is shown in Figure 16 for each of the three priors; portrayed are the posterior means (solid lines) along with two posterior standard-deviation intervals (dashed lines). The three panels are essentially the same, except for a proportional increase in variance moving from prior A to B to C. Presentations such as Figure 16 are not appropriate to identifying periods of smallest and largest conditional variance because (one suspects) the joint posterior distribution of annual averages of the h_t exhibits strong positive correlations. Engle (1983) discussed the question of periods of minimum and maximum conditional variance of inflation, and that issue can be addressed directly here. By constructing a set of 60 indicator variables for minima and maxima in each of the 30 full calendar years of the sample, the methods of Section 3 were used to produce the formal results of Table 5. It is essentially certain that 1951 or 1952 was the year of greatest conditional variance (a fact obscured in presentations such as Figure 16), with probabilities of about 93 percent for 1951 and 7 percent for 1952. The year of minimum variance is considerably more uncertain: With about 54 percent probability it was 1957 or 1959, and there are five years in the 1960s and 1970s for which the probability of being the minimum exceeds 1 percent. Differences among priors are trivial.

These are examples of functions of interest that could be employed to address questions about changes in the conditional variance in inflation using the ARCH linear model [equation (9)]. The exact choice of functions will depend on the taste of the investigator. Once the functions are

Conditional variance, Prior "A"

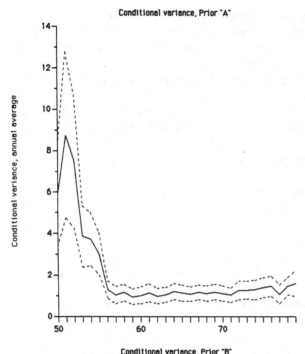

Conditional variance, Prior "B"

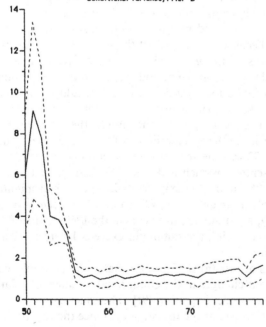

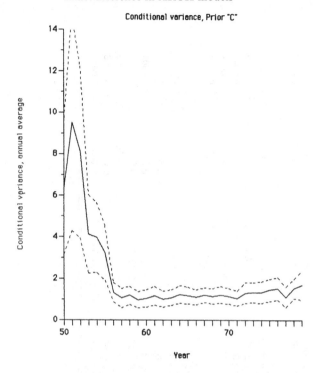

Figure 16. Average annual conditional variance. Solid line: mean value of posterior distribution of average conditional variance of inflation in each year. Dashed lines: two standard deviations above and below this posterior mean, respectively.

chosen, exact and formal results can be obtained routinely using the methods set forth here; and the evidence suggests that these results will not be sensitive to choices among diffuse priors.

5   Conclusion

The treatment of the ARCH linear model described here is the application of a paradigm for exact inference from aggregate economic time series. Thanks to increasingly cheap computing, it is practical to obtain the exact posterior distribution of any function of interest of the parameters subject to any diffuse prior. This is done through systematic exploration of the likelihood function, and the asymptotic sampling distribution theory for maximum-likelihood estimators provides the organization for this exploration. Diffuse priors may incorporate inequality restrictions that arise frequently in applied work but are impractical, if not impossible to

Table 5. *Maximum and minimum average annual conditional variances*

Year	Posterior probability under prior A		Posterior probability under prior B		Posterior probability under prior C	
	Probability	Numerical s.e.	Probability	Numerical s.e.	Probability	Numerical s.e.
Maximum						
1951	0.9302	0.0035	0.9304	0.0035	0.9311	0.0034
1952	0.0698	0.0035	0.0696	0.0035	0.0689	0.0034
Minimum						
1957	0.2232	0.0073	0.2190	0.0078	0.2112	0.0074
1959	0.3297	0.0072	0.3288	0.0074	0.3339	0.0074
1960	0.0743	0.0038	0.0754	0.0038	0.0812	0.0040
1961	0.0021	0.0007	0.0024	0.0009	0.0022	0.0008
1962	0.1002	0.0041	0.1008	0.0041	0.1020	0.0041
1963	0.0454	0.0030	0.0458	0.0031	0.0461	0.0031
1964	[a]		[a]		[a]	
1965	0.0051	0.0009	0.0055	0.0010	0.0055	0.0009
1968	0.0001	0.0001	0.0001	[a]	0.0001	[a]
1970	0.0011	0.0003	0.0011	0.0003	0.0011	0.0003
1971	0.0741	0.0031	0.0753	0.0032	0.0738	0.0031
1972	0.0017	0.0004	0.0017	0.0005	0.0016	0.0005
1974	0.0004	0.0002	0.0004	0.0002	0.0005	0.0002
1977	0.1427	0.0044	0.1438	0.0045	0.1408	0.0043

[a] Positive but less than 5×10^{-5}.

handle, in a classical setting. By choosing functions of interest appropriately, formal and direct answers to the questions that motivate empirical work can be obtained. The investigator can routinely handle problems in inference that would be analytical nightmares if attacked from a sampling-theoretic point of view and is left free to craft his models and functions more according to substantive questions and less subject to the restrictions of what asymptotic distribution theory can provide.

It is rightly objected that Bayesian inference, even under diffuse priors and despite the fact that conclusions may be insensitive to a wide range of these priors, is no substitute for a sampling-theoretic approach. Posterior distributions are conceptually distinct from sampling distributions, and posterior odds ratios are inconceivable substitutes for marginal significance levels. The objection is resolved by the fact that aggregate economic time series are much more amenable to Bayesian than to classical inference: These data nearly always pertain to unique environments incapable of reproduction even conceptually. The many practical attractions and technical advantages of the methods set forth here are based on this fact: They are simply the formalization of the sets of questions and answers often relegated to informal discussions at the ends of empirical papers.

This thesis has clear implications for the course of future research in econometrics. On the theoretical side, effort should be devoted more to problems in numerical analysis (like the choice and evaluation of importance functions for Monte Carlo integration) and less to exact sampling-theoretic work. On the applied side, we can look forward to spending less time trying to fit difficult questions into a limited set of analytical models and more time in the quantitative formalization of these questions with much less regard for analytical complexity. As we gain experience in the last endeavor and the price of computing continues to fall, this is what will happen.

REFERENCES

Engle, R. F. 1982. "Autoregressive Conditional Heteroscedasticity with Estimates of the Variance of United Kingdom Inflation." *Econometrica* 50: 987–1008.
    1983. "Estimates of the Variance of U.S. Inflation Based on the ARCH Model." *Journal of Money, Credit and Banking* 15: 286–301.
Engle, R. F., and T. Bollerslev. 1986. "Modelling the Persistence of Conditional Variances." *Econometric Reviews* 5: 1–50.
Geweke, J. 1986. "Exact Inference in the Inequality Constrained Normal Linear Regression Model." *Journal of Applied Econometrics* 1: 127–41.
    1987. "Bayesian Inference in Econometric Models Using Monte Carlo Integration." Duke University ISDS Discussion Paper 87-02, April.
Gourieroux, C., A. Holly, and A. Monfort. 1982. "Likelihood Ratio Test, Wald Test, and Kuhn–Tucker Test in Linear Models with Inequality Constraints on the Regression Parameters." *Econometrica* 50: 63–80.

Kloek, T., and H. K. Van Dijk. 1978. "Bayesian Estimates of Equation System Parameters: An Application of Integration by Monte Carlo." *Econometrica* 46: 1–19.

Monahan, J. F. 1983. "Full Bayesian Analysis of ARMA Time Series Models." *Journal of Econometrics* 21: 307–31.

Van Dijk, H. K., and T. Kloek. 1980. "Further Experience in Bayesian Analysis Using Monte Carlo Integration." *Journal of Econometrics* 14: 307–28.

1983. "Monte Carlo Analysis of Skew Posterior Distributions: An Illustrative Econometric Example." *The Statistician* 32: 216–23.

CHAPTER 6

Control of a linear regression process with unknown parameters

Nicholas M. Kiefer and Yaw Nyarko

1   Introduction

Applications of forms of control theory to economic policy making have been studied by Theil (1958), Chow (1975, 1981), and Prescott (1972). Many of the applications are approximations to the optimal policy – suggestions of how to improve existing practice using quantitative methods rather than development of fully optimal policies. Chow (1975) obtains the fully optimal feedback control policy for linear systems with known coefficients for a quadratic loss function and a finite time horizon. Chow (1981) argues that the use of control technique for the evaluation of economic policies is possible and essential under rational expectations. The use of optimal control for microeconomic planning is fully established. An early analysis with many practical suggestions is Theil (1958). Optimal control theory has also been useful in economic theory, in analyzing the growth of economies as well as the behavior over time of economic agents.

The problem of control of a stochastic economic system with unknown parameters is far less well studied. Zellner (1971, Chapter 11) studied the two-period control problem for a normal regression process with a conjugate prior and quadratic loss function. He obtained an approximate solution to the problem and compared it with two other solutions – the "here and now" solution, in which the agent chooses a fixed action for both periods at the beginning of the first period, and a "sequential updating" solution, in which the agent chooses the first-period policy without regard to its information value and then updates his beliefs on the basis of first-period experience before calculating the second-period policy. The sequential updating solution was studied further and compared with the

We are indebted to many conference participants, to our discussant Ingmar Prucha, and to two referees for useful comments. The revision of this chapter was supported by the National Science Foundation.

105

certainty equivalence rule by Harkema (1975). The optimal policy, as expected, yields a higher expected reward than the alternative policies. Prescott (1972) developed an approximation to the optimal control solution for a linear dynamic system with unknown coefficients, a finite horizon, and quadratic loss. Chow (1975, Chapter 10) developed a control policy for a linear dynamic equation system with unknown parameters, quadratic loss, and a finite horizon but no learning about the parameters over the period of control. Chow (1975, Chapter 11) provided an approximate solution for the control problem with learning. Taylor (1974) examined a simple regression case and considered asymptotic properties of estimates and policies when an agent uses least-squares control policies (i.e., in each period the agent chooses a policy as if unknown parameters were equal to their current least-squares estimates). He found that the sequence of slope estimates is consistent when the intercept is known. Anderson and Taylor (1976), in work closely related to an example we carry through here, presented simulation results for the least-squares control rule when both the slope and intercept are unknown. They found apparent convergence of the policy variable. Jordan (1985) followed up on this work by establishing conditions under which the sequence of parameter estimates obtained by following the least-squares control rule are consistent. The related problem of maximizing an unknown function has been studied (see Kushner and Clark 1978) without the parametric representation favored in economics, where parameters are sometimes directly interpretable.

We study the problem of controlling a linear regression process with unknown parameters. We use a stochastic control framework that makes explicit the trade-off between current expected reward and the information value of an action. An agent's information about unknown parameters is represented by a probability distribution. The model is set up in Section 2; Section 3 shows the existence of optimal policies. This chapter concentrates attention on the sequence of "beliefs" held by the agent. Section 4 shows that the agent's beliefs converge to some limit, which may or may not be concentrated on the true parameter value. Proofs are given in Section 5. Related results on the sequence of actions are given by Kiefer and Nyarko (1986).

2   The model

In this section we sketch the general framework we wish to study. Let Ω' be a complete and separable metric space, F' its Borel field, and (Ω', F', P') a probability space. On (Ω', F', P') define the stochastic process $\{\epsilon_t\}_1^\infty$, the *shock process,* which is unobserved by the agent. The shock process is assumed to be independent and identically distributed, with the common marginal distribution $p(\epsilon_t \mid \phi)$ depending on some parameter ϕ in R^h that is unknown to the agent. Assume that the set of probability measures $\{p(\cdot \mid \phi)\}$ is continuous in the parameter ϕ (in the weak topology of measures) and that for any ϕ, $\int \epsilon p(d\epsilon \mid \phi) = 0$. Let $\bar{X}$, the *action space*, be a compact subset of R^k. Define $\Theta = R^1 \times R^k \times R^h$ be the parameter space. If the "true parameter" is $\theta = (\alpha, \beta, \phi) \in \Theta$ and the agent chooses an action $x_t \in \bar{X}$ at date t, the agent observes y_t, where

$$y_t = \alpha + \beta x_t + \epsilon_t \tag{2.1}$$

and where ϵ_t is chosen according to $p(\cdot \mid \phi)$.

Let $\tilde{\Theta}$ be the Borel field of Θ, and let $P(\Theta)$ be the set of all probability measures on $(\Theta, \tilde{\Theta})$. Endow $P(\Theta)$ with its weak topology, and note that $P(\Theta)$ is then a complete and separable metric space (see, e.g., Parthasarathy 1967, Chapter II, Theorems 6.2 and 6.5). Let $\mu_0 \in P(\Theta)$ be the *prior probability* on the parameter space with a finite first moment.

The agent is assumed to use Bayes's rule to update the prior probability at each date after any observation of (x_t, y_t). For example, in the initial period, date 1, the prior distribution is updated after the agent chooses an action x_1 and observes the value of y_1. The updated prior, that is, the posterior, is then $\mu_1 = \Gamma(x_1, y_1, \mu_0)$, where $\Gamma : \bar{X} \times R^1 \times P(\Theta) \to P(\Theta)$ represents the Bayes rule operator. If the prior μ_0 has a density function, the posterior may be easily computed. In general, the Bayes rule operator may be defined by appealing to the existence of certain conditional probabilities (see Appendix). Under standard conditions the operator Γ is continuous in its arguments, and we assume this throughout. Any $\{x_t, y_t\}$ process will therefore result in a posterior process $\{\mu_t\}$, where, for all $t = 1, 2, \ldots,$

$$\mu_t = \Gamma(x_t, y_t, \mu_{t-1}). \tag{2.2}$$

Let $\bar{H}_n = P(\Theta) \prod_{i=1}^{n-1} [\bar{X} \times R^1 \times P(\Theta)]$. A *partial history* h_n at date n is any element $h_n = (\mu_0, (x_1, y_1, \mu_1), \ldots, (x_{n-1}, y_{n-1}, \mu_{n-1})) \in \bar{H}_n$; h_n is said to be admissible if equation (2.2) holds for all $t = 1, 2, \ldots, n-1$. Let H_n be the subset of $\bar{H}_n$ consisting of all admissible partial histories at date n.

A *policy* is a sequence $\pi = \{\pi_t\}_{t=1}^{\infty}$, where, for each $t \geq 1$, the policy function $\pi_t : H_t \to \bar{X}$ specifies the date t action $x_t = \pi_t(h_t)$ as a Borel function of the partial history h_t in H_t at that date. A policy function is *stationary* if $\pi_t(h_t) = g(\mu_t)$ for each t, where the function $g(\cdot)$ maps $P(\Theta)$ into $\bar{X}$. Note that μ_t can be regarded as a state variable at date t, containing all relevant information about the parameters provided by the partial history h_t.

Define $(\Omega, F, P) = (\Theta, \tilde{\Theta}, \mu_0)(\Omega', F', P')$. Any policy π then generates a sequence of random variables $\{(x_t(\omega), y_t(\omega), \mu_t(\omega)\}_{t=1}^{\infty}$ on (Ω, F, P), as described above, using (2.1) and (2.2) (the technical details are stated in the Appendix).

For any $n = 1, 2, \ldots$, let F_n be the subfield of F generated by the random variables (h_n, x_n). Notice that $x_n \in F_n$ but y_n and $\mu_n \in F_{n+1}$. Next define $F_\infty = V_{n=0}^\infty F_n$.

We now discuss the utility and reward functions and define the optimality criterion. Let $u : \bar{X} \times R^1 \to R^1$ be the utility function, and in particular, $u(x_t, y_t)$ is the utility to the agent when action x_t is chosen at date t and the observation y_t is made. We assume:

(A.1) u is bounded above and continuous.

The reward function $r : \bar{X} \times P(\Theta) \to R^1$ is defined by

$$r(x_t, \mu_{t-1}) = \int_\Theta \int_R u(x_t, y_t) p(d\epsilon_t \mid \phi) \mu_{t-1}(d\alpha \, d\beta \, d\phi), \qquad (2.3)$$

where $y_t = \alpha + \beta x_t + \epsilon_t$.

Let δ in $(0, 1)$ be the discount factor. Any policy π generates a sum of expected discounted rewards equal to

$$V_\pi(\mu_0) = \int \sum_{t=1}^\infty \delta^t r(x_t(\omega), \mu_{t-1}(\omega)) P(d\omega), \qquad (2.4)$$

where the (x_t, μ_t) processes are those obtained using the policy π. A policy π^* is said to be an *optimal policy* if, for all policies π and all priors μ_0 in $P(\Theta)$,

$$V_{\pi^*}(\mu_0) \geq V_\pi(\mu_0). \qquad (2.5)$$

The processes (x_t, y_t) corresponding to an optimal policy are called *optimal processes*. Even though the optimal policy π^* (when it exists) may not be unique, the function $V(\mu_0) = V_{\pi^*}(\mu_0)$ is always well defined and will be referred to as the *value function*.

3   The existence theorem

We now indicate that stationary optimal policies exist and that the value function is continuous.

Theorem 3.1.   *A stationary optimal policy $g : P(\Theta) \to \bar{X}$ exists. The value function V is continuous on $P(\Theta)$, and the following functional equation holds:*

$$V(\mu_{t-1}) = r(x_1, \mu_{t-1}) + \delta \int V(\mu_t) p(d\epsilon_t \mid \phi) \mu_{t-1}(d\alpha \, d\beta \, d\phi), \quad (3.1)$$

where $\mu_t = \Gamma(x_t, y_t, \mu_{t-1})$ and $y_t = \alpha + \beta x_t + \epsilon_t$ and the integral is taken over $\Theta \times R^1$.

Proof: Let $S = \{f: P(\Theta) \to R \mid f$ is continuous and bounded$\}$. Define T: $S \to S$ by

$$Tw(\mu_0) = \max_{x \in \bar{X}} r(x, \mu_0) + \delta \int V(\mu_1) p(d\epsilon_1 \mid \phi) \mu_0(d\alpha \, d\beta \, d\phi), \quad (3.2)$$

where $\mu_1 = \Gamma(x, y_1, \mu_0)$ and $y_1 = \alpha + \beta x + \epsilon_1$. One can easily show that for $w \in S$, $Tw \in S$; also, T is a contraction mapping. Hence, there exists a $v \in S$ such that $v = Tv$. Replacing w with v in (3.2) then results in (3.1); and since $v \in S$, v is continuous. Finally, it is immediate that the solution to the maximization exercise in (3.2) (replacing w with v) results in a stationary optimal-policy function [one should consult Blackwell (1965) or Maitra (1968) and Schal (1979) for the details of the preceding arguments].   Q.E.D.

4   Convergence properties of posterior process

In this section the convergence properties of the posterior process $\{\mu_t\}$ for arbitrary (i.e, not necessarily optimal) policies are studied.

The main results of this section may be described as follows. Proposition 4.1 shows that the posterior process always converges (in the weak topology of measures) with probability 1. However, the limiting probability μ_∞ may or may not be concentrated on the true parameter. Proposition 4.2 indicates that if there exists a strongly consistent estimator – be this the ordinary least-squares (OLS) estimator, the maximum-likelihood estimator, or some other – the posterior process necessarily converges to the true parameter.

In Section 4.1 the model is simplified somewhat (in particular, assume that the distribution of shocks is known and further that $k = 1$ so as to have a simple regression equation $y = \alpha + \beta x + \epsilon$). Under this simplification, some characterization of the limiting distribution can be provided. In particular, if for some ω in Ω, $x_t(\omega)$ does not converge to a limit, the limiting posterior distribution for that ω in Ω is concentrated on the "true" parameter value. Alternatively, if $x_t(\omega)$ does converge to some $x(\omega)$, say, the posterior process converges to a limiting probability with support a subset of the set $\{\alpha', \beta': \alpha' + \beta' x(\omega) = \alpha + \beta x(\omega)\}$, where α, β represent the "true" parameter values.

4.1   *Convergence of* $\{\mu_t\}$

First we prove that under the very general conditions of Sections 2 and 3, the posterior process converges for P almost everywhere (a.e.) ω in Ω to a well-defined probability measure (with the convergence taking place in the weak topology).

Note that for any Borel subset D of the parameter space Θ, if we suppress the ω's and let, for some fixed ω, $\mu_t(D)$ represent the mass that measure $\mu_t(\omega)$ assigns to the set D,

$$\mu_t(D) = E[1_{\{\theta \in D\}} \mid F_t]. \tag{4.1}$$

Define a measure μ_∞ on Θ by setting, for each Borel set D in Θ,

$$\mu_\infty(D) = E[1_{\{\theta \in D\}} \mid F_\infty]. \tag{4.2}$$

The proposition that follows shows that μ_∞ is the limiting posterior distribution and is indeed a well-defined probability measure.

Proposition 4.1. *The posterior process $\{\mu_t\}$ converges, for P-a.e. ω in Ω, in the weak topology, to the probability measure μ_∞.*

Recall P is the probability on Ω. Define P_θ to be the conditional distribution of P on Ω given the value θ in Θ. Here, P_θ should be interpreted as the distribution of histories – sequences $\{x_t, y_t\}$ – given values of the parameters of the regression equation and of the shock process θ. The proof of the following proposition is due to Schwartz (1965, Theorem 3.5, p. 14). Let 1_θ be the point mass at θ.

Proposition 4.2. *Suppose there exists an F_∞-measurable function g such that for μ_0-a.e. θ in Θ, $g(\omega) = \theta$, P_θ-a.e. Then for μ_0-a.e. θ in Θ, $\mu_\infty(\omega) = 1_\theta$, P_θ-a.e.*

The existence of a strongly consistent estimator is equivalent to the existence of a function g with the properties stated in Proposition 4.2.

4.2   Simple regression equation model

In this section a few simplifying assumptions are introduced to enable some rather strong characterizations of the convergence properties of the posterior process. These assumptions reduce the model to the situation of a simple regression equation. In particular, suppose that condition (S) holds:

Condition (S): The shock process has a distribution that is known to the agent and possesses finite second moment; $k = 1$, so that the action space $\bar{X}$ is a subset of R^1.

Proposition 4.3 shows that if the x_t process does not converge, the posterior process converges to the point mass on the true parameter value.

Note, however, that nonconvergence of the x_t process is not necessary for convergence of μ_t to point mass.

Let $B = \{\omega : x_t(\omega) \text{ does not converge}\}$, and recall that 1_θ is the point mass at θ.

Proposition 4.3. *For μ_0-a.e. θ in Θ, the posterior process $\mu_t(\omega)$ converges to 1_θ for P_θ-a.e. ω in B.*

Define on B^C, the set where $x_t(\omega)$ converges, $x(\omega) = \lim_{t \to \infty} x_t(\omega)$. In Proposition 4.4, it is shown that if the x_t process does converge to $x(\omega)$, the posterior process converges to a limiting probability with support a subset of the set $\{(\alpha', \beta') : \alpha' + \beta' x(\omega) = \alpha + \beta x(\omega)\}$, where α, β represent the true parameter values.

Proposition 4.4. *For μ_0-a.e. $\theta = (\alpha, \beta)$ in Θ, the posterior process $\mu_t(\omega)$ converges to a limiting distribution $\mu_\infty(\omega)$ with support a subset of the set $\{(\alpha', \beta') : \alpha' + \beta' x(\omega) = \alpha + \beta x(\omega)\}$ for P_θ-a.e. ω in B^C.*

5 Proofs

Proof of Proposition 4.1

The proof may be summarized as follows: We use equation (4.1) to show that for any Borel set D in Θ, $\mu_t(D)$ is a martingale sequence and apply the martingale convergence theorem to show that μ_t converges weakly to μ_∞. This argument does not assure us that the limit is a probability measure. However, the sequence of probability measures $\mu_t(\omega)$ for fixed ω is tight, and Prohorov's theorem can be applied to deduce that μ_∞ is a probability measure.

A sequence of probability measures v_n on Θ is said to be tight if, for all $\epsilon > 0$, there exists a compact set K^ϵ such that $v_n(K^\epsilon) \geq 1 - \epsilon$ for all n. Claim 5.1 establishes the tightness of $\{\mu_t\}$.

Claim 5.1. *For P-a.e. ω in Ω, the sequence of probability measures $\{\mu_t(\omega)\}$ is tight.*

Proof: Let K_r be the closed (compact) ball with center the origin and radius r. It suffices to show that for P-a.e. ω in Ω,

$$\lim_{r \to \infty} \left[\inf_t \mu_t(K_r)(\omega) \right] = 1. \tag{5.1}$$

However, using Chebyshev's inequality,

$$\mu_t(\Theta - K_r) = P(\|\theta\| > r \mid F_t) < E[\|\theta\| \mid F_t]/r,$$

so

$$\mu_t(K_r) \geq 1 - E[\|\theta\| \mid F_t]/r. \tag{5.2}$$

One can check that $\{E[\|\theta\| \mid F_t]\}$ is a positive martingale sequence and so converges to $E[\|\theta\| \mid F_\infty]$ (see, e.g., Chung 1974, Theorem 9.4.8, p. 340). We assumed that μ_0 has finite first moment, which implies that $E[\|\theta\|] < \infty$, which in turn implies that $E[\|\theta\| \mid F_\infty] < \infty$, P-a.e. Hence, $\sup_t E[\|\theta\| \mid F_t] = L < \infty$, P-a.e. Using this in (5.2) results in

$$\inf_t \mu_t(K_r) \geq 1 - \sup_t E[\|\theta\| \mid F_\infty]/r = 1 - L/r. \tag{5.3}$$

Taking limits as $r \to \infty$ then results in (5.1). This concludes the proof of Claim 5.1.   Q.E.D.

Proof of Proposition 4.1 (continued)

Let U be the subclass of F made up of sets of the following kind: First, since Θ is separable, let $\{s_1, s_2, s_3, \ldots\}$ be a separant; let B_n^k be the ball of radius $1/n$ and center s_k; then define U as the set of all finite intersections of the balls B_n^k, where $k = 1, 2, \ldots$ and $n = 1, 2, \ldots$. One may check that U is countable.

Next, for any fixed set D, $\mu_t(D) = E[1_{\{\theta \in D\}} \mid F_t]$, so using Chung (1974, Theorem 9.4.8, p. 340), the sequence $\{\mu_t(D)\}$ can be shown to be a positive martingale, and so the martingale convergence theorem applies, and we conclude that $\mu_t(D)$ converges with P probability 1 to $\mu_\infty(D)$. Since the set U is countable, convergence holds on all of U, simultaneously, with P probability 1. Then we check that U satisfies conditions (i) and (ii) of Billingsley (1968, Theorem 2.2, p. 14), so, from that Theorem, μ_t converges weakly to μ_∞ with P probability 1.

Finally, from Claim 5.1, for P-a.e. ω in Ω, the sequence of posterior distributions is tight. Hence, using Prohorov's theorem (see, e.g., Billingsley 1968, Theorem 6.1, p. 37), we may conclude that μ_∞ is a probability measure (P-a.e.).   Q.E.D.

Proof of Proposition 4.2

A stronger version of this proposition is stated and proved later in Lemma 5.4.

Comment on Proof of Proposition 4.3

The idea behind the proof of Proposition 4.3 is the following. Suppose first that $x_t(\omega) = x'$ for all t and for all ω. Then $y_t(\omega) = \alpha + \beta x' + \epsilon_t(\omega)$, and $\sum_{t=1}^{n} y_t(\omega)/n = \alpha + \beta x' + \sum_{t=1}^{n} \epsilon_t/n$. However, by the strong law of large numbers, $\lim_{n\to\infty} \sum_{t=1}^{n} \epsilon_t/n = 0$, P-a.e., so $y' = \alpha + \beta x'$ if we define $y' = \lim_{n\to\infty} \sum_{t=1}^{n} y_t(\omega)/n$; in particular, the agent will learn that the true parameter will satisfy this relation in the limit. Next, if $x_t(\omega)$ does not converge but alternates between two numbers x' and x'', it is obvious that applying the preceding argument first to the even sequence $\{x_{2t}\}_{t=1}^{\infty}$ and then to the odd sequence $\{x_{2t-1}\}_{t=1}^{\infty}$, the two equations $y' = \alpha + \beta x'$ and $y'' = \alpha + \beta x''$ will be obtained, where $y' = \sum_{t=1}^{\infty} y_{2t}$ and $y'' = \sum_{t=1}^{\infty} y_{2t-1}$, from which one may compute the true parameters α and β. In this situation the agent will learn the true parameters in the limit. This idea is behind the proof of Proposition 4.3.

In the preceding example, the law of large numbers had to be applied first to the even time subsequence and then to the odd subsequence. In Lemma 5.1, it is shown that the law of large numbers may be applied to a very large set of time subsequences. As indicated in Lemma 5.3, using the result of Lemma 5.1, one can compute the true parameter in a manner very similar to that explained in the preceding example (i.e., by solving two simultaneous equations involving the true parameters α and β). Lemma 5.4 states that if the true value can be computed, beliefs converge to point mass at the true value.

Proof of Proposition 4.3

Define $1_{\{\omega \in K\}}$ equal to 1 if $\{\omega \in K\}$ and equal to zero otherwise, where K is any subset of Ω. For any $1 < m$, define

$$N_k(\omega) = \inf\left\{n: \sum_{t=1}^{n} 1_{\{1 \le x_t(\omega) \le m\}} = k\right\}$$

if the set in brackets, $\{\cdot\}$, is nonempty and equal to infinity otherwise. Notice that for each k, $N_k(\omega)$ is a stopping time, that is, $\{\omega: N_k(\omega) = t\} \in F_t$ for each t.

Lemma 5.1. *There exists a set A in F with $P(A) = 1$ such that for all rational numbers ℓ and m, with $\ell < m$, and for all $\omega \in A$,*

$$\lim_{k\to\infty} \frac{1}{k} \sum_{t=1}^{N_k(\omega)} \epsilon_t(\omega) 1_{\{\ell \le x_t(\omega) \le m\}} = 0, \tag{5.4}$$

where the N_k are those corresponding to the ℓ and m.

Proof: Fix an ℓ and m with $\ell < m$. For ease of notation, drop the ω's in the random variables $\epsilon_t(\omega)$ and $x_t(\omega)$, and define, for fixed $\ell \ge m$, $\ell_t = 1_{\{\ell < x_t < m\}}$.

If, for some $s < \infty$, $N_k(\omega) = \infty$ for all $k \geq s$, then

$$\sum_{t=1}^{N_k(\omega)} \epsilon_t 1_t = \sum_{t=1}^{s} \epsilon_t 1_t < \infty \quad \text{for all } k \geq s,$$

and (5.4) follows immediately. If $N_k(\omega) < \infty$ for all k, then $\sum_{t=1}^{T} 1_t \to \infty$ and

$$\lim_{k \to \infty} \frac{1}{k} \sum_{t=1}^{N_k(\omega)} \epsilon_t 1_t = \lim_{T \to \infty} \frac{\sum_{t=1}^{T} \epsilon_t 1_t}{\sum_{t=1}^{T} 1_t}. \tag{5.5}$$

Since for $t' \geq t$, $\epsilon_{t'}$ is independent of $\{1_1, \ldots, 1_t\}$, (5.4) follows from (5.5) and Lemma 5.2 due to Taylor (1974).

Hence, if for fixed ℓ and m with $\ell < m$, $A(\ell, m)$ denotes the set on which (5.4) holds, $P(A(\ell, m)) = 1$. Define A to be the intersection over all rational numbers $\ell < m$ of the sets $A(\ell, m)$; then $P(A) = 1$, and A satisfies the conclusion of the lemma.   Q.E.D.

Lemma 5.2.   *Let $\{v_t\}$ be a sequence of independent random variables with mean zero and uniformly bounded variance. Let $\{z_t\}$ be a sequence of random variables such that for each t, t' with $t' > t$, $y_{t'}$ is independent of $\{z_1, \ldots, z_t\}$; then for almost every realization with $\sum_{t=1}^{T} z_t^2 \to \infty$,*

$$\lim_{T \to \infty} \frac{\sum_{t=1}^{T} z_t v_t}{\sum_{t=1}^{T} z_t^2} = 0. \tag{5.6}$$

Proof: One applies Taylor (1974, Lemmas 1–3) with minor modifications.   Q.E.D.

In Lemma 5.3, on the set where x_t does not converge, there exists a consistent estimator for the true parameter.

Lemma 5.3.   *There exists an F_∞-measurable function g such that $g(\omega) = \theta$, P_θ-a.s. on the set where x_t does not converge, that is, such that if B is the set where x_t does not converge,*

$$P_\theta(\{\omega : g(\omega) = \theta\} \cap B) = P_\theta(B). \tag{5.7}$$

Proof: Construct such a function g. To ease the exposition, assume that $\bar{X} = [0, 1]$. One may check that, since $\bar{X}$ is assumed compact, this simplifying assumption is without loss of generality.

Let $\bar{Q}$ be the set of rational numbers in $\bar{X}$, and let $\bar{x}(\omega) = \lim \sup x_t(\omega)$ and $\underline{x}(\omega) = \lim \inf x_t(\omega)$. Proceed to define two random variables $h(\omega)$ and $h'(\omega)$ taking values in $\bar{Q}$ and such that $\underline{x}(\omega) < h'(\omega) < h(\omega) < \bar{x}(\omega)$. Define the function $h : \bar{X} \times \bar{X} \to Q$ as follows. First, any integer $k = 1, 2, \ldots$ can be uniquely written as $k = 2^{n+1} + p$, where $n = 1, 2, \ldots$ and $0 \leq p \leq 2^{n+1} - 1$; so define $s_k = (2p+1)/2^n$, where $k = 2^{n-1} + p$. The sequence $\{s_k\}$

is therefore a sequence of rational numbers in $\bar{X} = [0, 1]$. Define $t(x, x') = \inf\{k : s_k \in [x, x']\}$ if $x < x'$ and $t(x, x') = 0$ if $x \geq x'$; and $h(x, x') = s_{t(x, x')}$ with $s_0 = 0$. Hence, h takes values in $\bar{Q}$, and one can check that h is Borel measurable. [In fact, to prove the measurability of h, note that $t(x, x') = 1_{\{x < x'\}} \sum_{t=1}^{\infty} r_t$, where r_t is the indicator function that equals 1 when $s_k \in [x, x']^c$ for all integers $k < t$ and $s_t \in [x, x']$ and zero otherwise (with $r_1 = 1$). Because $1_{\{x > x'\}}$ and r_t (for each t) are Borel measurable, we obtain the measurability of $t(x, x')$; the measurability of h then follows from $h(x, x') = s_{t(x, x')} = \sum_{k=1}^{\infty} s_k 1_{\{t(x, x') = k\}}$.]

Next, we define the random variable $h(\omega) = h(\bar{x}(\omega), \underline{x}(\omega))$ (note the abuse of notation!). Since $\bar{x}$ and $\underline{x}$ are both F_∞-measurable and $h(x, x')$ is Borel measurable, we obtain that $h(\omega)$ is F_∞-measurable. We have therefore constructed an F_∞-measurable random variable $h(\omega)$ taking values in $\bar{Q}$ and such that on B, $\underline{x}(\omega) < h(\omega) < \bar{x}(\omega)$. By replacing $\bar{x}(\omega)$ with $h(\omega)$ and repeating the preceding construction, we obtain an F_∞-measurable random variable $h'(\omega)$ taking values in $\bar{Q}$ and such that on B, $\underline{x}(\omega) < h'(\omega) < h(\omega)$.

We now need some notation and a few definitions to construct the function g. Let

$$\bar{I}_t = 1_{\{h \leq x_t \leq 1\}}; \qquad \bar{N}_k = \begin{cases} \inf\{n : \sum_{t=1}^{n} \bar{I}_t = k\} & \text{if well-defined,} \\ \infty & \text{otherwise;} \end{cases}$$

$$\bar{X}_k = \frac{1}{k} \sum_{t=1}^{\bar{N}_k} x_t \bar{I}_t; \qquad \bar{Y}_k = \frac{1}{k} \sum_{t=1}^{\bar{N}_k} y_t \bar{I}_t; \qquad \bar{\epsilon}_k = \frac{1}{k} \sum_{t=1}^{\bar{N}_k} \bar{\epsilon}_t \bar{I}_t. \qquad (5.8)$$

Define $\underline{N}_k$, $\underline{X}_k$, $\underline{Y}_k$, and $\underline{\epsilon}_k$ in a manner similar to $\bar{N}_k$, $\bar{X}_k$, $\bar{Y}_k$, and $\bar{\epsilon}_k$ but replace $\bar{I}_t$ with $\underline{I}_t = 1_{\{0 \leq x_t \leq h'\}}$. Finally, define $g : \Omega \to \Theta$ by $g(\omega) = (0, 0)$ on B^c and $g(\omega) = (g^\alpha(\omega), g^\beta(\omega))$ on B, where (dropping the ω's for clarity)

$$g^\alpha = \lim_{k \to \infty} \frac{\bar{X}_k \cdot \underline{Y}_k - \underline{X}_k \cdot \bar{Y}_k}{\bar{X}_k - \underline{X}_k} \quad \text{and} \quad g^\beta = \lim_{k \to \infty} \frac{\bar{Y}_k - \underline{Y}_k}{\bar{X}_k - \underline{X}_k}. \qquad (5.9)$$

The remainder of the proof is devoted to showing that the random variable g just constructed is well defined and satisfies the conclusions of the lemma.

Recall that $B = \{\omega : \underline{x}(\omega) < \bar{x}(\omega)\}$. On B, notice that $\underline{X}_k < h' < h < \bar{X}_k$, $\bar{N}_k(\omega) < \infty$, and $\underline{N}_k(\omega) < \infty$ for all k sufficiently large. Because $y_t = \alpha + \beta x_t + \epsilon_t$,

$$\frac{1}{k} \sum_{t=1}^{\bar{N}_k} y_t \bar{I}_t = \alpha \frac{1}{k} \sum_{t=1}^{\bar{N}_k} \bar{I}_t + \beta \frac{1}{k} \sum_{t=1}^{\bar{N}_k} x_t \bar{I}_t + \frac{1}{k} \sum_{t=1}^{\bar{N}_k} \epsilon_t \bar{I}_t. \qquad (5.10)$$

One can check that $(1/k) \sum_{t=1}^{\bar{N}_k} \bar{I}_t = 1$ for all k. Hence, (5.10) becomes

$$\bar{Y}_k = \alpha + \beta \bar{X}_k + \bar{\epsilon}_k. \qquad (5.11)$$

Similarly, one can show that

$$Y_k = \alpha + \beta \underline{X}_k + \epsilon_k. \tag{5.12}$$

Solving (5.11) and (5.12) for β yields

$$\beta = \frac{(\bar{Y}_k - \underline{Y}_k) - (\bar{\epsilon}_k - \underline{\epsilon}_k)}{\bar{X}_k - \underline{X}_k}. \tag{5.13}$$

Let A be the set where the conclusion of Lemma 5.1 holds, so that $P(A) = 1$. For any fixed $\theta = (\alpha, \beta)$, let A_θ be the set of ω's in A whose first coordinate is θ (recall $\Omega = \Theta\Omega'$). On the set A, since h and h' are both rational numbers, both $\bar{\epsilon}_k$ and $\underline{\epsilon}_k$ tend to 0 as $k \to \infty$. Hence, on $A_\theta \cap B$, taking limits on (5.13) leads to

$$\beta = \lim_{k \to \infty} \frac{\bar{Y}_k - \underline{Y}_k}{\bar{X}_k - \underline{X}_k}. \tag{5.14}$$

By a procedure similar to that used in deriving (5.14), one obtains, on $A_\theta \cap B$,

$$\alpha = \lim_{k \to \infty} \frac{\bar{X}_k \cdot \underline{Y}_k - \underline{X}_k \cdot \bar{Y}_k}{\bar{X}_k - \underline{X}_k}. \tag{5.15}$$

From (5.14) and (5.15), for all ω in $A_\theta \cap B$, $g(\omega) = \theta$. But $P_\theta(A_\theta) = 1$. Hence, $P_\theta(\{\omega : g(\omega) = \theta\} \cap B) = P_\theta(\{\omega : g(\omega) = \theta\} \cap A_\theta \cap B) = P_\theta(A_\theta \cap B) = P_\theta(B)$. Since, clearly, $g \in F_\infty$, this completes the proof of Lemma 5.3.

Q.E.D.

The final step in the proof of Proposition 4.3 involves showing that on the set where there exists a consistent estimator for the true parameter, the posterior distribution will converge to point mass on the true parameter. Since Lemma 5.3 implied the existence of a consistent estimator on the set B, Lemma 5.4 concludes the proof of Proposition 4.3.

Lemma 5.4.   *Suppose there exists an F_∞-measurable function g and a set $B \in F_\infty$ such that for μ_0-a.e. θ in Θ,*

$$P_\theta(\{\omega : g(\omega) = \theta\} \cap B) = P_\theta(B).$$

Then for μ_θ-a.e. θ in Θ,

$$P_\theta(\{\omega : \mu_\infty(\omega) = 1_\theta\} \cap B) = P_\theta(B), \tag{5.16}$$

where 1_θ is the point mass at θ.

Proof: To make things precise, in particular to indicate that the true parameter can be considered a random variable (with distribution μ_0), let

$\pi(\omega) \in \Theta$ be the projection of $\omega \in \Omega = \Theta\Omega'$ onto its first coordinate, Θ. Define $C = \{\omega: \mu_t(\omega) \to 1_{\pi(\omega)}$ in the weak topology$\}$ and $C_\theta = \{\omega: \mu_t(\omega) \to 1_\theta$ in the weak topology$\}$.

We seek to show that for μ_0-a.e. θ in Θ,

$$P_\theta(C_\theta \cap B) = P_\theta(B). \tag{5.17}$$

Now,

$$P(C \cap B) = \int_\Theta P_\theta(C_\theta \cap B)\mu_0(d\theta) \quad \text{and} \quad P(B) = \int_\Theta P_\theta(B)\mu_0(d\theta). \tag{5.18}$$

To prove (5.17), it suffices to prove that

$$P(C \cap B) = P(B). \tag{5.19}$$

For if (5.19) holds, using (5.18) yields

$$\int_\Theta P_\theta(C_\theta \cap B)\mu_0(d\theta) = \int_\Theta P_\theta(B)\mu_0(d\theta), \tag{5.20}$$

which implies, since $P_\theta(C_\theta \cap B) < P_\theta(B)$ for all θ, that (5.17) holds.

We have shown in Proposition 3.1 that $P(\{\omega: \mu_t(\omega) \to \mu_\infty(\omega)$ in the weak topology$\}) = 1$. Hence, to prove (5.19), we need to show that if D is any Borel subset of Θ, and we denote by $\mu_\infty(D)_{(\omega)}$ the mass that the measure $\mu_\infty(\omega)$ assigns to the set D, then

$$\mu_\infty(D)_{(\omega)} 1_{\{\omega \in B\}} = 1_{\{\pi(\omega) \in D\}} 1_{\{\omega \in B\}} \quad P\text{-a.e.} \tag{5.21}$$

Using the definition of g and B,

$$P(\{\omega: g(\omega) = \pi(\omega)\} \cap B) = \int P_\theta(\{\omega \mid g(\omega) = \theta\} \cap B)\mu_0(d\theta)$$

$$= \int P_\theta(B)\mu_0(d\theta) = P(B). \tag{5.22}$$

Noting that $B \in F_\infty$ and $g \in F_\infty$, if D is any Borel subset of Θ (by definition of μ_∞, dropping the ω's for ease of exposition),

$$\mu_\infty(D)_{(\omega)} 1_{\{\omega \in B\}} = E[1_{\{\pi \in D\}} \mid F_\infty] 1_B$$

$$= E[1_{\{\pi \in D\}} 1_B \mid F_\infty] \quad \text{[since } B \in F_\infty]$$

$$= E[1_{\{g \in D\}} 1_B \mid F_\infty] \quad \text{[using (5.22)]}$$

$$= 1_{\{g \in D\}} 1_B \quad \text{[since } g \text{ and } B \in F_\infty]$$

$$= 1_{\{\pi \in D\}} \cdot 1_B \quad P\text{-a.e.} \quad \text{[using (5.22)].}$$

This proves (5.19) and completes the proof. Q.E.D.

Proof of Proposition 4.4

Define on B^c,

$$x(\omega) = \lim_{t \to \infty} x_t(\omega).$$

We will indicate below that for P-a.e. ω in B^c,

$$y(\omega) = \lim_{n \to \infty} \frac{1}{n} \sum_{t=1}^{n} y_t(\omega)$$

is well defined. Let $M(\omega) = \{(\alpha', \beta') \in \Theta : \alpha' + \beta' x(\omega) = y(\omega)\}$. The proof of the proposition is complete if we show that for P-a.e. ω in B^c,

$$\pi(\omega) \in M(\omega) \quad \text{and} \quad \mu_\infty(M(\omega))_{(\omega)} = 1, \tag{5.23}$$

where for any Borel set D in Θ, we define $\mu_\infty(D)_{(\omega)}$ to be the mass assigned to the set D by the probability measure $\mu_\infty(\omega)$.

Remark: First note that for each ω, $M(\omega)$ is a closed subset of Θ and is hence a Borel subset of Θ. Next,

$$\{\omega \in B^c : \pi(\omega) \in M(\omega)\} = \{\omega \in B^c : \alpha(\omega) + \beta(\omega) x(\omega) = y(\omega)\}$$

is clearly in F since B^c, $\pi(\omega)$, $x(\omega)$, and $y(\omega)$ are in F; hence, the random variable $\mu_\infty(M(\omega))_{(\omega)} = E[1_{\{\pi(\omega) \in M(\omega)\}} | F_\infty]$ is F-measurable. The expressions in (5.23) are therefore all well defined.

Since $y_t(\omega) = \alpha(\omega) + \beta(\omega) x_t(\omega) + \epsilon_t(\omega)$, where $(\alpha(\omega), \beta(\omega)) = \pi(\omega)$,

$$\frac{1}{n} \sum_{t=1}^{n} y_t(\omega) = \alpha(\omega) + \beta(\omega) \frac{1}{n} \sum_{t=1}^{n} x_t(\omega) + \frac{1}{n} \sum_{t=1}^{n} \epsilon_t(\omega). \tag{5.24}$$

From the strong law of large numbers,

$$\lim_{n \to \infty} \frac{1}{n} \sum_{t=1}^{n} \epsilon_t = 0 \quad P\text{-a.e.}$$

(see, e.g., Chung 1974, Theorem 5.4.2, p. 126). Hence, taking limits in (5.24), we obtain, for P-a.e. ω in B^c,

$$y(\omega) = \alpha(\omega) + \beta(\omega) x(\omega) \quad P\text{-a.e.} \tag{5.25}$$

[Notice that this implies that P-a.e. $y(\omega)$ is well-defined whenever $x(\omega)$ is.] From (5.25), $\pi(\omega) \in M(\omega)$ for P-a.e. ω in B^c.

Next, $\pi(\omega) \in M(\omega)$ for P-a.e. ω in B^c implies that $1_{\{\pi(\omega) \in M(\omega)\}} \cdot 1_{B^c} = 1_{B^c}$ P-a.e.; hence, noting that $1_{B^c} \in F_\infty$,

$$\mu_\infty(M(\omega))_{(\omega)} \cdot 1_{B^c} = E[1_{\{\pi(\omega)\in M(\omega)\}} | F_\infty] \cdot 1_{B^c} = E[1_{\{\pi(\omega)\in M(\omega)\}} \cdot 1_{B^c} | F_\infty]$$
$$= E[1_{B^c} | F_\infty] = 1_{B^c} \ P\text{-a.e.} \tag{5.26}$$

This shows that (5.23) holds and concludes the proof.   Q.E.D.

Appendix

Bayes rule operator

Let $P(dy_t \, d\theta \, | \, x_t, \mu_{t-1})$ be the joint distribution on $R^1 \times \Theta$ obtained as follows: An element θ in Θ is first chosen according to the probability μ_{t-1}; then, given this chosen value of $\theta = (\alpha, \beta, \phi)$, y_t is chosen according to the relation $y_t = \alpha + \beta x_t + \epsilon_t$, where ϵ_t has the distribution $p(\cdot \, | \, \phi)$. Next, define $P(dy_t \, | \, x_t, \mu_{t-1})$ to be the marginal distribution of $P(dy_t \, d\theta \, | \, x_t, \mu_{t-1})$ on R^1. We now apply Parthasarathy (1967, Chapter V, Theorem 8.1) to obtain the existence of a conditional probability measure on Θ, $\Gamma(d\theta \, | \, x_t, y_t, \mu_{t-1})$, which, for fixed (x_t, μ_{t-1}), is measurable in y_t, and where

$$P(dy_t \, d\theta \, | \, x_t, \mu_{t-1}) = P(dy_t \, | \, x_t, \mu_{t-1}) \cdot \Gamma(d\theta \, | \, x_t, y_t, \mu_{t-1}).$$

The conditional probability $\Gamma(d\theta \, | \, x_t, y_t, \mu_{t-1})$ defines the Bayes rule operator $\Gamma(x_t, y_t, \mu_{t-1})$.

Random variables $\{x_t, y_t, \mu_t\}$

We now provide technical details behind construction of the $\{x_t, y_t, \mu_t\}$ processes. Recall $(\Omega, F, P) = (\Theta, \tilde{\Theta}, \mu_0)(\Omega', F', P')$. Any policy π generates a sequence of random variables $\{(x_t, y_t, \mu_t\}_{t=1}^\infty$ on (Ω, F, P) as follows: First consider $\{\epsilon_t\}$ as a stochastic process on (Ω, F, P) rather than on (Ω', F', P') by $\epsilon_t(\omega) = \epsilon_t(\omega')$, where ω' is the second coordinate of ω (recall $\Omega = \Theta \times \Omega'$). Here, μ_0 is given a prior; define $x_1(\omega) = \pi_0(\mu_0)$, $y_1(\omega) = \alpha + \beta x_1(\omega) + \epsilon_1(\omega)$, and $\mu_1(\omega) = \Gamma(x_1(\omega), y_1(\omega), \mu_0)$, where α and β are obtained from the first coordinate of ω (recall $\Omega = \Theta \times \Omega'$). Since both π_0 and Γ are Borel functions (recall Γ is continuous), observe that x_1, y_1, and μ_1 are (Borel measurable) random variables on (Ω, F, P).

Next, suppose that the random variables x_i, y_i, and μ_i have been defined for $i = 1, \dots, t-1$; then we may define, inductively, x_t, y_t, μ_t by putting $h_t(\omega) = (\mu_0; (x_1(\omega), y_1(\omega), \mu_1(\omega)), \dots, (x_{t-1}(\omega), y_{t-1}(\omega), \mu_{t-1}(\omega)))$ and

$$x_t(\omega) = \pi_t(h_t(\omega)), \qquad y_t(\omega) = \alpha + \beta x_t(\omega) + \epsilon_t(\omega),$$

$$\mu_t(\omega) = \Gamma(x_t(\omega), y_t(\omega), \mu_{t-1}(\omega)).$$

Since π_t is Borel measurable, x_t, y_t, μ_t are (measurable) random variables.

REFERENCES

Anderson, T. W. and J. Taylor. 1976. "Some Experimental Results on and Statistical Properties of Least Squares Estimates in Control Problems." *Econometrica* 44: 1289–1302.

Billingsley, P. 1968. *Convergence of Probability Measures.* New York: Wiley.

Blackwell, D. 1965. "Discounted Dynamic Programming." *Annals of Mathematical Statistics* 36: 2226–35.

Chow, G. C. 1975. *Analysis and Control of Dynamic Economic Systems.* New York: Wiley.

——— 1981. *Econometric Analysis by Control Methods.* New York: Wiley.

Chung, K. L. 1974. *A Course in Probability Theory,* 2d ed. New York: Academic.

Harkema, R. 1975. "An Analytical Comparison of Certainty Equivalence and Sequential Updating." *Journal of the American Statistical Association* 70: 348–50.

Jordan, J. S. 1985. "The Strong Consistency of the Least Squares Control Rule and Parameter Estimates." Manuscript, University of Minnesota.

Kiefer, N. and Y. Nyarko. 1986. "Optimal Control of a Linear Process with Learning." Manuscript, Cornell University.

Kushner, H. and D. Clark. 1978. *Stochastic Approximation Methods for Constrained and Unconstrained Systems.* New York: Springer-Verlag.

Maitra, A. 1968. "Discounted Dynamic Programming in Compact Metric Spaces." *Sankhya, Series A* 30: 211–16.

Parthasarathy, K. 1967. *Probability Measures on Metric Spaces.* New York: Academic.

Prescott, E. 1972. "The Multiperiod Control Problem Under Uncertainty." *Econometrica* 40: 1043–58.

Schal, M. 1979. "On Dynamic Programming and Statistical Decision Theory." *Annals of Statistics* 7: 432–45.

Schwartz, L. 1965. "On Bayes Procedures." *Z. Wahrscheinlichkeits-theorie* 4: 10–26.

Taylor, J. B. 1974. "Asymptotic Properties of Multiperiod Control Rules in the Linear Regression Model." *International Economic Review* 15: 472–84.

Theil, H. 1958. *Economic Forecasts and Policy.* Amsterdam: North-Holland.

Zellner, A. 1971. *An Introduction to Bayesian Inference in Econometrics.* New York: Wiley.

CHAPTER 7

Some tests of nonparametric regression models

Adonis John Yatchew

1   Introduction

Consider the following multivariate regression model:

$$y_t = g(\mathbf{x}_t) + \epsilon_t, \quad t = 1, \dots, T, \tag{1}$$

where boldface denotes vectors, g is a continuous function from a compact subset P of R^k to R^d, and the ϵ_t are independently and identically distributed (i.i.d.) with mean zero and covariance matrix Σ. Without introducing additional assumptions on g (in particular, g need not lie in a prespecified parametric family), we are interested in obtaining consistent estimates of Σ.

This chapter provides such estimators that are based on the following simple idea: Suppose y and x are scalars, the x's are being drawn from, say, an absolutely continuous distribution on the unit interval, and for any sample, the data are reordered *so that the x's are in increasing order.* Consider now the following estimator of σ^2, the variance of ϵ_t:

$$\hat{\sigma}^2 = \frac{1}{2T} \sum [y_t - y_{t-1}]^2$$

$$= \frac{1}{2T} \sum [\epsilon_t - \epsilon_{t-1}]^2 + \frac{1}{2T} \sum [g(x_t) - g(x_{t-1})]^2$$

$$+ \frac{2}{2T} \sum [\epsilon_t - \epsilon_{t-1}][g(x_t) - g(x_{t-1})]. \tag{2}$$

Examining the three components in the expansion of $\hat{\sigma}^2$, we note that the first term converges to σ^2. Furthermore, as the unit interval gets packed with observations on x, the average distance between successive x_t's goes

The author is especially grateful to Larry G. Epstein for the many hours of discussion on this and related topics and for originally suggesting the problem. Angelo Melino also provided much useful input.

121

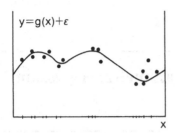

$y = g(x) + \varepsilon$

Figure 1

to zero (see Figure 1). But g is a continuous function, so that the average of the squared successive differences $[g(x_t) - g(x_{t-1})]^2$ also goes to zero; hence, the second term goes to zero. Finally, the third term is an average of variables $[\epsilon_t - \epsilon_{t-1}]$ that have a mean of zero multiplied by weights $[g(x_t) - g(x_{t-1})]$ that are going to zero, so that the third term also goes to zero. Thus, the estimator in (2) converges to σ^2.[1]

This heuristic argument provides the main intuition behind the consistency of such differencing estimators. In order to extend the results to higher dimenions of the domain P, we reorder the $\mathbf{x}$'s so that the average squared distance between them goes to zero as sample size gets large. The extension to the case where g is a vector function is straightforward. Finally, higher order powers of $[y_t - y_{t-1}]$ may be used to consistently estimate higher order moments.

The next problem is to try to establish the rate of convergence of such estimators; such a result would be useful if the estimator were to be used for inference purposes. To understand our results on rates of convergence, let P be the unit square and suppose our T observations on $\mathbf{x}, \mathbf{x}_1, \ldots, \mathbf{x}_T$ are distributed uniformly so that each $\mathbf{x}_t$ "occupies" an area $1/T$ and the distance between adjacent points is $1/T^{1/2}$. Suppose the data are reordered so that in fact $\|\mathbf{x}_t - \mathbf{x}_{t-1}\|$ is $1/T^{1/2}$, where $\|\cdot\|$ denotes Euclidean distances (see Figure 2). We now introduce the following additional assumption that restricts the variability of the regression function: We assume g satisfies a Lipschitz condition of the form $|g(\mathbf{x}_t) - g(\mathbf{x}_\tau)| \leq L \|\mathbf{x}_t - \mathbf{x}_\tau\|$. Consider now the two-dimensional version of (2):

$$\hat{\sigma}^2 = \frac{1}{2T} \sum [y_t - y_{t-1}]^2$$

$$= \frac{1}{2T} \sum [\epsilon_t - \epsilon_{t-1}]^2 + \frac{1}{2T} \sum [g(\mathbf{x}_t) - g(\mathbf{x}_{t-1})]^2 +$$

---

[1] After completing this chapter, I discovered a one-line reference to a differencing type estimator in the one-dimensional case in Rice (1984).

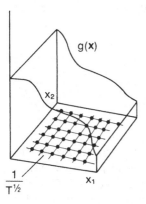

g(x)

x_2

$\frac{1}{T^{1/2}}$

x_1

Figure 2

$$+ \frac{2}{2T} \sum [\epsilon_t - \epsilon_{t-1}][g(\mathbf{x}_t) - g(\mathbf{x}_{t-1})]. \tag{2'}$$

So long as fourth moments of ϵ_t exist, the variance of the first term is $O(1/T)$, and so the first term is $O_p(1/T^{1/2})$, where O_p denotes big order of probability. Indeed, the first term, suitably normalized, is asymptotically standard normal.

For the second term we have

$$\frac{1}{2T} \sum [g(\mathbf{x}_t) - g(\mathbf{x}_{t-1})]^2 \leq \frac{1}{2T} \sum [L^2 \|\mathbf{x}_t - \mathbf{x}_{t-1}\|^2]$$

$$= \frac{L^2}{2T} \sum \left[\frac{1}{T^{1/2}}\right]^2 = \frac{L^2}{2T}; \tag{3}$$

that is, the second term is $O(1/T)$. If the dimensionality of P is k, the distance between adjacent points becomes $1/T^{1/k}$, and equation (3) implies a rate of convergence of $O(1/T^{2/k})$; the rate of convergence of the second term becomes progressively slower in higher dimensions as the rate at which the domain gets "packed" with observations slows.

The third term of equation (2') will have a rate of convergence somewhere between the rates of the first two terms. Thus, the rate of convergence of $\hat{\sigma}^2$ is determined by the rates of convergence of the first two terms, whichever converges more slowly.

The ideas described thus far may be used to develop tests for a variety of hypotheses on the regression function g, including hypotheses of significance, symmetry, homogeneity, separability, and specification.

Consider the hypothesis of the significance of the variable x_2 in a scalar regression function $g(x_1, x_2)$. If g is indeed constant with respect to x_2, reordering data solely according to x_1 will give a consistent estimator of σ^2. This estimator can be compared to an estimator where the data are reordered according to both x_1 and x_2, thus yielding a test. Tests for symmetry and homogeneity also follow from judicious reordering (and possibly transformations) of the data.

As a final example, suppose one wishes to test whether g lies in a parametric family of functions F. From a least-squares procedure (see, e.g., White 1981) one may obtain an estimator of σ^2 that coverges to $\sigma^2 + \delta$, where δ is a measure of the distance of g from F (δ is zero if g is in the family). A test procedure may then be devised by comparing the estimator of the variance to the differencing estimator proposed in this chapter.

The preceding heuristic arguments comprise the main ideas in this chapter; what remains is to demonstrate more precise versions of the arguments. We will be adopting the simplest possible assumptions that allow us to accomplish this.

It is worthwhile to contrast the preceding approach to that in the standard nonparametrics literature; there, one might proceed by first estimating g (there are many such estimators) using the residuals to estimate the variance and then proceeding to testing.[2] In our approach, on the other hand, it is not even clear that there is any implied *consistent* estimator of g. In spirit, however, our estimator is similar to many of those in the nonparametric regression literature in the sense that these estimators are based on the notion that observations on y at points $\mathbf{x}$ close to $\mathbf{x}^0$ contain useful information about the conditional distribution at $\mathbf{x}^0$.

The chapter is organized as follows: Section 2 demonstrates consistency for a class of estimators based on the foregoing notion of differencing. Section 3 develops the results on convergence rates. Section 4 develops testing procedures for a variety of hypotheses, and Section 5, the concluding section, discusses some extensions.

2   Consistent estimation of Σ

For completeness, we state all the assumptions needed for our proof of consistency at this point.

---

[2] Rao (1983) and Coullomb (1981) contain many references. Various consistency results may be found in Nadaraja (1970), Stone (1977), Devroye (1978), Geffroy (1980), and Gallant (1981). Results on rates of convergence may be found in Singh and Tracy (1977), Craven and Wahba (1979), Stone (1980), and Cox (1983). These typically depend on the dimensionality of the domain k. Relatively little attention, however, has been paid to the testing of specific hypotheses about nonparametric regression function; however, see Nadaraja (1983), Breiman and Meisel (1976), Gallant (1981), and Epstein and Yatchew (1985).

Assumption 1. For the model $y = g(x) + \epsilon$, g is a continuous function from P, a compact subset of R^k, to R^d.

Assumption 2. The ϵ_t are i.i.d. with zero mean and covariance matrix Σ.

Assumption 3. The x_t are i.i.d. with absolutely continuous distribution on P and independently of the ϵ_t.

In Assumption 3 assume absolute continuity because if there are any mass points in the distribution of x, say, at x_0, then Σ [and $g(x_0)$] may be estimated consistently using the observations on y at x_0.

The heuristics in the introduction suggest that so long as we choose reorderings of the data such that the average distance between successive x_t goes to zero, our differencing estimator will eventually converge to the true Σ.

Formally, let $PM(T)$ denote the set of all permutations of the integers $1, \ldots, T$. An *ordering rule* is a sequence $\{\phi_T\}_1^\infty$ such that, for each T, ϕ_T: $\times_{t=1}^T P \to PM(T)$, that is, ϕ_T assigns a permutation to every collection of observations $x_1, \ldots, x_T$.

An ordering rule is called proper if the following two conditions are satisfied:

P1 For each $T \to \infty$ and $\Pi \in PM(T)$, $\phi_T^{-1}(\Pi)$ is a Borel subset of $\overset{T}{\underset{t=1}{\times}} P$;

$$(4)$$

P2 $\lim_{T \to \infty} \frac{1}{T} \sum_{t=2}^T \|x_{\Pi^{-1}(t)} - x_{\Pi^{-1}(t-1)}\| = 0$ if $(x_1, x_2, \ldots, x_T, \ldots) \in \overset{\infty}{\underset{t=1}{\times}} P$.

$$(5)$$

The role of condition (4) is to ensure that the estimators defined in what follows are measurable. Condition (5) ensures that along the path joining $x_1, \ldots, x_T$, the average distance between points goes to zero as T gets large.

There are many examples of proper ordering rules: First, consider the nearest-neighbor algorithm (Rosenkrantz, Stearns, and Lewis 1977).

For any T and $x_1, \ldots, x_T$, reorder the points as follows:

1. Start with x_1.
2. At any stage proceed to the point not yet chosen that is nearest to the last point selected.
3. Break ties in 2 by selecting the point with the lowest subscript.

Formally, for each T and $(x_1, \ldots, x_T)$, let $\phi_T(x_1, \ldots, x_T) = \Pi_T$ where $\Pi_T(1) = 1$, and inductively for each $k > 1$, $\Pi_T(t) = k$ if and only if

$$k = \min\{i : i \notin S^k \equiv \{\Pi_T^{-1}(1), \dots, \Pi_T^{-1}(k-1)\} \text{ and}$$

$$\|\mathbf{x}_i - \mathbf{x}_{\Pi_T^{-1}(k-1)}\| \le \|\mathbf{x}_j - \mathbf{x}_{\Pi_T^{-1}(k-1)}\| \; \forall j \notin S^k\}.$$

Lemma 1.   *The ordering rule defined by the nearest-neighbor algorithm is a proper ordering rule.*

Note (Rosenkrantz et al. 1977) that the nearest-neighbor algorithm can be programmed to operate in time proportional to T^2, where T is the number of data points.

A further class of proper ordering rules is described in the following corollary:

Corollary 1.   *Fix $K \ge 1$. Let $\{\phi_T\}_1^\infty$ be an ordering rule that satisfies* (4) *and such that*

$$\frac{1}{T} \sum_{t=2}^T \|\mathbf{x}_{\Pi^{-1}(t)} - \mathbf{x}_{\Pi^{-1}(t-1)}\|$$

$$\le K \min\left\{\frac{1}{T} \sum_{t=2}^T \|\mathbf{x}_{\psi^{-1}(t)} - \mathbf{x}_{\psi^{-1}(t-1)}\|, \; \psi \in \text{PM}(t)\right\} \tag{6}$$

for all $T \to 0$ and $(\mathbf{x}_1, \dots, \mathbf{x}_T) \in \times_{t=1}^T P$. Then the ordering rule is proper.

If $K = 1$, there is equality in (6), and ϕ_T reorders the data so that the sum of the distances between successive points is minimized. This is a version of the traveling-salesman problem. In fact, any $K \ge 1$ and inequality (6) suffices to provide a proper ordering rule. Note that for $K = 2$ there exist efficient algorithms to find the desired reordering that can be programmed to operate in time proportional to T^2 (see Rosenkrantz et al. 1977, pp. 572–3). Such algorithms invariably satisfy (4).

Now turn to one of the two central results of this chapter.

Theorem 1.   *Let $\{\phi_T\}_1^\infty$ be a proper ordering rule, and define*

$$\hat{\Sigma}_T = \frac{1}{2T} \sum_{t=2}^T [\mathbf{y}_t^* - \mathbf{y}_{t-1}^*][\mathbf{y}_t^* - \mathbf{y}_{t-1}^*]', \tag{7}$$

where $\mathbf{y}_t^* = \mathbf{y}_{\Pi_T^{-1}(t)}$, $\Pi_T = \phi_T(\mathbf{x}_1, \dots, \mathbf{x}_T)$. Then $\hat{\Sigma}_T$ is measurable and converges almost surely (a.s.) to Σ as $T \to \infty$.

The analogue of equation (2) becomes

$$\hat{\Sigma}_T = \frac{1}{2T} \sum_{t=2}^T [\epsilon_t^* - \epsilon_{t-1}^*][\epsilon_t^* - \epsilon_{t-1}^*]'$$

$$+ \frac{1}{2T} \sum_{t=2}^T [g(\mathbf{x}_t^*) - g(\mathbf{x}_{t-1}^*)][g(\mathbf{x}_t^*) - g(\mathbf{x}_{t-1}^*)]' +$$

$$+ \frac{1}{2T} \sum_{t=2}^{T} [g(\mathbf{x}_t^*) - g(\mathbf{x}_{t-1}^*)][\epsilon_t^* - \epsilon_{t-1}^*]'$$

$$+ \frac{1}{2T} \sum_{t=2}^{T} [\epsilon_t^* - \epsilon_{t-1}^*][g(\mathbf{x}_t^*) - g(\mathbf{x}_{t-1}^*)]'. \tag{8}$$

(As in the statement of Theorem 1, sequences reordered according to the given ordering rule are denoted by asterisks.)

The proof of Theorem 1 demonstrates that the first term converges a.s. to Σ (by a law of large numbers), the third and fourth terms converge a.s. to zero matrices, and the second term converges to the zero matrix for *any* sequence $\{\mathbf{x}_1, \mathbf{x}_2, \ldots\}$.

That Theorem 1 provides many consistent estimators for Σ is clear since any proper ordering rule will do. But it is further highlighted by the fact that a rescaling of the exogenous $\mathbf{x}_t$'s, where each component $\mathbf{x}_{it}$, $i = 1, \ldots, k$, is rescaled differently, may change $\hat{\Sigma}_T$ even if the ordering rule is fixed. This is the case, for example, when the ordering rule is based on the nearest-neighbor or traveling-salesman algorithms.

Finally, we may say something about the bias of our estimator in finite samples. It is immediate from (8) that

$$\frac{T}{T-1} E(\hat{\Sigma}_T) = \Sigma + \frac{1}{2(T-1)} E\left[\sum_{t=2}^{T} [g(\mathbf{x}_t^*) - g(\mathbf{x}_{t-1}^*)][g(\mathbf{x}_t^*) - g(\mathbf{x}_{t-1}^*)]' \right] \tag{9}$$

so that $E\{[T/(T-1)]\hat{\Sigma}_T\}$ exceeds Σ by a positive semidefinite matrix.

3   Rate of convergence of $\hat{\Sigma}_T$

Replace the original assumption about how the $\mathbf{x}_t$ are obtained with the following:

Assumption 3′.   Let the domain P be the unit cube in R^k, and for each T, distribute $\mathbf{x}_1, \ldots, \mathbf{x}_T$ uniformly in the domain so that $\|\mathbf{x}_t - \mathbf{x}_{t-1}\| = T^{-1/k}$ and so that no pair of points is closer together than $T^{-1/k}$ ($\mathbf{x}_1$ may be placed at the origin).

Roughly speaking, we are taking the domain P, which has volume 1, dividing it up into regions of volume $1/T$, and placing a point in each such region. If we reorder the data for each T according to the nearest-neighbor algorithm, it is immediate that

$$\frac{1}{T} \sum_{t=2}^{T} \|\mathbf{x}_t^* - \mathbf{x}_{t-1}^*\|^2 = O(T^{-2/k}), \tag{10}$$

where asterisks denote reordered sequences.

Furthermore, the average squared distance along the traveling sales-man and K times the traveling-salesman paths [see equation (6)] are of the same order.

In addition to modifying Assumption 3, we introduce the following:

Assumption 4.   The vector function g satisfies a Lipschitz condition for any component g_i of g:

$$|g_i(\mathbf{x}_t) - g_i(\mathbf{x}_\tau)| \le L\|\mathbf{x}_t - \mathbf{x}_\tau\| \quad \forall \mathbf{x}_t, \mathbf{x}_\tau \in P,$$

which restricts the variability of the regression function, although alter-nate assumptions, such as bounding the total variation, would probably work as well.

Under Assumptions 1, 2, 3', and 4, we have the following, which is the main result of this section:

Theorem 2.   *Define $\hat{\Sigma}_T$ as in Theorem 1 and suppose the asterisk indi-cates sequences reordered according to an ordering rule for which* (10) *holds; then the rate of convergence of $\hat{\Sigma}_T$ to Σ is*

$$O_p(\max\{T^{-1/2}, T^{-2/k}\}),$$

where k is the dimension of P.

Examining the expansion in (8) and keeping in mind the heuristics in the introduction, the first term is $O_p(T^{-1/2})$, the second term is $O(T^{-2/k})$, and the last two terms have a stochastic rate of convergence between $T^{-1/2}$ and $T^{-2/k}$.

The following corollary is immediate:

Corollary 2.   *Suppose $k \le 3$, ϵ possesses fourth-order moments, and all the conditions of Theorem 2 are satisfied; then $\hat{\Sigma}_T$ appropriately stan-dardized is asymptotically unit normal.*

The result follows directly from the fact that as long as P has dimen-sionality less than or equal to 3, the second, third, and fourth terms of (8) are converging to zero quickly enough so that in large samples, the sto-chastic behavior of $\hat{\Sigma}_T$ is determined by the first term.

It is worth commenting on Assumption 3', which is fairly restrictive. This assumption simplifies our derivations by providing equation (10). Under the original Assumption 3, we would need the (probabilistic) rates of growth of squared distances along paths for various algorithms. In the case of the sum of (unsquared) distances along a path, much is known.

For example, for an *arbitrary* sequence of points in a k-dimensional set of bounded diameter, the following is true:

$$\frac{1}{T} \sum \|\mathbf{x}_t^* - \mathbf{x}_{t-1}^*\| = O(T^{-1/k}), \tag{11}$$

where the $\mathbf{x}_t^*$ have been reordered according to the traveling-salesman algorithm (see Moran 1982). Other results may be found in Verblunsky (1951), Few (1955), and Beardwood, Halton, and Hammersley (1958), and Lawler et al. (1985).

In the case of the sum of squared distances along a path, apparently little is known. Newman (1982) demonstrates that for an *arbitrary* distribution of points on the unit square, the *minimum sum of squared distances* along a path joining all points is bounded above by 4. Higher dimension cases, however, are not presented.

An alternative approach that should prove useful would be to divide the domain into regions of area (or volume) $1/T^{1-\delta}$, where $\delta > 0$ is close to zero. If the $\mathbf{x}$'s are being drawn from a uniform distribution on the domain, Kolchin, Sevastyanov, and Chistyakov (1978, pp. 4–5) provide formulas for the mean and the variance of the number of empty cells. These results could then be used to establish bounds on (probabilistic) rates of growth of squared distances along paths where contiguous regions are visited in succession and all points within a region are exhausted before leaving the region.

4 Applications to hypothesis testing

The results developed in the previous sections may be used to obtain tests of a variety of hypotheses; for expositional purposes, we will restrict ourselves to a scalar function g.

The idea is to compute two estimators of the variance: The estimator of Section 2 and a second estimator that is consistent only under the null hypothesis. The two estimators are then compared; if the null hypothesis is true, the two estimators should not be significantly different from zero.

Results such as those in Corollary 2 may be used to establish the approximate large-sample distribution of the estimators. Such distributions inevitably will depend on the fourth-order moments of ϵ, but these moments may be estimated consistently using higher order powers in, for example, equation (2). (The proof is analogous to that of Theorem 1.) However, a much harder problem is to establish the joint distribution of the two estimators and *in particular their covariance*. In this chapter, we circumvent this problem by dividing the sample in two so that the two estimators are independent. This procedure, however, undoubtedly reduces the efficiency of the estimators and the power of the tests.

In the examples that follow, we are drawing observations

$$\{(y_t, x_{1t}, x_{2t})\}_1^{2T}$$

on the model $y = g(x_1, x_2) + \epsilon$ and applying a proper ordering rule to observations $T+1, \ldots, 2T$ to obtain $\hat{\sigma}^2$, a consistent estimator of σ^2.

4.1   *Significance*

We wish to test

$$H_0: g(x_1, x_2) = g(x_1, x_2') \quad \forall (x_1, x_2), (x_1, x_2') \in P,$$

$$H_1: g(x_1, x_2) \neq g(x_1, x_2') \quad \text{for some } (x_1, x_2), (x_1, x_2') \in P,$$

and we will say x_2 is insignificant if H_0 is true.

Reorder observations $1, \ldots, T$ so that the observations on x_1 are in non-decreasing order: $\{(y_t^{**}, x_{1t}^{**}, x_{2t}^{**})\}_1^T$, where the double asterisks denote the reordered observations. Of course, this is equivalent to applying the obvious proper ordering rule to the data $\{(y_t, x_{1t})\}_1^T$. Define

$$\bar{\sigma}^2 = \frac{1}{2T} \sum_2^T [y_t^{**} - y_{t-1}^{**}]^2. \tag{12}$$

Then we have the following result:

Theorem 3

$$\frac{\hat{\sigma}^2 - \bar{\sigma}^2}{\sqrt{2\eta/T}} \overset{A}{\sim} N(0,1) \quad under \ H_0,$$

where $\eta = E\epsilon^4$.

It is easy to show that under the null hypothesis, arranging the first T observations according to the variable x_1 leads to a proper ordering rule so that $\bar{\sigma}^2$ is a consistent estimator of σ^2. Furthermore, the dimensionality of the model is low enough so that Corollary 2 yields asymptotic normality for both $\hat{\sigma}^2$ and $\bar{\sigma}^2$, and splitting the sample ensures independence of the two estimators. Finally, a consistent estimator of η is given by

$$\hat{\eta} = \frac{1}{4T} \sum_1^{2T} [y_t^* - y_{t-1}^*]^4 - 3 \left[\frac{1}{4T} \sum_1^{2T} [y_t^* - y_{t-1}^*]^2 \right]^2, \tag{13}$$

where all the data have been reordered according to a proper ordering rule using both explanatory variables. (The proof is straightforward and parallels that of Theorem 1.)

Extensions to higher dimensions of this test procedure are straightforward. For example, one may test the significance of x_2 and x_3 in the model

$y = g(x_1, x_2, x_3) + \epsilon$. However, even the approximate probability statements provided for by Corollary 2 are invalid beyond three dimensions.

4.2   Symmetry

Various economic hypotheses involve some notion of symmetry of the effects of two (or more) variables. For example, we may want to test whether the marginal propensity to consume out of asset income is the same as from labor income, which is just a test of equality of two coefficients in the linear model. More generally, one may want to test whether exchanging the two variables leaves the regression function unchanged. That is, suppose we test

$$H_0: g(x_1, x_2) = g(x_2, x_1) \quad \forall(x_1, x_2) \in P,$$

$$H_1: g(x_1, x_2) \neq g(x_2, x_1) \quad \text{for some } (x_1, x_2) \in P.$$

Revise observations $1, \ldots, T$ as follows: For those observations where $x_{1t} \leq x_{2t}$, replace (y_t, x_{1t}, x_{2t}) with (y_t, x_{2t}, x_{1t}). The revised observations $1, \ldots, T$ now lie to one side of the hyperplane $x_1 = x_2$. Apply a proper ordering rule to the revised observation $1, \ldots, T$ and obtain $\hat{\sigma}^2$ as in equation (12). Theorem 3 then applies. Other forms of symmetry may be tested in a similar way.[3]

4.3   Homogeneity of degree zero

Suppose we wish to test the hypotheses

$$H_0: g(\lambda x_1, \lambda x_2) = g(x_1, x_2) \quad \forall(x_1, x_2) \in P,$$

$$H_1: g(\lambda x_1, \lambda x_2) \neq g(x_1, x_2) \quad \text{for some } (x_1, x_2) \in P.$$

In addition to our previous assumptions assume P is a subset of the positive quadrant of R^2 and is bounded away from zero. If g is homogeneous of degree zero,

$$y = h[x_2/x_1] + \epsilon \tag{14}$$

for some continuous h, and if g satisfies a Lipschitz condition, so does h.

---

[3] Larry Epstein has pointed out that testing of linear separability or additivity can be transformed into a test of symmetry (as defined in section 4.2). Suppose, under H_0, $g(x_1, x_2) = f_1(x_1) + f_2(x_2)$. Let

$$h(x_1, x_1', x_2, x_2') = g(x_1, x_2) + g(x_1', x_2') = f_1(x_1) + f_2(x_2) + f_1(x_1') + f_2(x_2')$$
$$= f_1(x_1) + f_2(x_2') + f_1(x_1') + f_2(x_2) = h(x_1, x_1', x_2', x_2).$$

Hence, additivity implies that the third and fourth arguments of h are interchangeable. A procedure analogous to that of this section may be used to devise a test. The difficulty is that since h is four-dimensional, Corollary 2 does not apply immediately.

Reorder observations $1, \ldots, T$ so that the observations on x_2/x_1 are in nondecreasing order and apply the estimator $\bar{\sigma}^2$ of equation (12) to the reordered data. Theorem 4 then applies.

4.4   *Specification*

Suppose we wish to test the hypotheses

$$H_0: g \in F, \qquad H_1: g \notin F,$$

where F is a parametric family of functions indexed by a finite dimensional parameter Θ. Given sufficient regularity assumptions (see, e.g., White 1981), $\bar{\sigma}^2$, suitably standardized, is asymptotically normal where $\bar{\sigma}^2$ is the usual estimator of σ^2 based on a nonlinear regression using observations $1, \ldots, T$. Theorem 3 then applies and we have a specification test.

5   Extensions and conclusions

The basic idea of this chapter is that consistent estimates of the variance of the residual in a continuous regression model may be obtained by differencing observations that are close in the domain, an idea reminiscent of the first differencing used in panel data to remove individual effects.

Certain extensions are immediate; for example, continuity of g may be replaced by the assumption that g is discontinuous on a set of measure zero relative to the probability measure on the domain. Furthermore, higher order moments of ϵ (if they exist) can also be estimated simply by taking cubes, fourth powers, and so on, instead of squares.

Other extensions worth investigating include relaxing the Lipschitz assumption as well as relaxing the assumption that the domain of g be compact. For example, if x, a scalar argument, had a normal distribution, one would still expect that the average distance between (reordered) x's would go to zero as sample size became large. (Just look at the distribution of $1/T$ times the *range* of a collection of i.i.d. normal variables.)

Appendix

Proof of Lemma 1

Fix $\{\mathbf{x}_t\}_1^\infty x_t \in P$ and let M be the maximum Euclidean distance between any two points in P. For given $\delta > 0$, the compactness of P implies that there exist a finite number, say, q, of neighborhoods of diameter δ that cover P. For each $T > 0$ consider the path corresponding to the nearest-neighborhood algorithm that joins $\mathbf{x}_1, \ldots, \mathbf{x}_T$. Along such a path and for each neighborhood there can be at most one step of length more than δ that begins in the neighborhood and ends outside it. Thus, the average distance traveled along the path is no greater than $qM/T + \delta$, which converges to δ as $T \to \infty$. Since δ was chosen arbitrarily, (5) is proven.

Consider now the vector-valued random variable of length $\binom{T}{2}$ that enumerates the distances between each pair of points $\mathbf{x}_t, \mathbf{x}_\tau, t, \tau : 1, ..., T$, $t \neq \tau$. The itinerary (and hence Π) is completely determined by these distances and the nearest-neighbor algorithm. Measurability of ϕ_T follows straightforwardly.

Proof of Corollary 1

Only condition (5) need be demonstrated. Suppose $K = 1$; then this is the shortest path through the points and hence must be no longer than a path generated by the nearest-neighbor algorithm, and hence, by Lemma 1, the average distance between points must go to zero. But then for any fixed K, K times the average distance also goes to zero.

Proof of Theorem 1

Consider a typical entry in the matrix $\hat{\Sigma}_T$, say, $\hat{\sigma}_{ij}$, and denote reordered sequences with asterisks; then, following (8),

$$\hat{\sigma}_{ij} = \frac{1}{2T} \sum_2^T (\epsilon_{it}^* - \epsilon_{i(t-1)}^*)(\epsilon_{jt}^* - \epsilon_{j(t-1)}^*)$$

$$+ \frac{1}{2T} \sum_2^T (g_i(\mathbf{p}_t^*) - g_i(\mathbf{p}_{t-1}^*))(g_j(\mathbf{p}_t^*) - g_j(\mathbf{p}_{t-1}^*))$$

$$+ \frac{1}{2T} \sum_2^T (g_i(\mathbf{p}_t^*) - g_i(\mathbf{p}_{t-1}^*))(\epsilon_{jt}^* - \epsilon_{j(t-1)}^*)$$

$$+ \frac{1}{2T} \sum_2^T (\epsilon_{it}^* - \epsilon_{i(t-1)}^*)(g_j(\mathbf{p}_t^*) - g_j(\mathbf{p}_{t-1}^*)). \tag{A.1}$$

By the strong law of large numbers, the first term converges a.s. to σ^2. Since g_i and g_j are continuous on the compact set P, they are uniformly bounded by, say, B. Furthermore, they are uniformly continuous, and hence, for all $\Delta > 0$, there exists $\delta > 0$ such that $\mathbf{p}, \mathbf{q} \in P$, and $\|\mathbf{p} - \mathbf{q}\| < \delta$; then $(g_i(\mathbf{p}) - g_i(\mathbf{q}))(g_j(\mathbf{p}) - g_j(\mathbf{q})) < \Delta^2$. Given T and $p_1, ..., p_T$, let $S(T) = \{t \in \{1, ..., T\} : \|\mathbf{p}_t^* - \mathbf{p}_{t-1}^*\| > \delta\}$. Then

$$\frac{1}{2T} \sum_2^T |(g_i(\mathbf{p}_t^*) - g_i(\mathbf{p}_{t-1}^*))(g_j(\mathbf{p}_t^*) - g_j(\mathbf{p}_{t-1}^*))|$$

$$\leq \frac{1}{2T} \sum_{t \in S(T)} |(g_i(\mathbf{p}_t^*) - g_i(\mathbf{p}_{t-1}^*))(g_j(\mathbf{p}_t^*) - g_j(\mathbf{p}_{t-1}^*))| + \frac{\Delta^2}{2} \leq$$

$$\leq \frac{(2B)^2 \cdot \#S(T)}{2T} + \frac{\Delta^2}{2},$$

where $\#S(T)$ is the cardinality of the set $S(T)$. Since $\{\phi_T\}_1^\infty$ is a proper ordering rule, $\#S(T)/T \to 0$ as $T \to \infty$. Thus, for *any* sequence $\{\mathbf{p}_t\}_1^\infty$,

$$\lim_{T \to \infty} \frac{1}{2T} \sum_2^T |(g_i(\mathbf{p}_t^*) - g_i(\mathbf{p}_{t-1}^*))(g_j(\mathbf{p}_t^*) - g_j(\mathbf{p}_{t-1}^*))| \leq \frac{\Delta^2}{2}. \tag{A.2}$$

Since Δ was arbitrary, the second term of equation (A.1) converges surely to zero.

By the Cauchy–Schwartz inequality,

$$\left| \frac{1}{2T} \sum_2^T (g_i(\mathbf{p}_t^*) - g_i(\mathbf{p}_{t-1}^*))(\epsilon_{jt}^* - \epsilon_{j(t-1)}^*) \right|$$

$$\leq \left[\frac{1}{2T} \sum_2^T (g_i(\mathbf{p}_t^*) - g_i(\mathbf{p}_{t-1}^*))^2 \right]^{1/2} \left[\frac{1}{2T} \sum_2^T (\epsilon_{jt}^* - \epsilon_{j(t-1)}^*)^2 \right]^{1/2}.$$

But by (A.2), the first term on the right side converges to zero, and by the law of large numbers, the second term on the right side converges a.s. to a constant. Hence, the third and fourth terms of (A.1) converge a.s. to zero.

Measurability is straightforward to verify.

Proof of Theorem 2

Consider the expansion of a typical entry in the matrix $\hat{\Sigma}_T$ as given in equation (A.1).

The first term converges to σ_{ij} at a rate $O_p(T^{-1/2})$. For the second term we have

$$\frac{1}{2T} \sum [g_i(\mathbf{p}_t^*) - g_i(\mathbf{p}_{t-1}^*)][g_j(\mathbf{p}_t^*) - g_j(\mathbf{p}_{t-1}^*)] \leq \frac{1}{2T} \sum L^2 \|\mathbf{p}_t^* - \mathbf{p}_{t-1}^*\|^2,$$

which converges to zero at a rate $O(T^{-2/k})$.

Finally, by the Cauchy–Schwartz inequality, the third and fourth terms converge to zero at a rate that is an average of the rates of convergence of the first two terms, that is, at $O_p(T^{-1/2-1/k})$.

Since the rate of convergence of $\hat{\sigma}_{ij}$ is determined by the slowest rate of convergence of its components, the desired result follows.

REFERENCES

Beardwood, J., J. Halton, and J. Hammersley. 1958. "The Shortest Path through Many Points." *Proceedings of the Cambridge Philosophical Society* 55: 299–327.

Breiman, L. and W. S. Meisel. 1976. "General Estimates of the Intrinsic Variability of Data in Nonlinear Regression Models." *Journal of the American Statistical Association* 71: 301–7.

Coullomb, G. 1981. "Estimation Non-paramétrique de la Régression: Revue Bibliographique." *International Statistical Review* 49: 75–93.

Cox, D. D. 1983. "Asymptotics for M-Type Smoothing Splines." *Annals of Statistics* 11: 530–51.

Craven, P. and G. Wahba. 1979. "Smoothing Noisy Data with Spline Functions: Estimating the Correct Degree of Smoothing by the Method of Generalized Cross-Validation." *Numerische Mathematique* 31: 377–403.

Devroye, L. P. 1978. "The Uniform Convergence of Nearest Neighbour Regression Function Estimation and Their Application in Optimization." *IEEE Transactions on Information Theory* IT-24: 142–51.

Epstein, L. and A. Yatchew. 1985. "Nonparametric Hypothesis Testing Procedures and Applications to Demand Analysis." *Journal of Econometrics* 30: 149–69.

Few, L. 1955. "The Shortest Path and the Shortest Road through *n* Points." *Mathematica* 2: 141–4.

Gallant, A. R. 1981. "Unbiased Determination of Production Technologies." *Journal of Econometrics* 15: 211–45.

Geffroy, J. 1980. "Etude de la Convergence du Regrossogramme." *Publication of the Institute of Statistics, University of Paris* 25: 41–56.

Kolchin, V., B. Sevastyanov, and V. Chistyakov. 1978. *Random Allocations.* New York: Wiley.

Lawler, E., J. Lenstra, A. Rinnooy Kan, and D. Shmoys. 1985. *The Travelling Salesman Problem.* New York: Wiley.

Moran, S. 1982. "On the Length of Optimal TSP Circuits in Sets of Bounded Diameter." Technical Report No. 235, Technion, Haifa.

Nadaraja, E. 1970. "Remarks on Nonparametric Estimates of Density Functions and Regression Curves." *Theory Probability Applications* 15: 139–42.

——— 1983. "A Limit Distribution of the Square Error Deviation on Nonparametric Estimators of the Regression Function." *Z. Wahrscheinlichkeitstheorie verw. Gebiete* 64: 37–48.

Newman, D. J. 1982. *A Problem Seminar.* New York: Springer-Verlag.

Rao, B. L. S. P. 1983. *Nonparametric Functional Estimation.* Toronto: Academic.

Rice, J. 1984. "Bandwidth Choice for Nonparametric Regression." *Annals of Statistics* 12: 1215–30.

Rosenkrantz, D., R. Stearns, and P. Lewis. 1977. "An Analysis of Several Heuristics for the Travelling Salesman Problem." *SIAM Journal of Computing* 6: 563–81.

Singh, R. S. and D. S. Tracy. 1977. "Strongly Consistent Estimators of *k*th Order Regression Curves and Rates of Convergence." *Z. Wahrscheinlichkeitstheorie verw. Gebiete* 40: 339–48.

Stone, C. 1977. "Consistent Nonparametric Regression." *Annals of Statistics* 5: 595–645.

——— 1980. "Optimal Rates of Convergence for Nonparametric Estimators." *Annals of Statistics* 8: 1348–60.

Verblunsky, S. 1951. "On the Shortest Path Through a Number of Points." *Proceedings of the American Mathematical Society* 2: 905–13.

White, H. 1981. "Consequences and Detection of Misspecified Nonlinear Regression Models." *Journal of the American Statistical Association* 76: 419–33.

PART II

Linear time series modeling

CHAPTER 8

A central-limit result for instrumental variables estimators of linear time series models

Lars Peter Hansen

1   Introduction

This chapter derives central-limit approximations for products of two linear time series processes. We are interested in these approximations because of the occurrence of such products in instrumental variable and least-squares estimators of linear time series models. In many applications the admissible instrumental variables are uncorrelated with the contemporaneous disturbance vector but not necessarily with all leads and lags of the disturbance vector. In addition, the disturbance vector may be correlated over time.

Suppose d_t is a vector of disturbance terms for an econometric model at time t. This disturbance vector can be expressed as a function of variables that are observed by the econometrician and an unknown parameter vector to be estimated. For the estimation problems considered, this disturbance vector is an optimal forecast error of some random vector given an information set. Consequently, variables in the conditioning information set are orthogonal to the disturbance term. Let z_t denote a matrix with the same number of columns as there are entries in d_t. An instrumental variables estimator can be constructed that exploits the unconditional moment restrictions,

$$E(z_t d_t) = 0, \tag{1}$$

as long as there are at least as many moment restrictions as there are parameters to estimate, and the moment restrictions are not redundant. The derivation of the asymptotic distribution for the instrumental variables

Financial support for this work was supplied by the National Science and Sloan Foundations. Helpful comments were made by John Heaton, Masao Ogaki, and the referees.

estimator depends on the central-limit approximation for the sequence of scaled partial sums of $\{z_t d_t : t \geq 1\}$. This chapter focuses exclusively on the central-limit approximation.

We consider two estimation environments that have different implications for the cross products

$$E(z_{t-\tau} d_t) \quad \text{for} \quad \tau > 0. \tag{2}$$

In neither of the two estimation environments is it necessarily true that

$$E(z_{t-\tau} d_t) = 0 \quad \text{for} \quad \tau < 0. \tag{3}$$

In other words, the instrumental variables are not strictly exogenous.

In the first estimation environment, d_t is a forecast error conditioned on a finite number of current and past values of a vector of variables. Some of the models considered in Hansen and Hodrick (1983) have this feature. In these models, sufficiently long lags of the variables in the conditioning information set may be correlated with the disturbance term, and the disturbance term itself may be serially correlated. For instance, this phenomenon occurs in vector autoregressive approximations to more complicated forecasting equations. In this first estimation environment the expected cross products in (2) are not necessarily zero.

In the second estimation environment, the conditioning information set is infinite dimensional and contains lagged values of all variables in the set. Other models considered in Hansen and Hodrick (1983) and models considered in Hansen and Sargent (1982) have this feature. It is still true in these models that the process $\{d_t : t = 1, 2, \ldots\}$ can be serially correlated. In this second estimation environment, the expected cross products in (2) are zero.

The central-limit approximations derived here apply to both of these estimation environments. The additional moment restrictions that hold for the second estimation environment allow the approximations to be valid in a larger set of circumstances. Our analysis without the additional moment restrictions is patterned after Hall and Heyde's (1980) derivation of the asymptotic distribution of sample autovariances.

Throughout the analysis assume that the disturbances (entries of d_t) and instrumental variables (entries of z_t) have time-invariant moving-average representations in terms of a vector martingale difference sequence that is stationary, ergodic, and conditionally homoscedastic. With this assumption, best linear predictors of the disturbance and instrumental variable processes coincide with conditional expectations. This collection of assumptions is commonly used to study the asymptotic properties of the quasi-maximum-likelihood estimators of linear time series processes using Gaussian likelihood functions (e.g., see Kohn 1979).

To obtain central-limit approximations, one must restrict the temporal dependence of the product processes formed by multiplying the instrumental variables by the disturbances. Since the underlying processes are linear, we restrict the temporal dependence of the product processes by restricting the moving-average coefficients of the individual processes. The restrictions on the moving-average coefficients are most conveniently stated in terms of restrictions on their Fourier transforms.

Our analysis follows an approach suggested by Gordin (1969). We approximate time series averages of the product processes by martingale difference sequences. The sense of approximation is mean square, and results for Cesaro sums of Fourier series are used in validating these approximations. In Section 2 some notation is introduced and a set of assumptions presented that will be maintained throughout. Section 3 shows that the components of product processes of instrumental variables and disturbances can be represented as sums of two mean-square convergent sequences. In Section 4 martingale difference sequences are constructed that are subsequently used to approximate the product processes. Section 5 shows that each of the mean-square convergent series used to represent the product processes can be approximated appropriately by the corresponding martingale difference sequences constructed in Section 4. Finally, in Section 6 some concluding remarks relate the analysis in this chapter to the rest of the literature.

2 Basic assumptions and notation

Let (Ω, A, Pr) denote the underlying probability space. We will generate stochastic processes on this space using a transformation S mapping Ω onto Ω that is one to one, measurable, measure preserving, and ergodic. In addition, S^{-1} is assumed to be measurable. Let B be a subsigma algebra of A such that $\{B_t: -\infty < t < +\infty\}$ is strictly increasing, where

$$B_t = \{b_t: b_t = S^{-t}(b) \text{ for some } b \in B\}. \tag{4}$$

Suppose w is an n-dimensional random vector satisfying the next assumption.

Assumption 1. The w is measurable with respect to B, $E(w \,|\, B_{-1}) = 0$, $E(|w|^4) < +\infty$, and $E(ww' \,|\, B^{-1}) = I$.

Then $\{w_t: -\infty < t < +\infty\}$ is a martingale difference sequence adapted to $\{B_t: -\infty < t < +\infty\}$, where

$$w_t(\omega) = w[S^t(\omega)]. \tag{5}$$

Throughout this chapter subscripts on random variables define new random variables via (5).

Let G be a closed in mean-square linear space containing random variables of the form

$$g = \sum_{\tau=0}^{\infty} \alpha_\tau \cdot w_{-\tau}, \tag{6}$$

where $\{\alpha_\tau : t \geq 0\}$ is a sequence of n-dimensional vectors of real numbers satisfying

$$\sum_{\tau=0}^{\infty} |\alpha_\tau|^2 < \infty. \tag{7}$$

By mean-square convergence, we mean $L^2(\text{Pr})$ convergence on the space of random variables on (Ω, A, Pr). The closed in mean-square linear space G_t is defined to be

$$G_t = \{g_t : g_t(\omega) = g[S^t(\omega)] \text{ for some } g \in G\}. \tag{8}$$

Consider the particular probability space with collection of sample points given by $[-\pi, \pi]$, sigma algebra given by the Borel subsets of $[-\pi, \pi]$, and the probability measure given by Lebesgue measure scaled by $1/2\pi$. Let L^p be the space of complex-valued random variables on this particular probability space with finite absolute pth moments. Also, let $\|\cdot\|_p$ denote the corresponding norm.

We will view a particular member of G as a component of a disturbance term in an econometric model. This member is denoted e and is represented as

$$e = \sum_{\tau=0}^{\infty} \epsilon_\tau \cdot w_{-\tau}, \tag{9}$$

where $\{\epsilon_\tau : t \geq 0\}$ satisfies the square summability condition (7). Let

$$e^*(\theta) = \sum_{\tau=0}^{\infty} \epsilon_\tau \exp(-i\theta\tau), \tag{10}$$

where the infinite sum in (10) converges in L^2. The function e^* is the Fourier transform of the moving-average coefficients of e. The random variable e_t is a component of the vector d_t alluded to in the introduction. All functions with an asterisk will have domain $[-\pi, \pi]$.

A second member of G will be viewed as an instrumental variable used to estimate parameters of interest in the econometric model. This random variable is denoted h and is represented as

$$h = \sum_{\tau=0}^{\infty} \gamma_\tau \cdot w_{-\tau}. \tag{11}$$

Let

$$h^*(\theta) = \sum_{\tau=0}^{\infty} \gamma_\tau \exp(-i\theta\tau), \tag{12}$$

where the infinite sum on the right side of (12) also converges in L^2. The random variable h_t is an entry of the matrix of instrumental variables z_t alluded to in the introduction.

We consider two distinct sets of assumptions. The first set of assumptions is indexed by two positive integers q and p that are used to restrict e^* and h^*, respectively.

Assumption 2. Let $|e^*| \in L^p$ and $|h^*| \in L^q$, where $(2/p) + (2/q) = 1$.

Notice that there is a trade-off between the restrictions imposed on e^* and h^* by Assumption 2. When p and q are both 4, Assumption 2 imposes the same restrictions on both the disturbance and instrumental variables processes. Consistent with both of the estimation environments described in the introduction, assume:

Assumption 3. Let $E(eh) = 0$.

In the second set of assumptions, the counterpart to Assumption 2 restricts e^* more severely but does not restrict h^*.

Assumption 2'. There exists a version of e^* that is continuous on $[-\pi, \pi]$ and $e^*(-\pi) = e^*(\pi)$.[1]

Consistent with the second estimation environment described in the introduction, we assume:

Assumption 3'. Let $E(eh_{-t}) = 0$ for all $t \geq 0$.

One commonly used definition of strict exogeneity is that

$$E(eh_{-t}) = 0 \quad \text{for all} \quad t. \tag{13}$$

Assumptions 3 and 3' are relaxations of strict exogeneity. Clearly, Assumption 3' is more restrictive than Assumption 3. Hansen and Sargent (1982) give some examples of rational expectations models for which Assumption 3' is applicable.

---

[1] A sufficient condition for Assumption 2' is that the moving-average coefficients $\{\epsilon_\tau : \tau \geq 0\}$ be absolutely summable.

The goal in this chapter is to obtain a central-limit result for $\{P_T(eh): T \geq 1\}$, where

$$P_T(eh) \equiv (1/T)^{1/2}(e_1 h_1 + e_2 h_2 + \cdots + e_T h_T). \tag{14}$$

3   Martingale difference decomposition

The first step in our analysis is to obtain a martingale difference decomposition for eh. Both e and h can be represented as mean-square convergent series. Hence, the product eh can be represented as the product of such series. This section shows that eh can also be represented as the sum of two mean-square convergent series. The terms in each of the series are martingale differences.

Note that

$$E(eh \mid B_{-t}) - E(eh \mid B_{-t-1}) = (w_{-t} \cdot \gamma_t)E(e \mid B_{-t-1}) + (w_{-t} \cdot \epsilon_t)E(h \mid B_{-t-1})$$
$$+ \epsilon_t'(w_{-t}w_{-t}' - I)\gamma_t. \tag{15}$$

Calculating bounds on the second moments of the four components yields

$$E\{(w_{-t} \cdot \gamma_t)^2[E(e \mid B_{-t-1})]^2\} = E\{E[(w_{-t} \cdot \gamma_t)^2 \mid B_{-t-1}][E(e \mid B_{-t-1})]^2\}$$
$$= |\gamma_t|^2 E\{[E(e \mid B_{-t-1})]^2\}$$
$$\leq |\gamma_t|^2 E(e^2); \tag{16}$$

$$E\{(w_{-t} \cdot \epsilon_t)[E(h \mid B_{-t-1})]^2\} \leq |\epsilon_t|^2 E\{[E(h \mid B_{-t-1})]^2\}$$
$$\leq |\epsilon_t|^2 E(h^2); \tag{17}$$

$$E[(w_{-t} \cdot \gamma_t)^2(w_{-t} \cdot \epsilon_t)^2] \leq E(|w_{-t}|^4)|\gamma_t|^2|\epsilon_t|^2; \tag{18}$$

and

$$(\gamma_t \cdot \epsilon_t)^2 \leq |\gamma_t|^2|\epsilon_t|^2. \tag{19}$$

Since $\{(w_{-t} \cdot \gamma_t)E(e \mid B_{-t-1}): t \geq 0\}$ is a sequence of orthogonal random variables and

$$\sum_{t=0}^{\infty} |\gamma_t|^2 < \infty, \tag{20}$$

$$\sum_{t=0}^{\infty} (w_{-t} \cdot \gamma_t)E(e \mid B_{-t-1}) \tag{21}$$

converges in mean square. Similarly,

$$\sum_{t=0}^{\infty} (w_{-t} \cdot \epsilon_t)E(h \mid B_{-t-1}) \tag{22}$$

and

$$\sum_{t=0}^{\infty} \epsilon_t'(w_{-t}w_{-t}' - I)\gamma_t \tag{23}$$

converge in mean square. Consequently,

$$\left\{ \sum_{t=0}^{\tau} [E(eh \mid B_{-t}) - E(eh \mid B_{-t-1})] : \tau \geq 1 \right\} \tag{24}$$

converges in mean square.

This series must also converge to the same random variable in L^1. To prove that the infinite series equals eh, note that

$$E(eh \mid B_{-\tau}) = E(e \mid B_{-\tau})E(h \mid B_{-\tau}) + \sum_{t=0}^{\tau-1} \gamma_t \cdot \epsilon_t. \tag{25}$$

Now $\{E(e \mid B_{-\tau}) : \tau \geq 1\}$ and $\{E(h \mid B_{-\tau}) : \tau \geq 1\}$ converge in mean square to zero, and the sequence of real numbers

$$\left\{ \sum_{t=0}^{\tau-1} \gamma_t \cdot \epsilon_t : \tau \geq 1 \right\} \tag{26}$$

converges to zero because $E(eh)$ is zero. It follows from the Cauchy-Schwarz inequality that $\{E(eh \mid B_{-\tau}) : \tau \geq 1\}$ converges in L^1 to zero. Therefore,

$$eh = \sum_{t=0}^{\infty} [E(eh \mid B_{-t}) - E(eh \mid B_{-t-1})], \tag{27}$$

and eh has a finite second moment.

Substituting from (15) yields

$$eh = u^+ + v^+, \tag{28}$$

where

$$u^+ = \sum_{t=0}^{\infty} w_{-t} \cdot [\epsilon_t E(h \mid B_{-t-1}) + \gamma_t E(e \mid B_{-t-1})] \tag{29}$$

and

$$v^+ = \sum_{t=0}^{\infty} \epsilon_t'(w_{-t}w_{-t}' - I)\gamma_t. \tag{30}$$

The infinite series in (29) and (30) are both mean-square convergent. Instead of expressing eh as the product of two mean-square convergent series, equations (28)–(30) express eh as the sum of two mean-square convergent series. In general, u^+ and v^+ are correlated; however, in the special case in which w is normally distributed conditioned on B_{-1}, u^+ and v^+ are uncorrelated because the third moments of w conditioned on B_{-1} are zero.

The terms in both (29) and (30) are martingale differences since

$$E\{w \cdot [\epsilon_t E(h_t \mid B_{-1}) + \gamma_t E(e_t \mid B_{-1})] \mid B_{-1}\} = 0 \tag{31}$$

and

$$E(ww' - I \mid B_{-1}) = 0. \tag{32}$$

The martingale difference decomposition for u^+ is particularly convenient because

$$E\{w\cdot[\epsilon_t E(h\,|\,B_{-t})+\gamma_t E(e\,|\,B_{-t})]w\cdot[\epsilon_\tau E(h\,|\,B_{-\tau})+\gamma_\tau E(e\,|\,B_{-\tau})]\}$$
$$= E\{[\epsilon_t E(h\,|\,B_{-t})+\gamma_t E(e\,|\,B_{-t})]\cdot[\epsilon_\tau E(h\,|\,B_{-\tau})+\gamma_\tau E(e\,|\,B_{-\tau})]\}. \quad (33)$$

Consequently, autocovariances for the process generated by u^+ calculated by assuming that w is normally distributed conditioned on B_{-1} are correct even when w is not normally distributed.

4   Martingale difference sequences

In this section we construct two random variables denoted u and v that generate martingale difference sequences. Roughly speaking, these random variables are obtained by taking the terms in the infinite-series representations of u^+ and v^+ and shifting them forward t time periods. This shift in indices alters the correlation properties of the resulting time series. Appropriately scaled time series averages, however, are approximately the same with or without this shift in indices. This latter result will be established in Section 5.

The construction of u takes place in several stages. First we construct two mean-square convergent sequences of n-dimensional random vectors. Define

$$x^j \equiv \sum_{t=0}^{j} \gamma_t \frac{j-t}{j} e_t = \frac{1}{j} \sum_{\tau=1}^{j} \sum_{t=0}^{\tau-1} \gamma_t e_t, \quad (34)$$

$$T_\tau(h^*)(\theta) \equiv \sum_{t=-\tau+1}^{\tau-1} \gamma_t \exp(-i\theta t), \quad (35)$$

$$C_j(h^*) \equiv \frac{1}{j} \sum_{\tau=1}^{j} T_\tau(h^*), \quad (36)$$

where γ_t is zero for strictly negative values of t. Likewise, define y^j, $T_\tau(e^*)$, and $C_j(e^*)$ using $\{\epsilon_t: t \geq 1\}$, h, and e^* in place of $\{\gamma_t: t \geq 1\}$, e, and h^*. The sequence $\{T_\tau(\cdot): \tau \geq 1\}$ consists of the Fourier series approximations of the function in the argument, and $\{C_j(\cdot): j \geq 1\}$ consists of the first Cesaro means of the Fourier series approximations.

It turns out that when Assumptions 1–3 are satisfied, both $\{x^j: j \geq 1\}$ and $\{y^j: j \geq 1\}$ converge in mean-square (Pr) to random vectors denoted x and y, respectively. To see this, first note that each component of $\{C_j(h^*): j \geq 1\}$ converges in L^q to the corresponding component of h^* (e.g., see Edwards 1979, p. 87). Next consider $\{x^j: j \geq 1\}$. The process generated by $x^j - x^\tau$ has the spectral density matrix

$$[C_j(h^*)(-\theta) - C_\tau(h^*)(-\theta)]e^*(\theta)'e^*(-\theta)[C_j(h^*)(\theta) - C_\tau(h^*)(\theta)]'. \quad (37)$$

It follows from the Holder inequality that

$$E[|x^j - x^\tau|^2]^{1/2} \le \||C_j(h^*) - C_\tau(h^*)||e^*|\|_2$$
$$\le (\||C_j(h^*) - C_\tau(h^*)|\|_q)(\||e^*|\|_p). \tag{38}$$

Therefore, $\{x^j: j \ge 1\}$ is mean-square (Pr) Cauchy. An entirely similar argument can be used to show that $\{y^j: j \ge 1\}$ is mean-square Cauchy. Using the same logic, it can be shown that the stochastic processes generated by x and y can be represented as two-sided moving averages of the process generated by w.

When Assumption 2' is used in place of Assumption 2, the same implications exist. Consider first $\{x^j: j \ge 1\}$. Note that the components of $\tau \ge 1$ converge in L^2 to corresponding components of h^*. Again, $\{C_j(h^*): j \ge 1\}$ converges in L^2 to h^*. Since e^* is continuous on the compact set $[-\pi, \pi]$, the function $|e^*|$ has a maximum on that same domain. It then follows from the first inequality in (38) that $\{x^j: j \ge 1\}$ is mean-square Cauchy.

Consider next $\{y^j: j \ge 1\}$. The continuity of e^* is sufficient for $\{C_j(e^*): j \ge 1\}$ to converge uniformly to e^* (e.g., see Edwards 1979, p. 87). Also, the process generated by $y^j - y^\tau$ has the spectral density matrix

$$[C_j(e^*)(-\theta) - C_\tau(e^*)(-\theta)]h^*(\theta)'h^*(-\theta)[C_j(e^*)(\theta) - C_\tau(e^*)(\theta)]'. \tag{39}$$

Hence,

$$E[|y^j - y^\tau|^2]^{1/2} \le \||C_j(e^*) - C_\tau(e^*)||h^*|\|_2. \tag{40}$$

The uniform convergence of $\{C_j(e^*): j \ge 1\}$ implies that $\{y^j: j \ge 1\}$ is mean-square (Pr) Cauchy.

Using this same logic, it follows that the matrix of Fourier transforms of the moving-average coefficients for x is $h^*(\theta)e^*(\theta)'$ and the corresponding matrix for y is $e^*(\theta)h^*(\theta)'$ for frequency θ. All entries of these matrices are in L^2.

Define

$$E(x^j \mid B_{-1}) \equiv c^j, \tag{41}$$

$$E(x \mid B_{-1}) \equiv c, \tag{42}$$

$$E(y^j \mid B_{-1}) \equiv d^j, \tag{43}$$

$$E(y \mid B_{-1}) \equiv d. \tag{44}$$

The expectations operator conditioned on B_{-1} is equal to the least-squares projection operator projecting onto G_{-1} when the domain of the operators is taken to be G_t for any t. Since least-squares projection operators are mean-square continuous, $\{c^j: j \ge 1\}$ converges in mean-square to c and $\{d^j: j \ge 1\}$ to d. This convergence implies that

$$\lim_{j \to \infty} E[(c^j + d^j) \cdot (c + d)] = E[(c + d) \cdot (c + d)]. \tag{45}$$

The first of the two random variables constructed in this section is

$$u \equiv w \cdot (c+d). \tag{46}$$

Note that

$$E(u \mid B_{-1}) = E(w \mid B_{-1}) \cdot (c+d) = 0 \tag{47}$$

since the elements of c and d are measurable with respect to B_{-1}. Also,

$$E(u^2) = E[\mid c-d \mid^2] = \frac{1}{2\pi} \int_{-\pi}^{\pi} \mid c^*(\theta) + d^*(\theta) \mid^2 d\theta, \tag{48}$$

where $\mid \cdot \mid^2$ of a matrix argument is the trace of the matrix times its conjugate transpose,

$$c^*(\theta) = [h^*(-\theta)e^*(\theta)']_+, \tag{49}$$

and

$$d^*(\theta) = [e^*(-\theta)h^*(\theta)']_+. \tag{50}$$

In (49) and (50), the operator $[\cdot]_+$ is defined to be the Fourier transform of the Fourier coefficients corresponding to strictly positive integers where the Fourier coefficient of c^* for index τ is given by

$$\frac{1}{2\pi} \int_{-\pi}^{\pi} \exp(i\theta\tau)c^*(\theta) \, d\theta, \tag{51}$$

and the Fourier coefficients of d^* are defined similarly. Formulas (49) and (50) are obtained by expressing x and y as two-sided sums of $\{w_t: -\infty < t < +\infty\}$ and calculating their projections onto G_{-1}. Note that

$$\sum_{t=0}^{\infty} \mid \gamma_t \epsilon_t' \mid \leq \left(\sum_{t=0}^{\infty} \mid \gamma_t \mid^2 \sum_{t=0}^{\infty} \mid \epsilon_t \mid^2 \right)^{1/2}. \tag{52}$$

Hence,

$$\Delta = \sum_{t=0}^{\infty} \gamma_t \epsilon_t' \tag{53}$$

is well defined. Also, note that

$$c^*(\theta) + d^*(-\theta)' + \Delta = h^*(-\theta)e^*(\theta)', \tag{54}$$

where $c^*(\theta)$, $d^*(-\theta)'$, and Δ are orthogonal matrix functions on $[-\pi, \pi]$ since the integrals over $[-\pi, \pi]$ of any one of these functions times the conjugate transpose of any of the other functions is zero. Consequently,

$$\frac{1}{2\pi} \int_{-\pi}^{\pi} h^*(-\theta)e^*(\theta)'e^*(-\theta)h^*(\theta)' \, d\theta =$$

$$= \frac{1}{2\pi} \int_{-\pi}^{\pi} [c^*(\theta)c^*(-\theta)' + d^*(-\theta)'d^*(\theta)] \, d\theta + \Delta\Delta', \quad (55)$$

and

$$\frac{1}{2\pi} \int_{-\pi}^{\pi} h^*(-\theta)e^*(\theta)' \, d\theta$$

$$= \frac{1}{2\pi} \int_{-\pi}^{\pi} [c^*(\theta)d^*(-\theta)' + d^*(-\theta)'c^*(\theta)] \, d\theta + \Delta^2. \quad (56)$$

Combining these results and taking traces yields

$$E(u^2) = \frac{1}{2\pi} \int_{-\pi}^{\pi} |h^*(\theta)|^2 |e^*(\theta)|^2 \, d\theta + \frac{1}{2\pi} \int_{-\pi}^{\pi} [e^*(\theta) \cdot h^*(-\theta)]^2 \, d\theta$$

$$- \text{tr}(\Delta^2 + \Delta\Delta'). \quad (57)$$

When Assumption 3′ is satisfied, $[e^*(-\theta)'h^*(\theta)]_+ = e^*(-\theta)'h^*(\theta)$. Thus, the trace of the integral on the left side of (56) is zero. In this case

$$E(u^2) = \frac{1}{2\pi} \int_{-\pi}^{\pi} [h^*(\theta) \cdot h^*(-\theta)][e^*(\theta) \cdot e^*(-\theta)] \, d\theta - \text{tr}(\Delta\Delta' + \Delta^2). \quad (58)$$

In any event, we have shown that u generates a martingale difference sequence with a finite variance.

A second random variable that generates a martingale difference sequence is given by

$$v \equiv w'\Delta w = \sum_{t=0}^{\infty} \gamma_t' ww' \epsilon_t = \sum_{t=0}^{\infty} \gamma_t'(ww' - I)\epsilon_t. \quad (59)$$

Since

$$|v| \leq \sum_{t=0}^{\infty} |\gamma_t| |\epsilon_t| |w|^2, \quad (60)$$

v has a finite second moment. Finally,

$$E(v \mid B_{-1}) = \text{tr}[E(\Delta ww' \mid B_{-1})] = \text{tr}(\Delta) = 0, \quad (61)$$

which proves that v generates a martingale difference sequence with a finite variance.

In general, u and v will be correlated. When w is normally distributed conditioned on B_{-1}, however, they are uncorrelated because the third moments of w conditioned on B_{-1} are zero. Also, the variance of v takes on a particularly simple form because fourth moments of w can be calculated as products of second moments. More precisely,

$$E(v^2) = E(w'\Delta w)E(w'\Delta w) + \text{tr}[\Delta E(ww')\Delta E(ww')]$$

$$+ \text{tr}[\Delta E(ww')\Delta' E(ww')]$$

$$= \text{tr}(\Delta^2 + \Delta\Delta'). \quad (62)$$

5   Martingale difference approximation

We now derive a central-limit theorem. We have already established that u and v generate stationary and ergodic martingale difference sequences with finite variances. It follows from Billingsley (1961) that $\{P_T(u+v): T \geq 1\}$ converges in distribution to a normally distributed random variable with mean zero and variance $E[(u+v)^2]$. To derive a central-limit approximation for $eh = u^+ + v^+$, we will show that $\{P_T(u-u^+): T \geq 1\}$ and $\{P_T(v-v^+): T \geq 1\}$ converge in mean square to zero. It then follows that $\{P_T(u^+ + v^+): T \geq 1\}$ converges in distribution to a normally distributed random variable with mean zero and variance $E[(u+v)^2]$.

Consider first $\{P_T(v-v^+): T \geq 1\}$. It follows from (30) and (59) that

$$v - v^+ = \sum_{t=0}^{\infty} \gamma_t'(ww'-I)\epsilon_t - \sum_{t=0}^{\infty} \gamma_t'(w_{-t}w_{-t}'-I)\epsilon_t. \tag{63}$$

Let

$$w^+ = \text{vec}(ww'-I), \tag{64}$$

where vec stacks the rows of a matrix. Then w^+ has a finite second moment, and $E(w^+ \mid B_{-1}) = 0$ (Assumption 1). Also,

$$v - v^+ = \sum_{t=0}^{\infty} (\gamma_t \otimes \epsilon_t) \cdot w^+ - \sum_{t=0}^{\infty} (\gamma_t \otimes \epsilon_t) \cdot w_{-t}^+. \tag{65}$$

Define

$$v^*(\theta) = \sum_{t=0}^{\infty} (\gamma_t \otimes \epsilon_t) - \sum_{t=0}^{\infty} (\gamma_t \otimes \epsilon_t) \exp(-i\theta t) \tag{66}$$

and

$$P_T^*(\theta) = \left(\frac{1}{T}\right)^{1/2} \sum_{t=1}^{T} \exp(i\theta t). \tag{67}$$

Then

$$E[|P_T(v-v^+)|^2] = \frac{1}{2\pi} \int_{-\pi}^{\pi} |P_T^*(\theta)|^2 v^*(\theta)' E(w^+ w^{+\prime}) v^*(-\theta)\, d\theta. \tag{68}$$

Since

$$\sum_{t=0}^{\infty} |(\gamma_t \otimes \epsilon_t)| < \infty, \tag{69}$$

v^* is continuous on $[-\pi, \pi]$. Furthermore, v^* is zero at $\theta = 0$, which implies that

$$\lim_{T \to \infty} \int_{-\pi}^{\pi} |P_T^*(\theta)|^2 v^*(\theta)' E(w^+ w^{+\prime}) v^*(-\theta)'\, d\theta = 0 \tag{70}$$

(e.g., see Edwards 1979, p. 87). Therefore, $\{P_T(v-v^+): T \geq 1\}$ converges in mean square (Pr) to zero.

Consider next $\{P_T(u-u^+):T \geq 1\}$. To obtain an expression for the limit of $\{E[P_T(u^+)^2]:T \geq 1\}$, initially suppose that w is normally distributed conditioned on B_{-1}. In this case

$$E\{[P_T(eh)]^2\} = E\{[P_T(u^+)]^2\} + E\{[P_T(v^+)]^2\}. \tag{71}$$

Furthermore,

$$E[(eh)(e_{-t}h_{-t})] = E(eh)E(e_{-t}h_{-t}) + E(hh_{-t})E(ee_{-t}) + E(eh_{-t})E(e_{-t}h)$$
$$= E(hh_{-t})E(ee_{-t}) + E(eh_{-t})E(e_{-t}h). \tag{72}$$

Suppose that Assumption 2 is satisfied. Then the sequences $\{E(hh_{-t}): -\infty < t < +\infty\}$, $\{E(ee_{-t}): -\infty < t < +\infty\}$, $\{E(eh_{-t}): -\infty < t < +\infty\}$, and $\{E(e_{-t}h): -\infty < t < +\infty\}$ are the Fourier coefficients of the functions $|h^*|^2$, $e^*(h^{*c})$, and $h^*(e^{*c})$, where functions with a c superscript are conjugated. The function $|h^*|^2$ is in L^{2q}, $|e^*|^2$ is in L^{2p}, and both $e^*(h^{*c})$ and $h^*(e^{*c})$ are in L^2. Now

$$\sum_{t=-j}^{j} E(hh_{-t})E(ee_{-t}) = \frac{1}{2\pi} \int_{-\pi}^{\pi} F_j(|h^*|^2)(\theta)F_j(|e^*|^2)(\theta)\, d\theta, \tag{73}$$

and

$$\sum_{t=-j}^{j} E(eh_{-t})E(e_{-t}h) = \frac{1}{2\pi} \int_{-\pi}^{\pi} \{F_j[e^* \cdot h^*](\theta)\}^2\, d\theta. \tag{74}$$

It follows from the (L^{2q}, L^{2p}, L^2) convergence of the Fourier series approximations (e.g., See Edwards 1967, p. 100) and the Holder inequality that the limits as $j \to \infty$ on left sides of (73) and (74) exist and are equal to the corresponding integral of the limit functions. Consequently, the first-order Cesaro means of these series must converge to the same integrals. Note that

$$E[P_T(eh)^2] = \frac{1}{T} \sum_{t=1}^{T} (T-|t|)E[(eh)(e_{-t}h_{-t})]. \tag{75}$$

In light of (72)–(74) and (54),

$$\lim_{T \to \infty} E[P_T(eh)^2] = \frac{1}{2\pi} \int_{-\pi}^{\pi} |h^*(\theta)|^2 |e^*(\theta)|^2\, d\theta + \int_{-\pi}^{\pi} [e^*(\theta) \cdot h^*(-\theta)]^2\, d\theta$$
$$= E(u^2) + \mathrm{tr}(\Delta^2 + \Delta\Delta'). \tag{76}$$

We obtain the same conclusion when Assumptions 2′ and 3′ are imposed instead of Assumption 2. When Assumption 3′ is satisfied, (72) simplifies to become

$$E[(eh)(e_{-t}h_{-t})] = E(hh_{-t})E(ee_{-t}). \tag{77}$$

The spectral density function for the process generated by eh is given by the convolution

$$f^*(\theta) = \frac{1}{2\pi} \int_{-\pi}^{\pi} |e^*(\theta-\nu)|^2 |h^*(\nu)|^2 \, d\nu. \tag{78}$$

When Assumption 2' is satisfied, $|e^*|^2$ is continuous on $[-\pi, \pi]$ and is hence uniformly continuous. It follows that f^* is continuous on $[-\pi, \pi]$. Since f^* is continuous at zero,

$$\lim_{T\to\infty} E[P_T(eh)^2] = \lim_{T\to\infty} \frac{1}{2\pi} \int_{-\pi}^{\pi} P_T^*(\theta) f^*(\theta) \, d\theta$$

$$= f^*(0)$$

$$= \int_{-\pi}^{\pi} |h^*(\theta)|^2 |e^*(\theta)|^2 \, d\theta \tag{79}$$

(e.g., see Edward 1979, p. 87). Since $e^*(\theta) \cdot h^*(-\theta)$ viewed as a function of θ is in L^2, (74) continues to hold. Hence, Assumption 3' implies that

$$\frac{1}{2\pi} \int_{-\pi}^{\pi} [e^*(\theta) \cdot h^*(-\theta)]^2 \, d\theta = 0. \tag{80}$$

Substituting from (57) yields (76) for this case as well.

When w is normally distributed conditioned on B_{-1},

$$E(v^2) = \mathrm{tr}(\Delta^2 + \Delta\Delta'). \tag{81}$$

In light of (71) and (75)–(76),

$$\lim_{T\to\infty} E\{[P_T(u^+)^2]\} = E(u^2). \tag{82}$$

The discussion leading up to (82) presumed that w was normally distributed. We know that, in all circumstances,

$$\lim_{T\to\infty} E\{[P_T(v^+)]^2\} = \lim_{T\to\infty} E\{[P_T(v)]^2\} = E(v^2). \tag{83}$$

An incorrect assumption of normality only invalidates (81) and not (82) [see (33)].

Since u generates a martingale difference sequence,

$$E[P_T(u)^2] = E[(u)^2]. \tag{84}$$

Finally, consider $E[P_T(u)P_T(u^+)]$. Relation (29) gives a martingale difference decomposition of u^+. Using this decomposition, it follows that

$$E(u^+ u_t) = \begin{cases} 0 & \text{if } t > 0, \\ E\{(c+d) \cdot [\epsilon_t E(h \mid B_{-1}) + \gamma_t E(e \mid B_{-1})]\} & \text{if } t \le 0. \end{cases} \tag{85}$$

Using (85), (41), and (43) yields

$$E[P_T(u^+)P_T(u)] = E[(c^T + d^T) \cdot (c+d)]. \tag{86}$$

Taking limits and substituting from (45) gives

$$\lim_{T \to \infty} E[P_T(u^+)P_T(u)] = E[(c+d)\cdot(c+d)] = E(u^2).$$ (87)

Combining (82), (84), and (87) yields

$$\lim_{T \to \infty} E[P_T(u-u^+)^2] = 0.$$ (88)

We have now proved the following result.

Theorem. *Suppose Assumptions 1–3 or 1, 2', and 3' are satisfied. Then* $\{P_T(eh): t \geq 1\}$ *converges in distribution to a normally distributed random variable with mean zero and variance*

$$\lim_{T \to \infty} E[P_T(eh)^2] = E[(u+v)^2].$$ (89)

In general,

$$\lim_{T \to \infty} E[P_T(u^+)P_T(v^+)] \neq 0.$$ (90)

Consequently, third and fourth moments of w enter into the expression for the asymptotic variance. In some special cases, however, v is zero, which leads to a simplification of the asymptotic variance. For example, suppose that $n = 1$. Then Assumption 3 or Assumption 3' implies that $\Delta = 0$. Consequently, v given by (33) is zero. Alternatively, suppose that

$$e^*(\theta) = \sum_{j=0}^{\ell-1} \epsilon_j \exp(-i\theta)$$ (91)

and

$$h^*(\theta) = \sum_{j=\ell}^{\infty} \gamma_j \exp(-i\theta).$$ (92)

In this case e can be viewed as an ℓ step-ahead forecast error, and h is a random variable in the information set at the time of the forecast. Again Δ is zero, as is v. In these special cases, the asymptotic variance can be calculated using formulas for Gaussian processes.

Assumption 2 does not restrict e^* to be continuous as does 2'. In many applications of instrumental variable estimators, h has a nonzero mean. To accommodate this and still obtain a central-limit approximation appears to require restrictions in addition to Assumption 2. For instance, continuity of e^* at zero is sufficient (see Hansen 1985b). Consequently, Assumptions 1, 2', and 3' can accommodate nonzero means without strengthening.

So far, we have studied only the product of one component of a disturbance vector and one component of a vector of instrumental variables.

We specialized in this way only for notational convenience. Our analysis extends immediately to the case in which the restrictions apply to each component of a disturbance vector d and each entry of a matrix of instrumental variables z that is conformable with d. In this case the asymptotic covariance matrix is

$$\lim_{T \to \infty} E[P_T(zd)P_T(zd)'].$$ (93)

6   Relation to other research

This section compares our results to results reported in three papers. Hall and Heyde (1980, Theorem 6.7) derived the asymptotic distribution of sample autocovariances of a univariate time series. Their analysis is most closely related to our analysis when Assumptions 1–3 are imposed for p and q equal to 4 and n equal to 1. In addition, they gave sufficient (time domain) conditions for Assumption 2 to hold when p and q are 4. As noted in Section 5, when n is 1, Δ and hence v are zero. Consequently, the variance of the asymptotic distribution is just $E(u^2)$. The proof of our general result is patterned after the one used by Hall and Heyde.

When the disturbance vector d satisfies $E(d \mid B_{-\ell}) = 0$ and the entries of the matrix z are measurable with respect to $B_{-\ell}$, other auxiliary assumptions can be dispensed with. For instance, it is easy to relax the restrictions that w be conditionally homoscedastic and the entries of z have moving-average representations in terms of past values of w (e.g., see Hansen 1985a). This special case is of considerable interest in studying implications of rational expectation models.

Hansen and Sargent (1982), Hayashi and Sims (1983), and Hansen (1986) investigated the asymptotic efficiency of instrumental variables estimators for linear time series models. The analysis in this chapter can be combined with that of Hansen (1982) to obtain a derivation of the requisite asymptotic distribution presumed by these authors.

REFERENCES

Billingsley, P. 1961. "The Lindeberg–Levy Theorem for Martingales." *American Mathematical Society* 12: 788–92.

Edwards, R. E. 1967. *Fourier Series,* Vol. 2. New York: Holt, Rinehart and Winston.

1979. *Fourier Series,* Vol. 1, 2d ed. New York: Holt, Rinehart and Winston.

Gordin, M. I. 1969. "The Central Limit Theorem for Stationary Processes." *Soviet Mathematics Doklady* 10: 1174–6.

Hall, P., and C. C. Heyde. 1980. *Martingale Limit Theory and Its Application.* New York: Academic.

Hansen, L. P. 1982. "Large Sample Properties of Generalized Method of Moments Estimators." *Econometrica* 50: 1029–54.

1985a. "A Method for Calculating Bounds on the Asymptotic Covariance Matrices of Generalized Method of Moments Estimators." *Journal of Econometrics* 30: 203–38.

1985b. "Using Martingale Difference Approximations to Obtain Covariance Matrix Bounds for Generalized Methods of Moments Estimators." National Opinion Research Center Discussion Paper 85-16.

1986. "Asymptotic Covariance Matrix Bounds for Instrumental Variables Estimators of Linear Time Series Models." The University of Chicago, manuscript.

Hansen, L. P., and R. J. Hodrick. 1983. "Risk Averse Speculation in the Forward Foreign Exchange Market: An Econometric Analysis of Linear Models." In *Exchange Rates and International Macroeconomics,* J. A. Frenkel, Ed. Chicago, IL: University of Chicago Press.

Hansen, L. P., and T. J. Sargent. 1982. "Instrumental Variables Procedures for Estimating Linear Rational Expectations Models." *Journal of Monetary Economics* 9(3): 263–96.

Hayashi, F., and C. A. Sims. 1983. "Nearly Efficient Estimation of Time Series Models with Predetermined, But Not Exogenous, Instruments." *Econometrica* 51: 783–98.

Kohn, R. 1979. "Asymptotic Estimation and Hypothesis Testing Results for Vector Linear Time Series Models." *Econometrica* 47(4): 1005–30.

CHAPTER 9

Exact and approximate distribution of the *t* ratio test statistic in an AR(1) model

Alberto Holly and Georg Michael Rockinger

1   Introduction

In recent years there has been a number of papers on the distribution of the *t* ratio test statistic in an AR(1) model under different sets of assumptions. Nankervis and Savin (1985) considered an AR(1) model where the initial value of the lagged dependent variable is a known constant and were interested in the distribution of the *t* ratio test statistics for the autoregressive parameter when its value is in the neighborhood of unity. Nankervis and Savin (1984) also considered a stationary first-order autoregressive model with unknown intercept.

The Edgeworth expansion to the distribution of the *t* ratio test statistic up to $O(T^{-1/2})$ (where T is the sample size) was derived by Phillips (1977). Extending Phillips's result, Tanaka (1983) derived the Edgeworth expansion in the stationary AR(1) model with unknown constant mean and compared it with the distribution of the *t* ratio test statistic.

In the work of Nankervis and Savin (1984, 1985) and Tanaka (1983), Monte Carlo methods are used to investigate the finite-sample distribution of the *t* statistic. The purpose of this chapter is to explore an alternative way of deriving this finite-sample distribution in the case of a stationary first-order autoregresive model with no intercept,

$$y_t = \alpha y_{t-1} + u_t \quad (|\alpha| < 1), \tag{1}$$

where the u_t are independent and identically distributed as $\mathfrak{N}(0, \sigma^2)$.

Following the approach outlined in Daniels (1956), we derive in Section 2 the exact density function, given in an integral form, for the *t* ratio test statistic. We also derive in Section 3 a saddlepoint approximation.[1]

---

[1] Before presenting the main results of this chapter, we would like to mention that we tried (very hard) to obtain numerical results for selected values of α and T for the *t* ratio statistic. However, the computer program we have developed seems to give somewhat inaccurate numerical results. They seem to be sensitive to the boundaries of the integration

157

2   Finite-sample density function of t ratio test statistic

We define the $(T+1) \times (T+1)$ matrices C_1, C_2, and C_3 as[2]

$$C_1 = \begin{bmatrix} 0 & \frac{1}{2} & \cdots & 0 & 0 \\ \frac{1}{2} & 0 & \cdots & 0 & 0 \\ \vdots & \vdots & \ddots & \vdots & \vdots \\ 0 & 0 & \cdots & 0 & \frac{1}{2} \\ 0 & 0 & \cdots & \frac{1}{2} & 0 \end{bmatrix},$$

$$C_2 = \begin{bmatrix} 0 & 0 & \cdots & 0 & 0 \\ 0 & 1 & \cdots & 0 & 0 \\ \vdots & \vdots & \ddots & \vdots & \vdots \\ 0 & 0 & \cdots & 1 & 0 \\ 0 & 0 & \cdots & 0 & 1 \end{bmatrix},$$

$$C_3 = \begin{bmatrix} 1 & 0 & \cdots & 0 & 0 \\ 0 & 1 & \cdots & 0 & 0 \\ \vdots & \vdots & \ddots & \vdots & \vdots \\ 0 & 0 & \cdots & 1 & 0 \\ 0 & 0 & \cdots & 0 & 0 \end{bmatrix}.$$

Introducing

$$Z_i = y'C_i y \quad (i = 1, 2, 3),$$

$$X_i = y'C_i y / y'C_3 y \quad (i = 1, 2),$$

where $y' = (y_0, y_1, \ldots, y_T)$, we can write the ordinary least-squares estimators for α and σ^2 in (1) as

$$\hat{\alpha} = X_1, \qquad \hat{\sigma}^2 = \frac{1}{T-1}[Z_2 - X_1 Z_1],$$

and the t ratio test statistic as

$$t = \frac{X_1 - \alpha}{\sqrt{(X_2 - X_1^2)/(T-1)}}. \tag{2}$$

Footnote 1 *(cont.)*
domain. We have not been able to solve this problem in time for publication, but have made substantial progress in this direction and hope to present satisfactory numerical computations in the near future.

[2] The reader should note that our notation differs from that of Phillips (1977) in the sense that what we define as C_2 and C_3 are defined as C_3 and C_2, respectively, in Phillips's paper.

Since t is a simple transformation of X_1 and X_2, we shall derive its exact finite-sample density function from the joint distribution of X_1 and X_2. To be more specific, suppose that the joint density of X_1 and X_2, denoted as $f_{(X_1,X_2)}(x_1,x_2)$, is known and define two new random variables by

$$U_1 = X_1 - \alpha, \qquad U_2 = \sqrt{[1/(T-1)](X_2 - X_1^2)}.$$

Let $\mathfrak{D}(u_1,u_2)$ be the image of the domain of (X_1,X_2) under the transformation. The joint density of (U_1, U_2) is equal to

$$f_{(U_1,U_2)}(u_1,u_2) = 2(T-1)u_2 f_{(X_1,X_2)}[u_1+\alpha, (T-1)u_2^2+(u_1+\alpha)^2]$$

for $(u_1,u_2) \in \mathfrak{D}(u_1,u_2)$, and the density function of the t ratio test statistic is equal to

$$
\begin{aligned}
&f_t(\tau)\\
&= 2(T-1)\int_{\mathfrak{D}(u_2)} u_2^2 f_{(X_1,X_2)}[\tau u_2+\alpha, (T-1)u_2^2+(\tau u_2+\alpha)^2]\, du_2, \quad (3)
\end{aligned}
$$

where

$$\mathfrak{D}(u_2) = \{u_2 \text{ such that } (\tau u_2+\alpha, u_2) \in \mathfrak{D}(u_1,u_2)\}.$$

At this point, it is important to note that since we consider a stationary AR(1) model, the distribution of the t ratio test statistic does not depend on the parameter σ^2. Therefore, to simplify the notation, assume that $\sigma^2 = 1$ in all derivations.

2.1   Joint distribution of X_1 and X_2

Following the approach suggested in Daniels (1956), we shall derive the expression for the joint distribution of X_1 and X_2 from the Laplace transform of the joint distribution of Z_1, Z_2, and Z_3. Before doing so, it might be useful to briefly outline Daniels's approach.[3]

Let $V = (V_1, \ldots, V_{m+1})'$ be a random vector of order $m+1$, where V_{m+1} takes positive values, and suppose we are interested in the distribution of the random vector $X = (X_1, \ldots, X_m)'$, where $X_i = V_i/V_{m+1}$.

Let $f_V(v_1, \ldots, v_{m+1})$ and $f_X(x_1, \ldots, x_m)$ be the joint density functions of V and X, respectively. As is well known,

$$f_X(x_1,\ldots,x_m) = \int_0^\infty (v_{m+1})^m f_V(x_1 v_{m+1}, \ldots, x_m v_{m+1}, v_{m+1})\, dv_{m+1}. \quad (4)$$

It is often the case that the expression for $f_V(v_1, \ldots, v_{m+1})$ is more difficult to derive than the expression for the moment-generating function or the characteristic function of the distribution of V. For these cases, rather

---

[3] This approach has been used by Phillips (1976, 1978) to derive a saddlepoint approximation to the density of $\hat{\alpha}$.

than computing $f_X(x_1, \ldots, x_m)$ from (4), Daniels (1956) has suggested an alternative approach using the (multiple) Laplace transform of the distribution of V, which, as we will recall in what follows, is related to the moment-generating function.

Specifically, let $\xi = (\xi_1, \ldots, \xi_{m+1})'$ be a vector of $m+1$ real variables, and define E_R as the convex subset of $\mathbf{R}^{m+1}$ such that the moment-generating function

$$\mathfrak{M}|\xi| = \int_{\mathbf{R}^{m+1}} \exp(\xi'v) f_V(v) \, dv$$

exists.

Let $\theta = (\theta_1, \ldots, \theta_{m+1})'$ be a vector of $m+1$ complex numbers. We call the (multiple) Laplace transform of f_V, the complex function

$$L(\theta) = \int_{\mathbf{R}^{m+1}} \exp(\theta'v) f_V(v) \, dv.$$

It can be easily seen that $L(\theta)$ is defined in the following subset of $\mathbf{C}^{m+1}$,

$$E = \{\theta \in \mathbf{C}^{m+1}; \Re(\theta) = (\Re(\theta_1), \ldots, \Re(\theta_{m+1}))' \in E_R\},$$

where $\Re(\theta_j)$ $(j = 1, \ldots, m+1)$ denotes the real part of θ_j.

Now, let $\mathring{E}_R$ be the interior of E_R and define

$$\mathring{E} = \{\theta \in \mathbf{C}^{m+1}, \Re(\theta) \in \mathring{E}_R\}.$$

As is well known, the Laplace transform is analytic in $\mathring{E}$, and its derivatives can be obtained by derivation under the integral sign.[4] In addition, the function $f_V(v)$ can be recovered from $L(\theta)$ by means of an inverse transformation. Specifically, if a point $c = (c_1, \ldots, c_{m+1})'$ belongs to E_R, the integral

$$\left(\frac{1}{2\pi i}\right)^{m+1} \int_{c_1-i\infty}^{c_1+i\infty} \cdots \int_{c_{m+1}-i\infty}^{c_{m+1}+i\infty} \exp(-\theta'v) L(\theta) \, d\theta$$

over the product of the vertical contours converges absolutely and is equal to the function $f_V(v)$ at all its points of continuity. Assuming now that $f_V(v)$ is a continuous function of v,

$$f_V(x_1 v_{m+1}, \ldots, x_m v_{m+1}, v_{m+1})$$
$$= \left(\frac{1}{2\pi i}\right)^{m+1} \int_{c_1-i\infty}^{c_1+i\infty}$$
$$\cdots \int_{c_{m+1}-i\infty}^{c_{m+1}+i\infty} \exp[(-v_{m+1}(\theta_{m+1} + \theta_1 x_1 + \cdots + \theta_m x_m)] L(\theta) \, d\theta. \quad (5)$$

---

[4] The fact that $L(\theta)$ is an analytic function of several complex variables is proved, for example, in Bochner and Martin (1948). We shall use certain theorems from the theory of such functions that can be found, e.g., in Bochner and Martin (1948) and Fuks (1963).

Now, given $x = (x_1, \ldots, x_m)'$, we make the change of variables,

$$\theta_1 = \theta_1, \theta_2 = \theta_2, \cdots;$$

$$u = \theta_{m+1} + \theta_1 x_1 + \cdots + \theta_m x_m.$$

This change of variables defines an analytical (or holomorphic) mapping. This is in fact a pseudoconformal mapping since its Jacobian is equal to 1.[5] If a point $c = (c_1, \ldots, c_{m+1})'$ belongs to E_R, we define c_u as $c_u = c_{m+1} + c_1 x_1 + \cdots + c_m x_m$ and can write (5) as

$$f_V(x_1 v_{m+1}, \ldots, x_m v_{m+1}, v_{m+1})$$

$$= \frac{1}{2\pi i} \int_{c_u - i\infty}^{c_u + i\infty} \exp(-u v_{m+1}) \varphi(u, x) \, du, \qquad (6)$$

where

$$\varphi(u, x) = \left(\frac{1}{2\pi i}\right)^m \int_{c_1 - i\infty}^{c_1 + i\infty} \cdots \int_{c_{m+1} - i\infty}^{c_{m+1} + i\infty} L\left(\theta_1, \ldots, u - \sum_{j=1}^{m} \theta_j x_j\right) \prod_{k=1}^{m} d\theta_k.$$

We see from (6) that $f_V(x_1 v_{m+1}, \ldots, x_m v_{m+1}, v_{m+1})$ and $\varphi(u, x)$ constitute a transform pair, and

$$\varphi(u, x) = \int_0^\infty f_V(x_1 v_{m+1}, \ldots, x_m v_{m+1}, v_{m+1}) \exp(u v_{m+1}) \, dv_{m+1}.$$

We now see that

$$\frac{\partial^m \varphi(u, x)}{\partial u^m} = \int_0^\infty (v_{m+1})^m f_V(x_1 v_{m+1}, \ldots, x_m v_{m+1}, v_{m+1}) \exp(u v_{m+1}) \, dv_{m+1}$$

and, from (4), that the joint density of X can be written as

$$f_X(x_1, \ldots, x_m) = \left. \frac{\partial^m \varphi(u, x)}{\partial u^m} \right|_{u=0}.$$

To summarize the results obtained so far, the joint density of X can be obtained from

$$f_X(x_1, \ldots, x_m) = \frac{\partial^m}{\partial u^m} \left[\left(\frac{1}{2\pi i}\right)^m \int_{c_1 - i\infty}^{c_1 + i\infty} \right.$$

$$\left. \cdots \int_{c_m - i\infty}^{c_m + i\infty} L\left(\theta_1, \ldots, u - \sum_{j=1}^{m} \theta_j x_j\right) \prod_{k=1}^{m} d\theta_k \right] \qquad (7)$$

provided that $(\theta_1, \ldots, u - \sum_{j=1}^m \theta_j x_j)' \in \mathring{E}$. Furthermore, we can interchange the derivative and integral sign.

---

[5] This chapter uses some concepts and theorems from the theory of analytic (or holomorphic) mappings with nonzero Jacobians, and we refer the reader to Fuks (1963, pp. 103–16). At this point, it might be useful to recall that if not only a mapping itself but also its inverse mapping is analytic, such a mapping is said to be *pseudoconformal*. If the Jacobian of an analytic mapping is different from zero at a given point, this mapping is pseudo-

As we shall see in the following, it is frequently useful to make a further change of variables in (7) by means of a pseudoconformal mapping. We shall not consider here the general case and shall now turn to the derivation of the joint distribution of X_1 and X_2 for the situation of interest.

The moment-generating function of Z_1, Z_2, and Z_3 is equal to

$$\mathfrak{M}(\xi_1, \xi_2, \xi_3) = (\det \Sigma)^{-1/2}\{\det[\Sigma^{-1} - 2(\xi_1 C_1 + \xi_2 C_2 + \xi_3 C_3)]\}^{-1/2},$$

where Σ is the covariance matrix of y with (i, j)th element given by $\alpha^{|i-j|}/(1-\alpha^2)$.

We have

$$\mathfrak{M}(\xi_1, \xi_2, \xi_3) = (1-\alpha^2)(\det h_{T+1})^{-1/2}, \tag{8}$$

with

$$h_{T+1} = \begin{pmatrix} 1-2\xi_3 & \delta & 0 & \cdots & 0 & 0 \\ \delta & \beta & \delta & \cdots & 0 & 0 \\ \vdots & \vdots & \vdots & \ddots & \vdots & \vdots \\ 0 & 0 & 0 & \cdots & \beta & \delta \\ 0 & 0 & 0 & \cdots & \delta & 1-2\xi_2 \end{pmatrix},$$

where

$$\beta = 1+\alpha^2-2(\xi_2+\xi_3), \qquad \delta = -(\alpha+\xi_1).$$

Following Daniels (1956) and Phillips (1976), it is now convenient to define the matrix g_{T+1} to be the same as the matrix h_{T+1} except that the leading diagonal element is β rather than $1-2\xi_3$. It is easy to verify that

$$\det h_{T+1} = \det g_{T+1} + (2\xi_2-\alpha^2) \det g_T. \tag{9}$$

Moreover, as explained in the appendix, one can show that

$$\det g_T = \frac{1}{\lambda_2-\lambda_1}[(1-2\xi_2)(\lambda_2^T-\lambda_1^T)+\lambda_1\lambda_2(\lambda_1^{T-1}-\lambda_2^{T-1})], \tag{10}$$

where

$$\lambda_1, \lambda_2 = \tfrac{1}{2}[1+\alpha^2-2(\xi_2+\xi_3)$$
$$\pm([1+\alpha^2-2(\xi_2+\xi_3)]^2-4(\alpha+\xi_1)^2)^{1/2}]. \tag{11}$$

Using (9), we can compute $\det h_{T+1}$ and therefore $\mathfrak{M}(\xi_1, \xi_2, \xi_3)$.

If $\theta = (\theta_1, \theta_2, \theta_3)'$ is a vector of complex variables, we obtain the expression for the Laplace transform $L(\theta_1, \theta_1, \theta_2)$ by replacing ξ_1, ξ_2, and ξ_3 by θ_1, θ_2, and θ_3, respectively, in the expression for $\mathfrak{M}(\xi_1, \xi_2, \xi_3)$.

Footnote 5 *(cont.)*
conformal at this point. The expression "pseudoconformal" is used in the context of analytic mappings in distinction from the expression "conformal mapping" for analytic functions of one complex variable; a pseudoconformal mapping, generally speaking, does not preserve the angle between directions.

As already explained, for given values of x_1, x_2 we need to find the expression for

$$\varphi(u, x_1, x_2)$$

$$= -\frac{1}{4\pi^2} \int_{c_1-i\infty}^{c_1+i\infty} \int_{c_2-i\infty}^{c_2+i\infty} L(\theta_1, \theta_2, u-\theta_1 x_1 - \theta_2 x_2) \, d\theta_1 \, d\theta_2. \tag{12}$$

To this purpose, we shall use an idea of Daniels (1956) and Phillips (1976) and make the change of variables $(\theta_1, \theta_2, \theta_3) \to (w, \theta_2, u)$, where, as before, $u = \theta_3 + \theta_1 x_1 + \theta_2 x_2$, and the new variable w is defined by

$$w + \frac{1}{w} = \frac{1 + \alpha^2 - 2(\theta_2 + \theta_3)}{\alpha + \theta_1}. \tag{13}$$

We shall later consider in detail the domain of (w, θ_2, u). Before doing so, we shall first derive the expression for the integrand in (12).

It is easy to see that the Jacobian of the transformation $(\theta_1, \theta_2, \theta_3) \to (w, \theta_2, u)$ is equal to

$$J = -\frac{(1-w^2)p(u)}{(w^2 - 2x_1 w + 1)^2}, \tag{14}$$

where

$$p(u) = 1 + \alpha^2 + 2[\theta_2(x_2-1) - u] - 2x_1\alpha. \tag{15}$$

We shall assume that the Jacobian J is different from zero in the image of the domain of $(\theta_1, \theta_2, \theta_3)$ by the analytic mapping $(\theta_1, \theta_2, \theta_3) \to (w, \theta_2, u)$. Therefore, assume that $w^2 \neq 1$ and that $p(u) \neq 0$. In particular, for $u = 0$, assume that $p(0) = 1 + \alpha^2 - 2\theta_2(x_2-1) - 2x_1\alpha$ is different from zero. This is always verified when $|\alpha| < 1$ and $|x_1| < 1$. As noted earlier, if J is different from zero, the analytic mapping $(\theta_1, \theta_2, \theta_3) \to (w, \theta_2, u)$ is a pseudoconformal mapping.

Now, defining

$$L^*(w, \theta_2, u) \equiv L(\theta_1(w, u), \theta_2, u - \theta_1(w, u)x_1 - \theta_2 x_2) \tag{16}$$

we find that

$$\lambda_1 = (\alpha + \theta_1)w, \qquad \lambda_2 = (\alpha + \theta_1)/w$$

and

$$L^*(w, \theta_2, u) = \frac{(1-\alpha^2)^{1/2}(1-w^2)^{1/2}(w^2 - 2x_1 w + 1)^{(T+1)/2}}{[p(u)]^{(T-1)/2}}$$

$$\times (N_1 + N_2)^{-1/2}, \tag{17}$$

where

$$N_1 = [1 - 2\theta_2 - (2\theta_2 - \alpha^2)w^2](w^2 - 2x_1 w + 1)p(u)$$

$$+ (2\theta_2 - \alpha^2)(1 - 2\theta_2)(w^2 - 2x_1 w + 1)^2 - w^2 p^2(u) \tag{18}$$

and

$$N_2 = \{[(2\theta_2 - \alpha^2) - (1 - 2\theta_2)w^2]p(u) - (1 - 2\theta_2)(2\theta_2 - \alpha^2)(w^2 - 2x_1w + 1)\}$$
$$\times (w^2 - 2x_1w + 1)w^{2T} + p^2(u)w^{2T+2}. \tag{19}$$

From (14) and (19) we see that the integral $\varphi(u, x_1, x_2)$ given in (12) may be written as

$$\varphi(u, x_1, x_2) = -\frac{1}{4\pi^2} \iint_{\mathfrak{D}} \Psi(w, \theta_2, u) \, dw \, d\theta_2, \tag{20}$$

where

$$\Psi(w, \theta_2, u) = -\frac{(1 - \alpha^2)^{1/2}(1 - w^2)^{3/2}(w^2 - 2x_1w + 1)^{(T-3)/2}}{[p(u)]^{(T-3)/2}}$$
$$\times (N_1 + N_2)^{-1/2}. \tag{21}$$

The manifold $\mathfrak{D}$ in (20) is the Cartesian product of the curves

$$\Gamma_w \times]c_2 - i\infty, c_2 + i\infty[,$$

where Γ_w will be described in what follows.

The joint distribution of X_1 and X_2 is given by

$$f_X(x_1, x_2) = -\frac{1}{4\pi^2} \iint_{\mathfrak{D}} \frac{\partial^2}{\partial u^2}[\Psi(w, \theta_2, u)]\bigg|_{u=0} dw \, d\theta_2. \tag{22}$$

Defining

$$a = w^{2T+2} - w^2 \tag{23}$$

$$b = \{1 - 2\theta_2 - (2\theta_2 - \alpha^2)w^2 + [(2\theta_2 - \alpha^2) - (1 - 2\theta_2)w^2]w^{2T}\}$$
$$\times (w^2 - 2x_1w + 1) \tag{24}$$

$$c = (2\theta_2 - \alpha^2)(1 - 2\theta_2)(w^2 - 2x_1w + 1)^2(1 - w^{2T}) \tag{25}$$

and $p_0 = p(0)$, the expression for the joint density of X_1 and X_2 may be written as

$$f_{X_1, X_2}(x_1, x_2) = -\frac{(1 - \alpha^2)^{1/2}}{4\pi^2} \iint_{\mathfrak{D}} (1 - w^2)^{3/2}$$
$$\times (w^2 - 2x_1w + 1)^{(T-3)/2}[R_1 + R_2 + R_3 + R_4] \, dw \, d\theta_2, \tag{26}$$

where

$$R_1 = \frac{(T-3)(T-1)}{p_0^{(T+1)/2}(ap_0^2 + bp_0 + c)^{1/2}}, \tag{27}$$

$$R_2 = \frac{2(T-3)(2ap_0 + b)}{p_0^{(T-1)/2}(ap_0^2 + bp_0 + c)^{3/2}}, \tag{28}$$

$$R_3 = \frac{3(2ap_0 + b)^2}{p_0^{(T-3)/2}(ap_0^2 + bp_0 + c)^{5/2}}, \tag{29}$$

$$R_4 = -\frac{4a}{p_0^{(T-3)/2}(ap_0^2 + bp_0 + c)^{3/2}}. \tag{30}$$

Having obtained the expression for the integrand in (26), we now need to examine carefully the region $\mathfrak{D}$. Indeed, since $L(\theta_1, \theta_2, u - \theta_1 x_1 - \theta_2 x_2)$ is analytic in $\mathring{E}$, every contour in the integral (12) can be deformed in a rather arbitrary manner by replacing it with a rectifiable curve, provided this second path of integration is obtainable by a deformation of the vertical lines that does not require moving it through any singularities (poles or branch cuts) of the Laplace transform. This is also the case for the region $\mathfrak{D}$, and we shall now examine curve Γ_w.

2.2 Curve Γ_w

In order to compute the integral (26), we now need to consider in some detail the domain $\mathfrak{D}$. To this purpose, recall some well-known properties of the function defined by

$$\zeta(w) = w + 1/w$$

in the complex domain $\mathbf{C}$.[6]

The function $\zeta(w)$ is analytic in $\mathbf{C} - \{0\}$ with a simple pole at $w = 0$. If $w = re^{i\theta}$ $(r > 0)$, $\zeta(w) = u + iv$, it follows that

$$u = (r + 1/r) \cos \theta, \qquad v = (r - 1/r) \sin \theta.$$

The image under ζ of the circle $|w| = r$ is the ellipse of foci ± 2 and semi-axes $r + (1/r)$, $|r - (1/r)|$ for $r \neq 1$. For $r = 1$, the image under ζ of the unit circle $|w| = 1$ degenerates into the segment of endpoints ± 2. In addition, the image under ζ of a half line $r \to re^{i\theta}$ $(r > 0)$ is (for θ distinct from 0, $\pm \pi/2$ and π) a branch of a hyperbola of foci ± 2. On the other hand, since $\zeta(1/w) = \zeta(w)$, the image under ζ of the open unit disc $|w| < 1$ less the point 0, denoted as Ω, is identical to the image of the exterior of the unit disc $|w| > 1$. The function $\zeta(w)$ is a conformal mapping of either Ω or the exterior of the unit disc $|w| > 1$ onto $\Lambda = \mathbf{C} - \{[-2, 2]\}$ (the plane "cut" along the segment of endpoints ± 2).

At this point, it is crucial to make a distinction between the case where $|x_1| < 1$ and $|x_1| > 1$. Indeed, since $\hat{\alpha}$ is not the maximum-likelihood estimator of α, there is nothing in the ordinary least-squares (OLS) procedure that prevents $|\hat{\alpha}|$ from being greater than 1. As we shall see in what follows, the case where $|x_1| > 1$ is more complicated to treat than the case where $|x_1| < 1$.

---

[6] See, e.g., Dieudonné (1971).

First consider the case where $|x_1| < 1$. To see which path in the "punctured disc" Ω corresponds to a "legal" path in the θ_1 plane, examine the change of variables in (13) with $\theta_3 = u - \theta_1 x_1 - \theta_2 x_2$ and $u = 0$, that is,

$$w + \frac{1}{w} = \frac{1 + \alpha^2 - 2\theta_2(1 - x_2) - 2\theta_1 x_1}{\alpha + \theta_1}, \tag{31}$$

which gives

$$\theta_1 = \frac{[1 + \alpha^2 - 2\theta_2(1 - x_2) - 2\alpha x_1]w}{w^2 - 2x_1 w + 1} - \alpha. \tag{32}$$

This last expression corresponds to the successive transformations

$$\theta_1 = \frac{1 + \alpha^2 - 2\theta_2(1 - x_2) - 2\alpha x_1}{\zeta - 2x_1} - \alpha \tag{33}$$

and

$$\zeta = w + 1/w.$$

Now, writing (33) as

$$\zeta - 2x_1 = \frac{1 + \alpha^2 - 2\theta_2(1 - x_2) - 2\alpha x_1}{\alpha + \theta_1}$$

and putting $\theta_1 = \epsilon_1 + i\eta_1$, $\theta_2 = \epsilon_2 + i\eta_2$, for any permissible value ϵ_1, $\zeta \to 2x_1$ when $\eta_1 \to \infty$. It is not difficult to see that the limiting value $\zeta = 2x_1$ corresponds in the w plane to the points $x_1 \pm i(1 - x_1^2)^{1/2}$.

In addition, on examining the preceding transformations, it will be seen that the "punctured disc" Ω is mapped on the whole θ_1 plane cut along the parts of the real axis exterior to the interval

$$\left[-\frac{(1 + \alpha)^2 - 2\epsilon_2(1 - x_2)}{2(1 + x_1)}, \frac{(1 - \alpha)^2 - 2\epsilon_2(1 - x_2)}{2(1 - x_1)} \right].$$

To summarize the discussion so far on the integration paths, any "legal" path in the θ_1 plane running from $c_1 - i\infty$ through the gap in the real axis to $c_1' - i\infty$ corresponds to a path in Ω running from $x_1 - i(1 - x_1^2)^{1/2}$ to $x_1 + i(1 - x_1^2)^{1/2}$.

If we now return to the expression for the joint density of X_1 and X_2 given in (26), the presence of $(w^2 - 2x_1 w + 1)^{(T-3)/2}$ suggests the use of the saddlepoint method.[7] More precisely, for evaluating (29), choose a path of integration running from $x_1 - i(1 - x_1^2)^{1/2}$ to $x_1 + i(1 - x_1^2)^{1/2}$ and corresponding to the path of steepest descent. As is well known, this corresponds to a path passing through the saddlepoint of the integrand

---

[7] For a description of the application of the saddlepoint method in statistics and econometrics, see Daniels (1954, 1956), Phillips (1978), and Holly and Phillips (1979).

$(w^2 - 2x_1 w + 1)^{(T-3)/2}$ and such that the imaginary part of $w^2 - 2x_1 w + 1$ is constant. It is easy to verify that the integrand has a saddlepoint at $w = x_1$, through which the path of steepest descent is the straight line joining the points $x_1 - i(1 - x_1^2)^{1/2}$ and $x_1 + i(1 - x_1^2)^{1/2}$. We shall parameterize this path by t with $t \in \,]-1, 1[$ and $w = x_1 + it(1 - x_1^2)^{1/2}$. Obviously, this corresponds to a new change in variables, with $dw = i(1 - x_1^2)^{1/2} \, dt$. More specifically, the expression for the joint density of x_1 and x_2 may now be written as

$$f_{X_1, X_2}(x_1, x_2) = \frac{(1 - \alpha^2)^{1/2}(1 - x_1^2)^{(T-2)/2}}{4\pi^2} \int_{\theta_2 = -i\infty}^{+i\infty} \int_{t=-1}^{1}$$
$$\times [(1 - t^2)^{(T-3)/2}(1 - w^2)^{3/2}(R_1 + R_2 + R_3 + R_4)] \, d\theta_2 \, dt,$$
(34)

where now w is replaced by $x_1 + it(1 - x_1^2)^{1/2}$.[8]

Now consider the case where $|x_1| > 1$. Putting as before $\theta_1 = \epsilon_1 + i\eta_1$, $\theta_2 = \epsilon_2 + i\eta_2$ and applying the same arguments as before, it is easy to verify that Ω is now mapped on the whole θ_1 plane cut along the segment

$$\left[\frac{(1 - \alpha)^2 - 2\epsilon_2(1 - x_2)}{2(1 - x_1)} ; \frac{-(1 - \alpha)^2 + 2\epsilon_2(1 - x_2)}{2(1 + x_1)} \right].$$

We also see that for any permissible value ϵ_1, $\zeta \to 2x_1$, where $\eta_1 \to \infty$. However, in contrast with the previous case, the limiting value $\zeta = 2x_1$ now corresponds in the w plane to two points in the real axis $x_1 \pm (x_1^2 - 1)^{1/2}$. One of these points is in Ω, and the other one is in the exterior of the unit disc $|w| > 1$. Therefore, whether we restrict w to lie in Ω or not, the integration path Γ_w is necessarily a closed contour starting from and arriving to one of the preceding points. If we assume that $w \in \Omega$, we cannot apply the saddlepoint method, since the integrand has a saddlepoint at $w = x_1$ that belongs to the exterior of the unit disc $|w| > 1$. We therefore need to find a convenient closed path Γ_w lying in Ω.

This version is incomplete since we do not present the more convenient integration path Γ_w. We hope to be able to present in the near future a solution to the case where $|\hat{\alpha}|$ takes values greater than 1.

3   Saddlepoint approximation

The results presented in the previous section were exact. As in Daniels (1956) and Phillips (1978), we can derive an approximation to the distribution of the t ratio test statistic by neglecting the term $N_2(19)$. This

---

[8] At this point, it should be noted that on examining expressions (3) and (34), if α is changed to $-\alpha$, $f_t(\tau)$ is changed to $f_t(-\tau)$. In other words, the true density of the t ratio test statistic is symmetric.

approximation is justified by the fact that w belongs to the open unit disc $|w| < 1$ (less the point 0).

Similarly, neglecting the factor terms of w^{2T} in the expressions for a, b, and c and defining

$$b_a = [1 - 2\theta_2 - (2\theta_2 - \alpha^2)w^2](w^2 - 2x_1 w + 1), \tag{35}$$

$$c_a = (2\theta_2 - \alpha^2)(1 - 2\theta_2)(w^2 - 2x_1 w + 1)^2, \tag{36}$$

$$B_a(u) = [-w^2 p^2(u) + b_a p(u) + c_a]^{-1/2}, \tag{37}$$

$$R_1^a = \frac{(T-3)(T-1)}{p_0^{(T+1)/2}(-w^2 p_0^2 + b_a p_0 + c_a)^{1/2}}, \tag{38}$$

$$R_2^a = \frac{2(T-3)(-2w^2 p_0 + b_a)}{p_0^{(T-1)/2}(-w^2 p_0^2 + b_a p_0 + c_a)^{3/2}}, \tag{39}$$

$$R_3^a = \frac{3(-2w^2 p_0 + b_a)^2}{p_0^{(T-3)/2}(-w^2 p_0^2 + b_a p_0 + c_a)^{5/2}}, \tag{40}$$

$$R_4^a = \frac{4w^2}{p_0^{(T-3)/2}(-w^2 p_0^2 + b_a p_0 + c_a)^{3/2}}, \tag{41}$$

we obtain, similarly to (34), the following approximate density function of the joint distribution of X_1 and X_2,

$$f_{X_1, X_2}^a(x_1, x_2) = \frac{(1-\alpha^2)(1-x_1^2)^{(T-2)/2}}{4\pi^2} \int_{\theta_2 = -i\infty}^{+i\infty} \int_{t=-1}^{1}$$
$$\times (1-t^2)^{(T-3)/2}(1-w^2)^{3/2}(R_1^a + R_2^a + R_3^a + R_4^a)\, d\theta_2\, dt, \tag{42}$$

where w is replaced by $x_1 + it(1-x_1^2)^{1/2}$.

We now define

$$\phi(w) = (1-w^2)^{3/2} R_1^a [1 + (R_2^a/R_1^a) + (R_3^a/R_1^a) + (R_4^a/R_1^a)]. \tag{43}$$

We now expand $\phi(w)$ in a Taylor series about the value $w = x_1$ and integrate term by term in (42). Taking into account the expression for R_1^a, R_2^a, R_3^a and R_4^a, it is not difficult to show that a first approximation to $f_{X_1, X_2}^a(x_1, x_2)$ is

$$f_{(X_1, X_2)}^a(x_1, x_2) \sim f_{(X_1, X_2)}^{aa}(x_1, x_2)[1 + O(T^{-1})],$$

where

$$f_{X_1, X_2}^{aa}(x_1, x_2) = \frac{(T-3)(T-1)(1-\alpha^2)^{1/2}(1-x_1^2)^{(T+1)/2}\Gamma[(T-1)/2]}{4\pi^{3/2}\Gamma(T/2)}$$
$$\times \int_{-i\infty}^{+i\infty} \frac{d\theta_2}{\mathfrak{D}(\alpha, \theta_2, x_1, x_2)}, \tag{44}$$

$$\mathfrak{D}(\alpha, \theta_2, x_1, x_2) = p_0^{(T+1)/2}\{-x_1^2 p_0^2 + [1 - 2\theta_2 - (2\theta_2 - \alpha^2)x_1^2](1 - x_1^2)p_0$$
$$+ (2\theta_2 - \alpha^2)(1 - 2\theta_2)(1 - x_1^2)^2\}^{1/2}. \qquad (45)$$

Now, similarly as for the exact distribution, we obtain the following saddlepoint approximation of the density of the t ratio test statistic

$$f_t^a(\tau) = 2(T-1) \int_{\mathfrak{D}(u_2)} u_2^2 f_{X_1, X_2}^{aa}[\tau u_2 + \alpha, (T-1)u_2^2 + (\tau u_2 + \alpha)^2] \, du_2.$$

As shown in this chapter, it is possible to obtain integral expressions for both the exact distribution and a saddlepoint approximation of the t ratio test statistic in an AR(1) model. One of our objectives is to compute these densities by numerical integration. We have outlined some of the difficulties encountered, but believe we can solve them in the very near future and expect to publish numerical results very soon.

Appendix

This appendix derives the expression for the determinant of matrices of order $T \times T$ of the form

$$G_T = \begin{pmatrix} b & d & 0 & \cdots & 0 & 0 \\ d & b & d & \cdots & 0 & 0 \\ \vdots & \vdots & \vdots & \ddots & \vdots & \vdots \\ 0 & 0 & 0 & \cdots & b & d \\ 0 & 0 & 0 & \cdots & d & c \end{pmatrix}.$$

We obtain the expression for $\det g_T$ by replacing b, d, and c by β, δ, and $1 - 2\xi_2$, respectively.

Note that if we delete the first row and column of G_T, the remaining $(T-1) \times (T-1)$ matrix is of the same form as G_T, so we denote this matrix as G_{T-1}. Similarly, we denote G_{T-2} as the resulting matrix when the first two rows and columns are eliminated from G_T. Expanding $\det G_T$ on the first row yields

$$\det G_T = b \det G_{T-1} - d^2 \det G_{T-2}.$$

We shall now look for solutions of this difference equation of the form $\det G_T = \lambda^T$. Clearly, λ is a zero of the following second-degree polynomial:

$$\lambda^2 - b\lambda + d^2 = 0.$$

Therefore, provided $b^2 > 4d^2$, $\det G_T$ is of the form

$$\det G_T = A\lambda_1^T + B\lambda_2^T, \qquad (A.1)$$

where

$$\lambda_{1,2} = \tfrac{1}{2}[b \pm (b^2 - 4d^2)^{1/2}].$$

Using the initial conditions $\det G_0 = 1$ and $\det G_1 = c$,

$$A = \tfrac{1}{2}[1 + (2c - b)(b^2 - 4d^2)^{-1/2}], \tag{A.2}$$

$$B = \tfrac{1}{2}[1 - (2c - b)(b^2 - 4d^2)^{-1/2}]. \tag{A.3}$$

Now using the fact that $\lambda_1 + \lambda_2 = b$ and $\lambda_1 + \lambda_2 = (b^2 - 4d^2)^{1/2}$, it is easy to verify that A and B may be written as

$$A = \frac{c \doteq \lambda_2}{\lambda_1 - \lambda_2}, \qquad B = \frac{\lambda_1 - c}{\lambda_1 - \lambda_2}. \tag{A.4}$$

It follows from (A.1) and (A.4) that

$$\det G_T = \frac{1}{\lambda_1 - \lambda_2}[c(\lambda_1^T - \lambda_2^T) + \lambda_1 \lambda_2 (\lambda_2^{T-1} - \lambda_1^{T-1})]. \tag{A.5}$$

REFERENCES

Bochner, S. and W. T. Martin. 1948. *Several Complex Variables.* Princeton, NJ: Princeton University Press.

Daniels, H. E. 1954. "Saddlepoint Approximation in Statistics." *Annals of Mathematical Statistics* 25: 631–50.

———. 1956. "The Approximate Distribution of Serial Correlation Coefficients." *Biometrika* 43: 169–85.

Dieudonné, J. 1971. *Infinitesimal Calculus.* Paris: Hermann.

Fuks, B. A. 1963. *Introduction to the Theory of Analytic Functions of Several Complex Variables.* Providence, RI: American Mathematical Society.

Holly, A. and P. C. B. Phillips. 1979. "A Saddlepoint Approximation to the Distribution of the *k*-Class Estimator of a Coefficient in a Simultaneous System." *Econometrica* 47: 1527–47.

Nankervis, J. C. and N. E. Savin. 1984. "The Student's *t* Approximation in a Stationary First Order Autoregressive Model." Mimeo, City of London Polytechnic.

———. 1985. "Testing the Autoregressive Parameter with the *t* Statistics." *Journal of Econometrics* 27: 143–61.

Phillips, P. C. B. 1976. "Supplement to 'Large Deviation Expansions Applied to Tail Probabilities in a First Order Stochastic Difference Equation'." Mimeo, University of Birmingham.

———. 1977. "Approximations to Some Finite Sample Distributions Associated with a First Order Stochastic Difference Equation." *Econometrica* 45: 463–86.

———. 1978. "Edgeworth and Saddlepoint Approximations in the First-Order Noncircular Autoregression." *Biometrika* 65: 91–8.

Tanaka, K. 1983. "Asymptotic Expansions Associated with the AR(1) Model with Unknown Mean." *Econometrica* 51: 1221–31.

CHAPTER 10

The use of ARIMA models in unobserved-components estimation: an application to Spanish monetary control

Agustín Maravall

Time series analysts (often "econometricians") working in institutions involved with economic policy making or short-term economic analysis face two important professional demands: forecasting and unobserved components estimation (including seasonal adjustment). Estimation of unobserved components is overwhelmingly done in practice by using ad hoc filters; the most popular example is estimation of the seasonally adjusted series with the X11 or X11 ARIMA program.

Concerning forecasting, the decade of the seventies witnessed the proliferation of autoregressive integrated moving-average (ARIMA) models (Box and Jenkins 1970), which seemed to capture well the evolution of many series. Since this evolution is related to the presence of trend, seasonal, and noise variation, the possibility of using ARIMA models in the context of unobserved components was soon recognized. Since the early work of Grether and Nerlove (1970) on stationary series, several approaches have been suggested. I shall concentrate on one that is becoming, in my opinion, a powerful statistical tool in applied time series work [starting references are Cleveland and Tiao (1976) and Box, Hillmer, and Tiao (1978); more recent references are Bell and Hillmer (1984) and Maravall and Pierce (1987)]. In the context of an application related to the control of the Spanish money supply, I shall address the issues of model specification, estimation of the components, diagnostic checking of the results, and inference drawing.

1   Model specification

Let an observed series z_t be the sum of several independent components:

$$z_t = \sum_i z_{it}. \tag{1.1}$$

Let the ith component and the overall observed series follow the ARIMA processes:

$$z_{it} = \psi_i(B)a_{it}, \qquad \psi_i(B) = \theta_i(B)/\phi_i(B) \qquad [a_{it} \sim \text{n.i.i.d. } (0, \sigma_i^2)] \qquad (1.2)$$

and

$$z_t = \psi(B)a_t, \qquad \psi(B) = \theta(B)/\phi(B) \qquad [a_t \sim \text{n.i.i.d. } (0, \sigma_a^2)], \qquad (1.3)$$

where n.i.i.d. stands for normally identically independently distributed.

Although the approach can handle more general cases, I shall concentrate on the usual decomposition of a series z_t into trend (p_t), seasonal (s_t), and irregular (u_t) components:

$$z_t = p_t + s_t + u_t, \qquad (1.4)$$

where the three components are independent. Often, the two components p_t and u_t are considered jointly, so that z_t is decomposed as in

$$z_t = z_t^a + s_t, \qquad (1.5)$$

where $z_t^a = p_t + u_t$ is the seasonally adjusted series. Since u_t may be such that erratic short-term movements render the seasonally adjusted series a poor indicator of the underlying evolution of the series, trend estimation has often been recommended as an alternative or complement to seasonal adjustment. I consider, thus, separate estimation of p_t and u_t. By comparing the properties of the estimators of p_t and of z_t^a, some light will be shed on the relative virtues of using either of the two components.

In practice, at institutions such as the Bank of Spain, many hundreds of series are routinely decomposed as in (1.4) or (1.5), and it is impossible to perform a detailed univariate analysis of each series. There is, thus, a need for a standard model that approximates reasonably well a large number of series and hence that can be applied routinely. Besides this practical reason, when dealing with a large collection of time series, there are also a priori theoretical reasons for using some type of "common central model," perhaps letting just a few parameters differ across the series (Sims 1985).

An obvious candidate among ARIMA models is the airline model of Box and Jenkins (1970), given by

$$\nabla\nabla_{12}z_t = (1 - \theta_1 B)(1 - \theta_{12}B^{12})a_t, \qquad (1.6)$$

which has been found to approximate many series encountered in practice characterized by the presence of trend and seasonal variation. The model (1.6) contains three parameters. Since $\theta_1 = 1$ implies a deterministic trend and $\theta_{12} = 1$ implies a deterministic seasonal component, θ_1 and θ_{12} are related to the stability of the trend and seasonal components, respectively. The third parameter, σ_a^2, provides a measure of the size of the one-period-ahead forecast error. When $-1 < \theta_1 < 1$ and $0 < \theta_{12} < 1$, the model accepts a decomposition as in (1.4) (Hillmer and Tiao 1982).

The discussion will be clearer if we focus on a particular example. Consider the monetary aggregate targeted in Spanish monetary policy: the series of liquid assets in the hands of the public (the sum of currency, deposits in banks and savings institutions, and other liquid assets). Estimation of (1.6) for the logarithm of the monthly series, using the period 1973–85 ($T = 156$), yields $\theta_1 = -0.1915$ (SE $= 0.080$), $\theta_{12} = 0.6228$ (SE $= 0.069$), and $\sigma_a^2 = 0.138 \times 10^{-4}$. (The standard error of the one-period-ahead forecast is approximately equal to 0.37 percent of the level of the series.) The residual autocorrelation function (ACF) is relatively clean, and for example, the Box–Pierce–Ljung statistic for the first 24 autocorrelations is equal to 20.6, well below the critical value $\chi_{22}^2(0.05) = 33.9$.

The spectrum of the estimated model for z_t is given in Figure 1, part A. It displays peaks for the frequencies $\omega = 0$, associated with the trend, and $\omega = j\pi/6$, $j = 1, \ldots, 6$, associated with the one- to six-times-a-year seasonal frequencies. Writing $\nabla\nabla_{12} = \nabla^2 S$, where $S = 1 + B + \cdots + B^{11}$, the peak for $\omega = 0$ is induced by the factor ∇^2, whereas the peaks for $\omega = j\pi/6$, $j = 1, \ldots, 6$, are induced by the unit roots of S. Therefore, the models for the trend, seasonal, and irregular components will be of the type $\nabla^2 p_t = \alpha(B)b_t$, $Ss_t = \beta(B)c_t$, and u_t white noise, where $\alpha(B)$ and $\beta(B)$ are polynomials in B of finite order. From (1.4) and (1.6), consistency with the overall model implies

$$\theta(B)a_t = S\alpha(B)b_t + \nabla^2\beta(B)c_t + \nabla\nabla_{12}u_t, \tag{1.7}$$

where $\theta(B) = (1 - \theta_1 B)(1 - \theta_{12}B^{12})$. Since the left side of (1.7) is a moving average of order 13, we can set $\alpha(B)$ to be of order 2 and $\beta(B)$ to be of order 11, so that the three terms on the right side are also of order 13. Therefore, the models for the components are of the type

$$\nabla^2 p_t = (1 - \alpha_1 B - \alpha_2 B^2)b_t, \tag{1.8a}$$

$$Ss_t = (1 - \beta_1 B - \cdots - \beta_{11}B^{11})c_t, \tag{1.8b}$$

$$u_t \sim \text{white noise}, \tag{1.8c}$$

and for the seasonally adjusted series, the identity $z_t^a = p_t + u_t$ implies that z_t^a is an IMA(2, 2) model, say,

$$\nabla^2 z_t^a = (1 - \lambda_1 B - \lambda_2 B^2)d_t, \tag{1.8d}$$

where λ_1, λ_2, and σ_d^2 can be obtained from the models for p_t and u_t.

Equating the variance and autocovariances of the left and right sides of (1.7), a system of 14 equations is obtained. These equations express the

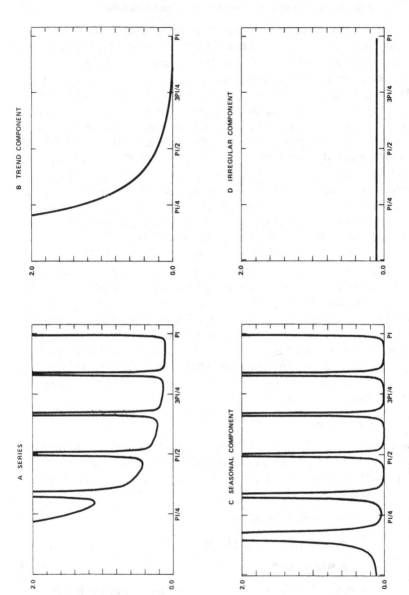

Figure 1. Spectra of series and components.

relationship between the parameters of the overall model and the unknown parameters in the components models. Since the number of the latter is 16 ($\alpha_1, \alpha_2, \beta_1, \ldots, \beta_{11}, \sigma_b^2, \sigma_c^2,$ and σ_u^2), there is an infinite number of structures of the type (1.8) that are compatible with the same model (1.6). The identification problem is similar to the one that appears in standard econometric models. The model for the observed series is the reduced form, whereas the models for the components represent the associated structural form. For a particular reduced form, there are an infinite number of structures from which it can be generated. In order to select one, additional information has to be incorporated. The traditional approach in econometrics has been to set a priori some parameters in the structural model equal to zero, rationalized as reflecting a priori economic theory information. In the case of our unobserved-components model, such a priori information is not available. We follow instead an alternative approach originally suggested by Box et al. (1978) and Pierce (1978). The additional information will be the requirement that separable white noise should not be a part of either the trend or the seasonal component and should go to the irregular component. The variance of the irregular component is thus maximized, and the resulting decomposition has been termed "canonical" by Hillmer and Tiao (1982). These two authors and Burman (1980) have developed methods for estimating the canonical components. For the case of the airline model, both methods imply the same decomposition.

Without loss of generality, let $\sigma_a^2 = 1$. All variances will then be expressed in units of σ_a^2. For $\theta_1 = -0.1915$, $\theta_{12} = 0.6228$, the models obtained for the components are

$$\nabla^2 p_t = (1 + 0.039B - 0.961B^2)b_t$$
$$= (1 + B)(1 - 0.961B)b_t, \tag{1.9a}$$

$$\nabla^2 z_t^a = (1 - 0.779B - 0.175B^2)d_t$$
$$= (1 + 0.182B)(1 - 0.961B)d_t, \tag{1.9b}$$

and

$$Ss_t = (1 + 2.019B + 2.487B^2 + 2.619B^3 + 2.481B^4 + 2.182B^5 + 1.800B^6$$
$$+ 1.365B^7 + 0.972B^8 + 0.568B^9 + 0.310B^{10} - 0.032B^{11})c_t. \tag{1.9c}$$

Furthermore, the innovation variances are given by

$$\sigma_b^2 = 0.234; \qquad \sigma_c^2 = 0.053; \qquad \sigma_u^2 = 0.108; \qquad \sigma_d^2 = 0.670. \tag{1.10}$$

Thus, for example, the irregular component variance is approximately 10 percent of the one-step-ahead forecast error variance, and hence the ran-

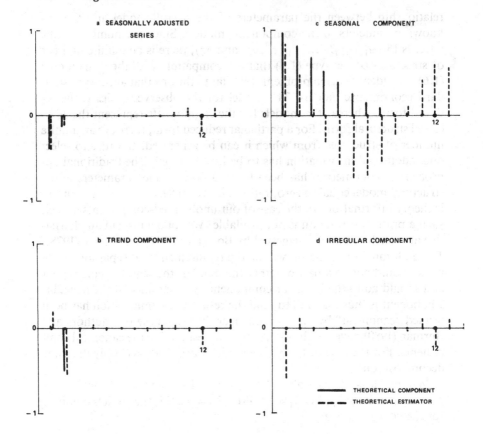

Figure 2. ACF of theoretical component and estimator.

dom character of the trend and seasonal components contributes heavily to the error in forecasting the overall series z_t.

The spectra of the components p_t, s_t, and u_t are displayed in Figure 1. (The spectrum of z_t^a is that of p_t plus a constant.) The ACF of $\nabla^2 p_t$ and Ss_t are given by the continuous line in Figure 2. Looking at the factorization of $\alpha(B)$ in (1.9a), the root $1+B$ induces the zero in the spectrum for $\omega = \pi$. The second root $1-0.961B$ is close to $1-B$ and hence nearly cancels out with one of the ∇'s on the right side of (1.9a). Therefore, the model for the trend can be rewritten as

$$\nabla p_t = (1+B)b_t + \delta,$$

where δ is a slowly changing parameter. Similarly, the seasonally adjusted series follows the model

$$\nabla z_t^a = (1 + 0.182B)d_t + \delta,$$

close to that of a random walk with a slowly changing drift. The model for the seasonal component is a relatively complicated expression. The zero in the spectrum is attained at the frequency $\omega = 0.9175\pi$, between the five- and six-times-a-year frequencies; the stationary component Ss_t displays a slowly decaying ACF.

Although the model for the trend depends on three parameters, the model for the seasonal component on 12, and the model for the irregular on 1, all those parameters are simply functions of θ_1 and θ_{12}. It can be seen that different values of θ_1 and θ_{12} have very little effect on the α-parameters of the trend component model and a moderate effect on the β-parameters of the model for the seasonal component. Different values of θ_1 and θ_{12}, however, have a strong effect on the variance of the component model innovations: More stable trends (i.e., larger values of θ_1) yield smaller values of σ_b^2, and more stable seasonal components (i.e., larger values of θ_{12}) yield smaller values of σ_c^2. Therefore, in terms of the structural parameters, different reduced-form parameters (θ_1 and θ_{12}) translate mostly into differences in the variances of the component model innovations, leaving the rest of the structure relatively unchanged. In general, the more random a component, the larger its innovation variance.

2   Estimation of components

2.1   *Minimum mean-squared error estimators*

Referring back to equations (1.2) and (1.3), when the information consists of a complete realization of z_t, denoted by $[z_t]$, the minimum mean-squared error (MMSE) estimator of the component z_{it} is given by

$$\hat{z}_{it} = k_i \frac{\psi_i(B)\psi_i(F)}{\psi(B)\psi(F)} z_t = \nu_i(B, F)z_t, \tag{2.1}$$

where $k_i = \sigma_i^2/\sigma_a^2$ and $F = B^{-1}$. Under our assumptions, this expression also yields the conditional mean $E(z_{it}|[z_t])$. The derivation of (2.1) for the stationary case can be found in Whittle (1963), and the extension to nonstationary series can be found in Cleveland and Tiao (1976) and Bell (1984).

For the airline model (1.6) and the component model of the type (1.8), writing for notational simplicity,

$$\theta = (1 - \theta_1 B)(1 - \theta_{12}B^{12}),$$

$$\alpha = 1 - \alpha_1 B - \alpha_2 B^2,$$

$$\beta = 1 - \beta_1 B - \cdots - \beta_{11} B^{11},$$

$$\lambda = 1 - \lambda_1 B - \lambda_2 B^2,$$

and letting a bar denote the same polynomial with B replaced by F, the filter $v_i(B,F)$ in (2.1) becomes

$$v_p(B,F) = k_b \frac{\alpha \bar{\alpha} S \bar{S}}{\theta \bar{\theta}} \qquad (2.2a)$$

for the trend component and

$$v_s(B,F) = k_c \frac{\alpha \bar{\alpha} \nabla^2 \bar{\nabla}^2}{\theta \bar{\theta}} \qquad (2.2b)$$

for the seasonal component. In the example we are analyzing, from (1.9) and (1.10) the two filters are easily obtained. They are centered and symmetric, and invertibility of the overall model guarantees convergence. The two filters are displayed in Figure 3.

The estimator of the irregular component is obtained as the residual, after the trend and seasonal component estimators have been removed. Hence,

$$\hat{u}_t = z_t - \hat{p}_t - \hat{s}_t = [1 - v_p(B,F) - v_s(B,F)]z_t, \qquad (2.3)$$

which eventually yields

$$\hat{u}_t = k_u \frac{\nabla \bar{\nabla} \nabla_{12} \bar{\nabla}_{12}}{\theta \bar{\theta}} z_t = k_u [\psi(B)\psi(F)]^{-1} z_t. \qquad (2.4)$$

Therefore, $\hat{u}_t$ estimated as the residual is the same as what would result from direct estimation using (2.1). More generally, it is irrelevant which two of the three components on the right side of (1.4) are estimated directly, leaving the third as the residual.

Returning to the Spanish money supply, estimates of the components were computed with a program developed by Burman and are displayed in Figure 4. (Notice that once the spectra of the components are known, the autocovariance functions are easily derived, and nothing more is needed to find the filters v_p and v_s. In particular, estimation of the components does not require the derivation of their ARIMA expressions.)

2.2   *Models for estimators*

Having derived expressions for the component models and for their MMSE estimators, by comparing the two it is seen that, as noted by Grether and Nerlove (1970), the model for a component is different from

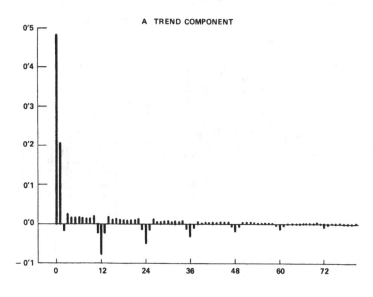

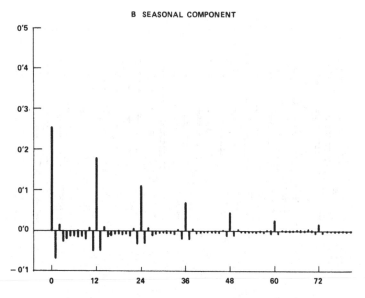

Figure 3. Filters for estimators.

A RATE OF GROWTH OF SEASONALLY ADJUSTED SERIES

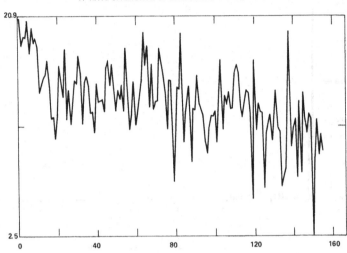

C SEASONAL COMPONENT

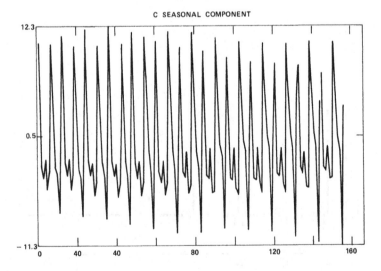

B RATE OF GROWTH OF TREND

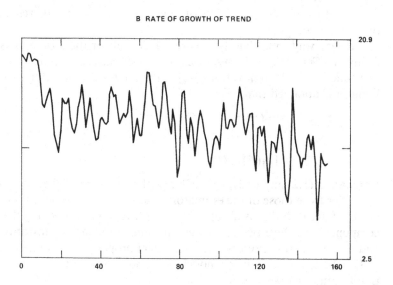

D IRREGULAR COMPONENT

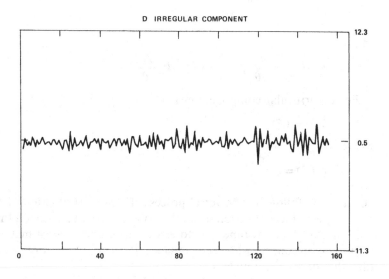

Figure 4. Estimated components.

the model for its estimator. It is of interest to look at the differences between the two.

An easy way to derive the theoretical model for the estimator is the following: Setting $z_t = \psi(B)a_t$ in (2.1), the estimator $\hat{z}_{it}$ can be expressed as a function of the innovations $[a_t]$ in the observed series. After simplifying, it is obtained that

$$\hat{z}_{it} = \psi_i(B)\eta_i(F)a_t, \tag{2.5}$$

where

$$\eta_i(F) = k_i[\psi_i(F)/\psi(F)]a_t. \tag{2.6}$$

Comparing (1.2) and (2.5), the ACF and the spectrum of the component will differ from those of the estimator because of the presence of $\eta_i(F)$ in (2.5), a filter in F that is always convergent. It is worth noticing that the component and the estimator require the same stationarity transformation and that estimation preserves the canonical property of a component.

For the case of the airline model, the expressions for the seasonal and trend estimators become

$$\nabla^2 \hat{p}_t = \alpha(B)\eta_p(F)a_t, \tag{2.7a}$$

$$S\hat{s}_t = \beta(B)\eta_s(F)a_t, \tag{2.7b}$$

where

$$\eta_p(F) = k_b \frac{\bar{\alpha}\bar{S}}{\bar{\theta}}, \qquad \eta_s(F) = k_c \frac{\bar{\beta}\bar{\nabla}^2}{\bar{\theta}}. \tag{2.8}$$

For the irregular component estimator

$$\hat{u}_t = \eta_u(F)a_t, \tag{2.9}$$

where

$$\eta_u(F) = k_u \frac{\bar{\nabla}\bar{\nabla}_{12}}{\bar{\theta}}, \tag{2.10}$$

and hence $\hat{u}_t$ follows the "inverse" process of the observed series. The estimator $\hat{u}_t$ is a linear function of innovations a_{t+j}, $j \geq 0$, so that although autocorrelated, at any time t, its forecast will be zero. The estimator $\hat{u}_t$ is seen to be stationary, with finite variance; this variance is always smaller than that of the theoretical u_t.

From expressions (2.7) to (2.10), ACFs and spectra of the theoretical estimators can be easily computed. For the example of the monetary aggregate series they are displayed in Figures 2 and 5, where they are compared to those of the theoretical components. Looking at the ACFs, it is seen that, for the seasonally adjusted series, MMSE estimation leaves practically unchanged the low-order autocorrelations, whereas it induces

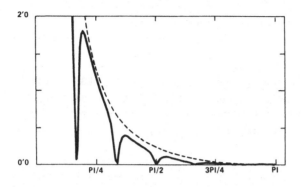

A TREND COMPONENT

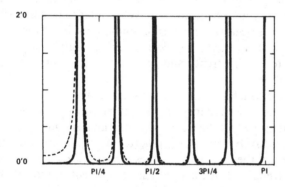

B SEASONAL COMPONENT

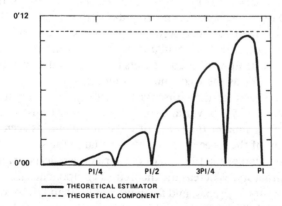

C IRREGULAR COMPONENT

THEORETICAL ESTIMATOR
THEORETICAL COMPONENT

Figure 5. Spectra of theoretical components and estimators.

Table 1. *Standard deviation of components*

	$\nabla^2 z_t^a$	$\nabla^2 p_t$	Ss_t	u_t
Theoretical component	1.05	0.67	1.38	0.33
Theoretical estimator	0.94	0.48	0.34	0.19

Note: $\mathrm{Corr}(\nabla^2\hat{p}_t, S\hat{s}_t) = 0.11$; $\mathrm{Corr}(\nabla^2\hat{p}_t, \hat{u}_t) = 0.06$; $\mathrm{Corr}(S\hat{s}_t, \hat{u}_t) = 0.05$.

some negative autocorrelation at lag 12. In the case of the trend, estimation lowers the value of ρ_1 and induces some negative autocorrelation at lag 12. For the seasonal component, the slow decay of the component ACF is replaced by a cycle of period 12 for the ACF of the estimator. In the case of the irregular component, the two ACFs differ markedly, with the estimator displaying negative autocorrelation at both low-order and seasonal lags. Finally, the negative autocorrelations at lag 12 induced in the seasonally adjusted series, trend, and irregular components are seen to be all equal to -0.19.

The spectra of the estimators display additional zeros that are implied by the unit roots in the denominators of the η_i filters. Let $\hat{g}_p(\omega)$, $\hat{g}_s(\omega)$, and $\hat{g}_u(\omega)$ denote the spectra of the trend, seasonal, and irregular component estimators, respectively. The zeros in $\hat{g}_p(\omega)$ and $\hat{g}_u(\omega)$ for the seasonal frequencies reflect the fact that, for these frequencies, the ratio of the variance of the trend and of the irregular component to that of the seasonal component is zero. Therefore, these frequencies will be ignored when estimating the trend or the irregular component. Similarly, the zero in $\hat{g}_s(\omega)$ and $\hat{g}_u(\omega)$ for $\omega = 0$ is explained by the fact that, for $\omega = 0$, the ratio of the variance of the seasonal or the irregular to that of the trend is zero. In relative terms, the difference between the two spectra is particularly noticeable for the case of the irregular component estimator, which is far from white noise. Its upward shape reflects the predominance of the trend component variance as the frequency becomes lower.

In all cases, the spectrum of the estimator lies below the spectrum of the component. Accordingly, the variance of the (stationary transformation of the) estimator is smaller than that of the component, as seen in Table 1. Since the sum of the three components is equal to the sum of the three estimators, the difference in the sum of the variances reflects covariances among the estimators. Whereas the theoretical components are uncorrelated, the estimators $\nabla^2\hat{p}_t$, $S\hat{s}_t$, and $\hat{u}_t$, in view of (2.7) and (2.9), will be correlated in general. These correlations can easily be computed and are also displayed in Table 1. Although nonzero, the correlations between the estimators are nevertheless small.

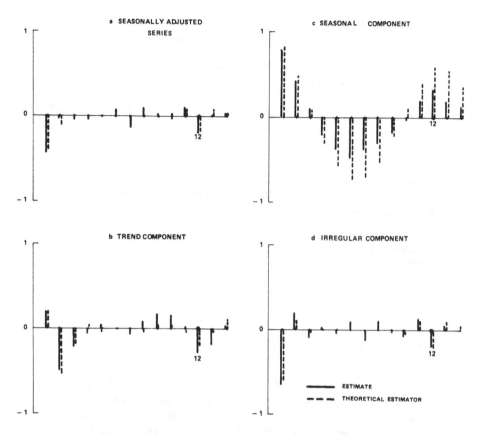

Figure 6. ACF of theoretical estimator and estimated components.

3   Diagnosis and inference

3.1   *Diagnosis*

An important virtue of a model-based approach to unobserved-compo-
nent estimation is that it provides the grounds for diagnostic checks by
comparing theoretical models with the obtained estimates. As we have
seen, the theoretical model to use in the comparison should be that of the
estimator, which can be quite different from that of the theoretical component.

Figure 6 exhibits the ACF of the stationary transformations of the theoretical estimators, derived from (2.7) and (2.9), and compares them with
the empirical ACF of the component estimates for the monetary aggregate series. For the seasonally adjusted series and the trend and irregular

Table 2. *Component moments: simulation*

	$\nabla^2 \hat{z}_t^a$	$\nabla^2 \hat{p}_t$	$S\hat{s}_t$	$\hat{u}_t$
(a) Lag-1 autocorrelation (ρ_1)				
Simulation	−0.39	0.18	0.84	−0.59
	(0.07)	(0.06)	(0.02)	(0.06)
Theoretical estimator	−0.40	0.18	0.83	−0.60
Estimate	−0.44	0.21	0.81	−0.64
(b) Lag-12 autocorrelation (ρ_{12})				
Simulation	−0.22	−0.22	0.52	−0.22
	(0.08)	(0.08)	(0.16)	(0.08)
Theoretical estimator	−0.19	−0.19	0.62	−0.19
Estimate	−0.19	−0.27	0.31	−0.18
(c) Standard deviation				
Simulation	0.96	0.49	0.33	0.19
	(0.04)	(0.03)	(0.06)	(0.01)
Theoretical estimator	0.94	0.48	0.34	0.19
Estimate	0.90	0.44	0.22	0.18

Note: Numbers in parentheses are standard errors.

components, the empirical and theoretical ACFs are in close agreement. In the case of the seasonal component, the shapes are also similar, although the empirical ACF dies off faster than the theoretical one.

In order for the comparison of the two ACFs to be meaningful, we need to have an idea of how close we can expect to get to the theoretical autocorrelations in a particular realization. To answer that question, 300 independent series were generated with the airline model with $\theta_1 = -0.1915$ and $\theta_{12} = 0.6228$. Each series consisted of 156 observations. The trend, seasonal, and irregular components were estimated, and the variance and ACF were computed for their stationary transformations. As shall be discussed in Section 3.2, the series of estimates obtained are contaminated at both ends by the replacement of starting and future observations by expectations. It was found, however, that the results changed very little when years were removed from both ends of the series, and the results reported are for the complete series of estimates.

The biases were found to be small, practically nonexistent for ρ_1 and for the variance, and slowly increasing for ρ_k as k gets larger. Table 2 reports the results for the estimators of ρ_1 and ρ_{12} and the standard deviation (σ) of the stationary transformation of the component estimators.

Table 2 displays also their theoretical values and the empirical estimates obtained for the monetary aggregate series. The comparison between the last rows in (a), (b), and (c) of Table 2 provides an overall check of the validity of the decomposition obtained. Considering the simulation results, the estimates obtained for the seasonally adjusted series, trend, and irregular components are comfortably in agreement with the theoretical estimators. For the seasonal component, however, both $\hat{\rho}_{12}$ and $\hat{\sigma}$ are borderline acceptable.

A similar simulation was carried out for a series half the length of the one considered in our example. The estimators had small biases and were reasonably precise. Comparison of the theoretical and empirical second moments of the stationary component estimators seems to provide a convenient, easy to compute check on the results. In the example we are considering, the check leads to (nonenthusiastic) acceptance of the results.

3.2   Inferences

An important issue of applied concern (see, e.g., Bach et al. 1976; Moore et al. 1981) is the error incurred in estimating the components. In the example we are considering of the Spanish monetary aggregate, since targets are set for the seasonally adjusted series, in order to judge whether targets are being met, it is important to know how accurately the seasonally adjusted series can be measured. Furthermore, the measurement error in the adjusted series should imply a range of tolerance for future targets. The model-based approach offers a convenient framework to address the issue (see, e.g., Pierce 1979, 1980; Hillmer 1985; Burridge and Wallis 1985).

There are several types of errors involved in the estimation of the components. Consider the estimator $\hat{z}_{it}$ given by (2.1). This is the final estimator of z_{it} obtainable when a complete realization of z_t is available. The error

$$\delta_{it} = z_{it} - \hat{z}_{it} \tag{3.1}$$

will be called the "final estimation error." The second type of error is related to the distortion induced at both ends of the component estimator series by the fact that starting and future values of the series are unknown. Direct inspection of the filters ν_p and ν_s in Figure 3 shows that the weight assigned to the observation z_T in the estimation of a component s_t or p_t is negligible when T and t are separated by more than 5 years [this is also evident from the results in Hillmer (1985)]. Considering the series length, the unknown starting values will only affect the early, distant years. We focus on the error induced by the lack of future observations, which shall be termed "revision error." As shown in Pierce (1980), the final estimation and the revision errors are independent of each other; therefore, I shall analyze the two separately.

(a)   *Final estimation error*

For notational simplicity, consider estimation of the first component. Equation (1.1) can be rewritten as

$$z_t = z_{1t} + Z_{1t},$$

where $Z_{1t} = \sum_{j \geq 2} z_{jt}$. Since all components follow ARIMA models, Z_{1t} will also be an ARIMA, and its expression will be of the type

$$\phi_1^* Z_{1t} = \theta_1^* g_t,$$

where g_t is white noise with variance σ_g^2, ϕ_1^* is the product of the AR polynomials of the components included in Z_{1t}, and θ_1^* is a moving average that can be obtained from the models for the components. Then it can be seen that (3.1) simplifies to

$$\delta_{1t} = \frac{\theta_1 \theta_1^*}{\theta} \epsilon_t, \tag{3.2}$$

where ϵ_t is white noise, with $\sigma_\epsilon^2 = \sigma_1^2 \sigma_g^2 / \sigma_a^2$ (Pierce 1979). Notice that the final estimation error for all components is an ARMA process, with the autoregressive polynomial always the same and equal to the moving-average polynomial of the model for the observed series. Since this model is invertible, the error will always be stationary.

For the airline model and the three-component decomposition (1.4), since it has to be that $\sum_i \delta_{it} = 0$, we need to consider final estimation errors of only two of the three components.

According to (3.2), the model for the final estimation error in the seasonally adjusted series can be expressed as

$$\theta \delta_{at} = \beta \lambda \epsilon_t.$$

Therefore, δ_{at} follows a stationay ARMA(13, 13) model with autoregressive polynomial $(1 - \theta_1 B)(1 - \theta_{12} B^{12})$; its ACF is displayed in the first column of Table 3, part (a).

To obtain the model for the trend final estimation error, we need the MA polynomial θ^* in the ARIMA representation of $Z_t = s_t + u_t$, which can be obtained by solving the system of covariance equations associated with $\theta^* g_t = \beta b_t + S u_t$. From (3.2), δ_{pt} then follows the model

$$\theta \delta_{pt} = \alpha \theta^* \epsilon_t,$$

again a stationary ARMA(13, 13) model. The ACF of δ_{pt} is displayed in the first column, part (b), of Table 3 and is remarkably close to that of

Table 3. *ACF of estimation errors*

Lag	Final estimation error	Revision error
(a) Seasonally adjusted series		
1	0.67	0.67
2	0.28	0.32
3	−0.03	0.03
4	−0.25	−0.20
5	−0.39	−0.35
6	−0.45	−0.43
7	−0.43	−0.44
8	−0.34	−0.37
9	−0.17	−0.22
10	0.06	0.01
11	0.36	0.33
12	0.63	0.63
(b) Trend		
1	0.68	0.61
2	0.24	0.35
3	−0.01	0.07
4	−0.20	−0.13
5	−0.32	−0.28
6	−0.37	−0.36
7	−0.35	−0.38
8	−0.27	−0.34
9	−0.13	−0.22
10	0.07	0.04
11	0.30	0.24
12	0.43	0.47

δ_{at}. These ACFs will be needed when computing the estimation error for alternative measures of the rate of change of a component.

Table 4 shows the variances of the final estimation error of the trend and of the seasonally adjusted series. They are similar, and in both cases, the standard deviation of the error is close to one-half of the standard deviation of the one-period-ahead forecast error of the overall series. In our example, the error in the final estimator of the seasonally adjusted series is of considerable size; however, no improvement in precision can be expected from using, alternatively, the trend.

(b)   *Revision error*
When estimating a component in order to obtain $\hat{z}_{it}$ by means of (2.1), a complete realization $[z_t]$ is needed. From (2.2), the filter v is convergent

Table 4. *Variance of estimation errors*

	Revision error	Error in final estimator	Total estimation error
Trend	0.231	0.217	0.448
Seasonally adjusted series	0.197	0.184	0.381

in B and in F; hence, it can be truncated. Still, at time T, when the last observation available is z_T, estimation of z_{it} for t close enough to T requires unknown future observations. As shown by Cleveland and Tiao (1976), a preliminary estimator can be obtained by applying (2.1) to the extended series $z_1, \ldots, z_T, \hat{z}_T(1), \hat{z}_T(2), \ldots$, where $\hat{z}_T(j)$ denotes the forecast of z_{T+j} with origin T. Accordingly, the preliminary estimator will be subject to revisions since, as new observations become available, forecasts will be updated and eventually replaced with observations. The difference between the preliminary and final estimator represents a measurement error in the former and will be called the revision error.

Consider first (concurrent) estimation of z_{it} at time t, the case of most applied interest. The revision in the concurrent estimator $\hat{z}_{it}^0$ is

$$r_{it}^0 = \hat{z}_{it} - \hat{z}_{it}^0 = \sum_{j=1}^{\infty} v_j(z_{t+j} - \hat{z}_t(j)) = \sum_{j=1}^{\infty} v_j e_t(j), \qquad (3.3)$$

where $e_t(j)$ denotes the jth period-ahead forecast error of z_t. From (1.3),

$$e_t(j) = a_{t+j} + \sum_{k=1}^{j-1} \psi_k a_{t+j-k},$$

and hence expression (3.3) can be rewritten as a moving average of future innovations $a_{t+1}, a_{t+2}, \ldots$. However, a more direct way of obtaining this moving-average representation is through the model derived for the estimators given by (2.5). Let $\zeta(B, F) = \psi_i(B)\eta_i(F)$. Then

$$\hat{z}_{it} = \zeta_i(B, F)a_t = \sum_{j=-\infty}^{\infty} \zeta_{ij} a_{t+j}. \qquad (3.4)$$

Since $E_t a_{t-j} = a_{t-j}$ for $j \geq 0$, and $E_t a_{t+j} = 0$ for $j > 0$, it follows that

$$\hat{z}_{it}^0 = E_t \hat{z}_{it} = \sum_{j=-\infty}^{0} \zeta_{ij} a_{t+j}, \qquad (3.5)$$

and subtracting (3.5) from (3.4), the revision is

$$r_{it}^0 = \sum_{j=1}^{\infty} \zeta_{ij} a_{t+j} = \zeta_i(F)a_{t+1}. \qquad (3.6)$$

Table 5. *Variance of revision error*

	r_t^0	r_t^{12}	r_t^{24}	r_t^{36}	r_t^{48}	r_t^{60}
Revision in trend	0.231	0.061	0.024	0.009	0.004	0.001
Revision in seasonally adjusted series	0.197	0.077	0.033	0.012	0.005	0.002

From expression (3.6) it is possible to derive properties of the revisions (Maravall 1986).

In a similar way, (3.4) can be used to derive the revision in any preliminary estimator. If $\hat{z}_{it}^n$ denotes the estimator of z_{it} obtained at time $t+n$ ($n \gtrless 0$),

$$\hat{z}_{it}^n = E_{t+n}\hat{z}_{it} = \sum_{j=-\infty}^{n} \zeta_{ij} a_{t+j},$$

and the revision in the preliminary estimator becomes

$$r_{it}^n = \hat{z}_{it} - \hat{z}_{it}^n = \sum_{j=n+1}^{\infty} \zeta_{ij} a_{t+j}. \tag{3.7}$$

Given that the filter $\zeta_i(B, F)$ is convergent in F, the revision is a stationary process. Notice that (3.7) implies that the change in the revision when the estimation period moves from T to $T+n$ is a moving average of order $n-1$ (Pierce 1980) and that updating an estimator when a new observation becomes available is equivalent to adding the last innovation multiplied by the corresponding ζ_i weight.

In the case of the airline model, from (2.7),

$$\zeta_p(B, F) = \frac{\alpha(B)\eta_p(F)}{\nabla^2}, \qquad \zeta_s(B, F) = \frac{\beta(B)\eta_s(F)}{S}, \tag{3.8}$$

where $\eta_p(F)$ and $\eta_s(F)$ are given in (2.8). For the particular example we are considering, Table 5 displays the variance of the revision in the concurrent estimator and of the revision after 1, 2, 3, 4, and 5 years of additional data have become available. It is seen that, after 5 years, the revision in the trend and in the seasonally adjusted series are negligible, so that the filter can be truncated safely. (In fact, more than 95 percent of the variance of the revision in the concurrent estimator of both components is explained by the first 3 years.)

Looking at Table 4, the revision error in the concurrent estimator of the trend is seen to be slightly larger than the revision in the concurrent estimator of the seasonal. For both components, the variance of the final estimation error is slightly smaller than that of the revision error. The two types of error in the estimators of the two components are all in the same approximate order of magnitude: The standard deviation of the error is close to 50 percent of the standard deviation of the innovations in the observed series.

One implication of the previous results is the following. In connection with the conduct of short-term monetary policy, Maravall and Pierce (1986) recently concluded, "why so much emphasis on seasonal adjustment? Perhaps attention should shift to estimation of a smoother signal less affected by revisions (possibly some type of trend)." For the case of the Spanish monetary aggregate the trend certainly provides a smoother signal, but it is not subject to smaller revisions, nor is it estimated with more precision. The trend estimator, in fact, performs slightly worse on both accounts.

Finally, seasonal adjustment of the Spanish monetary aggregate series has been done traditionally once a year instead of concurrently. This implies the use of the concurrent seasonal estimator for January and the projected seasonal components for the next 11 months. The variances of the revision error in the projected components are reported in Table 6. There is some gain from using concurrent adjustment: Averaging over the year, the improvement represents roughly a 15 percent reduction in the variance of the total estimation error.

4   Final remark: confidence intervals and rates of growth

I have analyzed the additive decomposition of the log of the series. The seasonal component obtained in this way is the log of the seasonal factor used in practice. Table 7 displays the confidence intervals (CIs) at the 95 and 67 percent levels for a seasonal factor estimated as 100. It is seen that the width of the 95 percent CI for the concurrent estimator represents 0.9 percent of the level of the series; for the 67 percent CI around the final estimator, the interval shortens to 0.32 percent.

Since targets are set for the rates of growth and not for the levels, it is of interest to see the effect of measurement error on the rates. The rate most widely used is the monthly rate of growth of the monthly series (annualized and expressed in percentage points); this rate is denoted T_{11}. Linearizing T_{11} and using Tables 3 and 4, the variances of the different measurement errors can be easily computed, and Table 8 presents the 95 percent CI for the concurrent and final estimator of the rate T_{11} for the seasonally adjusted series and for the trend. Roughly, the interval associated with the concurrent estimator is on the order of ± 5 percentage points, which narrows to ± 3 percentage points when the final estimator becomes available. If, for example, the T_{11} measured for the last month is 12 percent, the associated error implies that this measurement could be

Table 6. *Variance of revision error: seasonally adjusted series*

Revision in fore-casted component	Variance
Concurrent	0.197
1 month ahead	0.215
2 months ahead	0.246
3 months ahead	0.265
4 months ahead	0.274
5 months ahead	0.278
6 months ahead	0.279
7 months ahead	0.279
8 months ahead	0.282
9 months ahead	0.289
10 months ahead	0.305
11 months ahead	0.331

Table 7. *Confidence intervals around a seasonal factor of 100*

Level of confidence (%)	Concurrent estimator	Final estimator
95	99.54, 100.46	99.68, 100.32
67	99.78, 100.23	99.84, 100.16

Table 8. *Confidence interval for monthly rate of growth of monthly series (95% confidence level)*

	Concurrent estimator	Final estimator
Seasonally adjusted series	±4.45	±3.09
Trend	±5.02	±3.31

compatible with a true underlying growth between 7 and 17 percent, approximately. In other words, if the target for the present month growth is 12 percent, a measured growth between 7 and 17 percent could be taken as acceptable. The width of these intervals is unquestionably larger than

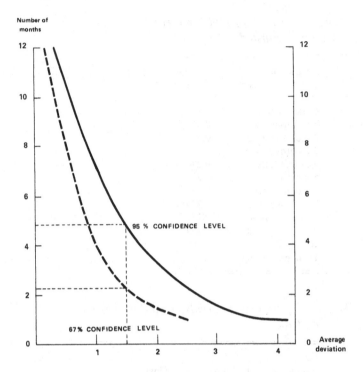

Figure 7. Average deviation in monthly rate of growth.

the tolerance ranges typically used in practice. Obviously, lowering the confidence level decreases the width of the interval: For example, the 67 percent CIs would be approximately one-half of those in Table 8.

Since the rate T_{11} of either the seasonally adjusted series or the trend is subject to large measurement errors, there is interest in attenuating its unreliability. One way to do this is to average consecutive T_{11} measures. For the seasonally adjusted series, Figure 7 shows the number of months needed to conclude that the target is not being met as a function of the average deviation with respect to the target. Thus, for example, if the average deviation is 1.5 percent, with a 67 percent confidence, it should have occurred over a period of at least 2 months in order to conclude that growth is significantly different from the one targeted. At the 95 percent level, at least 5 months would be needed.

Alternatively, rates different from T_{11} are also used. Of these, the most important is the monthly rate of growth of a 3-month moving average, annualized and expressed in percentage points. This rate is denoted T_{31}, and again, linearizing the rate and using Tables 3 and 4, it is possible to

Table 9. *Confidence interval for monthly rate of growth of 3-month moving average (95% confidence level)*

	Concurrent estimator	Final estimator
Seasonally adjusted series	±2.58	±1.82
Trend	±2.76	±1.96

estimate the associated measurement errors. Table 9 exhibits the 95 percent CI for the estimators of the T_{31} rate of the seasonally adjusted series and of the trend. The width of these intervals represents between 55 and 60 percent of the width of the intervals for the T_{11} rate.

Finally, I have emphasized the problems that estimation errors cause to the conduct of monetary policy. In terms of historical series, it is worth noticing that the standard deviation of the error in the final estimator of either component (seasonally adjusted series or trend) available with a 5-year delay represents (approximately) an annual growth of 1 percent, a small, yet not negligible, amount.

REFERENCES

Bach, G. L., P. D. Cagan, M. Friedman, C. G. Hildreth, F. Modigliani, and A. Okun. 1976. *Improving the Monetary Aggregates: Report of the Advisory Committee on Monetary Statistics.* Washington, DC: Board of Governors of the Federal Reserve System.

Bell, W. R. 1984. "Signal Extraction for Nonstationary Time Series." *Annals of Statistics* 12(2): 646-64.

Bell, W. R. and S. C. Hillmer. 1984. "Issues Involved with the Seasonal Adjustment of Economic Time Series." *Journal of Business and Economic Statistics* 2(4): 291-320.

Box, G. E. P., S. C. Hillmer, and G. C. Tiao. 1978. "Analysis and Modeling of Seasonal Time Series." In *Seasonal Analysis of Economic Time Series,* A. Zellner, Ed. Washington, DC: U.S. Department of Commerce, Bureau of the Census, pp. 309-34.

Box, G. E. P. and G. M. Jenkins. 1970. *Time Series Analysis: Forecasting and Control.* San Francisco: Holden Day.

Burman, J. P. 1980. "Seasonal Adjustment by Signal Extraction." *Journal of the Royal Statistical Society, Series A* 143: 321-37.

Burridge, P. and K. F. Wallis. 1985. "Calculating the Variance of Seasonally Adjusted Series." *Journal of the American Statistical Association* 80(391): 541-52.

Cleveland, W. P. and G. C. Tiao. 1976. "Decomposition of Seasonal Time Series: A Model for the X-11 Program." *Journal of the American Statistical Association* 71: 581-7.

Grether, D. M. and M. Nerlove. 1970. "Some Properties of 'Optimal' Seasonal Adjustment." *Econometrica* 38: 682–703.

Hillmer, S. C. 1985. "Measures of Variability for Model-Based Seasonal Adjustment Procedures." *Journal of Business and Economic Statistics* 3(1): 60–8.

Hillmer, S. C. and G. C. Tiao. 1982. "An ARIMA-Model Based Approach to Seasonal Adjustment." *Journal of the American Statistical Association* 77: 63–70.

Maravall, A. 1986. "Revisions in ARIMA Signal Extraction." *Journal of the American Statistical Association* 81: 736–40.

Maravall, A. and D. A. Pierce. 1986. "The Transmission of Data Noise into Policy Noise in U.S. Monetary Control." *Econometrica* 54(4): 961–79.

1987. "A Prototypical Seasonal Adjustment Model." *Journal of Time Series Analysis* 8: 177–93.

Moore, G. H., G. E. P. Box, H. B. Kaitz, J. A. Stephenson, and A. Zellner. 1981. *Seasonal Adjustment of the Monetary Aggregates: Report of the Committee of Experts on Seasonal Adjustment Techniques.* Washington, DC: Board of Governors of the Federal Reserve System.

Pierce, D. A. 1978. "Seasonal Adjustment When Both Deterministic and Stochastic Seasonality are Present." In *Seasonal Analysis of Economic Time Series,* A. Zellner, Ed. Washington, DC: U.S. Department of Commerce, Bureau of the Census, pp. 242–69.

1979. "Signal Extraction Error in Nonstationary Time Series." *Annals of Statistics* 7: 1303–20.

1980. "Data Revisions in Moving Average Seasonal Adjustment Procedures." *Journal of Econometrics* 14(1): 95–114.

Sims, C. A. 1985. "Comment on 'Issues Involved with the Seasonal Adjustment of Economic Times Series' by W. R. Bell and S. C. Hillmer." *Journal of Business and Economic Statistics* 3(1): 92–4.

Whittle, P. 1963. *Prediction and Regulation by Linear Least-Square Methods.* London: English Universities Press.

PART III

Chaotic attractor modeling

CHAPTER 11

The aggregation-theoretic monetary aggregates are chaotic and have strange attractors: an econometric application of mathematical chaos

William A. Barnett and Ping Chen

1 Introduction

A major methodological revolution is going on in the physical sciences at the present time as a result of dramatic recent advances in nonlinear dynamics.[1] During the past 10 years, the mathematics and physics literature on strange attractors, bifurcation theory, and deterministic chaos have acquired growing capabilities in many fields. Most of the major advances in these areas were produced through numerical iteration on nonlinear deterministic dynamical recursions and required the use of computers. Computing power is especially important in the continuous-time applications. Hence, the fact that most such advances occurred within the past 10 years is not surprising. Examples of the recent accomplishments of that literature include the production of deterministic explanations for brain wave behavior, memory retrieval, turbulence in fluids, insect population behavior, thermal convection dynamics, climatic behavior over centuries of data, chemically reacting systems, buckling beams, sunspot activity, nonlinear wave interactions in plasmas, solid-state physics, lasers, self-generation of the earth's magnetic field, magnetohydrodynamic flow, and

This research was partially supported by National Science Foundation Grant No. SOC-8305162 and the Welch Foundation. We are greatly indebted to Ilya Prigogine for inspiring this research and to Salam Fayyad for producing and providing the weekly Divisia monetary aggregates data. We benefited from comments by the participants at Ilya Prigogine's 1985 Brussels conference. Throughout this research we have benefited extensively from our interaction with Ilya Prigogine's Center for Studies in Statistical Mechanics and Harry Swinney's Center for Research in Nonlinear Dynamics, both located in the Department of Physics at the University of Texas at Austin.

[1] Furthermore, a strong case for the use of nonlinear dynamics as the fundamental general paradigm in science has been made by Prigogine (1980).

199

many other such phenomena that previously had been viewed as inherently stochastic and beyond existing theoretical modeling capabilities.[2] The applications have been both theoretical and empirical. Although the first definitive experimental observations of deterministic chaos in nature were produced by physicists only 3 years ago (in a number of papers published in 1983), it nevertheless already has become clear that low-dimensional chaos is common in nature.

The reason for the rapidly expanding interest in this literature is evident. The recent advances have generated the capability to produce deterministic solution paths that have the characteristics of stochastic processes and hence have the properties usually seen in real data.[3] Those results, in addition to being directly empirically useful, can be derived directly from the relevant structural theory without the need to introduce ad hoc additive or exogenous stochastics. Furthermore, the resulting solution paths can exhibit the appearance of unpredictability and of structural change, when in fact there has been no shift in the model's structure at all. In other words, empirically useful results, applicable even to very long run data, become available without the need to introduce *any* "free parameters" in the Lucas sense.

[2] For surveys of much of that literature, see, e.g., Barnett and Chen (1986), Ott (1981), Hofstadter (1985, Chapter 16), Collet and Eckmann (1980), Hao (1984), Schuster (1984), and Guckenheimer and Holmes (1983). Applications to economic theory were pioneered by Benhabib and Day (1980–2) and Stutzer (1980). For additional important contributions to economic theory, see Day (1982, 1983) and Grandmont (1985), whose theoretical contributions are relevant to distinguishing between the stable and the endogenously cyclical operating regimes in an overlapping generations model with continuous market clearing and rational expectations.

For an earlier use in empirical economic inference, see Brock (1986). Although that paper contained the first attempted empirical application to economics, it was not successful at detecting deterministic chaos. Our research in this paper and in Barnett and Chen (forthcoming) was successful at detecting chaos, perhaps because our sample sizes are about four times larger than those used by Brock and our data were produced from second-order ("superlative") index numbers, whereas Brock's data were produced from first-order (Laspeyres) index numbers. For a Monte Carlo study comparing the conventional econometric approach to structural inference and the nonparametric chaotic attractor approach, see Barnett and Choi (forthcoming).

Some particularly interesting applications to other fileds include Nicholis and Nicholis (1985), who applied deterministic chaos theory empirically to climatology, May (1976), and May and Oster (1976), whose research in this area is in ecology. One of the earliest pathbreaking works in the field is Lorenz (1963), which was extended by Hoppensteadt and Hyman (1977).

[3] In fact, Bunow and Weiss (1979) have shown that the very simple deterministic chaotic model produced by the tent map generates time paths, autocorrelation functions, and spectral power density functions appearing to be indistinguishable from those produced by pseudorandom numbers.

Once it is found that observed data can be explained from a chaotic attractor model, the possibility exists of recovering information about the unknown model that produced the observed data path. In this paper we report the results of an ongoing research project that has been successful in identifying economic chaotic attractors from long time series of unusually high quality data. In particular, those attractors can explain the dynamical behavior of the broad Divisia monetary aggregates and hence can reveal information about the nature of the dynamical system that produces the observed monetary services path over time. The revealed information produces a measure of the degree of controllability and of the degree of aggregation error for each of the various monetary aggregates considered. We shall use these results as a means of comparing the usefulness of the official simple sum monetary aggregates, the Divisia demand monetary aggregates, and the Divisia supply monetary aggregates in terms of their controllability and degree of imbedded aggregation error. Although there previously have been a number of successful applications of deterministic chaotic dynamics in economic theory, we believe that our results represent the first clearly successful empirical application.

2 New results from nonlinear dynamics

2.1 *Deterministic chaos*

The relevant mathematical theory deals with very deep modeling, in the sense that all sources of the system's dynamics are endogenized, so that the system itself then produces its own dynamics. In particular, let us define s_t to be the vector of state variables at period t. The state vector is of dimension S. The state vector is defined to contain all information that is relevant to the behavior of the economy during period $t+1$. In principle, the state variables could contain the value of every variable in the economy, in the world, and in the universe during every period up to and including period t. It therefore follows, almost tautologically, that there must exist a function f (called the *deterministic dynamical system*, or "law of motion") such that $s_{t+1} = f(s_t)$ for all t.[4] We need *not* assume that all or any of the state variables are actually observed. We also certainly need not assume that we know f. However, we do observe a variable m_t during period t. Clearly, m_t must depend on the state vector. Hence, there must exist an *observer function* g such that $m_t = g(s_t)$ for every t. The space that contains all possible paths of the state vector is called the *state space* and has dimension S.

---

[4] However, the existence of f is not strictly a tautology, since we require the nontrivial assumption that s_t has finite dimension, which furthermore must be independent of t.

Clearly, in reality, the dimension of that space is huge, and there is likely to be a tremendous number of choices of state vectors s_t and dynamical systems f that can explain the existing data on m_t deterministically. However, in the spirit of all economic theory and of all science, the literature on chaotic dynamics seeks to produce the *simplest* useful explanation for the observed data path. Hence, we shall be seeking the lowest dimensional state space that can be used to produce a self-generating deterministic explanation of the past, present, and future behavior of the data series m_t. We should expect that the resulting minimum dimension may be very low, since it has been shown that very simple small neoclassical economic models can produce richly complex chaotic dynamics. See, for example, Day (1985) and Grandmont (1985).

We present the theory entirely in discrete time, although an analogous continuous-time literature exists in terms of nonlinear differential equations. In the continuous-time case, the problem is stated in somewhat different terms. The observed variable m_t is stacked onto the state vector to produce a combined system vector of dimension $S+1$. The behavior of the combined system vector is assumed to evolve continuously over time in accordance with a system of nonlinear differential equations of first order in time. By repeated differentiation in time, the system of differential equations can be reduced to a single differential equation of order $S+1$ in the one variable m_t. Hence, we see that observations on only the one variable, m_t, are sufficient to permit us to go beyond its own one-dimensional space and to begin inferring information about the dynamical system f itself, which is defined over the unknown state space. In the continuous-time literature, it nevertheless is common to produce discrete observations from the continuous paths by a specific procedure. The discrete set of points produced by that procedure is called a "Poincaré map." In the rest of this paper, we consider only the discrete-time case. Nevertheless, all results discussed in this paper have their analogue in continuous time. For example, Guckenheimer and Holmes (1983, p. 116) observe in continuous time that "simple differential equations of dimension three or greater can possess solutions of stunning complexity."

If the function f is monotonically increasing or monotonically decreasing, the state vector will forever trend in one direction. Such simple trends do not produce interesting (i.e., stochastic appearing) results in this literature. As a result, it is assumed that f has at least one turning point, as would be the case, for example, if f were a parabola or any other folded function. One of the most remarkable results in this literature applies to the case of a one-dimensional state space, with a single-hump dynamical recursion relation f. In that case it has been found that most of the important limiting properties – Feigenbaum's (1978) two constants describing the onset of chaos – are almost entirely independent of the choice of function for f. Only the properties of f at the center of its turning point matter. This near independence of the properties of f in describing the onset of chaos is called *metrical universality*. Feigenbaum's famous results assume only that the turning point is quadratic.

Another important insight provided by these results is the inherent *irreversibility of time* in theory. This conclusion follows from the fact that the existence of a turning point in f renders f noninvertible as a function, since the inverse of f is set valued. In other words, although f is a function, the "inverse" of f is a correspondence. This characteristic of the model differs fundamentally from that of ordinary differential equations, which can, in principle, be integrated either forward or backward in time.

In applications, we might, for example, assume that our data had been detrended, so that f is not monotonic. Under the very general and highly abstract assumptions just made, it has been shown in the mathematics and physics literature that m_t can evolve over time in a remarkable number of ways, from simple convegence to a constant, to cycling, to deterministic chaos having the properties of almost any kind of informative stochastic process.[5] Much is now known about all of those possible regimes, including the conditions producing transition between regimes. The source of this theoretical richness is the feedback produced by the definition of the function f, which in mathematics is called a *coupled recurrence relation*. Feedback-induced dynamics is produced by the resulting nonlinear iterations on the function f at each encountered value of its arguments (except at convergence to fixed points of f). Beginning at some initial condition s_0, the sequences or paths produced for s_t and m_t by iteration on f are called the *orbits* or *trajectories*.

For our purposes, chaotic dynamical systems can be viewed as deterministic systems that produce solution paths that appear to be stochastic. In fact, as we shall see in what follows, a stochastic explanation is indeed natural in such cases and can be produced by defining a probability measure over the limiting range (attractor) set, despite the fact that the system that produced the path is itself entirely deterministic. In the case of a physical system, such a time path would appear to be "turbulent," or, upon detailed inspection, highly complex. Nevertheless, an entirely rigorous and formal definition for chaos exists in the mathematics literature. In particular, a time sequence is *chaotic,* or "turbulent," if the sequence has the following three properties: (1) *sensitive dependence* on the initial conditions (called the *seed*), (2) a form of stationarity,[6] and (3) nonperiodicity. Sensitive dependence on initial conditions is defined to mean

[5] For further details, see Ruelle and Takens (1971) and Li and Yorke (1975).

[6] In particular, the average correlation function must converge to zero as time tends to infinity. See Ott (1981, p. 656) for a formal statement of that assumption.

that if two initial conditions are very close together, the two induced time paths of m_t will initially diverge exponentially (i.e., as if produced stochastically).

The literature becomes noninformative in the case in which the data is *pure* white noise. In that case, any exact deterministic explanation would have to be infinitely complex, so that no possible finite amount of information about the state vector could produce any information whatsoever relative to m_{t+1}. In fact, even in that extreme worst case, chaotic dynamics can produce a close approximation to reality, since Sakai and Tokumaru (1980) have shown that the triangular recursion specification for f produces trajectories that appear to be white noise.[7] Furthermore, a literature exists on the use of systems with infinite degrees of freedom. See Guckenheimer and Holmes (1983, Section 7.6).

It is difficult to believe that the dynamic evolution of economic variables, observed to a finite degree of disaggregation, is beyond all possible explanation with a finite number of variables, and hence we believe that the recent developments in nonlinear dynamics should be empirically applicable to economic variables. We therefore believe that it should be possible empirically to recover some information about unknown dynamical systems from observed paths of economic variables. We should expect that the resulting unknown dynamical system will produce stochastic-appearing observed paths, and conditional subsystems will appear to be subject to stochastic shocks from outside the subsystem. Potential exceptions to these conclusions could result from the existence of nonnegligible (high noise-to-signal ratio) pure white noise induced by measurement error. As a result, data quality is of great importance in empirical applications of mathematical chaos to economics. In principle, it is also possible for noise to exist directly in the observer function or in the law of motion, but those possibilities are theoretically unconvincing and ad hoc. In any case, the literature on deterministic chaos with imbedded white noise is in its infancy and will be discussed only briefly.

Differences in opinions between the various macroeconomic schools of thought amount to differences in opinions about the degree of depth of modeling needed to capture the source of the system's dynamics. Keynesians often argue that the system's dynamics can be produced from within the structure of the private sector. The monetarist model requires endogenizing the central bank's reaction function. The literature on rational expectations modeling and on the related "new classical economics" has produced its own dynamical models, which typically require endogenizing private-sector expectations (especially about relative prices) consistently

---

[7] They also demonstrated that simple variations on that recursion produce trajectories that look like AR(1) processes. For a definition of the triangular recursion along with three other well-known recursions, see Bunow and Weiss (1979).

with the economy's structure and also endogenizing all sources of governmental shocks to the private sector; the resulting econometric specifications reveal the economy's "deep parameters." The linearity assumptions common in models in all three traditions have rarely been viewed as inherent in any of the three traditions but rather as simplifying local approximations.[8] In fact, formidable literatures on endogenous business cycles exist in each of the three traditions. For example, in the rational expectations tradition see Lucas (1981). The empirical inference techniques that we use from chaotic dynamics require no prior assumptions about the depth of modeling needed to endogenize the system's dynamics and hence are *not* dependent on one's view about the source of the system's dynamics.

2.2   *Strange-attractor theory*

Attractor sets, and especially "strange" attractors, play an important role in chaotic dynamics. We now define the concept of a strange attractor. First, collect together the cluster (limit) points of the sequence (s_t) into a set S called the *attractor*. The sequence (s_t) is produced, through its definition, by successive iterations on the function f. In the limit the orbits will be trapped, or "locked in," by that attractor set, so long as the initial condition s_0 is sufficiently close to the attractor set. The *basin,* or "domain of attraction," induced by an attractor set is the closure of the set of initial conditions ("seeds") such that the orbit originating at the initial condition will eventually be trapped by the attractor set.[9] Once trapped by the attractor set (i.e., for sufficiently large t), the orbit will wander within or near the attractor set forever, and the behavior of the trapped paths within the attractor set will be influenced by the geometry of the attractor set.

If the sequence converges to a fixed point then the attractor is a singleton set containing one limit point and therefore has dimension zero. Such a singleton attractor is called an attractor of period 1. We can imagine the sequence as drawn by some attraction to the limit point, so that the sequence necessarily eventually must converge to the limit point. If, however, the attractor set contains two points, the sequence will simultaneously be "attracted" by two separated points and therefore will oscillate between points in two separate sequences, each of which converges to a different limit point. The resulting limiting behavior that will be approached is called a 2-cycle, and the attractor is then called an attractor of

---

[8] However, the common linearity assumptions have been the subject of much recent criticism. See, e.g., Granger and Newbold (1974), Blatt (1978), Neftci (1978), Delong and Summers (1984), Hinich and Patterson (1985a), and Maravall (1983).

[9] See Guckenheimer and Holmes (1983, p. 34).

period 2. This can occur when the choice of the model's parameter values causes the height of the turning point of the function f to pass a critical point at which the original single limit point *bifurcates,* or "fissions," into two cluster points.[10] The height of the turning point of f is called the *knob setting*.

The transition to chaos through period doubling often proceeds as follows. As the parameters of the model are further shifted, the two cluster points, which coincided at their birth from the bifurcation, separate farther and farther apart. Eventually, succeeding bifurcation points will be passed at predictable values of the parameters. The number of cluster points doubles each time bifurcation occurs, since at bifurcation each cluster point spawns its own new 2-cycle and every point in the attractor bifurcates simultaneously. Hence, bifurcation produces period doubling. As we pass from one bifurcation point to the next, the distance between knob settings producing bifurcation gets smaller and smaller, with that distance being exactly predictable from a convergence rate constant called *Feigenbaum's number*. The potential richness of the sort of observed behavior that can be produced increases as the number of points in the attractor set increases. If the behavior is periodic, the attractor is a closed loop (a limit cycle). If the behavior is n-periodic, the attractor is an n-torus. In all of those cases, points that are initially close will remain close for all time.

In the limit, after the infinite sequence of bifurcations has converged, the attractor set can have an infinite number of points. In such cases, which can produce transition to "chaos," the attractor set usually will be a *fractal,* which is a Cantor set of fractional Hausdorf dimension. Fractals are the sets made famous by Mandelbrot (1977).[11] We then say that the attractor set is a chaotic, or *"strange," attractor*. The knob setting at convergence of the sequence of bifurcations to the fractal set is finite, so that convergence of the knob settings to the chaotic regime actually can be attained. Chaos is *not* an exceptional case that can be approached only in the unattainable limit.

It has been shown that the existence of a strange attractor is neither necessary nor sufficient for chaos. Nevertheless, in virtually all known

[10] In particular, if f has only one local maximum and one parameter and if the state space dimension S is integer 1, then this phenomenon is known to occur and the height of f at which the phenomenon occurs is known.

[11] Typically, a strange attractor is an infinitely folded sheet of infinite extent located in a bounded region. A line will typically cut the attractor an infinite number of times. A wealth of examples of fractal attractors has been produced in the theoretical literature on dynamical systems and in the experimental literature on fluid dynamics and chemical kinetics. See, e.g., Helleman (1981). While fractals have nonzero (in fact, fractional) Hausdorf measures, their Lebesgue measures are zero.

useful applications of chaos, a strange attractor exists. Hence, we shall equate the existence of chaotic dynamics with the existence of a strange attractor drawing the time path toward it. Some of the points in the attractor can be stable points, and some can be repellant points. The potential explanatory power of strange attractors is tremendous, since they can "attract" a sequence into deterministic behavior that is sufficiently complex and turbulent to appear to be stochastic. For example, in the chaotic regime the orbits produced from some seed values will converge to no attractor point. Such orbits are called aperiodic orbits. There will be sensitive dependence on initial conditions, so that points close together need not remain close together over all time, and in fact will, on average, initially diverge exponentially. However, such paths will not diverge indefinitely, since all orbits are eventually trapped within the attractor set, which is bounded.

Since orbits produced from nearby seeds may initially diverge rapidly (exponentially), a "statistical" view of the generated phenomena becomes natural.[12] In addition, there is a beautiful form of mathematical order that can be found in the resulting chaos. The resulting order is a deeper kind than the more transparent kind encountered prior to the transition to chaos. See Prigogine and Stengers (1984). In particular, strange attractors (as well as fractals in general) are characterized by an infinite regress of detail, with a neverending nesting of pattern within pattern as one looks increasingly closely at the appearance of the attractor set. This property of strange attractors is called *scale invariance*.[13] In the physical sciences it has been shown that *dissipative systems* often can produce mathematical chaos through the phenomenon of turbulence, where a dissipative system is defined to be a system that loses entropy as time passes, as through friction. Clearly, dissipative systems are the rule rather than the exception in nature.

2.3 *Empirical inference capabilities of chaotic dynamics and strange attractors*

There are a number of techniques widely used in physics to detect chaos, such as spectral analysis, computation of the maximum Lyapunov exponent, Poincaré sectioning, and subharmonic stroboscopy. However, not all of the approaches developed by physicists are applicable in economics because most of those methods require a large amount of data to

---

[12] Alternatively, if nearby orbits tend smoothly and systematically to get closer together over time, the system is deterministically stable and cannot produce stochastic-appearing behavior.

[13] In mathematics, the scale invariance property is possessed by all renormalization groups.

assure sufficient precision. For example, a typical power spectral analysis of deterministic chaos requires more than 10,000 data points. In this paper we use only those techniques that are potentially useful for detecting chaos with less than 1,000 data points. The physics literature on detecting and quantifying chaos is still in its infancy. Nevertheless, two techniques are potentially especially useful in economic applications. One is computation of the attractor's dimension, which to be useful must be finite, fractional, and small. The other is computation of the orbits' Lyapunov exponents. Two other techniques that can be useful even with small sample sizes are inspection of phase portraits and of autocorrelation functions. In addition, some classical statistical methods are applicable, including time series frequency domain techniques. In this section we shall discuss each of those five techniques, although we first describe the fundamental relationship between phase space and state space.

2.3.1   *Phase space embedding*

It can be shown that strange attractors are never topological manifolds, which have integer dimensions, but rather fractals, which are Cantor sets having noninteger dimensions and zero volumes (relative to Lebesgue measure). A measure-theoretic method based on the Hausdorf measure (through the Hausdorf covering theorem) exists for measuring the dimension of a fractal.[14] The resulting noninteger-valued dimension of a strange attractor is called its fractal dimension, which measures the number of independent degrees of freedom relevant to the system's dynamical behavior. In general, the dimension of a set is the amount of information needed to specify the position of a point on the set to within a given accuracy. If the attractor is a Euclidean object, any of the methods described in what follows for measuring attractor dimension produces the Euclidean dimension of the attractor. *The attractor is defined to be "strange" if and only if the attractor's dimension is noninteger-valued, that is, if the attractor is a fractal.*

The attractor set is a subset of the state space, although we typically have no measured values of the state vector s_t. We only have measured values of m_t. Hence, it is important to have a means of relating fractal dimension to the potential values of m_t. Takens (1980, p. 369) has done

---

[14] The measure-theoretic concept of the Hausdorf measure is easily understood as follows. Cover the points in the attractor with the minimum possible number of cubes of side length δ, and count the resulting number of cubes required. Call that minimum number $N(\delta)$, and let $\delta \to 0$. Then for sufficiently small δ, $N(\delta)$ will grow approximately proportionately to δ^{-H}, where H is the Hausdorf dimension of the attractor set. See Ott (1981, p. 660) for a more complete, although simplified, discussion. For a rigorous definition, see Guckenheimer and Holmes (1983, Definition 5.8.4, p. 285).

so through an embedding theorem, which can be understood as follows. Select a state vector from the basin set; produce the n-history (orbit) of m_t created from $n-1$ iterations on (g, f); then stack the resulting n values of m_t into an n-dimensional vector. If the first observation in the n-history is m_t, we can designate an n-history at t by $\mathbf{m}(n)_t$, where

$$\mathbf{m}(n)_t = (m_t, m_{t+1}, \ldots, m_{t+n-1}) \tag{2.1}$$

at each t.

In the discussion that follows, the lags usually will continue to be successive one-period lags to simplify exposition, although in practice the coordinates of phase space generally should be successive multiperiod lags. In that case, for preselected time delay of τ periods, we would have the n-history

$$\mathbf{m}(n, \tau)_t = (m_t, m_{t+\tau}, m_{t+2\tau}, \ldots, m_{t+(n-1)\tau}) \tag{2.2}$$

at each t. It is to be understood that whenever $\mathbf{m}(n)_t$ appears in an equation, it should be replaced in practice by $\mathbf{m}(n, \tau)_t$. The existence of the argument τ should be understood in the following discussion. An information theoretic criterion for selecting the time delay τ is provided by Fraser and Swinney (forthcoming).

The space of those n-histories $\mathbf{m}(n, \tau)_t$ for a fixed choice of n is called the *phase space,* and the selected value of n is called the *embedding dimension.* As defined in that manner, phase space has delay coordinates. The set of phase space trajectories for all possible initial conditions for the state vector within the basin set is called the *phase portrait* of the system. Sometimes the term *phase portrait* alternatively is used to refer to the trajectories of the n-histories produced in phase space by the actual observed data.

2.3.2 *Dimensionality measures*

Suppose the construction of $\mathbf{m}(n)_t$ for a fixed embedding dimension is repeated for each possible value of s_t within the basin set.[15] Designate the

---

[15] Most of the theorems cited in what follows were proved under the more restrictive assumption that the initial condition is within the attractor set rather than in the basin set. However, those theorems usually can be extended to the more realistic case of initial conditions within basin sets. The extended proofs would use Guckenheimer and Holmes (1983, Theorem 5.8.1, p. 282).

In empirical applications, the set of initial conditions is restricted to the set of state vector values that produced the set of observed values of m_t. In that case, we easily can produce the resulting n-histories as the successive observed n-histories $\mathbf{m}(n, \tau)_t$, $\mathbf{m}(n, \tau)_{t+\tau}, \ldots, \mathbf{m}(n, \tau)_{N-(n+1)\tau}$. The justification for that simplification is provided by the Grassberger–Procaccia theorem described later. It is also often informative simply to plot the resulting induced orbit through "phase space" (the space of n-histories) in the case of $n = 2$.

resulting set of n-history vectors by $J(n)$. Then the Hausdorf dimension of $J(n)$ is computed. This computation is repeated for successively larger values of n. Takens (1980, p. 369) proved that the limiting dimension of $J(n)$ as $n \to \infty$ equals the fractal dimension of the strange attractor in state space. We shall call that theorem the *Takens embedding theorem*. Hence, we can define the dimension of the strange attractor in state space in terms solely of n-histories, $\mathbf{m}(n)_t$, of observable values of m_t. In fact, Takens proved an even stronger result. He proved that there exists a deterministic dynamical system (coupled recursion relation) F_n in phase space for any fixed embedding dimension n such that a one-to-one correspondence exists between the dynamical properties (in particular, all conjugate invariants) of $\mathbf{s}_{t+1} = f(\mathbf{s}_t)$ in state space and the dynamical properties of $\mathbf{m}(n)_{t+1} = F_n(\mathbf{m}(n)_t)$ in phase space. Those invariant properties include the Lyapunov exponent (to be discussed later) as well as the dimension and entropy concepts. Hence, a strange attractor will exist in phase space if and only if a strange attractor exists in state space, and the dimensions of the attractors will be the same in both spaces. Clearly, in order to be able to measure that dimensionality in phase space, the embedding dimension must be selected to exceed the attractor dimension, since the attractor is a subset of the phase space for sufficiently large n.

The Hausdorf dimension of a strange attractor, whether computed in phase space or directly in state space, is extremely difficult to compute. As a result, more easily computed approximations have been proposed. The most notable examples are the Grassberger–Procaccia correlation dimension and the information dimension. It has been shown that the correlation dimension is always less than the information-theoretic "information dimension," which is always less than the Hausdorf fractal dimension.[16] Since the next integer larger than the fractal dimension is most commonly used as a lower bound to the state space dimension, the correlation dimension is the most conservative of the three. In fact, physical scientists now consider the Grassberger and Procaccia (1983a, b) method to be the best method because of its conservatism, its computational simplicity, and its own particular theoretical merits.[17]

We first define the Grassberger–Procaccia method of measuring the dimension of $J(n)$. The dimension measure resulting from that method is called the correlation dimension of $J(n)$, since the procedure uses the correlation function $C_n(\epsilon)$ defined by

---

[16] If the covering of the attractor is uniform, all three of the dimension measures will be equal. Otherwise, the three measures typically will be very close together.

[17] Also see Takens (1983) on that method. The theoretical argument for the superiority of the Grassberger–Procaccia method is that it gives more weight to neighborhoods of frequently visited points along an orbit, whereas the Hausdorf measure, being purely geometric, does not.

$$C_n(\epsilon) = \#\{(i, j): \|\mathbf{m}(n)_i - \mathbf{m}(n)_j\| < \epsilon, 1 \le i \le N_n, 1 \le j \le N_n\}/N_n^2, \qquad (2.3)$$

where $N_n = N - (n-1)\tau$ is the number of n-histories that can be produced from a sample of size N with time lag τ, and $\#A$ denotes the cardinality of (number of distinct points in) the set A.[18] In particular, the Grassberger-Procaccia correlation dimension of $J(n)$ is defined as

$$D(n) = \lim_{\epsilon \to 0} \lim_{N \to \infty} (\log_2 C_n(\epsilon)/\log_2 \epsilon). \qquad (2.4)$$

If we then take the limit as the embedding dimension goes to infinity, as suggested by the Takens embedding theorem, we get the correlation dimension of the strange attractor in state space,

$$D = \lim_{n \to \infty} D(n). \qquad (2.5)$$

In practice, with a well-behaved chaotic model, the value of $D(n)$ will "saturate" (i.e., attain its limit) at some finite level of n, called the saturation embedding dimension n_S. The correlation dimension of the strange attractor then is $D(n_S)$. At the opposite extreme, saturation is never attained if the data is white noise. In that case all dimensions of phase space are used by the data at every embedding dimension, and $D(n) = n$ at all n. As a result, $D = \infty$ for white noise.[19]

The reason for equation (2.4) is easily seen from the fact that at sufficiently small ϵ and large N, Grassberger and Procaccia showed that the correlation function can be written approximately in the form

$$\log_2 C_n(\epsilon) = \log_2 k + D(n) \log_2 \epsilon, \qquad (2.6)$$

where k is a constant. Hence, (2.4) follows by dividing (2.6) by $\log_2 \epsilon$ and letting $\epsilon \to 0$. From (2.6) we see that we alternatively can define $D(n)$ by

$$D(n) = \lim_{\epsilon \to 0} (\partial \log_2 C_n(\epsilon)/\partial \log_2 \epsilon), \qquad (2.7)$$

which is, in fact, the form used in practice. The procedure is to select a small value for ϵ but not to go all the way to zero, since data noise tends to dominate at extremely small values of ϵ. As a result, (2.7) must be used, rather than (2.4), since for small nonzero values of ϵ the intercept of the plot of $\log_2 C_n(\epsilon)/\log_2 \epsilon$ against $\log_2 \epsilon$ remains nonzero.

[18] The correlation function is more commonly called the correlation integral since it can be written in the form of an integral depending upon the indicator (Heaviside) function. The correlation function measures the correlation of points along an orbit. Since paths are eventually trapped by the attractor, points at sufficiently large t will be partially correlated, even with the most "chaotic" attractor. However, high correlation is unlikely as a result of the local exponential (i.e., "stochastic-appearing") divergence property of chaotic orbits.

[19] In the case of uniform noise, the noise level of the time series can be measured using the approach of Ben-Mizrachi, Procaccia, and Grassberger (1984).

In particular, $\log_2 C_n(\epsilon)$ is plotted against $\log_2 \epsilon$ to permit measurement of the slope $\partial \log_2 C_n(\epsilon)/\partial \log_2 \epsilon$ versus $\log_2 \epsilon$. At sufficiently low (i.e., sufficiently negative) values of $\log_2 \epsilon$, the slope will reach a plateau before noise begins to dominate and to produce further variation of the slope at even lower values of $\log_2 \epsilon$. The value of the slope along the plateau is used as $D(n)$.[20]

To permit easy identification of the boundaries of the plateau, the value of the slope is plotted against $\log_2 \epsilon$, and the resulting plot is inspected to find the left-hand boundary, $\log_2 \epsilon_L(n)$, and right-hand boundary, $\log_2 \epsilon_R(n)$, of the plateau at embedding dimension n. Having found the left- and right-hand limits of the linear region of the plot of $\log_2 C_n(\epsilon)$ versus $\log_2 \epsilon$, the values of $\log_2 C_n(\epsilon)$ are regressed linearly on $\log_2 \epsilon$. The points used in the regression are all of those points on the plot of $\log_2 C_n(\epsilon)$ versus $\log_2 \epsilon$ for values of $\log_2 \epsilon$ between $\log_2 \epsilon_L(n)$ and $\log_2 \epsilon_R(n)$. The slope of that linear regression is the estimate of $D(n)$. The procedure is repeated at increasing levels of n from $n = 1$ until the saturation embedding is attained. It is important not to exceed the lowest candidate for a saturation-embedding dimension, since the number of observations in phase space rapidly declines as the embedding dimension increases. With too few points in phase space, the ability to identify the linear region (2.6) quickly disappears.[21] By (2.5), the limiting value of $D(n)$, approximated by the value of $D(n)$ at the saturation-embedding dimension, is the fractal dimension D.[22]

We would expect from the Takens embedding theorem that D will measure the dimension of the strange attractor in state space, despite the fact that $D(n)$ at all finite n is produced from vectors in phase space. In fact, Grassberger and Procaccia have shown that D can indeed be written in terms of the state vectors s_t ($1 \leq t \leq N$) as

[20] Empirically, the use of the ratio in (2.4) is not a satisfactory substitute for the slope in (2.7), since for nonzero values of ϵ the intercept in (2.6) remains nonzero.

[21] There is no need to consider embedding dimensions exceeding $2D + 1$ by much. With less than 100,000 observations, the saturation-embedding dimension should be less than 8. With fewer than 1,000 dimensions, it should not be necessary to consider embedding dimensions exceeding $n = 6$.

[22] The procedure is described in detail in Swinney (1985), Wolf, Brandstater, and Swift (1985), and Ben-Mizrachi et al. (1984). Typically, convergence will be closely approached for n substantially less than N.

Unfortunately, in practice the procedure often must be somewhat altered, unless the data is of very high quality and produced from a well-designed experiment. The reason is that most data contains some noise that cannot be entirely explained deterministically. In such cases, the necessary modification of the previously described graphical procedure is described in Ben-Mizrachi et al. (1984). The modified procedure also produces a measure of the amount of noise in the data. The modification is necessitated by the fact that noise in the data produces fuzziness in the fractal patterns appearing in strange attractors.

$$D = \lim_{\epsilon \to 0} (\log_2 C(\epsilon)/\log_2 \epsilon), \tag{2.8}$$

where

$$C(\epsilon) = \lim_{N \to \infty} \#\{(i,j): \|s_i - s_j\| < \epsilon, 1 \le i \le N, 1 \le j \le N\}/N^2. \tag{2.9}$$

The correlation function usually is adjusted to eliminate (i,j) pairs such that $i = j$. In that case (2.3) and (2.4) become

$$C_n^*(\epsilon)$$
$$= \#\{(i,j): \|\mathbf{m}(n)_i - \mathbf{m}(n)_j\| < \epsilon, 1 \le i \le N_n, 1 \le j \le N_n, i \ne j\}/(N_n^2 - N_n) \tag{2.10}$$

and

$$C^*(\epsilon)$$
$$= \lim_{N \to \infty} \#\{(i,j): \|s_i - s_j\| < \epsilon, 1 \le i \le N, 1 \le j \le N, i \ne j\}/(N^2 - N). \tag{2.11}$$

In our work, we use these adjusted correlation functions.[23]

For sufficiently large n, N, the limiting correlation dimension can be found with reasonable accuracy. Grassberger and Procaccia showed that the limiting correlation dimension D is less than, but nevertheless closely approximates, the Hausdorf fractal dimension of the strange attractor. We use the Grassberger–Procaccia procedure for computing fractal dimensions for strange attractors.

The next integer larger than that fractal dimension of the strange attractor clearly provides a lower bound to the dimension of the space that can contain the attractor. Furthermore, since the attractor set is a subset of the state space, it follows that the next integer larger than the fractal dimension also provides a lower bound to the dimension of the state space that could contain state vector paths (s_t) capable of producing the observed orbit of m_t. Since the Grassberger–Procaccia correlation dimension D is less than the Hausdorf fractal dimension, we see that the correlation dimension D of the strange attractor is also a lower bound to the dimension of the state space S.

The preceding conclusions, including the existence of the postulated limits, will hold if the state vector orbits are generated in accordance with a deterministic dynamical model consistent with the existence of (f, g). This is a powerful result, since it provides a *lower bound to the number of variables that can be used to produce an entirely theoretical explanation for endogenous evolution of m_t.* That result follows from the fact

[23] In practice, there is no need to divide by N^2 in (2.9), or to divide by $N_n^2 - N_n$ in (2.10), since division of (2.9) or (2.10) by constants only affects the intercept in (2.6) without affecting the slope, and it is the slope that is the value of $D(n)$ that we compute by this procedure. As a result, in our computations we dropped the constant divisors.

that $m_t = f(s_t)$, and the dimension of s_t is S. It is important, however, to recognize that the simplest chaotic deterministic model that can produce the observed path of m_t need not be the model that actually produced the observed data. In fact, in experimental applications the fractal dimension is typically very much smaller than the number of variables that actually produced the observed data.[24] Only when the attractor is not chaotic ("strange") is that lower bound tight.[25]

As mentioned, a path drawn toward a strange attractor can appear to be a stochastic process, despite its totally deterministic origins. In addition, it is possible to define a probability measure on the attractor set in terms of the distribution of points throughout the set. In that manner it becomes possible to interpret the path as the realizations of a stochastic process, with a fully deterministic explanation of the source of the probability measure. That explanation for stochastic behavior becomes entirely conventional if the measure on the attractor set and the set of possible paths is used to induce a probability distribution on the basin set, which is defined to be the closure of the set of initial conditions from which all possible solution paths begin. The result is a link between the deterministic structural theory and the probability distribution of the observed stochastic process that produces the observed data.

If the fractal dimension is infinite, the path becomes infinitely complicated to explain deterministically and could only be embedded in an infinite-dimensional state space. An infinite number of variables is needed to explain the path "deterministically." This would happen if, in fact, *no* deterministic explanation could exist, so that the real world is just white noise, no matter how deeply we might delve into the source of the observed dynamics.

There is a semiempirical formula used to estimate the needed sample size. For example, with the Mackey–Glass model, the minimum number of data points needed to permit estimation of the attractor's dimension has been estimated to be $N_{min} = 21.5^D$, where D is the attractor dimension.[26] As a result, in that case a sample size of at least 460 is needed to permit measurement of the dimension of an attractor of dimension 2, whereas a sample of size 10,000 is needed to permit measurement of the dimension of an attractor of dimension 3. With less than 1,000 observations, the largest dimension that could reasonably be measured in that

---

[24] For example, with the Mackey–Glass equation with $\tau = 17$, the correlation dimension of the fractal is 1.95, so the minimum dimension of the state space is 2. However, the actual dimension of the state space is 600. See Ben-Mizrachi et al. (1984, Figure 3).

[25] If the attractor is a manifold rather than a fractal, so that the attractor has integer-valued dimension, then the correlation dimension $D(n)$ is exactly equal to the state space dimension for sufficiently large imbedding dimension n.

[26] See Wolf et al. (1985).

case would be a fractional dimension between 2 and 3. Clearly, current methods permit discovery only of low-dimensional attractors with economic data.

The standard error of the dimensionality estimate can be acquired using the probability measure proposed by Takens (1984).

2.3.3   *Lyapunov exponent as test for chaos*

The *Lyapunov exponent* provides a different sort of information. The Lyapunov exponent characterizes the nature of the wandering behavior of chaotic orbits. Trajectories initially close to each other are considered, and the long-run average rate at which they diverge or converge over time is computed in various locally defined orthogonal directions. It can be shown that the behavior of all of the trajectories drawn by the attractor can be characterized by a finite number of Lyapunov exponents. One exponent is necessarily zero, and some others are negative. With a well-defined system, the sum of all Lyapunov exponents will be negative. Of particular interest is the largest of the Lyapunov exponents, since its reciprocal measures the limits of deterministic predictability of the long-run evolution of the path (m_t).[27] If the dynamics is chaotic, there will be at least one positive Lyapunov exponent, which reflects the exponential divergence of orbits from nearby initial conditions. *The positivity of the largest Lyapunov exponent can be used as the definition of mathematical chaos.* As a result, the sign of the maximum Lyapunov exponent is more important than its numerical value. The maximum Lyapunov exponent can distinguish between strange attractors and ordinary integer-dimensional (topological manifold) attractors. As a result, the method is useful to distinguish between chaos and periodic processes. The method is not powerful at distinguishing between chaos and white noise. That comparison is most effectively investigated in terms of the behavior of the autocorrelation function.

Formally, the Lyapunov exponents can be defined as follows, in terms of orbits in state space. Let f^k designate the composition of f with itself k times; so, for example, f^3 is defined by $f^3(s_t) = f(f(f(s_t)))$. Let H_{kt} be the Hessian matrix of $f^k(s_t)$, and let $a_{it}(k)$ be the ith eigenvalue of H_{kt} with the eigenvalues ordered such that $a_{1t}(k) \geq a_{2t}(k) \geq \cdots \geq a_{St}(k)$, where S is the dimension of the state vector s_t. The ith Lyapunov exponent, $\lambda_i(t)$, is defined by

$$\lambda_i(t) = \lim_{k \to \infty} (1/k) \log_2 a_{it}(k), \quad i = i, \dots, S, \tag{2.12}$$

where $\lambda_i(t)$ is independent of evolution time for all s_t within the attractor set once the orbit has become completely trapped by the attractor set.

[27] See Shaw (1981).

Hence, the Lyapunov exponents are considered only within the attractor set. The vector of Lyapunov exponents, $(\lambda_1(t), \lambda_2(t), ..., \lambda_S(t))$, is called the *Lyapunov spectrum*. The maximum Lyapunov exponent is

$$\bar{\lambda}(t) = \max\{\lambda_i(t): i = 1, ..., S\}. \tag{2.13}$$

We present equation (2.12) in terms of the state vectors rather than in terms of the observed variables m_t only for notational convenience. In practice, the analogous definition in phase space, with f replaced by $g(f)$, is used, so that (2.12) can be computed from the observed data. Because of the relationship between state space and phase space, Lyapunov exponents computed in either space at sufficiently large embedding dimensions would be the same.

We compute the largest Lyapunov exponents, $\bar{\lambda}(t)$, using the algorithm in Wolf et al. (1984).[28] Their paper also provides a means of dealing with noise through the use of a low-pass filter.[29] That algorithm can be shown to converge to the largest Lyapunov exponent for an infinite sample size and to produce an approximation to that Lyapunov exponent for a finite sample size.[30]

The Wolf et al. algorithm produces a plot of values of the maximum Lyapunov exponent, $\bar{\lambda}(t)$, against evolution time t at fixed time intervals over an appropriate range. In theory, $\bar{\lambda}(t)$ should be completely independent of t within the attractor, but in empirical applications some variation will occur. As a result, a plateau of the plot is sought over which the value of $\bar{\lambda}(t)$ is stable. The evolution time at the start of the plateau is designated by t_S, and the evolution time at the end of the plateau is designated by t_E. The computed values of $\bar{\lambda}(t)$ for t between t_S and t_E are then averaged to acquire the estimate $\bar{\lambda}^*$ of the maximum Lyapunov exponent on the attractor.

It should be observed that tests with the Rossler and Lorenz attractors demonstrate that precise calculation of the Lyapunov exponents requires high precision in experimental data. Since round-off error in economic data usually exceeds that needed for precise measurement of Lyapunov exponents, the value of the maximum Lyapunov exponent acquired with economic data should be expected to be imprecisely estimated. Neverthe-

---

[28] That algorithm has been shown to be the most robust one available by Vastano and Kostelich (in press) with experimental data. Also see Oseledec (1968, Theorem 2.1). The FORTRAN computer coding for the algorithm was published in the paper by Wolf et al. (1984).

[29] Other work on deterministic chaos with random noise includes Wolf and Swift (1984), Ben-Mizrachi et al. (1984), Crutchfield and Farmer (1982), Brock and Dechert (this volume), and Matsumoto and Tsuda (1983). That literature is very limited and very new.

[30] See Bennettin et al. (1980).

less, since only its sign is most important, we often can expect to be able to acquire useful information from Lyapunov exponents with economic data.

The Lyapunov spectrum is closely related to the dimensionality of the attractor set. Kaplan and Yorke (1978) have conjectured that the information dimension of the attractor set can be computed as a direct function of the Lyapunov spectrum, although the formula requires knowledge of the entire Lyapunov spectrum vector, not just of the value of the maximum Lyapunov exponent.

2.3.4 Inspection of phase portraits

An informal exploratory data analysis often is useful in uncovering chaotic dynamics. The approach is to plot the n-histories in a two-dimensional phase space with preselected time delay. In other words, for $n = 2$ and a preselected value for τ we plot the value of the two-dimensional vector $\mathbf{m}(n, \tau)_t$ in phase space at each t. The geometric pattern that appears is compared with the patterns that previously have been shown to be produced by systems that have known properties. For example, periodic motion with period equal to $T = k\tau$ is known to produce a phase portrait with k points in a closed orbit. At the other extreme, pure white noise produces a uniform cloud of data points in phase space. Chaos produces complex, nonuniform phase portraits, such as those of the Henon attractor, the Rossler model, and the Mackey–Glass model.[31] As a result, an initial inspection of phase portraits is useful, although the more formal methods described in the foregoing should follow.

2.3.5 Inspection of autocorrelation function

Another form of useful preliminary exploratory data analysis is inspection of the autocorrelation function. The autocorrelation function used in this manner is the conventional one used in statistical time series analysis. In particular, let $\mathrm{var}(\mathbf{m})$ be the variance of the sample $\mathbf{m} = (m_1, \ldots, m_N)$, and let $\mathrm{cov}(t, \bar{t})$ be the covariance of m_t and $m_{\bar{t}}$. Then the autocorrelation function is defined as

$$G(t, \bar{t}) = \mathrm{cov}(t, \bar{t})/\mathrm{var}(\mathbf{m}). \tag{2.14}$$

It is common to plot $G(t, \bar{t})$ against $\bar{t}$ at fixed t, since the properties of the resulting plot are known for many kinds of models. For example, it is known that the autocorrelation function is an oscillating cosine function for a periodic process. The autocorrelation function is a delta function

---

[31] See, e.g., Gibson and Jeffries (1984), Henon (1976), Rossler (1976), and Mackey and Glass (1977).

(spike at the origin) for white noise, since m_t is then totally uncorrelated with $m_{\bar{t}}$ for any $\bar{t} \neq t$.[32] For deterministic chaos, the autocorrelation function first exhibits fast decay at an exponential rate and then residual oscillations with slow deacy.[33] In the limit, as the orbit is completely trapped by the attractor, the asymptotic behavior is independent of the initial conditions. In other words, the correlation function has a long fat tail declining asymptotically to zero at the right. Furthermore, with deterministic chaos the characteristic decorrelation time, T_{AC}, is roughly on the order of the inverse of the largest positive Lyapunov exponent.[34] The characteristic decorrelation time is defined to be the minimum time for the correlation function to decay to e^{-1}. Completely stable processes that converge asymptotically to a single point also produce autocorrelation functions that may have a tail on the right. However, in the case of chaos, the tail remains thicker after the initial exponential decay than the tail produced by a stable system having a singleton attractor.

2.3.6   *Time series statistical inference methods*

Computations of correlation dimensions and maximum Lyapunov exponents can produce convincing evidence of deterministic chaos. However, those tests use point estimates having unknown statistical properties. The reason is that they are based directly on the definition of chaos and hence on deterministic mathematics. Nevertheless, as observed here, a stochastic interpretation can be given to the orbits produced from chaotic dynamics, and the distribution of the process can be derived directly from the deterministic dynamics.[35] There have not yet been many results produced that exploit the stochastic interpretation. However, a statistical test for chaos based on Hinich's (1982) bispectral test of nonlinearity has been proposed by Ashley and Patterson (1985). They showed that the Hinich test can test a nonlinearity property necessary for some chaotic recursions.[36] The test is based on the use of classical statistical methods, and hence the test has known power. However, the condition tested is not sufficient for chaos and is necessary only for some chaotic recursions, which include some of the most important chaotic recursions. Nevertheless, the

---

[32] See Otnes and Enochson (1972).

[33] See Grossman and Sonneborn-Schmick (1982).

[34] See Nicholis and Nicholis (1985).

[35] See, e.g., Shaw (1981) for the derivation and use of an invariant probability measure, based on the Hausdorf measure, over a strange attractor. They then further define the information-theoretic dimensionality and entropy of the attractor induced by the probability distribution. For the definition of the asymptotic probability measure, see Guckenheimer and Holmes (1983, p. 283).

[36] For a related alternative bispectral test for linearity of stationary time series, see Rao and Gabr (1980). See Maravall (1983) for an approach using the autocorrelation function of the squared residuals from fitted ARIMA models.

Hinich nonlinearity test is important, since the nonlinearity property is central to the difference in behavior between such chaotic models as those of Day and Grandmont on the one hand and such well-known models as the many Keynesian linear macroeconometric models and the Lucas-type linear rational expectations models on the other hand.[37]

We are not aware of any direct test of mathematical chaos based on classical statistical theory, although the approach of Kalaba and Testfatsion (1980) may be adaptable to that purpose.

3   Data requirements

3.1   *The issue*

As discussed, data quality is very important in applying the currently existing techniques for uncovering the dynamics of nonlinear systems. The white noise produced from measurement error complicates the use of existing methods for extracting information from strange attractors, since such data error produces fuzzy appearance in strange attractor sets. In addition, it seems reasonable to presume that the variable used as the measured variable m_t should be an "important" one, since the empirical techniques currently available for extracting empirical information from chaotic orbits use the observed orbit of only one variable to reconstruct the dynamics of the complete (simplest compatible) system in state space.

It is important to recognize that there is no inherent reason to believe that economic data is more noisy than data produced in the physical sciences. Many techniques from classical statistics require most variables to be exogenous. But fully nonstochastic exogenous variables usually can be acquired only as control variables in controlled experiments. As a result, it is often believed that inference procedures applied to economic data, which typically are not produced from controlled experiments, are greatly complicated by "noisy" economic data. Whereas simultaneity bias created by endogeneity of many variables is certainly a problem for classical statistical inference procedures, endogeneity is *not* a problem for the use of strange-attractor theory. The distinction between endogenous and exogenous variables is irrelevant to chaos, and in fact the power of chaotic dynamics lies in its ability to produce stochastic-appearing solution paths. The usefulness of fully deterministic mathematical chaos requires only that the data be of high quality, so that large amounts of white noise produced by measurement error not be present.

---

[37] Patterson (1983) has developed a computer algorithm that can implement the Hinich test. Applications rejecting linearity with stock market data can be found in Hinich and Patterson (1985a, b).

There is no reason to believe that *completely disaggregated* economic data need inherently be any more noisy, in the sense of possessing high measurement error, than data produced from controlled experiments in the physical sciences. But, of course, almost all available economic data is aggregated both over goods and over economic agents, and aggregation can indeed induce white noise into the aggregated data. Hence, the problem for the empirical use of deterministic chaos and strange-attractor theory is not that economic data is not produced from controlled experiments, but rather that the data is aggregated and aggregation bias can induce noise into the aggregated data.

Most governmental data is produced from Laspeyres or Paasche indexes, which are only first-order approximations to the true aggregation-theoretic aggregate. The resulting second-order remainder terms could possibly produce a troublesome amount of noise for the nonlinear inference procedures currently available from the physics literature. Although the money supply would be an "important" variable, the official Federal Reserve System simple-sum monetary aggregates are not even first-order approximations and hence have first-order remainder terms, which certainly are too large for our purposes. In addition, the techniques that we seek to use in this research benefit substantially from the largest possible sample sizes.

We believe that a data series potentially well suited to the objectives of this research is the weekly data on the Divisia monetary aggregates. Barnett's Divisia monetary aggregates are second-order approximations to the exact aggregation-theoretic monetary service flows produced by the corresponding monetary asset components. As a result, the remainder terms are only third order and have been shown to be less than the round-off error in the component data. Furthermore, the monetary service flows in the economy are important variables. In addition, Fayyad (1986) provided that data in weekly form over a sample period adequate for the use of the techniques described here. We use both the Divisia demand monetary aggregates and Divisia supply monetary aggregates as data in our tests for chaos. For purposes of comparison, we also use the official simple-sum monetary aggregates and IBM common stock daily returns. We present the relevant economic theory briefly. For a fuller presentation, see Barnett (1987).

3.2   *Divisia monetary aggregates*

Barnett (1980a; 1981a, Chapter 7) introduced the use of neoclassical aggregation and index number theory into monetary economics. His Divisia aggregates, based on Diewert's (1976) superlative class of index numbers, measure the economy's flow of monetary services as perceived by the users of those monetary services. As a result, the relevant aggregation theory is that produced by neoclassical consumer and factor demand theory. Much empirical research now exists on that subject; and as would be expected from the theory, the empirical research is mostly related to demand-side empirical tests. See, for example, Barnett (1982b, 1983a, 1984) and Barnett, Offenbacher, and Spindt (1981, 1984). More recently, Barnett (1987) introduced the Divisia supply monetary aggregates, which are based on supply-side aggregation theory with a conventional neoclassical model of financial intermediary monetary asset supply. A very similar model of a financial firm, originated by Hancock (1985, 1986), has been employed by Hancock (1987) empirically to investigate supply-side monetary aggregation.

Unfortunately, as shown both theoretically and empirically in this paper, the aggregation-theoretic exact money demand aggregate need not always equal the aggregation-theoretic exact money supply aggregate. This potential complication can arise, even if both aggregates are produced from Divisia aggregation over the same components and *even if the markets in all monetary components are continually cleared.* This paradox is caused by the existence of required reserves having regulated zero rates of return. That regulatory constraint produces an implicit tax on financial intermediation in terms of foregone investment interest. Financial intermediaries receive zero return on part of their deposits and a market return on the rest. However, depositors receive the same marginal return on every dollar deposited in a given account.

Both the Divisia demand and Divisia supply monetary aggregates depend jointly on component quantities and user cost prices, which are functions of after-tax component yields. As a result, even if all component markets are continually cleared, the demand and supply aggregates can differ, since the "after (implicit) tax" component yields seen by financial intermediaries and depositors are not the same. The implicit tax on required reserves produces a regulatory wedge between the user cost paid by the demander of the asset and the user cost received by the supplier of the asset.

In brief, a classical regulatory wedge appears between the two sides of the aggregated money market as a result of the asymmetric taxation on the two sides of the market. Complications of the same sort are produced in many goods markets, including money markets, by the differences in the *direct* taxation rates on the two sides of the market.

If the difference between a Divisia demand monetary aggregate and the corresponding Divisia supply monetary aggregate were small, we could use only one of them. The result would be a substantial simplification in modeling, since we then could use an aggregate money demand and aggregate money supply function to produce a market that can be cleared in the monetary aggregate. For that to be the case, the difference between the Divisia demand monetary aggregate and the Divisia supply monetary aggregate would have to be statistically insignificant, so that we could treat each as a drawing from the same distribution. Barnett, Hinich, and Weber (1986) have shown that the difference between the spectrum of the Divisia demand monetary aggregates and the corresponding Divisia supply monetary aggregates is statistically insignificant at all frequencies, and that the coherences between the Divisia demand and Divisia supply monetary aggregates are very high at all frequencies. Nevertheless, through the use of a Hilbert transform method, they showed that subtle dynamic differences exist between the corresponding indexes at high frequencies. Since we are dealing explicitly with nonlinear dynamics, we therefore use both the Divisia demand and Divisia supply monetary aggregates.

4   Demand-side monetary aggregation and index number theory

4.1   *Aggregation theory*

Demanders of monetary assets are treated as either maximizing intertemporal utility subject to a sequence of budget constraints or as maximizing the discounted present value of profits subject to given technology, expressed as an intertemporal transformation function. Real balances of each monetary asset appear in the utility or transformation function. That utility or transformation function is the derived function shown in general equilibrium theory always to exist if money has positive value in equilibrium.[38] In short, we begin with conventional neoclassical theory applicable both to consumer demand for monetary assets and to firm demand for monetary assets. We further assume that the utility or transformation function for each economic agent is blockwise weekly separable in the current-period portfolio of monetary assets. For tests of that assumption, see Serletis (1987) and Fayyad (1986).

Barnett (1980a, 1987) has proved that the economic agent, whether a consumer or firm, then can be viewed as solving a simple conditional current-period decision problem, since the first- and second-order conditions for solving that problem are included among the necessary conditions for solving the economic agent's full intertemporal joint optimization problem. That current-period conditional decision is of the form

---

[38] See, e.g., Arrow and Hahn (1971), Fischer (1974), Phlips and Spinnewyn (1982), and Samuelson and Sato (1984).

Maximize $u(\mathbf{m}_t)$ subject to $\mathbf{m}_t' \boldsymbol{\pi}_t = y_t,$ $\qquad\qquad$ (4.1)

where $\mathbf{m}_t = (m_{1t}, \dots, m_{nt})'$ is the economic agent's current-period real balances of the n monetary assets, $\boldsymbol{\pi}_t = (\pi_{1t}, \dots, \pi_{nt})'$ is the vector of real user cost prices of those assets, and y_t is current-period real expenditure on the services of monetary assets. The function u is the weakly separable subfunction (category subutility function or category subproduction function) that is nested within the full intertemporal transformation function or utility function. Hence, in the case of a firm, u is a subproduction function, and in the case of a consumer, u is a subutility function. The function u is monotonically increasing and strictly quasi-concave.

Barnett (1978, 1980a) has proved that the real user cost price of monetary asset i, for either a firm or a consumer, is

$$\pi_{it} = (R_t - r_{it})/(1 + R_t), \qquad\qquad (4.2)$$

where R_t is the "benchmark" rate measuring the maximum expected rate of return available in the economy and r_{it} is the own rate of return on monetary asset i.

In the general case, the exact economic quantity aggregate produced by decision (4.1) is the distance function, treated as a function of $\mathbf{m}_t$ at fixed reference level u_0. The distance function $d(u_0, \mathbf{m}_t)$ is defined in implicit form by

$$u(\mathbf{m}_t/d(u_0, \mathbf{m}_t)) = u_0. \qquad\qquad (4.3)$$

Equation (4.3) has an interesting geometric interpretation. We see that $d(u_0, \mathbf{m}_t)$ is the factor by which $\mathbf{m}_t$ must be deflated to reduce (or increase) the level of u to the fixed reference level u_0.

When deflated by its value in a base period, the distance function becomes the Malmquist quantity index, which is dual to the famous Konüs true cost-of-living index. In the special case of homotheticity of the function u, the Malmquist index becomes the function u deflated by its value in the base period. Hence, in that elementary case the function u is itself the quantity aggregator function.

4.2   *Index number theory*

At this point we see that we can estimate the exact monetary quantity index for a consumer or firm by estimating the function u. If u is linearly homogeneous then u is itself the quantity aggregator function. If u is not linearly homogeneous then the distance function, which is derivable from u, is the exact quantity aggregator function. However, estimation of u produces an aggregate that depends both on the empirical specification of u and the estimator of its parameters. In practice, index numbers that are specification and estimator dependent are rarely used by data-producing governmental agencies.

The solution to that practical problem is to use nonparametric methods to estimate the unknown exact aggregator function of aggregation theory. The field of statistical index number theory exists precisely for that purpose. Statistical index numbers are defined to be functions only of the data and not of any unknown parameters, although statistical quantity index numbers do depend jointly on prices as well as quantities. On the other hand, the aggregation-theoretic exact-quantity aggregator function, which does contain unknown parameters, depends only on quantity data.

In recent years it has become increasingly clear from new theoretical results that the best statistical quantity index in continuous time is the Divisia index, and that the best quantity index in discrete time is the Törnqvist (Simpson's rule) discrete-time approximation to the Divisia index.[39] In continuous time with homogeneous u, the Divisia index tracks the exact aggregator function without error. In discrete time, the Törnqvist approximation to the Divisia index (which we call simply the Divisia index in discrete time) tracks the exact economic aggregator function with very low error, regardless of whether u is homogeneous. That result has been shown to hold even when the function u is shifting over time. See Caves, Christensen, and Diewert (1982a, b).

The Divisia index, whether in discrete or continuous time, computes the growth rate of the quantity aggregate as a weighted average of the growth rates of the component quantities. The weights are the expenditure shares. In continuous time, the weight applied to the growth rate of component i at instant t is the ith good's instantaneous share $s_{it} = m_{it}\pi_{it}/\mathbf{m}_t'\pi_t$. In discrete time, the weight applied to the growth rate of component i during period t is the ith good's average share

$$\bar{s}_{it} = \tfrac{1}{2}(s_{it} + s_{i, t-1}),$$

where s_{it} is this period's share and $s_{i, t-1}$ is last period's share.[40]

5   Supply-side monetary aggregation and index number theory

5.1   *Aggregation theory*

Financial intermediaries are suppliers of monetary assets. Such firms will be treated as maximizing the discounted present value of profits subject to

[39] See, e.g., Caves, Christensen, and Diewert (1982a, b) and Diewert (1980a, b, 1981).

[40] The microeconomic theory used in this section is available in detail in Barnett (1987). Relevant index number theory can be found in Barnett (1980b, 1981b, 1982a, 1983b, in

given technology, expressed as an intertemporal transformation function. Real balances of produced monetary assets are outputs in the transformation function. We assume that the transformation function is blockwise weakly separable in the current-period vector of monetary assets produced. For empirical tests of that assumption, see Hancock (1987).

Barnett (1987) has proved that the financial intermediary then can be viewed as solving a simple current-period problem, since solution to that conditional decision is necessary for solution to the firm's full intertemporal decision. That current-period conditional decision is to select the value of the monetary asset output quantity vector μ_t to

$$\text{Maximize } \mu_t' \gamma_t \text{ subject to } f(\mu_t; \mathbf{k}_t) = M_t, \tag{5.1}$$

where $\mu_t = (\mu_{1t}, \dots, \mu_{Nt})'$ is the current-period produced real balances of the financial intermediary's N outputs, $\gamma_t = (\gamma_{1t}, \dots, \gamma_{Nt})'$ is the vector of real user cost prices of those assets, $\mathbf{k}_t$ is the vector of reserve requirement ratios applying to the N assets, and M_t is total aggregate production of monetary services. In short, the financial intermediary maximizes revenue conditionally upon given (perhaps from a prior stage decision in aggregates) production of monetary services, which, in turn, is a function of factor quantities employed. The function f is the weakly separable subfunction that is nested within the transformation function. The function f is called the factor requirement function and is monotonically increasing and strictly *convex*. The constraint in decision (5.1) defines the production possibility surface at a given level of factor usage, since M_t is a function of factor quantities. The production possibility surface is concave to the origin.

It can be proved (see Barnett 1987) that the real user cost price of monetary asset i produced by the financial intermediary is

$$\gamma_{it} = [(1 - k_{it})R_t - r_{it}]/(1 + R_t), \tag{5.2}$$

where R_t is the maximum yield that the financial intermediary can earn on an additional dollar of loans, and r_{it} is the yield paid by the financial intermediary on monetary asset (deposit account type) i. For a nearly identical result (except for a puzzling difference in the discount rate in the denominator), see Hancock (1985, 1986).[41]

---

press), Allen and Diewert (1981), Denny and Pinto (1978), and Diewert (1978, 1980a, 1981). Results relevant to the economic aggregation theory used in Section 2.1 can be found in Berndt and Christensen (1973), Fuss (1977), and Christensen, Jorgenson, and Lau (1975).

[41] Hancock's user cost formulation also includes explicit transactions costs, which we do not incorporate, although our yields could be viewed as net of transactions costs. The issues raised and the approach used in what follows would not be affected, although the data would be altered. Incorporation of Hancock's transactions costs adjustments could produce a worthwhile extension of our empirical work.

Clearly, the user cost in equation (5.2) would equal the user cost in equation (4.2) if k_{it} were zero. We find that under some fairly common simplifying assumptions about the equality of interest rates seen on both sides of the markets, the user cost of monetary asset i would be the same for every firm demanding that asset, every consumer demanding that asset, and every financial intermediary producing that asset if there were no required reserves for that asset.

Observe that revenue can be written in the form

$$\mu_t' \gamma_t = \mu_t' \pi_t + R_t \mathbf{k}_t' \mu_t / (1 + R_t), \tag{5.3}$$

where π_t is the monetary asset demanders' user costs from (4.2). It therefore is clear that the second term on the right side of (5.3) is the discounted (to the beginning of the time interval) present value of the implicit tax "paid" by the financial intermediary as a result of the existence of the reserve requirements. If we do not discount by dividing by the denominator, we acquire the end-of-period tax, which is the foregone interest on required reserves. The discounted, or end-of-period, tax could be evaluated in nominal, rather than real, dollars by measuring μ_t in nominal dollars.

In the general case, the exact economic quantity aggregate produced by decision (5.1) is the output distance function treated as a function of μ_t at a fixed reference level of factor quantities. The output distance function has definition and interpretation analogous to those for the input distance function defined in equation (4.3). See Barnett (1987). When deflated by its value in a base period, the output distance function becomes the Malmquist output quantity index. In the special case of linear homogeneity of the function f, the Malmquist output quantity index becomes the function f deflated by its value in the base period. Hence, in that elementary case, f is itself the output quantity aggregator function.

5.2   *Index number theory*

The problem of acquiring a nonparametric approximation to the exact output quantity aggregate again arises, although we now are dealing with an output quantity aggregate, and again the best known statistical index is the Divisia index in continuous time or its Törnqvist (Simpson's rule) approximation in discrete time. The formula is the same as that described in Section 4.2, but with quantities demanded **m** replaced by quantities supplied μ_t and with paid user costs π_t replaced by received user costs γ_t.[42]

---

[42] For a detailed presentation of the microeconomic theory relevant to Section 3, see Barnett (1987). For results relevant to microeconometric modeling of this economic theory, see Berndt and Khaled (1979), Brown, Caves, and Christensen (1979), Denny and Pinto (1978), and Lau (1978).

Since π_t need not equal γ_t when reserve requirements are nonzero, the Divisia demand monetary aggregate need not equal the Divisia supply monetary aggregate computed over the same component quantities, even when all component markets are cleared. A regulatory wedge exists. For further theoretical discussion of the implications of that wedge, along with a geometric illustration in the case of one consumer and one financial intermediary, see Barnett, Hinich, and Weber (1986).

6   Results

We applied the tests of chaos described in the preceding to the four Divisia demand monetary aggregates, the four Divisia supply monetary aggregates, and the four simple-sum monetary aggregates. For comparison, we also produced phase portraits and autocorrelation function plots for 2,000 successive observations on IBM daily common stock returns, beginning on July 2, 1962. The monetary aggregate data was weekly data beginning in January 1969.[43] At the M1, M2, and M3 levels of monetary aggregation, our data included the 807 weekly observations beginning in January 1969 and ending in July 1984. At the highest level of aggregation, called L by the Federal Reserve, our data included 798 weekly observations beginning in January 1969. The remaining nine observations at the L level of aggregation were not yet available.

We detrended using log-linear detrending. Our data therefore consists of the residuals of an ordinary least-squares linear regression of the logarithm of the aggregate on time. Since log-linear detrending removes the neutral constant growth rate trend, we believe that log-linear detrending is the appropriate form of detrending for these tests with economic data. We use the following abbreviations for the detrended monetary aggregate data series. The Divisia monetary demand aggregates that aggregate over the components of M1, M2, M3, and L are denoted by DDM1, DDM2, DDM3, and DDL, respectively. The corresponding Divisia monetary supply aggregates are denoted by DSM1, DSM2, DSM3, and DSL, respectively. The corresponding official Federal Reserve simple-sum monetary aggregates are SSM1, SSM2, SSM3, and SSL, respectively. As a check on the robustness of the detrending method, we reran all of our tests using log cubic smoothed data. In that case, our data consists of the residuals of an ordinary least-squares regression of the logarithm of the data on a third-order polynomial in time. We designate log cubic smoothing by appending the superscript C to the aggregates symbol. For example, DDM2^C designates log cubic smoothed Divisia demand M2. Although we see no

[43] Our data source is Fayyad (1986).

particular theoretical merit to log cubic detrending, it does produce a convenient test for robustness to the theoretically attractive log-linear detrending.

The successful cases were DDM2, DDM3, DDL, DSM2, SSM2, and DDM2^C. Those data series passed all of our tests for mathematical chaos and for the existence of a strange attractor. In all other cases, a finite correlation dimension could not be found, since no linear region, (2.6), could be found in the plots of $\log_2 C_n(\epsilon)$ against $\log_2 \epsilon$ for any low embedding dimension n. In those unsuccessful cases we conclude either that the data is very noisy or that the aggregate cannot be controlled using a small number of instruments, since the minimum dimensionality of the state space is extremely large. We now describe the results in detail for the successful cases.

6.1   *Phase space portraits*

Figure 1 contains phase space portraits in four cases with embedding dimension $n = 2$. Cases 1 and 2 provide useful reference examples for comparison with cases 3 and 4. Case 1 presents the phase portrait for 2,000 observations of IBM common stock daily returns. The nearly uniform cloud of points closely resembles the phase portrait of pure Gaussian white noise. Those results would not contradict the efficient market theory for common stock returns. Case 2, on the other hand, is the phase portrait for 1,000 observations from a known strange attractor, the Henon attractor. The pattern is clearly not that of a uniform cloud but is more complex than the pattern from a simple stable or periodic system.

Cases 3 and 4 present the phase portrait produced by DDM3 and DDM2^C, respectively. The phase portrait for SSM2 closely resembles that of DDM2^C, and the phase portraits for the other successful cases (DDM2, DDL, and DSM2) closely resemble the phase portrait for DDM3. As a result, we only display the phase portraits for DDM3 and DDM2^C. In each of these cases, the time delay is 20 weeks. The selection of time delay in the display of phase portraits is somewhat arbitrary.

In cases 3 and 4, we see patterns not resembling those of white noise and too complex to be those of simple stable or periodic systems. The patterns are characterized by several foldings and twists. Case 4 is characterized by more twists than case 3. Although inspection of a phase portrait alone cannot produce a conclusive inference, the elementary exploratory data analysis displayed in Figure 1 suggests that our successful cases are probably chaotic and probably have strange attractors. Comparison with case 2 as well as with other well-known cases of theoretical chaos, such as the Whisker mapping and the Rossler model, suggests that the underlying

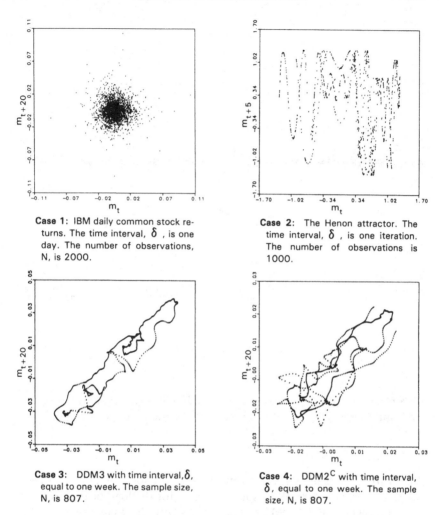

Case 1: IBM daily common stock returns. The time interval, δ, is one day. The number of observations, N, is 2000.

Case 2: The Henon attractor. The time interval, δ, is one iteration. The number of observations is 1000.

Case 3: DDM3 with time interval, δ, equal to one week. The sample size, N, is 807.

Case 4: DDM2^C with time interval, δ, equal to one week. The sample size, N, is 807.

Figure 1. Phase portraits consisting of phase space plots of the n-histories when embedding dimension $n = 2$.

strange attractors for our successful cases have very complex structure, as is entirely possible with fractal geometry. The patterns in cases 3 and 4 are suggestive of a geometrically twisted variant of Rossler spiral chaos, with the variation from the known Rossler case being greater in case 4 than in the less twisted case 3. As a result, the chaos apparently exhibited by DDM2, DDM3, DDL, and DSM2 appear to be of a more familiar form than the very complex chaos apparently exhibited by DDM2^C and SSM2.

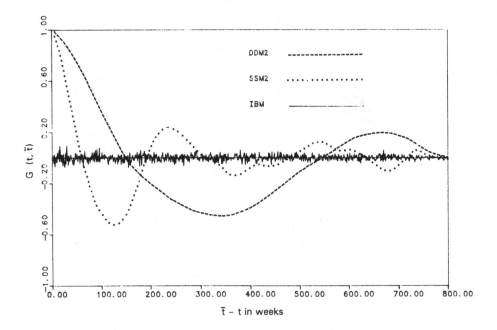

Figure 2. Autocorrelation functions $G(t, \bar{t})$ plotted vs. $\bar{t} - t$. Sample size is 807 weeks.

Since phase portraits are not easily used to differentiate between chaos and multiperiodic orbits, further tests are needed.

6.2   *Autocorrelation function plots*

In Figure 2 we display the autocorrelation functions $G(t, \bar{t})$, with $\bar{t} - t$ varying from 0 to 800. We display the plots for the log-linear detrended monetary aggregates DDM2 and SSM2. As with the phase portraits, the plot for DDM2^C closely resembles that for SSM2, whereas the plots for the other successful cases (DDM3, DDL, and DSM2) all closely resemble the autocorrelation plot for DDM2. As a result, we only present the results for DDM2 and SSM2 in Figure 2.

For comparison, we also present the autocorrelation function plot for our observations on IBM common stock daily returns.[44] That reference case produces an autocorrelation function closely resembling the delta function (spike at the origin) characterizing pure white noise. The other

[44] In order to keep all sample sizes the same in all figures, we used only the first 807 observations from our 2,000 observations on IBM common stock daily returns.

plots all produce initial exponential decay followed by thick tails apparently converging asymptotically to the time axis. That pattern is characteristic of chaos. The characteristic decorrelation time T_{AC} in each case was computed and tabulated in the last column of Table 3. None of the autocorrelation plots resembles an oscillating cosine function, which would be produced by a periodic process. As is evident from Figure 2 and from the characteristic decorrelation times, the initial exponential decay of the autocorrelation function for SSM2 (and therefore also for DDM2^C) is rapid, although certainly not as rapid as the infinitely fast decay of a delta function.

6.3   Correlation dimension

The correlation dimension of a strange attractor is particularly informative. The first step in the computation of the correlation dimensions for our successful cases is displayed in Figure 3. In that figure we plot $\log_2 C_n(\epsilon)$ against $\log_2 \epsilon$ for embedding dimensions $1, \ldots, 6$. We used a time delay τ of 5 weeks, which has been found from experience in the physics literature and from our own numerical tests with our monetary aggregates data to provide robust results. The existence of linear regions at low values of $\log_2 \epsilon$ is evident. Also evident is the existence of a saturation (asymptotic) slope approached at a sufficiently high value of the embedding dimension. It was our inability to find linear regions at low values of $\log_2 \epsilon$ that led us to rule out all of the monetary aggregates other than DDM2, DDM3, DDL, DSM2, SSM2, and DDM2^C as candidates for deterministic chaos.

To permit identification of the slope plateau, the value of the slope of each plot in Figure 3 is plotted against $\log_2 \epsilon$ and displayed in Figure 4.[45] The resulting plots are inspected to find the left-hand boundary, $\log_2 \epsilon_L(n)$, and the right-hand boundary, $\log_2 \epsilon_R(n)$, of the slope plateau at each embedding dimension n. Those boundaries are tabulated in Table 1 for $n = 3, 4, 5, 6$. The plateaus are most stable in the cases of DDM2, DSM2, and DDM3, with DDM2 and DSM2 producing as stable and broad a plateau as could be expected from even the highest quality experimental data. In Figures 3 and 4 we do not display DDL or DDM2^C, since the plots for DDL closely resemble those of DDM3, and the plots for DDM2^C closely resemble those for SSM2.

Using the points in Figure 3 between $\log_2 \epsilon_L(n)$ and $\log_2 \epsilon_R(n)$, we regress $\log_2 C_n(\epsilon)$ linearly on $\log_2 \epsilon$ at each n. The slopes are the estimates of $D(n)$ tabulated for $n = 3, \ldots, 6$ in Table 2. Inspection of those values

---

[45] The slopes were acquired from adjacent points by computing the ratios of first differences along each axis.

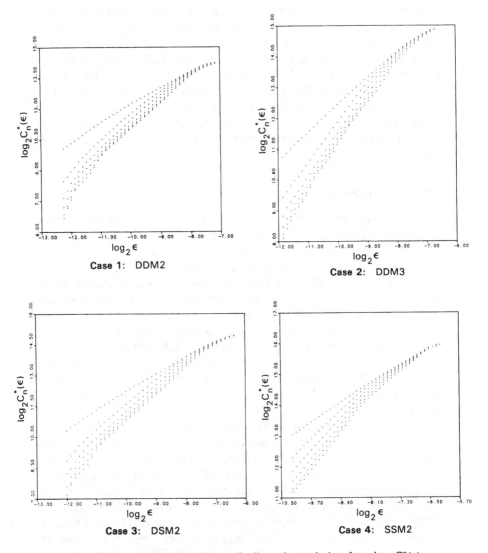

Figure 3. Plots of logarithm of adjusted correlation function $C_n^*(\epsilon)$ vs. logarithm of ϵ for embedding dimensions $n = 1, 2, ..., 6$. Plots rotate downward and to the right as n increases, with limit function approached closely at $n = 5$.

produces our estimates of the limits of $D(n)$ as $n \to \infty$. The result is our estimates of the correlation dimension, D, of the strange attractor. Those estimates of D are displayed in the last column of Table 2. In extrapolating as $n \to \infty$, the sample size in phase space declines and hence the flat

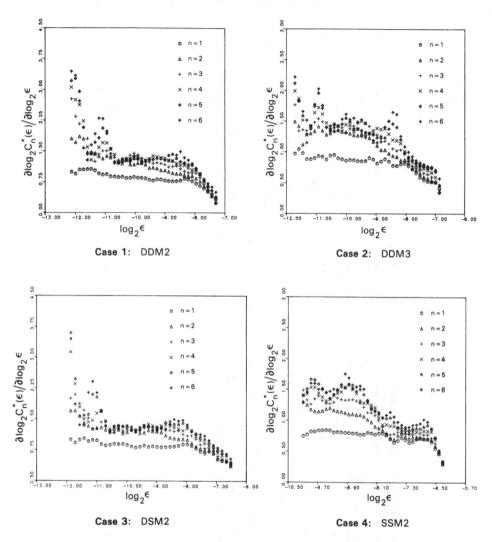

Figure 4. Plots of slopes of Figure 3 curves against $\log_2 \epsilon$ for embedding dimensions $n = 1, 2, ..., 6$. Linear regions of curves in Figure 3 can be identified from flat regions in Figure 4.

region in Figure 4 gets smaller as the embedding dimension increases. Hence, the estimated values of $D(n)$ decline in precision as n increases; and the sample size has already become rather small at $n = 6$. Our decision to set $D = 1.5$ rather than 1.6 for SSM2 reflects our judgment of the low precision of the $D(6)$ estimate.

Table 1. *Left- and right-hand boundaries of linear regions of plots in Figure 3*

Aggregate	$\log_2 \epsilon_L(3)$	$\log_2 \epsilon_R(3)$	$\log_2 \epsilon_L(4)$	$\log_2 \epsilon_R(4)$	$\log_2 \epsilon_L(5)$	$\log_2 \epsilon_R(5)$	$\log_2 \epsilon_L(6)$	$\log_2 \epsilon_R(6)$
DDM2	−11.48	−9.13	−11.48	−9.00	−11.48	−9.13	−11.48	−9.13
DDM3	−11.59	−9.22	−11.19	−9.36	−10.67	−9.49	−10.67	−9.62
DDL	−11.53	−10.06	−11.42	−10.27	−11.53	−10.37	−11.53	−10.48
DSM2	−11.00	−8.69	−10.42	−8.54	−10.42	−8.83	−10.57	−8.54
SSM2	−9.99	−8.46	−9.69	−8.56	−9.58	−8.46	−9.48	−8.36
DDM2^C	−10.23	−8.58	−9.96	−8.67	−9.59	−8.76	−9.59	−8.86

Note: $\log_2 \epsilon_L(n)$ designates left-hand boundary of $\log_2 \epsilon$ at which stable (flat) region of Figure 3 begins for embedding dimension n. Correspondingly, $\log_2 \epsilon_R(n)$ designates right-hand boundary of that stable region. Boundaries are acquired from inspection of Figure 4 at embedding dimensions $n = 3, \ldots, 6$.

Table 2. *Calculation of correlation dimension $D(n)$ in n-dimensional phase space for $n = 3, \ldots, 6$ and estimated correlation dimension D of strange attractor*

Aggregate	Number of observations (weeks)	$D(3)$	$D(4)$	$D(5)$	$D(6)$	D (estimated at saturation)
DDM2	807	1.34 (0.01)	1.36 (0.01)	1.40 (0.03)	1.42 (0.04)	1.4
DDM3	807	1.43 (0.004)	1.45 (0.01)	1.44 (0.01)	1.47 (0.02)	1.5
DDL	798	1.36 (0.01)	1.44 (0.02)	1.48 (0.02)	1.54 (0.03)	1.5
DSM2	798	1.28 (0.01)	1.30 (0.01)	1.27 (0.01)	1.27 (0.01)	1.3
SSM2	807	1.32 (0.002)	1.44 (0.01)	1.50 (0.01)	1.57 (0.01)	1.5
DDM2[C]	807	1.19 (0.01)	1.27 (0.01)	1.28 (0.02)	1.19 (0.01)	1.3

Note: D is approached at saturation embedding dimension. For embedding dimension $n = 3, \ldots, 6$, correlation dimension $D(n)$ is estimated slope of linear region of corresponding plot in Figure 3, where left- and right-hand boundaries of linear region are listed in Table 1. Numbers in parentheses are standard errors of ordinary least-squares slope estimators.

Since the attractors are fractals (strange attractors), the correlation dimensions are all fractional. In each case, the correlation dimension estimate is between 1.3 and 1.5. Hence, the minimum dimension of the state space is 2 for discrete-time models in each of our successful cases. From Figure 4, the procedure described in Ben-Mizrachi, Procaccia, and Grassberger (1984) can be used to estimate the amount of uniform white noise in the data. We find that about 1 percent noise exists in DDM2 and DDM3, and about 2 percent noise exists in DDL, DSM2, SSM2, and DDM2[C].

Recall that m_t is not an element of the state vector s_t, although m_t is a function of the state vector. Hence, the state space does not include the path of the observed variable m_t. As a result, the minimum dimension of the space that could contain the path of the augmented vector $(\mathbf{m}_t, \mathbf{s}_t)$ is 3 in each of our successful cases. If we were to impute our results to a continuous-time world, the convention is to use the augmented vector $(m_t, \mathbf{s}_t)$ as the state vector, since the differential equation system that describes the evolution of the system continuously over time contains the

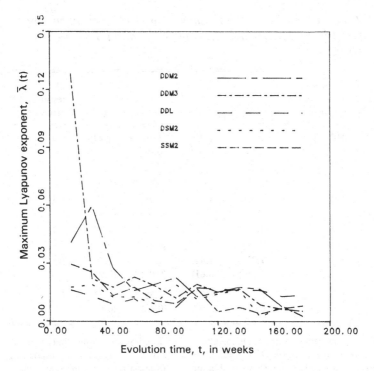

Figure 5. Maximum Lyapunov exponents plotted vs. time, with evolution times varying from 15 to 180 weeks at 15-week intervals.

augmented vector of variables. Hence, if the results of our computation were imputed to continuous time, the minimum state space dimension in our successful cases would be 3.

Although the values of $D(n)$ have not fully converged at $n = 5$, the values of $D(5)$ are reasonably close to the saturation values. Furthermore, the sample size of the observed n-histories in phase space has become somewhat small for our purposes at $n = 6$. Hence, we have chosen $n = 5$ to be the saturation-embedding dimension for our computation of the Lyapunov exponent in the next section. We also continue to use $\tau = 5$ for that computation for the same purpose of robustness.

6.4   *Maximum Lyapunov exponents*

Figure 5 contains the plots of the maximum Lyapunov exponents $\bar{\lambda}(t)$ against evolution time t. The values of the maximum Lyapunov exponents are computed at 15-week intervals, which we found to be adequate for identification of the plateau of each plot. We provide the plot for each

Table 3. *Maximum Lyapunov exponent calculation in phase space*

Aggregate	Number of observations (weeks)	t_S	$\lambda(t_S)$	t_E	$\lambda(t_E)$	λ^*	λ^{*-1}	T_{AC}
DDM2	807	45	0.0275	150	0.0165	0.0184	54.3	99
DDM3	807	30	0.0220	135	0.0170	0.0180	55.6	94
DDL	798	45	0.0129	180	0.0120	0.0122	82.0	94
DSM2	798	45	0.0126	135	0.0164	0.0136	73.5	100
SSM2	807	45	0.0133	105	0.0169	0.0135	74.1	41
DDM2^C	807	45	0.0205	165	0.0148	0.0140	71.4	49

Note: Time delay $\tau = 5$ weeks, embedding dimension $n = 5$, and 15-week intervals between computed Lyapunov exponents. Symbols: t_S = start time (initial evolution time, in weeks) for stable region of $\lambda(t)$ from Figure 5; t_E = end time (terminal evolution time, in weeks) for stable region of $\lambda(t)$ from Figure 5; $\lambda(t)$ = value of maximum Lyapunov exponent (see equation 2.11) at t; λ^* = average value of $\{\lambda(t_S), \lambda(t_S + 15), \lambda(t_S + 30), ..., \lambda(t_E)\}$, values of $\lambda(t)$ computed at 15-week intervals from t_S to t_E; T_{AC} = characteristic decorrelation time (time to decay to e^{-1}) of autocorrelation function.

of the successful log-linear detrended cases, DDM2, DDM3, DDL, DSM2, and SSM2.

By inspection of the plots in Figure 5, we determined the evolution time t_S at the start of the plateau and the evolution time t_E at the end of the plateau for each of the cases displayed in the figure. We tabulated those boundary times, along with the corresponding values $\bar{\lambda}(t_S)$ and $\bar{\lambda}(t_E)$ of the maximum Lyapunov exponent. The average values of $\bar{\lambda}(t)$ for t between t_S and t_E were then computed and displayed as $\bar{\lambda}^*$ in Table 3. It is those average values that are of interest, since they estimate the value of the maximum Lyapunov exponent on the attractor set. In each case, $\bar{\lambda}^*$ is positive, as is required for chaos. The plateau is particularly stable in the cases of DDM2 and DDM3, where DDM3 provides practically a textbook case of deterministic chaos. The somewhat less stable plateaus in the other cases reflect the existence of more data noise of a sort that cannot be explained by chaos.

Although the Lyapunov exponent is not easily used to differentiate between chaos and white noise, the positive Lyapunov exponents are powerful tests against periodic processes, and the autocorrelation and phase portrait plots already have ruled out white noise for the successful monetary aggregate cases.

Table 3 also provides Lyapunov exponent results for DDM2^C, which also produces a positive value for $\bar{\lambda}^*$. With log cubic detrending, DDM2 was the only monetary aggregate found in our research to be successfully modeled by deterministic chaos, so we display only its results in the log cubic detrending case. We present its results only as a test of robustness to the detrending method.

A check of our computations can be acquired by calculating the reciprocal of $\bar{\lambda}^*$, since the value of that reciprocal should be of the same order of magnitude as the value of the characteristic decorrelation time T_{AC} computed from the autocorrelation function. Those two values are tabulated in the last two columns of Table 3. They are about as close together in general order of magnitude as is typically the case.

7   Conclusions

The monetary aggregates DDM2 and DDM3 possess the characteristics of mathematical chaos very clearly. The monetary aggregates DDL, DSM2, and SSM2 possess those characteristics rather well, but with more noise being evident. Those results combined with the very low estimated state space dimensions suggest one of the following two conclusions. The remaining aggregates that do not produce well-defined dimensions are either (1) low-quality noisy aggregates having substantial aggregation or data error, or (2) good-quality aggregates that cannot be controlled by a small number of control variables, so that the state space dimension must be very large.

These results are consistent with the relevant aggregation theory. At the lowest level of aggregation, M1, little substitution has been internalized by aggregation, and hence many explanatory variables should be expected to be in the demand function and supply function for DDM1, DSM1, or SSM1. It therefore should be expected that those aggregates should be volatile and difficult to control without the use of many policy instruments. In other words, the minimum dimension of the state space must be large.

The fact that the Divisia demand aggregates worked better than the simple-sum aggregates is precisely as should be expected from the aggregation theory. The simple-sum index is not even a first-order approximation to the exact aggregation-theoretic aggregate, and such zero-order approximations produce tremendous aggregation error. We should expect to find extremely high noise in the simple-sum monetary aggregates. The exception was the simple-sum M2 aggregate. We do not know the reason for the favorable results with SSM2; however, it has been observed previously that M2 is the only simple-sum monetary aggregate that has ever been found to perform well in comparisons with the Divisia monetary aggregates in other tests. In particular, when judged relative to information-theoretic criteria, simple-sum SSM2 has been found to be a good indicator of unemployment. See Barnett (1982b).

The fact that DDL possessed more noise than DDM2 and DDM3 probably results from the fact that the quality of the data needed to go from the M3 level of aggregation to the higher L level of aggregation is not as good as that used in the M3 level of aggregation. In fact, the data availability problem at the L level of aggregation has led the Federal Reserve to compute L with much longer time delays than any of the other monetary aggregates. Similarly, the quality of data used in the supply-side Divisia monetary aggregates is not as high as that used in computing the demand-side Divisia monetary aggregates, since the user cost formulas needed in the computation of the supply-side Divisia monetary aggregates contain, in theory, many transaction costs on which no data exists. In addition, the Divisia demand monetary aggregates directly measure the economy's monetary service flow. But the regulatory wedge (created by the existence of required reserves paying no interest) between the demand and supply Divisia monetary aggregates produces distance between the Divisia supply monetary aggregates and the economy's monetary service flow.

The robustness of our conclusions to the detrending method is not high, although there is no particular reason to believe that it should be high. However, log-linear detrending is justified by economic theory, since that form of detrending removes the neutral constant growth rate trend. We conclude that DDM2 and DDM3 are high-quality aggregates that are likely to be controllable more easily than any of the other monetary aggregates. If, for example, the minimum state dimension of 2 were the *actual* state dimension, only two instruments would be necessary to permit perfect control of the aggregate. If only one of the state variables were a controlled policy instrument, it would need only to be used to offset the effects on the monetary aggregate of the one remaining uncontrolled variable. In reality, of course, we should expect that the actual state dimension is much higher than 2, since the lower bound produced by the correlation dimension is *very* conservative.

We also conclude that the literature on mathematical chaos and strange attractors are applicable to economics when very high-quality and carefully aggregated data, such as DDM2 and DDM3, are used. The relevant aggregation theory must be used to avoid inducing excessive noise in the data through aggregation error.

REFERENCES

Allen, R. C. and W. E. Diewert. 1981. "Direct Versus Implicit Superlative Index Number Formulae." *Review of Economics and Statistics* 63: 430–5.

Arrow, K. J. and F. H. Hahn. 1971. *General Competitive Analysis.* San Francisco: Holden-Day.

Ashley, R. and D. Patterson. 1985. "Linear Versus Nonlinear Macroeconomies: A Statistical Test." Virginia Polytechnic Institute, Blacksburg, VA.

Barnett, W. A. 1978. "The User Cost of Money." *Economic Letters* 1(2): 145–9.

　1980a. "Economic Monetary Aggregates: An Application of Index Number and Aggregation Theory." *Journal of Econometrics* 14: 11–48.

　1980b. "Economic Monetary Aggregates: Reply." *Journal of Econometrics* 14: 57–9.

　1981a. *Consumer Demand and Labor Supply: Goods, Monetary Assets, and Time.* Amsterdam: North-Holland.

　1981b. "The New Monetary Aggregates: A Comment." *Journal of Money, Credit, and Banking* 13: 485–9.

　1982a. "Divisia Indices." In *Encyclopedia of Statisical Sciences,* Vol. 2, S. Kotz and N. L. Johnson, Eds. New York: Wiley.

　1982b. "The Optimal Level of Monetary Aggregation." *Journal of Money, Credit, and Banking* 14(4, pt. 2): 687–710.

　1983a. "New Indices of Money Supply and the Flexible Laurent Demand System." *Journal of Business and Economic Statistics* 1(1): 7–23.

　1983b. "Understanding the New Divisia Monetary Aggregates." *Review of Public Data Use* 11: 349–55.

　1984. "Recent Monetary Policy and the Divisia Monetary Aggregates." *American Statistician* 38: 165–72.

　1987. "The Economic Theory of Monetary Aggregation." In *New Approaches to Monetary Economics, Proceedings of the Second International Symposium in Economic Theory and Econometrics,* W. Barnett and K. Singleton, Eds. Cambridge: Cambridge University Press.

　In press. "Developments in Monetary Aggregation Theory." *Econometric Reviews.*

Barnett, W. A. and P. Chen. 1986. "Economic Theory as a Generator of Measurable Attractors." *Mondes en Developpement* 14(453); reprinted in I. Prigogine and M. Sanglier, Eds., *Laws of Nature and Human Conduct: Specificities and Unifying Themes.* Brussels: G.O.R.D.E.S., pp. 209–24.

　Forthcoming. "Deterministic Chaos and Fractal Attractors as Tools for Nonparametric Dynamical Econometric Inference." *International Journal of Mathematical Modeling.*

Barnett, W. and S. Choi. Forthcoming. "A Comparison Between the Conventional Econometric Approach to Structural Inference and the Nonparametric Chaotic Attractor Approach." In *Economic Complexity: Chaos, Sunspots, Bubbles, and Nonlinearity, Proceedings of the Fourth International Symposium in Economic Theory and Econometrics,* W. Barnett, J. Geweke, and K. Shell, Eds. Cambridge: Cambridge University Press.

Barnett, W. A., M. J. Hinich, and W. E. Weber. 1986. "The Regulatory Wedge Between the Demand-Side and Supply-Side Aggregation Theoretic Monetary Aggregates." *Journal of Econometrics* 33: 165–85.

Barnett, W. A., E. K. Offenbacher, and P. A. Spindt. 1981. "New Concepts of Aggregated Money." *Journal of Finance* 36: 497–505.

　1984. "The New Divisia Monetary Aggregates." *Journal of Political Economy* 92(6): 1049–85.

Benhabib, J. and R. H. Day. 1980. "Erratic Accumulation." *Economics Letters* 6(2): 113–17.

　1981. "Rational Choice and Erratic Behavior." *Review of Economic Studies* 48: 459–71.

　1982. "A Characterization of Erratic Dynamics in the Overlapping Generation Model." *Journal of Economic Dynamics and Control* 4: 27–55.

Ben-Mizrachi, A., P. Procaccia, and I. Grassberger. 1984. "Characterization of Experimental (Noisy) Strange Attractors." *Physical Review A* 29: 975.

Bennettin, G., L. Galgani, A. Giorgilli, and J. M. Strelcyn. 1980. "Lyapunov Characteristic Exponents for Smooth Dynamical Systems: A Method for Computing All of Them." *Meccanica* 15: 9.

Berndt, E., and L. Christensen. 1973. "The Internal Structure of Functional Relationships: Separability, Substitution, and Aggregation." *Review of Economic Studies* 40(3): 403–10.

Berndt, E. and M. S. Khaled. 1979. "Parametric Productivity Measurement and Choice among Flexible Functional Forms." *Journal of Political Economy* 87(6): 1220–45.

Blatt, J. M. 1978. "On the Econometric Approach to Business-Cycle Analysis." *Oxford Economic Papers* 30: 292–300.

Brock, W. 1986. "Distinguishing Random and Deterministic Systems: Abridged Version." *Journal of Economic Theory* 40(1): 168–94.

Brock, W. and W. D. Dechert. "Theorems on Distinguishing Deterministic and Random Systems." In *Dynamic Econometric Modeling, Proceedings of the Third International Symposium in Economic Theory and Econometrics*, W. Barnett, E. Berndt, and H. White, Eds. Cambridge: Cambridge University Press, this volume.

Brown, R. S., D. Caves, and L. Christensen. 1979. "Modelling the Structure of Cost and Production for Multiproduct Firms." *Southern Economic Journal* 46(1): 256–73.

Bunow, B. and G. H. Weiss. 1979. "How Chaotic is Chaos? Chaotic and Other 'Noisy' Dynamics in the Frequency Domain." *Mathematical Biosciences* 47: 221–37.

Caves, D. W., L. R. Christensen, and W. E. Diewert. 1982a. "Multilateral Comparisons of Output, Input, and Productivity Using Superlative Index Numbers." *Economic Journal* 92: 73–86.

1982b. "The Economic Theory of Index Numbers and the Measurement of Input, Output, and Productivity." *Econometrica* 50: 1393–1414.

Christensen, L. R., D. W. Jorgenson, and L. J. Lau. 1975. "Transcendental Logarithmic Utility Functions." *American Economic Review* 65: 367–83.

Collet, P. and J. Eckmann. 1980. *Iterated Maps on the Interval as Dynamical Systems*. Basel: Birkhauser.

Crutchfield, J. P. and J. D. Farmer. 1982. "Fluctuations and Simple Chaotic Dynamics." *Physics Report* 92: 45–82.

Day, R. 1982. "Irregular Growth Cycles." *American Economic Review* 72: 406–14.

1983. "The Emergence of Chaos from Classical Economic Growth." *Quarterly Journal of Economics* 54: 201–13.

1985. "Dynamical Systems Theory and Complicated Economic Behavior." *Environment and Planning B: Planning and Design* 12: 55–64.

Delong, J. and L. Summers. 1984. "Are Business Cycles Symmetric?" Harvard Institute of Economic Research Discussion Paper 1076.

Denny, M. and C. Pinto. 1978. "An Aggregate Model with Multi-Product Technologies." In *Production Economics: A Dual Approach to Theory and Applications*, Vol. 2, M. Fuss and D. McFadden, Eds. Amsterdam: North-Holland, pp. 53–70.

Diewert, E. W. 1976. "Exact and Superlative Index Numbers." *Journal of Econometrics* 4: 115–45.

242   **William A. Barnett and Ping Chen**

1978. "Superlative Index Numbers and Consistency in Aggregation." *Econometrica* 46(4): 883-900.

1980a. "Aggregation Problems in the Measurement of Capital." In *The Measurement of Capital,* D. Usher, Ed. Chicago: University of Chicago Press (for the N.B.E.R.), pp. 433-538.

1980b. "Reply by Diewert." In *The Measurement of Capital,* D. Usher, Ed. Chicago: University of Chicago Press (for the N.B.E.R.), p. 538.

1981. "The Economic Theory of Index Numbers: A Survey." In *Essays in the Theory and Measurement of Consumer Behaviour in Honour of Sir Richard Stone,* A. Deaton, Ed. Cambridge: Cambridge University Press, pp. 163-208.

Fayyad, S. 1986. "Monetary Asset Component Grouping and Aggregation: An Inquiry into the Definition of Money." Doctoral Dissertation, University of Texas at Austin, Austin, TX.

Feigenbaum, M. J. 1978. "Quantitative Universality for a Class of Nonlinear Transformations." *Journal of Statistical Physics* 19: 25-52.

Fischer, S. 1974. "Money and the Production Function." *Economic Inquiry* 12(4): 517-33.

Fraser, A. and H. Swinney. Forthcoming. "Using Mutual Information to Find Independent Coordinates for Strange Attractors." *Physical Reviews A.*

Fuss, M. 1977. "The Demand for Energy in Canadian Manufacturing." *Journal of Econometrics* 5: 89-116.

Gibson, G. and C. Jeffries. 1984. "Observation of Period Doubling and Chaos in Spin-Wave Instabilities in Yttrium Iron Ganet." *Physics Reviews A* 29: 811-18.

Grandmont, J. M. 1985. "On Endogenous Competitive Business Cycles." *Econometrica* 53: 995-1045.

Granger, C. W. J. and P. Newbold. 1974. *Forecasting Economic Time Series.* New York: Academic.

Grassberger, P. and I. Procaccia. 1983a. "Measuring the Strangeness of Strange Attractors." *Physica* 90: 189-208.

1983b. "Characterization of Strange Attractors." *Physical Review Letters* 50(5): 346-9.

Grossmann, S. and B. Sonneborn-Schmick. 1982. "Correlation Decay in the Lorenz Model as a Statistical Physics Problem." *Physics Reviews A* 25: 2371-84.

Guckenheimer, J. and P. Holmes. 1983. *Nonlinear Oscillations, Dynamical Systems, and Bifurcations of Vector Fields.* New York: Springer-Verlag.

Hancock, D. 1985. "The Financial Firm: Production with Monetary and Nonmonetary Goods." *Journal of Political Economy* 93: 859-80.

1986. "A Model of the Financial Firm with Imperfect Asset and Deposit Elasticities." *Journal of Banking and Finance* 10(1): 37-54.

1987. "Aggregation of Monetary Goods: A Production Model." In *New Approaches to Monetary Economics, Proceedings of the Second International Symposium in Economic Theory and Econometrics,* W. Barnett and K. Singleton, Eds. Cambridge: Cambridge University Press.

Hao, B.-L. 1984. *Chaos.* Singapore: World Scientific.

Helleman, R., Ed. 1981. *Nonlinear Dynamics.* New York Academy of Sciences, New York.

Henon, M. 1976. "A Two Dimensional Mapping with a Strange Attractor." *Communications in Mathematical Physics* 50: 69-77.

Hinich, M. 1982. "Testing for Gaussianity and Linearity of a Stationary Time Series." *Journal of Time Series Analysis* 3(3): 1969–76.

Hinich, M. and D. Patterson. 1985a. "Evidence of Nonlinearity in Stock Returns." *Journal of Business and Economic Statistics* 3: 69–77.

1985b. "Identification of the Coefficients in a Nonlinear Time Series of the Quadratic Type." *Journal of Econometrics* 30: 112–21.

Hofstadter, D. 1985. *Metamagical Themas: Questioning for the Essence of Mind and Pattern*. New York: Basic Books, Chapter 16, pp. 364–95.

Hoppensteadt, F. and J. Hyman. 1977. "Periodic Solutions of a Logistic Difference Equation." *SIAM Journal on Applied Mathematics* 32: 73–81.

Kalaba, R. and L. Testfatsion. 1980. "A Least-Squares Model Specification Test for a Class of Dynamic Nonlinear Economic Models with Systematically Varying Parameters." *Journal of Optimization Theory and Applications* 32(4): 537–67.

Kaplan, J. and J. Yorke. 1978. "Chaotic Behavior of Multidimensional Difference Equations." In *Functional Differential Equations and the Approximation of Fixed Points, Lecture Notes in Mathematics*, Vol. 73, H. O. Peitgen and H. O. Walther, Eds. Berlin: Springer, p. 228.

Lau, L. J. 1978. "Applications of Profit Functions." In *Production Economics: A Dual Approach to Theory and Applications*, Vol. 1, M. Fuss and D. McFadden, Eds. Amsterdam: North-Holland, pp. 133–215.

Li, T-Y and J. A. Yorke. 1975. "Period Three Implies Chaos." *American Mathematical Monthly* 82: 985–92.

Lorenz, E. N. 1963. "Deterministic Nonperiodic Flow." *Journal of the Atmospheric Sciences* 20: 120–41.

Lucas, R. E. 1981. *Studies in Business Cycle Theory*. Cambridge, MA: MIT Press.

Mackey, M. C. and L. Glass. 1977. "Oscillation and Chaos in Physiological Control Systems." *Science* 197: 287–9.

Mandelbrot, B. 1977. *Fractals, Form, Chance, and Dimension*. San Francisco: Freeman.

Maravall, A. 1983. "An Application of Nonlinear Time Series Forecasting." *Journal of Business and Economic Statistics* 1(1): 66.

Matsumoto, K. and I. Tsuda. 1983. "Noise-Induced Order." *Journal of Statistical Physics* 31: 87–106.

May, R. M. 1976. "Simple Mathematical Models with Very Complicated Dynamics." *Nature* 261: 459–67.

May, R. M. and G. F. Oster. 1976. "Bifurcations and Dynamic Complexity in Simple Ecological Models." *American Naturalist* 220: 573–99.

Neftci, S. N. 1978. "A Time-Series Analysis of the Real Wages–Employment Relationship." *Journal of Political Economy* 86: 281.

Nicholis, C. and G. Nicholis. 1984. "Is There a Climatic Attractor?" *Nature* 311: 529–32.

1985. "Reconstruction of the Dynamics of the Climatic System from Time Series Data." Free University of Brussels, preprint.

Oseledec, V. 1968. "A Multiplicative Ergodic Theorem: Lyapunov Characteristic Numbers for Dynamical Systems." *Transactions Moscow Mathematical Society* 19: 197–231.

Otnes, R. K. and L. Enochson. 1972. *Digital Time Series Analysis*. New York: Wiley.

Ott, E. 1981. "Strange Attractors and Chaotic Motions of Dynamical Systems." *Review of Modern Physics* 53: 655–71.

Patterson, D. 1983. "BISPEC: A Program to Estimate the Bispectrum of a Stationary Time Series." *American Statistician* 37: 323–4.

Phlips, L. and F. Spinnewyn. 1982. "Rationality Versus Myopia in Dynamic Demand Systems." In *Advances in Econometrics,* vol. 1, R. L. Basmann and G. F. Rhodes, Eds. Greenwich, CT.: JAI Press, pp. 3–33.

Prigogine, I. 1980. *From Being to Becoming.* New York: Freeman.

Prigogine, I. and I. Stengers. 1984. *Order out of Chaos: Man's New Dialogue with Nature.* New York: Bantam.

Rao, S. and M. M. Gabr. 1980. "A Test for Linearity of Stationary Time Series." *Journal of Time Series Analysis* 1: 145.

Rossler, O. E. 1976. "Different Types of Chaos in Two Simple Differential Equations." *Zeitschrift für Naturforschung* 31A: 1664–70.

Ruelle, D. and F. Takens. 1971. "On the Nature of Turbulence." *Communications in Mathematical Physics* 20: 167–92.

Sakai, H. and H. Tokumaru. 1980. "Autocorrelations of a Certain Chaos." *IEEE Transactions on Acoustics, Speech and Signal Processing* V.I. ASSP-28(5): 588–90.

Samuelson, P. A. and R. Sato. 1984. "Unattainability of Integrability and Definiteness Conditions in the General Case of Demand for Money and Goods." *American Economic Review* 74(4): 588–604.

Schuster, H. G. 1984. *Deterministic Chaos: An Introduction.* Weinheim (Federal Republic of Germany): Physik-Verlag.

Serletis, A. 1987. "Monetary Asset Separability Tests." In *New Approaches to Monetary Economics, Proceedings of the Second International Symposium in Economic Theory and Econometrics,* W. Barnett and K. Singleton, Eds. Cambridge: Cambridge University Press.

Shaw, R. 1981. "Strange Attractors, Chaotic Behavior, and Information Flow." *Zeitschrift für Naturforschung* 36A: 80.

Stutzer, M. 1980. "Chaotic Dynamics and Bifurcations in a Macro Model." *Journal of Economic Dynamics and Control* 2: 353–76.

Swinney, H. 1985. "Observations of Complex Dynamics and Chaos." In *Fundamental Problems in Statistical Mechanics VI,* E. G. D. Cohen, Ed. Amsterdam: Elsevier North-Holland.

Takens, F. 1980. "Detecting Strange Attractors in Turbulence." In *Dynamical Systems and Turbulence,* D. Rand and L. Young, Eds. Warwick 1980, Lecture Notes in Mathematics No. 898. Berlin: Springer-Verlag, pp. 366–82.

——— 1983. "Distinguishing Deterministic and Random Systems." In *Nonlinear Dynamics and Turbulence,* G. Borenblatt, G. Iooss, and D. Joseph, Eds. Boston: Pitman, pp. 315–33.

——— 1984. "On the Numerical Determination of the Dimension of an Attractor." Unpublished manuscript.

Vastano, J. and E. J. Kostelich. In press. "Comparison of Algorithms for Determining Lyapunov Exponents from Experimental Data." In *Entropies and Dimensions,* G. Meyer-Kress, Ed. Berlin: Springer-Verlag.

Wolf, A., A. Brandstater, and J. Swift. 1985. "Comment on Recent Calculations of Fractional Dimension of Attractors." University of Texas at Austin, preprint.

Wolf, A. and J. Swift. 1984. "Progress in Computing Lyapunov Exponents from Experimental Data." In *Statistical Physics and Chaos in Fusion Plasmas,* C. W. Holton, Jr. and L. E. Reichl, Eds. New York: Wiley.

Wolf, A., J. Swift, H. Swinney, and J. Vastano. 1984. "Determining Lyapunov Exponents from a Time Series." Department of Physics, University of Texas at Austin, Austin, TX.

CHAPTER 12

Theorems on distinguishing deterministic from random systems

W. A. Brock and W. D. Dechert

1   Introduction

Recently there has been much interest in chaotic dynamical systems and empirical tests on time series for the presence of deterministic chaos. A survey and exposition of some of this activity and especially empirical methodology is contained in Barnett and Chen (this volume) and Brock (1986). Deterministic chaos can look random to the naked eye and to some statistical tests such as spectral analysis.

In Brock and Dechert (1986) it is shown how a simple map from the closed interval $[-\frac{1}{2}, \frac{1}{2}]$ to itself can be used to generate a time series of pseudorandom numbers $\{x_t\}$ that are uniformly distributed on $[-\frac{1}{2}, \frac{1}{2}]$. This is well known. Brock and Dechert also show how this time series generates a Hilbert space of pseudorandom variables that is mean-square norm isometrically isomorphic to the Hilbert space of random variables generated by white noise $\{\epsilon_t\}$, where $\{\epsilon_t\}$ is an independent and identically distributed (i.i.d.) sequence of random variables. Since the Wold decomposition theorem implies that a large class of stationary stochastic processes can be represented as a moving average of white noise (Anderson 1971, pp. 420–1), the Brock and Dechert result shows that examination of the empirical spectrum or, equivalently, the empirical autocovariance function of a time series $\{a_t\}$ cannot tell the analyst whether $\{a_t\}$ was generated by a deterministic mechanism or a stochastic mechanism. Something else is needed to distinguish deterministic from random systems.

The purpose of this chapter is twofold.

First, in Sections 2 and 3 we discuss some recent notions of dimension of a time series $\{a_t\}$ put forth by natural scientists, in particular, the correlation dimension of Grassberger and Procaccia (1983a, b) and Takens (1984). It is shown that if $\{a_t\}$ is generated by a stochastic process then its dimension is infinite, whereas if $\{a_t\}$ is "deterministically" generated then its dimension is finite. We provide rigorous mathematical proofs of these assertions for the Grassberger and Procaccia (1983b) correlation dimension. Our precise statements and proofs appear to be new. We have only found heuristic assertions of the theorems stated and proved here and in the literature. We believe that it is important to have precise statements and proofs of these two basic properties of the Grassberger–Procaccia (GP) correlation dimension since the GP measure of dimension is the dominant one in empirical work. Our methods of proof reveal the regularity conditions needed on the system generating $\{a_t\}$ for the GP measure computed from $\{a_t\}$ to uncover the dimension of the attractor of the unknown law of motion generating $\{a_t\}$. It turns out that some fairly involved mathematics, such as the ergodic theorem of dynamical systems theory and measure theory, is needed to formulate and prove these results.

Second, in Section 4 we formulate a precise theorem and proof that the Wolf et al. (1985) algorithm converges to the largest Lyapunov exponent. The Wolf et al. algorithm uses the observed time series $\{a_t\}$ to compute an estimate of the largest Lyapunov exponent. We have not seen a rigorous proof that it converges when the underlying unknown law of motion must be observed through a measuring device or observer function. Since this is the case in applied work, it is important to locate sufficient conditions for Lyapunov exponent estimation. Here again the mathematics does not seem to be easy.

Since a discussion of the applications of these two ideas (dimensions and Lyapunov exponents) to economics is in Barnett and Chen (1986) and Brock (1986), we shall be brief on such exposition. The chapter ends with Section 5, a summary.

2   Correlation dimension: deterministic chaos

We mentioned in the previous section that the sequences $\{a_t\}$ are of the form

$$a_t = h(x_t), \qquad x_t = F(x_{t-1}),$$

where both h and F are deterministic functions that can behave like the typical realization of a stationary stochastic process. This motivates a search for tests that can be performed on the observed series $\{a_t\}$ to distinguish whether it is generated by a deterministic system such as (2.1) or a stationary stochastic process. To discuss this matter precisely, we need to lay some groundwork. Since much of this groundwork is laid out in Barnett and Chen (1986) and Brock (1986), we proceed briskly here in order to save space. The reader is referred to Barnett and Chen (1986) and Brock (1986) for an exposition of notions of "dimension" and why they are useful. The reader is referred to Brock (1986) for a discussion of why the groundwork and definitions take the form they do here.

Definition 2.1 (Takens 1983). The time series of real numbers $\{a_t\}_{t=1}^{\infty}$ has a *smoothly* (i.e., at least C^2) *deterministic* explanation if there exists a *system* (h, F, x_0) such that $h: R^n \to R$, $F: R^n \to R^n$ are smooth and

$$a_t = h(x_t), \qquad x_t = F(x_{t-1}), \quad t = 1, 2, \ldots \; (x_0 \text{ given}). \qquad (2.1)$$

There is an analogue of this definition for continuous-time systems where $x_t = F(x_{t-1})$ is replaced by $dx/dt = F(x)$, but to save space, we concentrate on discrete-time systems. Also, Takens (1983, pp. 316-17) only requires that h, F be Lipschitz. In order that $\{a_t\}$ behave erratically and still be generated by (2.1), we need the notion of deterministic chaos.

To define *deterministic chaos,* we need a definition of *chaotic attractor.* The best definition seems to be unsettled in the literature (Guckenheimer and Holmes 1983, p. 256). The definition that works best for what we want to do is that of Guckenheimer and Holmes (p. 256):

Definition 2.2. An *attractor* is an indecomposable, closed, invariant set Λ with the property that, given any $\epsilon > 0$, there is a set U of positive Lebesgue measure in the ϵ-neighborhood of Λ such that $x \in U$ implies that the ω-limit set of x is contained in Λ and the forward orbit of x is contained in U.

Following Wolf et al. (1985), we say that the attractor is *chaotic* if the largest Lyapunov exponent (to be defined later) is positive. For later work we need existence of an orbit that densely covers the entire attractor.

Definition 2.3 (Guckenheimer and Holmes 1983, p. 237). A closed invariant set Λ is *topologically transitive* if F has an orbit that is dense in Λ.

We will also need, in order to position ourselves for use of the Oseledec (1968) multiplicative ergodic theorem and for the work of ergodic theory in general, that our attractor Λ and dynamical system F come equipped with a unique ergodic invariant measure ρ.

Maintained Hypothesis 2.1. *The time series $\{a_t\}_{t=1}^{\infty}$ has a C^2 deterministic explanation (h, F, x_0), where F has a unique compact attractor that is topologically transitive and is equipped with a unique invariant ergodic measure ρ that has a continuous density $\rho(dx) \equiv j(x)\, dx$. Furthermore, the forward orbit $\{x_t\}_{t=0}^{\infty}$ determined by x_0 is dense in Λ, and the largest Lyapunov exponent (to be defined later) is positive.*

Since we are interested in studying the properties of chaotic attractors with an invariant measure that is "spread out" (as opposed to concentrated on a finite number of points), we included the hypothesis that the *largest* Lyapunov exponent is positive. When this exponent is positive, the trajectories of the dynamical systems $x_{t+1} = F(x_t)$ have a tendency to spread out locally, which results in an attractor with positive dimension.

Let us try to explain the ingredients of the maintained Hypothesis 2.1 that can be tested by looking at $\{a_t\}$. For later work and to explain some implications of Hypothesis 2.1, we need:

Definition 2.4 (Guckenheimer and Holmes 1983, pp. 283–4). Let F: $R^n \to R^n$ define a discrete dynamical system. Assume F is C^1. Fix $x \in R^n$. Let $F^i(x)$ denote the ith iterate of F. Suppose that there are subspaces $V_i^{(1)} \supset V_i^{(2)} \supset \cdots \supset V_i^{(n)}$ in the tangent space at $F^i(x)$ and numbers $\mu_1 \geq \mu_2 \geq \cdots \geq \mu_n$ that depend on x with the properties that

  (a) $DF(V_i^{(j)}) = V_{i+1}^{(j)}$, $i = 0, 1, \ldots$;
  (b) $\dim V_i^{(j)} = n + 1 - j$, $i = 0, 1, \ldots$;
  (c) $\lim_{N \to \infty} (1/N) \ln \|D_x F^N(v)\| = \mu_j$ for all $v \in V_0^{(j)} - V_0^{(j+1)}$, $\|v\| = 1$.

Then the μ_j are called the *Lyapunov exponents* of F at x. A basic tool is the Oseledec multiplicative ergodic theorem.

Theorem 2.1 (Oseledec 1968; Guckenheimer and Holmes 1983, p. 284; Benettin et al. 1976). *Let F be C^2. Let F and its attractor Λ possess an ergodic invariant (Guckenheimer and Holmes 1983, p. 280) measure ρ. Then there is a ρ-measurable set $\Lambda_1 \subseteq \Lambda$ with $\rho(\Lambda_1) = \rho(\Lambda)$, and for all $x \in \Lambda_1$, Lyapunov exponents exist.*

Remark: One can get by with F being $C^{1+\theta}$ for some $\theta > 0$. See Ruelle (1979).

Remark: Since $\dim V_0^{(1)} = n + 1 - 1 = n$, as pointed out by Bennettin et al. (1976, p. 2339), if one chooses the vector v in (c) "at random," one finds $\mu_j = \mu_1$. Ergodicity of ρ implies (Katok 1980, p. 138) that μ_1 is *independent* of x. Hence, we will speak of *the* largest Lyapunov exponent of (F, Λ, ρ).

Taken's theorem (Theorem 2.2) establishes, for $m \geq 2n + 1$, that the dynamics of $x_{t+1} = F(x_t)$ on Λ is equivalent to a dynamics of m-histories a_{t+1}^m on $J_m(\Lambda)$. Here "smooth" means, as always, at least C^2, where $J_m(x) = (h(x), h(F/x)), \ldots, h(F^{m-1}(x))$.

Theorem 2.2 (Takens 1980, p. 369). *Let $\mathfrak{N}$ be a compact manifold of dimension n. For pairs (h, F), where $F: \mathfrak{N} \to \mathfrak{N}$ is a smooth diffeomorphism and where $h: \mathfrak{N} \to R$ is a smooth function, it is a generic property that the map $J_m: \mathfrak{N} \to R^m$ is an embedding provided that $m \geq 2n + 1$. That is, J_m is one-to-one and onto $J_m(\mathfrak{N})$.*

Takens gives an analogue of this theorem for flows. The importance of this theorem for us here is that the dynamics of $x_{t+1} = F(x_t)$ on $\Lambda \subseteq R^n$ are generically equivalent to the dynamics of $a_{t+1}^m = J_m \circ F \circ J_m^{-1}(a_t^m) \equiv \psi_m(a_t^m)$ for $m = 2n+1$. Here $\circ$ means composition. We state this as the *invariance principle:* Generically, conjugacy invariants of F and the attractor Λ are preserved by J_m for $\psi_m \equiv J_m \circ F \circ J_m^{-1}$ and the attractor $J_m(\Lambda)$. The first invariant that we study is *the correlation dimension.*

Let us explain the meaning of the correlation dimension and its relationship to the more intuitive notion of limit capacity defined by Takens (1980) as the *rate* of growth of the cardinality of a minimal ϵ-spanning set that covers Λ as $\epsilon \to 0$. If Λ is an n-dimensional manifold, the cardinality of a minimal ϵ-spanning set that covers Λ will increase like ϵ^{-n} as $\epsilon \to 0$.

Definition 2.5. The *correlation dimension* α of (F, Λ, x_0) is given by (when the limits below exist)

$$C(\epsilon) = \lim_{N \to \infty} \#\{(x_i, x_j) \mid \|x_i - x_j\| < \epsilon, 1 \le i, j \le N\}/N^2, \qquad (2.2)$$

$$\alpha = \lim_{\epsilon \to 0} \ln C(\epsilon)/\ln \epsilon, \qquad (2.3)$$

where $x_i \equiv F^i(x_0)$, $i = 1, 2, \ldots$, and $\#\{\ \}$ is the cardinality of the set.

The correlation dimension has nice properties. We have not found formal statements and proofs of the properties developed in what follows for the correlation dimension in the natural science literature. We do this here. Theorems 2.3 and 2.4 are from Brock (1986).

Theorem 2.3. *The correlation dimension is independent of any two norms* $\|\cdot\|_1$.

Proof: See Brock (1986).

Remark: The correlation dimension can be defined in a general metric space framework (S, d) such as the limit capacity. The same argument as the foregoing shows that the correlation dimension, similar to the limit capacity, is independent of any two equivalent distances d, d'.

The second nice property of the correlation dimension is given by:

Theorem 2.4. *Under Hypothesis 2.1, α_m is (generically) independent of m for $m \ge 2n+1$.*

Proof: See Brock (1986).

A third property of the correlation dimension requires some work to prove. But the meaning is simple: The correlation dimension gives dimension n to objects we think should have dimension n.

Theorem 2.5.   *Assume Hypothesis 2.1. If Λ is an n-dimensional manifold (with boundary) that possesses an invariant measure ρ with $\rho(dx) = j(x)\,dx$, $j(x) > 0$, for all $x \in \Lambda$, j continuous, then $\alpha_m = n$, generically, for $m \geq 2n+1$.*

Proof: The proof will be developed in a sequence of lemmas.

Lemma 2.1.   *Let $S \subseteq \Lambda \times \Lambda$ be measurable with respect to the product measure $\rho_2 \equiv \rho \times \rho$ on $\Lambda \times \Lambda$. Then*

$$\lim_{N \to \infty} \#\{(i,j) \mid 1 \leq i, j \leq N, (x_i, x_j) \in S\}/N^2 = \int_S d\rho_2 \equiv \rho_2(S).$$

Proof: We first establish this for ρ-measurable rectangles $A_1 \times A_2$, $A_1 \subseteq \Lambda$, $A_2 \subseteq \Lambda$, extend it to finite sums of measurable rectangles, and then extend it to monotone sequences of finite sums of measurable rectangles. It is easy to see from the definition of the indicator function I_A of any set A and the mean ergodic theorem that

$$\#\{(i,j) \mid 1 \leq i, j = N, (x_i, x_j) \in A_1 \times A_2\}/N^2$$
$$= \sum_{i=1}^{N} \sum_{j=1}^{N} I_{A_1 \times A_2}(x_i, x_j)/N^2 = \left(\sum_{i=1}^{N} I_{A_1}(x_i)\right)\left(\sum_{j=1}^{N} I_{A_2}(x_j)\right)\Big/N^2$$
$$\to \rho(A_1)\rho(A_2) \equiv \rho_2(A_1 \times A_2); \quad N \to \infty. \tag{2.4}$$

The mean ergodic theorem applies because, under Hypothesis 2.1, ρ is the unique, ergodic, invariant measure for (F, Λ).

Now let A be a finite disjoint sum of rectangles $A = \bigcup_{k=1}^{K} A_{1k} \times A_{2k}$; then $I_A = \sum I_{A_{1k} \times A_{2k}}$. Now

$$\rho_2^*(A) \equiv \lim_{N \to \infty} \sum_{i=1}^{N} \sum_{j=1}^{N} I_A(x_i, x_j)/N^2$$
$$= \sum_{k=1}^{K} \lim_{N \to \infty} \left(\sum_{i=1}^{N} \sum_{j=1}^{N} I_{A_{1k} \times A_{2k}}(x_i, x_j)\right)\Big/N^2$$
$$= \sum_{k=1}^{K} \rho_2(A_{1k} \times A_{2k}) = \rho_2(A). \tag{2.5}$$

We have two set functions (measures) ρ_2^* and ρ_2 that agree on the field of measurable rectangles; therefore, ρ^* extends uniquely to a measure we still denote by ρ_2^* on the σ-field generated by the field of measurable rectangles and $\rho_2^* = \rho_2$ (Loève 1963, p. 87).

For completeness we include a direct argument to finish the proof. By the ρ_2 measurability of S, we can find a sequence of increasing and decreasing sets $B_k \downarrow S$, $A_k \uparrow S$, where each A_k, B_k is a finite disjoint sum of measurable rectangles, $k = , 2, \ldots$. Now

$$\rho_2(B_k) = \overline{\lim_{N \to \infty}} \sum_{i=1}^{N} \sum_{j=1}^{N} I_{B_k}/N^2 \geq \overline{\lim_{N \to \infty}} \sum_{i=1}^{N} \sum_{j=1}^{N} I_S/N^2$$

$$\geq \lim_{N \to \infty} \sum_{i=1}^{N} \sum_{j=1}^{N} I_S/N^2 \geq \lim_{N \to \infty} \sum_{k=1}^{N} \sum_{j=1}^{N} I_{A_k}/N^2 = \rho_2(A_k). \qquad (2.6)$$

Take k to infinity in both sides of (2.6) to finish the proof. Q.E.D.

Lemma 2.2. *There are positive constants $\underline{K}, \bar{K}$ such that*

$$\underline{K}\epsilon^n \leq \rho_2(S_\epsilon) \leq \bar{K}\epsilon^n,$$

where

$$S_\epsilon \equiv \{(x, y) \mid x \in \Lambda, y \in \Lambda, \|x - y\| < \epsilon\}. \qquad (2.7)$$

Proof:

$$\rho_2(S_\epsilon) = \int_{\{(x,y)\,|\,\|x-y\|<\epsilon\}} \rho_2(dx, dy) = \int_x dx \int_{\{y\,|\,\|x-y\|<\epsilon\}} g(x, y)\, dy, \qquad (2.8)$$

where g is the density function of ρ_2. But $g > 0$ and continuous on compact $\Lambda \times \Lambda$ implies

$$0 < (\min g)V_\epsilon \leq \int_{\{y\,|\,\|x-y\|<\epsilon\}} g(x, y)\, dy \leq (\max g)V_\epsilon < \infty, \qquad (2.9)$$

where V_ϵ is the n-volume of the ϵ-ball about x (which is independent of x) and the minimum and maximum are taken over $\Lambda \times \Lambda$. To finish the proof, integrate both sides of (2.9) with respect to x, and use $\rho(\Lambda) = 1$ together with the fact that Λ is an n-manifold implies that the n-volume of an ϵ-ball about x is on the order ϵ^n. Q.E.D.

Remark: The definition of ρ_2 implies that $g(x, y) = j(x)j(y)$, but this extra structure is not needed in the proof. All that is needed is continuity and positivity of g on $\Lambda \times \Lambda$.

Corollary

$$C(\epsilon) \equiv \lim_{N \to \infty} \#\{(i, j) \mid 1 \leq i, j \leq N, \|x_i - x_j\| < \epsilon\}/N^2 = \rho_2(S_\epsilon), \qquad (2.10)$$

where S_ϵ is defined in equation (2.7).

Proof: This obviously follows from Lemma 2.1 provided that S_ϵ is ρ_2 measurable for each ϵ. It is easy to adapt Loève (1963, p. 135) to show that S_ϵ is ρ_2 measurable. Q.E.D.

Proof of Theorem 2.5:   Since we know that, generically, the correlation dimension is J_m invariant for $m \geq 2n+1$, we need only show that

$$\lim_{\epsilon \to 0} \ln \rho_2(S_\epsilon)/\ln \epsilon = n.$$

But this follows from (2.8).   Q.E.D.

The assumptions of this theorem are too strong. We want to allow attractors that have nonintegral limit capacity and correlation dimension such as those generated by the Henon and Feigenbaum maps. Hence, this theorem is of use only to show that the correlation dimension is a "sensible" notion of dimension in that it, similar to the limit capacity, assigns n to objects we think of as n-dimensional. We can weaken our maintained Hypothesis 2.1 to include some of these cases:

Hypothesis 2.2.   *The time series $\{a_t\}_{t=1}^\infty$ has a C^2 deterministic explanation (h, F, x_0), where F has a unique compact attractor Λ that is topologically transitive and is equipped with a unique invariant ergodic measure ρ that satisfies, for all $x \in \Lambda$,*

$$a\epsilon^{\alpha(x)} \leq \rho(N_\epsilon(x) \cap \Lambda) \leq b\epsilon^{\alpha(x)} \tag{2.11}$$

for $a > 0$, $\alpha(x) > 0$, $\alpha \in L^1(\rho)$, $0 < \epsilon \leq \epsilon_0$ (for some fixed $\epsilon_0 > 0$) and where $N_\epsilon(x)$ is the ϵ-neighborhood of x.

That this hypothesis is weaker than Hypothesis 2.1 can be shown by letting $\alpha(x) = m$ for some integer $m = 1, 2, \ldots$ in (2.11). In this case we have the following:

Lemma 2.3.   *If $\alpha(x) = m$ then ρ is absolutely continuous with respect to Lebesgue measure μ on R^m.*

Proof: Suppose $A \subset \Lambda$ and $\mu(A) = 0$. Then there exist open sets $G_1 \supset G_2 \supset \cdots \supset A$ with $\mu(G_n) < 2^{-n}$. Furthermore, for $\{x_i\}$ dense in Λ there exists $\epsilon_{n,i}$, $i = 1, 2, \ldots$, with $\sum_{i=1}^\infty \epsilon_{n,i}^m \leq 2^{-n+1}$ such that

$$G_n = \bigcup_{i=1}^\infty N_{\epsilon_{n,i}}(x_i).$$

Then

$$\rho(A) \leq \rho(G_n \cap \Lambda) \leq \sum_{i=1}^\infty \rho(N_{\epsilon_{n,i}}(x_i) \cap \Lambda)$$

$$\leq b \sum_{i=1}^\infty \epsilon_{n,i}^m \leq b 2^{-n+1},$$

and hence, $\rho(A) = 0$.   Q.E.D.

Our fundamental result is that the correlation coefficient is the ρ-essential infimum of the exponent $\alpha(x)$. Some of the proofs have been omitted here and can be found in Brock and Dechert (1986).

Lemma 2.4. *The following limit exists:*

$$\lim_{\epsilon \to 0} \frac{\ln \int_\Lambda \epsilon^\alpha \, d\rho}{\ln \epsilon} = \alpha_*,$$

where α_* is the ρ-essential infimum of α over Λ.

Proof: See Brock and Dechert (1986).

That the correlation coefficient equals the essential infimum of the exponent function $\alpha(x)$ now follows from:

Theorem 2.6. *Under Hypothesis 2.2 the correlation coefficient is*

$$\lim_{\epsilon \to 0} \frac{\ln C(\epsilon)}{\ln \epsilon} = \alpha_*.$$

Proof: From Brock and Dechert (1986), we get that

$$a \int \epsilon^\alpha \, d\rho \le \int_\Lambda \rho(N_\epsilon(x) \cap \Lambda)\rho(dx) \le b \int_\Lambda \epsilon^\alpha \, d\rho.$$

From Lemma 2.2 and its corollary,

$$C(\epsilon) = \int_\Lambda \rho(N_\epsilon(x) \cap \Lambda)\rho(dx)$$

and hence

$$\frac{\ln a}{\ln \epsilon} + \frac{\ln \int_\Lambda \epsilon^\alpha \, d\rho}{\ln \epsilon} \ge \frac{\ln C(\epsilon)}{\ln \epsilon} \ge \frac{\ln b}{\ln \epsilon} + \frac{\ln \int_\Lambda \epsilon^\alpha \, d\rho}{\ln \epsilon}.$$

Applying Lemma 2.4 to both sides of these equalities yields

$$\lim_{\epsilon \to 0} \frac{\ln C(\epsilon)}{\ln \epsilon} = \alpha_*. \qquad \text{Q.E.D.}$$

This theorem shows that the correlation coefficient picks up the smallest exponent of the ergodic measure ρ over the subsets of Λ with positive ρ measure.

Takens (1980) showed that the limit capacity of Λ is greater than or equal to its Hausdorf dimension, whereas Grassberger and Procaccia (1983a) argue that, in general, the Hausdorf dimension is greater than or equal to the correlation coefficient. We show directly that under our hypotheses the limit capacity is greater than or equal to the correlation coefficient. First, for the sake of completeness, we use the following from Takens (1980, pp. 374–5):

> Let $s(\epsilon)$ be the maximal cardinality of a subset of Λ such that no two points have distance less than ϵ; such a set is called a maximal ϵ-separated set.
>
> Let $r(\epsilon)$ be the minimal cardinality of a subset of Λ such that Λ is the union of the ϵ-neighborhoods of its points; such a set is called a minimal ϵ-spanning set.

Then Takens shows that

$$r(\epsilon) \le s(\epsilon) \le r(\epsilon/2), \tag{2.12}$$

and he defines the limit capacity of Λ as

$$D(\Lambda) = \lim_{\epsilon \to 0} \inf \frac{\ln r(\epsilon)}{-\ln \epsilon} = \lim_{\epsilon \to 0} \inf \frac{\ln s(\epsilon)}{-\ln \epsilon},$$

where the equality of the two inferior limits follows from (2.12).

Theorem 2.7.   *Under Hypothesis 2.2, $D(\Lambda) \ge \alpha_*$, where α_* is the essential infimum of $\alpha(x)$ over Λ.*

Proof: For each $\epsilon > 0$ let J_ϵ be a minimal ϵ-spanning subset of Λ. Without loss in generality we may assume that for each $x \in J_\epsilon$, $\alpha(x) \ge \alpha_*$. This follows from the fact that $\rho(\{x \in \Lambda \mid \alpha(x) < \alpha_*\}) = 0$ and no set of ρ-measure zero has a nonempty interior. [By condition (2.11), every ϵ-neighborhood in Λ has positive ρ-measure.] Then

$$1 = \rho\left(\bigcup_{x \in J_\epsilon} N_\epsilon(x) \cap \Lambda \right) \le \sum_{x \in J_\epsilon} \rho(N_\epsilon(x) \cap \Lambda)$$
$$\le b \sum_{x \in J_\epsilon} \epsilon^{\alpha(x)} \le b\epsilon^{\alpha_*} r(\epsilon).$$

By taking logarithms,

$$0 \le \ln b + \alpha_* \ln \epsilon + \ln r(\epsilon),$$

and hence

$$\lim_{\epsilon \to 0} \inf \frac{\ln r(\epsilon)}{-\ln \epsilon} \ge \alpha_*. \qquad \text{Q.E.D.}$$

3   Correlation dimension: stochastic case

Noise can enter in two basic ways: (i) through the measuring apparatus or observer h and (ii) through the unknown (to the scientist) law of motion

F. Intuitively, the dimension of $\{a_t\}_{t=0}^{\infty}$ should be infinite if the noise is nondegenerate. To see this heuristically, look at $\{a_t^m\}, \{a_t^{m+1}\}$. Given that $\{a_t^m\}$ fills m cubes, we would expect $\{a_t^{m+1}\}$ to fill $m+1$ cubes provided that the conditional density of a_{t+m} on $a_t^m = (a_t, a_{t+1}, \ldots, a_{t+m-1})$ is nondegenerate. It seems surprisingly difficult to turn this heuristic argument into precise mathematics.

We present two main results in this section. First, we locate precise sufficient conditions for a stochastic process $\{a_t\}$ to have infinite correlation dimension. Second, we locate sufficient conditions on how the noise enters the observer and the law of motion for the sufficient conditions to be satisfied.

Let a metrically transitive strictly stationary stochastic process $\{a_t\}_{t=0}^{\infty}$ (Doob 1953, p. 458) be given. Using the maximum norm, look at the definition of the correlation integral for embedding dimension m:

$$C_m(\epsilon) = \lim_{N \to \infty} \#\{(i,j) \mid 1 \le i, j \le N, \|a_i^m - a_j^m\| < \epsilon\}/N^2$$

$$= \int_{A_\epsilon} g_m(u_0^m) g_m(v_0^m) \, du_0^m \, dv_0^m, \qquad (3.1)$$

where

$$A_\epsilon \equiv \{(u_0^m, v_0^m) \mid \|u_0^m - v_0^m\| < \epsilon\}.$$

Here

$$g_m(u_0^m) = f(u_0^m), \qquad u_0^m = (u_0, u_1, \ldots, u_{m-1}) \qquad (3.2)$$

denotes the density of a_t^m (which is independent of t by strict stationarity). The right side of (3.1) follows from the mean ergodic theorem (Doob 1953, p. 465) and the fact that measurable functions of metrically transitive strictly stationary stochastic (MTSSS) processes are MTSSS (Doob 1953, p. 458).

Lemma 3.1. *For each* $m = 1, 2, \ldots,$ *let the range of* $\{a_t^m\}$ *be* R^m *and let the probability measure* $P_m(S) \equiv \mathrm{Prob}\{a_t^m \in S\}$ *possess a bounded density* $f_{0,\ldots,m-1}$ *on* R^m. *Then the correlation dimension* $\alpha_m \ge m$ *for all* m.

Proof: We must show, for all $m = 1, 2, \ldots,$

$$\lim_{\epsilon \to 0} \ln C_m(\epsilon)/\ln \epsilon \ge m. \qquad (3.3)$$

To do this, look at the right side of (3.1) putting $g_m = f_{0,\ldots,m-1}$ to ease typing. We have

$$C_m(\epsilon) = \int_{V_0^m} \int_{N_\epsilon(u_0^m)} g_m(u_0^m) g_m(v_0^m) \, du_0^m \, dv_0^m, \qquad (3.4)$$

where $N_\epsilon(u_0^m)$ denotes the m-ball of radius ϵ centered at $u_0^m \in R^m$. Since g_m is bounded, $\sup g_m = \bar{g}_m < \infty$. Estimate $C_m(\epsilon)$ as

$$C_m(\epsilon) \le \bar{g}_m V_m(\epsilon) \equiv \bar{C}_m(\epsilon), \tag{3.5}$$

where $V_m(\epsilon)$ is the R^m-Lebesgue volume of the m-ball $N_\epsilon(u_0^m)$. Since

$$V_m(\epsilon) = k_m \epsilon^m \quad \text{for some } k_m > 0, \tag{3.6}$$

taking $\lim_{\epsilon \to 0} \ln(\cdot)/\ln \epsilon$ of both sides of (3.5) yields the result.   Q.E.D.

This lemma and proof are worth discussing in detail. Some kind of regularity condition is necessary to get $\alpha_m \ge m$ for all $m = 1, 2, \ldots$ if a_t takes on only a finite number of values but is i.i.d. Then the correlation dimension of $\{a_t^m\}$ is zero for each m. A direct condition on $g_m(\cdot)$ may be found as follows.

Suppose that g_m is C^1 so that [recall that the closure of $N_m(u_0^m)$ is compact]

$$\int_{N_\epsilon(u_0^m)} g_m(v_0^m) \, dv_0^m = \int_{N_\epsilon(u_0^m)} g_m(u_0^m + v_0^m - u_0^m) \, dv_0^m$$

$$= (g_m(u_0^m) + O(\epsilon)) V_m(\epsilon), \tag{3.7}$$

where $O(\epsilon) \to 0$ as $\epsilon \to 0$. See this by expanding $g_m(u_0^m + v_0^m - u_0^m)$ in a Taylor series about u_0^m and use $\|v_0^m - u_0^m\| < \epsilon$ for v_0^m in $N_\epsilon(u_0^m)$. Now (3.4) and (3.7) imply

$$C_m(\epsilon) = V_m(\epsilon) \int (g_m(u_0^m) + O(\epsilon)) g_m(u_0^m) \, du_0$$

$$= V_m(\epsilon) \left[\int g_m^2(u_0^m) \, du_0^m + O(\epsilon) \right]. \tag{3.8}$$

We have:

Corollary. *Suppose g_m is C^1. Then $\int g_m^2 \, du_0^m > 0$ implies*

$$\lim \ln C_m(\epsilon)/\ln(\epsilon) = m. \tag{3.9}$$

Proof: The proof is obvious from (3.8).   Q.E.D.

It is now clear that some form of nondegeneracy of g_m is needed in order to get $\alpha_m = m$. A set Λ_m of positive R^m-Lebesgue measure will do. Let us locate conditions on $h(x_t, \eta_t)$, $x_{t+1} = F(x_t, v_{t+1})$ for g_m to be positive on Λ_m for each m. To do this, write

$$g_{m+1}(a_t, a_{t+1}, \ldots, a_{t+m}) \equiv f_{0,\ldots,m}(a_t, a_{t+1}, \ldots, a_{t+m})$$

$$= f_m^*(a_{t+m} \mid a_t^m) g_m(a_t^m). \tag{3.10}$$

Here $f_{m|0,\ldots,m-1}$ denotes the conditional density of a_{t+m} given a_t^m. We shorten the notation to f_m^* to ease typing.

To get some insight into the kind of degeneracy of g_m that prevents $\alpha_m = m$, look at the case where $\{\eta_t\}$, $\{\nu_t\}$ are deterministic at their means $\bar{\eta}$, $\bar{\nu}$. By Taken's theorem (1980, p. 369–71), generically, the map J_m is one-to-one for $m = 2n+1$ when $F: R^n \to R^n$. Hence, $f_{m|0,\ldots,m-1}$ is degenerate at the point

$$\bar{a}_{t+m} \equiv h(F^m(x_t)) = h(F^m(J_m^{-1}(a_t^m))) \equiv q_m(a_t^m).$$

That is, for $m \geq 2n+1$ given a_t, observations from $t+m$ or a_{t+m}, a_{t+m+1}, ..., are deterministic. Hence, for $m \geq 2n+1$, $g_m^2 > 0$ only on a set of Lebesgue measure zero in R^m. This violates the condition of the corollary. Also note that, in this case, g_m cannot be differentiable on R^m because it "spikes" on a set of Lebesgue measure zero. Yet g_m is a density. The area under it must be 1. Since $\int_{\Lambda_m} g_m \, du_0^m = 1$, g_m places nondegenerate mass on a set of Lebesgue measure zero. This Dirac-delta-like behavior causes the order of $C_m(\epsilon)$ to be less than m for ϵ near zero.

In order to locate conditions on $h(x_t, \eta_t)$, $F(x_t, \nu_t)$, for positivity of f_m, divide the discussion into two cases: (i) $\{\nu_t\}$ is deterministic at mean value $\bar{\nu}$, and (ii) $\{\eta_t\}$ is deterministic at mean value $\bar{\eta}$. We treat (i) first. Assume η is scalar valued and $h(x, \eta)$ is invertible in η. Then, abusing notation for probability densities,

$$\text{Prob}\{h(x_{t+m}, \eta_{t+m}) = u_m \mid a_t^m = u_0^m\}$$

$$= \int \text{Prob}\{\eta_{t+1} = h_2^{-1}[u_m, F(x, \bar{\nu})] \mid a_t^m = u_0^m\}$$

$$\times \text{Prob}\{x_{t+m-1} = x \mid a_t^m = u_0^m\} \, dx$$

$$= \int f_\eta(h_2^{-1}[u_m, F(x, \bar{\nu})]) f_{x|u_0^m}(x \mid u_0^m) \, dx,$$

where f_η, $f_{x|u_0^m}$ denote the density of η_{t+1} and the conditional density of x_{t+m-1} given $a_t^m = u_0^m$, respectively. By the assumption of independence, η_{t+1} is independent of information up to and including date t. We have:

Theorem 3.1. *If*

$$\int_{u_0^m, u_m} \left\{ \left[\int_x f_\eta(h^{-1}[u_m, F(x, \bar{\nu})]) f_x \mid u_0^m(x \mid u_0^m) \, dx \right] g_m(u_0^m) \right\}^2 du_0^m \, du_m > 0$$

then

$$\lim_{\epsilon \to 0} \ln C_{m+1}(\epsilon)/\ln \epsilon = m+1.$$

Proof: The quantity { } is g_{m+1}. The results follows from the corollary.
$$\text{Q.E.D.}$$

It is easy to generalize this kind of result when $\bar{v}$ is replaced by v_{t+1} so that there is noise in the law of motion. One then obtains

$$f_m(u_m \mid u_0^m) = \int f_\eta(h_2^{-1}[u_m, F(x, v)]) f(v) f_{(x \mid u_0^m)} \, dx \, dv,$$

and an obvious analogue of Theorem 3.1 may be stated. One can see that what is needed to get "enough" nondegeneracy of the conditional density $f_m(u_m \mid u_0^m)$, so that $\alpha_{m+1} = m+1$, is a nondegeneracy of $h(x, \eta)$ in η and/ or a nondegeneracy of $h(F(x, v), \eta)$ in η. We have not been able to get by with less nondegeneracy than that embodied in the preceding theorem.

4   Calculating largest Lyapunov exponent: deterministic case

Calculation of the largest Lyapunov exponent μ_1 is based on formulas (a)–(c) of Definition 2.4 and the Oseledec Theorem 2.1. We briefly explain the Wolf et al. (1985) algorithm for estimating the largest Lyapunov exponent following the exposition in Brock (1986).

For each embedding dimension form the time series $\{a_t^m\}_{t=1}^{N_m}$ of m-histories. Start the algorithm by locating the nearest neighbor $a_{t_1''}^m \neq a_1^m$ to the initial m-history a_1^m. Let $d_1^{(1)} = \|a_{t_1''}^m - a_1^m\|$. Note that $d_1^{(1)}$ is the smallest *positive* distance $\|a_t^m - a_1^m\|$. Select a positive integer q, set $d_2^{(1)} = \|a_{t_1'+q}^m - a_{1+q}^m\|$, and store $g_1(q) = d_2^{(1)}/d_1^{(1)}$. This ends the first iteration. Now enter the main program loop.

Ideally, in order to start the second iteration, we would like to find a new m-history $a_{t_2}^m$ near a_{1+q}^m whose angle $\theta(a_{t_2}^m - a_{1+q}^m, a_{t_1'+q}^m - a_{1+q}^m)$ is near zero. In this way we mimic Definition 2.4(c) of the Lyapunov exponent as closely as possible with $a_{t_1'}^m - a_1^m$ determining v through $J_m(\cdot)$. Definition 2.4(b) shows that except for hairline cases $\lim(1/N) \ln \|D_x F^N(v)\| = \mu_1$, the *largest* Lyapunov exponent, because the set $V_0^{(1)} - V_0^{(2)}$ has full Lebesgue measure.

Motivated by this strategy, choose t_2 to minimize the penalty function

$$p(a^m - a_{1+q}^m, a_{t_1'+q}^m - a_{1+q}^m) \equiv \|a_t^m - a_{1+q}^m\| + \hat{w} |\theta(a_t^m - a_{1+q}^m, a_{t_1'+q}^m - a_{1+q}^m)| \tag{4.1}$$

subject to the nondegeneracy requirement $a_t^m \neq a_{1+q}^m$. Here $\hat{w}$ is a penalty weight on the deviation $|\theta|$ from zero. Store

$$g_2(q) \equiv d_2^{(2)}/d_1^{(2)}, \qquad d_1^{(2)} \equiv \|a_{t_2}^m - a_{1+q}^m\|, \qquad d_2^{(2)} \equiv \|a_{t_2+q}^m - a_{1+2q}^m\|. \tag{4.2}$$

This ends iteration 2. Continue in this manner.

For iteration k, store

$$g_k(q) \equiv d_2^{(k)}/d_1^{(k)}, \qquad d_1^{(k)} \equiv \|a_{t_k}^m - a_{1+(k-1)q}^m\|, \qquad d_2^{(k)} \equiv \|a_{t_k+q}^m - a_{1+kq}^m\|,$$

$$(4.3)$$

where t_k minimizes $p(a_t^m - a_{1+(k-1)q}^m, a_{t_{k-1}+q}^m - a_{1+(k-1)q}^m)$ subject to $a_t^m \neq a_{1+(k-1)q}^m$. Continue until $k = K$, where K solves $\max\{k \mid 1 + kq \leq N_m\}$. Set

$$\hat{\lambda}_q \equiv \frac{1}{K} \sum_{k=1}^{K} \ln \frac{d_2^{(k)}/d_1^{(k)}}{q}. \qquad (4.4)$$

It is possible to show that, generically, Hypothesis 2.1 implies that an idealized version of the Wolf et al. algorithm converges to the largest Lyapunov exponent μ_1 of (F, Λ, ρ) ρ almost everywhere. In order to see this, consider first the quantity

$$\|a_{t_1(\xi)+kq}^m - a_{1+kq}^m\| / \|a_{t_1(\xi)}^m - a_1\| \equiv R_m(\xi, w, r), \qquad (4.5)$$

where

$$a_{t_1(\xi)}^m - a_1^m = \xi w + o(\xi), \qquad r \equiv kq, \qquad (4.6)$$

for a fixed direction vector w. Here $o(\xi)$ is a function of ξ such that $o(\xi)/\xi \to 0$, $\xi \to 0$. The idea we are trying to capture is that of taking a sequence of "nearest neighbors" $a_{t_1(\xi)}^m$ converging to $a_1^m \equiv J_m(x_1)$ along the direction vector w in the tangent space $T_{a_1^m}$ to $J_m(\Lambda)$ at $J_m(x_1)$. By the definition of $T_{a_1^m}$, we may find vectors $a_{t_1(\xi)}^m$ satisfying (4.6) provided that $\{a_t^m\}_{t=1}^{\infty}$ is dense in $J_m(\Lambda)$. The density of $\{a_t^m\}_{t=1}^{\infty}$ in $J_m(\Lambda)$ follows by $\{x_t\}$ lying on the orbit, which is dense in Λ by topological transitivity (cf. Hypothesis 2.1). We may now state and prove:

Theorem 4.1. *Under Hypothesis 2.1, for Lebesgue almost all $w \in T_{a_1}^m$, for ρ almost all x_1,*

$$\lim_{r \to \infty} (\lim_{\xi \to 0} \ln(R_m(\xi, w, r)))/r = \mu_1 \equiv \lim_{r \to \infty} (\ln\|D_{x_1} F^r(v)\|/r).$$

Proof: Since $a_{t_1(\xi)}^m \in J_m(\Lambda)$ there is an $x_{t_1(\xi)} \in \Lambda$ such that

$$a_{t_1(\xi)}^m - a_1^m = J_m(x_{t_1(\xi)}) - J_m(x_1) = \xi w + o(\xi). \qquad (4.7)$$

Divide both sides of (4.7) by ξ and take ξ to zero to obtain

$$\lim_{\xi \to 0} (a_{t_1(\xi)}^m - a_1^m)/\xi = D_{x_1} J_m v = w, \qquad (4.8)$$

where

$$v \equiv \lim(x_{t_1(\xi)} - x_1)/\xi. \qquad (4.9)$$

Hence, generically, for $m \geq 2n+1$, the direction vector $w \neq 0$ in $T_{a_1^m}$ determines the direction vector $v \neq 0$ in T_{x_1} – the tangent space to Λ at $x_1 \in \Lambda$.

With this groundwork we may assert

$$\lim_{\xi \to 0} R_m(\xi, w, r)$$

$$= \lim_{\xi \to 0} (\|J_m \circ F'(x_1 + \xi v + o(\xi)) - J_m \circ F'(x_1)\| / \|J_m(x_1 + \xi v + o(\xi)) - J_m(x_1)\|)$$

$$= \|D_{F'(x_1)} J_m D_{x_1} F'(v)\| / \|D_{x_1} J_m(v)\| \equiv R_m(0, w, r). \tag{4.10}$$

Now put

$$A \equiv D_{F'}(x_1) J_m, \qquad B \equiv D_{x_1} F', \tag{4.11}$$

and take $\|\cdot\|$ to be the Euclidean norm. Then

$$\|ABv\| \equiv [(ABv)'(ABv)]^{1/2} = [v'B'A'ABv]^{1/2} \equiv [y'A'Ay]^{1/2}, \tag{4.12}$$

where $y \equiv Bv$ and X' denotes the transpose of X. Now, generically, $A'A$ is positive definite and nonsingular for $m \geq 2n+1$. This is so because A is generically of full rank for $m \geq 2n+1$ (cf. Taken's Theorem 2.2). Since A is continuous in x_1 over $x_1 \in \Lambda$ and Λ is compact,

$$\underline{\eta}^{1/2} \|y\| \leq (y'A'Ay)^{1/2} \leq \bar{\eta}^{1/2} \|y\|, \tag{4.13}$$

where

$$0 < \underline{\eta} \equiv \min_{x_1 \in \Lambda} \min_{|y|=1} y'A'Ay \tag{4.14}$$

$$\bar{\eta} \equiv \max_{x_1 \in \Lambda} \max_{|y|=1} y'A'Ay < \infty. \tag{4.15}$$

Using the lower and upper bound of (4.14) and, without loss of generality, putting $\|v\| = 1$, we have, from (4.10),

$$\mu_1 = \lim_{r \to \infty} (\ln[\underline{\eta}^{1/2} \|D_{x_1} F'(v)\| / \|D_{x_1} J_m(v)\|]/r)$$

$$\leq \lim_{r \to \infty} (\ln[\|ABv\| / \|D_{x_1} J_m(v)\|]/r) \equiv \lim_{r \to \infty} (\ln R_m(0, w, r)/r)$$

$$\leq \lim_{r \to \infty} (\ln[\bar{\eta}^{1/2} \|D_{x_1} F'(v)\| / \|D_{x_1} J_m(v)\|]/r) = \mu_1 \tag{4.16}$$

Equation (4.16) follows because by the Oseledec theorem for ρ almost all x_1 for Lebesgue almost all v, $\|v\| = 1$, we have

$$\mu_1 = \lim_{r \to \infty} (\ln \|D_{x_1} F'(v)\| / r).$$

Furthermore,

$$\lim_{r \to \infty} (\ln[\eta^{1/2} \|D_{x_1} J_m(v)\|]/r) = 0 \quad \text{for } \eta > 0 \text{ and } \|D_{x_1} J_m(v)\| > 0.$$

To finish the proof, observe that $\|D_{x_1} J_m(v)\| > 0$ generically for Lebesgue almost all v for $m \geq 2n+1$ by Taken's Theorem 2.2.   Q.E.D.

In practice, given a finite data set $\{a_t^m\}_{t=1}^{N_m}$, the Wolf et al. algorithm calculates an approximation to μ_1. First, the nearest neighbor a_{t_1} determines to an approximation a direction w through (4.6), which in turn determines v through (4.7) and (4.8). This is yet still another approximation. Second, for evolution time q the vector $a_{t_1+q}^m - a_{1+q}^m = J_m(F^q(x_{t_1})) - J_m(F^q(x_1))$ can be expected to become a progressively poorer approximation to $D_{x_1}J_m \circ F^q(v)$ as q increases. For this reason the Wolf et al. algorithm tries to find a new nearest neighbor $a_{t_2}^m$ to a_{1+q}^m on the line segment connecting $a_{t_1+q}^m$ and a_{1+q}^m. In practice, of course, the distance of $a_{t_2}^m$ from this line segment must be traded off against the distance of $a_{t_2}^m$ from a_{1+q}^m. We do this by minimizing a penalty function such as (4.1) where the analyst may weigh the angle θ by his choice of $\hat{w}$. This induces yet another approximation.

Finally, for a finite data set, the average in (4.4) is necessarily a finite average. The following theorem shows that an idealized form of the Wolf et al. algorithm converges to μ_1.

Theorem 4.2. *Assume Hypothesis 2.1. Fix q and, for each $k = 1, 2, \ldots$, select a new vector $a_{t_{k+1}(\xi)}$ in the line segment connecting $a_{t_k(\xi)+q}$ and a_{1+kq}. Form the ratios*

$$g_k(q, \xi) = d_2^{(k)}(\xi)/d_1^{(k)}(\xi) \tag{4.17}$$

and the sum $\hat{\lambda}_q(\xi, k)$ as in (4.3) and (4.4), respectively. Let the sequence $a_{t_1(\xi)}^m$ be determined as in Theorem 4.1:

$$a_{t_1(\xi)}^m - a_1^m = \xi w + o(\xi). \tag{4.18}$$

Then

$$\lim_{k \to \infty} \lim_{\xi \to 0} \lambda_1(\xi, k) = \mu_1. \tag{4.19}$$

Proof: See Brock and Dechert (1986).

Remark: Bennettin et al. (1976) and references in Wolf et al. (1985) prove this theorem for the case where x is observable. Our statement and proof seem to be the only one available for the case where x can only be observed indirectly through an observer function $h(x)$.

5   Summary and conclusions

This chapter has attempted to develop the mathematics of two central concepts of applied chaos theory: (i) the correlation dimension and (ii) the algorithmic computation of the largest Lyapunov exponent. This was done for the case where the data must be observed through an observer, as in Takens (1980, 1983). We have only found heuristic arguments in the literature for this case, which is the important one for applied work where the underlying system is not known but must be "reconstructed." The level of rigor chosen is that typical of modern mathematical economics and theoretical econometrics.

Sufficient conditions on a stochastic process were located so that its correlation dimension is infinite. Sufficient conditions on a deterministic dynamical system were located so that the correlation dimension is finite. The arguments that we developed reveal the regularity that is necessary to get these results. Our arguments also reveal the regularity needed so that the correlation dimension calculated from m-histories $\{a_t^m\}$ of data is the same as the correlation dimension of the underlying dynamical system, $x_t = F(x_{t-1})$. It is obvious from the fact that a Bernoulli i.i.d. sequence taking values in $\{0, 1\}$ yields a correlation dimension of zero that some regularity is necessary to get infinite dimension for a stochastic process.

The Wolf et al. (1985) algorithm for Lyapunov exponent computation is put in a formal mathematical setting where the ergodic theory of dynamical systems may be applied to prove generic almost sure convergence to the largest Lyapunov exponent. This is done for the case where the attractor under scrutiny must be reconstructed through m-histories, as in Takens (1980, 1983, 1984). We have not seen a proof for this case, which is the important one in applied work. The argument reveals the regularity conditions that must be placed upon the Takens reconstruction map in order to get convergence. The quality of the convergence depends on the numerical condition of the derivative matrix of the reconstruction map.

Brock and Dechert (1986) contains more leisurely discussion of the preceding results as well as (i) a proof of the statement that any covariance stationary process can be approximated in mean-square norm by a one-dimensional deterministic process, (ii) a general symmetry-based non-linearity test, and (iii) limited results on when aggregation of deterministic processes preserves invariants such as the correlation dimension and the largest Lyapunov exponent.

REFERENCES

Anderson, T. W. 1971. *The Statistical Analysis of Time Series.* New York: Wiley.
Barnett, W. and P. Chen. "The Aggregation Theoretic Monetary Aggregates are Chaotic and Have Strange Attractors." This volume.
Bennettin, G., L. Galgani, and J. Streleyn. 1976. "Kolmogorov Entropy and Numerical Experiments." *Physical Review A* 14(6): 2338–45.

Brock, W. 1986. "Distinguishing Random and Deterministic Systems: An Expanded Version." *Journal of Economic Theory* 90(1): 168–95.

Brock, W. and W. Dechert. 1986. "Theorems on Distinguishing Deterministic from Random Systems: Expanded Version." Department of Economics, University of Wisconsin, Madison and University of Houston.

Doob, J. 1953. *Stochastic Processes*. New York: Wiley.

Grassberger, P. and I. Procaccia. 1983a. "Characterization of Strange Attractors." *Physical Review Letters* 50(5): 346–9.

1983b. "Measuring The Strangeness of Strange Attractors." *Physica* 9D: 189–208.

Guckenheimer, J. and P. Holmes. 1983. *Nonlinear Oscillations, Dynamical Systems, and Bifurcations of Vector Fields*. New York: Springer-Verlag.

Katok, A. 1980. "Lyapunov Exponents, Entropy, and Periodic Orbits for Diffeomorphisms." *Publication de l'Institut des Hautes Etudes Scientifiques* 51: 137–74.

Loève, M. 1963. *Probability Theory*. Princeton, NJ: Van Nostrand.

Oseledec, V. 1968. "A Multiplicative Ergodic Theorem: Lyapunov Characteristic Numbers for Dynamical Systems." *Transactions of the Moscow Mathematical Society* 19: 197–231.

Ruelle, D. 1979. "Ergodic Theory of Differentiable Dynamical Systems." *Publication de l'Institut des Hautes Etudes Scientifiques* 50: 27–58.

Takens, F. 1980. "Detecting Strange Attractors in Turbulence." In *Dynamical Systems and Turbulence,* Warwick 1980, Lecture Notes in Mathematics No. 898, D. Rand and L. Young, Eds. Berlin: Springer-Verlag, pp. 366–82.

1983. "Distinguishing Deterministic and Random Systems." In *Nonlinear Dynamics and Turbulence,* G. Borenblatt, G. Iooss, and D. Joseph, Eds. Boston: Pitman, pp. 315–33.

1984. "On the Numerical Determination of the Dimension of an Attractor." Unpublished manuscript.

Wolf, A., J. Swift, H. Swinney, and J. Vastano. 1985. "Determining Lyapunov Exponents from a Time Series." *Physica* 16D: 285–317.

PART IV

Applications

CHAPTER 13

Investment and sales: some empirical evidence

Andrew B. Abel and Olivier J. Blanchard

This chapter attempts to give a structural interpretation to the distributed lag of sales on investment at the two-digit level in U.S. manufacturing. It first presents a simple model that captures the various sources of lags and their respective implications. It then estimates the model using both data on investment and sales as well as direct information on the sources of lags. The spirit of the chapter is exploratory; the model is used mainly as a vehicle to construct, present, and interpret the data.

Lags in the response of investment expenditures to sales can be attributed to four main sources. The first is expectations. Investment depends on future sales, which themselves depend on current and past sales. The next two come from technology. One, costs of adjustment, is internal to the firm. The other, delivery lags, is external to the firm. Together they imply that the firm is neither willing nor able to adjust its capital stock completely and instantaneously to movements in sales. The last source is financial. Although the theory describes investment orders, data are about investment expenditures, which are related to orders by a distributed lag. Section 1 presents a model that incorporates these four sources explicitly and shows their respective implications.

Section 2 presents the basic investment and sales characteristics for 13 industries. It estimates a reduced-form relation of investment on sales and the capital stock, showing common patterns and differences across industries.

Given the existence of data on orders and deliveries by sector of origin, one can construct direct estimates of delivery lags by type of good. Given information on the composition of capital by industry, one can

We thank Nobu Kiyotaki for excellent research assistance and Jim Hines, Andy Lo, Jim Medoff and Jeff Zax for help along the way. Financial assistance from the National Science Foundation and the Sloan Foundation is gratefully acknowledged.

269

construct estimates of delivery lags by sector of destination. These estimates are presented in Section 3.

Section 4 examines the stochastic behavior of sales in each industry. It shows substantial differences in univariate representations of sales across industries. There appears to be a relation between the degree of persistence of sales and the size of the effect of sales on investment, which supports the hypothesis that the stochastic behavior of sales is an important determinant of the distributed-lag effect of sales on investment.

A formal test of the theory is finally carried out in Section 5, through estimation of the structural model presented in Section 1.

Section 6 reviews and assesses the main results.

1   Flexible accelerator model

We specify a flexible accelerator model. That is, we work under the maintained hypotheses that there is a causal relation from sales to investment and that no factors other than sales affect investment.[1] Although we do not believe that either of these two assumptions is correct, we see this shortcut as appropriate for a first look at the data.[2] We assume that investment behavior is characterized by[3]

[1] Even if we take as given that investment depends on demand, there are three possible candidates: production, orders, and sales (shipments). Production data must be constructed using finished goods inventory data and are not of high quality. This leaves orders or shipments. Which one is appropriate depends on the technology. If the technology is a "referee report" technology in which orders are shelved until processed, capital requirements are more closely related to shipments. If the technology is a "pipeline" technology, in which production takes time and production starts upon receipt of orders, orders are more appropriate. Not knowing which technology is more appropriate, we have done estimation both using shipments and using orders. Because of space constraints, we only report results using shipments here; results using orders are not qualitatively different.

[2] To state more explicitly our position, we believe that the relation from shipments to investment is indeed largely causal [see Blanchard (1986)]. We also believe, based on our reading of empirical work on investment, that leaving out the cost of capital is unlikely to bias the coefficients on sales substantially and is an acceptable first step.

[3] The equations in the text can be derived from the following cost minimization problem. The firm, taking sales as given, chooses a sequence of orders $\{I_t\}$ so as to minimize

$$E\left\{ \sum_{i=0}^{\infty} b^i \left[a(cS_{t+i} - K_{t+i} + e_{t+i})^2 + p\left(\sum_{j=0}^{n} \omega_j I_{t+i-j} \right) + d(I_{t+i-n})^2 \right] \middle| \Omega_t \right\}$$

subject to $K_{t+i} = (1-\theta)K_{t+i-1} + I_{t+i-n}$. Investment expenditures are then given by

$$X_{t+i} = \sum_{j=0}^{n} \omega_j I_{t+i-j},$$

where all variables are as defined in the text. In addition, b is the discount factor, assumed constant, and p is the price of new capital goods, also assumed constant. The values a, c, and d are structural parameters, and e_t is the disturbance term affecting cost. The first term in the objective function gives the cost of producing S given K. The second gives

$$I_t = \lambda(K_{t+n}^* - K_{t+n-1}) + \theta K_{t+n-1} + \xi_t, \quad 0 < \lambda < 1; \tag{1}$$

$$K_{t+n}^* = \alpha(1-\sigma) \sum_{i=0}^{\infty} \sigma^i E(S_{t+n+i} \mid \Omega_t), \quad 0 < \sigma < 1, \ \alpha > 0; \tag{2}$$

$$K_{t+n} = (1-\theta)K_{t+n-1} + I_t; \tag{3}$$

$$X_t = \sum_{i=0}^{n} \omega_i I_{t-i}, \quad \omega_i \geq 0 \ \forall i, \ \sum_{i=0}^{n} \omega_i = 1; \tag{4}$$

where:

K_t = capital in place at beginning of period t

K_{t+n}^* = level of capital desired as of time t for beginning of period $t+n$

I_t = investment orders at time t for delivery at beginning of period $t+n$

X_t = investment expenditures in period t

S_t = sales in period t

ξ_t = disturbance term

Ω_t = information set at time t, which includes at least current and lagged sales

Consider first the case where firms face *costs of adjustment* of capital but not delivery lags, so that $n = 0$. In this case, investment orders, expenditures, and deliveries are identical. From equation (1), net investment is equal to a fraction λ of the gap between desired and actual capital plus a disturbance term; gross investment is equal to net investment plus replacement investment, θK_{t-1}. Desired capital in turn depends on the sequence of expected future sales with discount factor σ; α is the steady-state ratio of capital to sales.

Costs of adjustment give two important parameters, a gap parameter λ and a discount parameter σ. These are not, strictly speaking, technological parameters.[4] We shall however treat them as structural parameters.

Consider now the case where firms also face *delivery lags*. Delivery lags are formalized in the simplest possible way by assuming that capital is

current payments on current and past investment orders, and the third describes costs of installation of newly delivered capital goods.

The coefficients α, σ, and λ in equations (1) and (2) are functions of the underlying coefficients a, b, c, d, and θ. The disturbance term ξ_t in (1) is a linear combination of expectations held as of time $t-n$ about e_{t+i}, $i \geq 0$. We do not attempt to recover those underlying coefficients and thus start directly with equations (1)–(4).

[4] For example, an increase in the convexity of the costs of adjustment, d, reduces λ and increases σ: Firms adjust more slowly and look at expected sales further in the future. There is also a simple relation between σ and λ that holds when equations (1)–(4) are derived from the preceding minimization problem. It is given by $\lambda = 1 - (\sigma/b)$. Thus, if we were to specify b a priori, we could impose that restriction on λ and σ. We do not impose it in what follows.

delivered and ready to use n periods after it is ordered.[5] This modifies all four equations. At time t, there is nothing the firm can do about its capital stock until time $t+n$ (orders cannot be canceled). Thus, in equation (1), orders close a fraction of the gap between the expected desired capital stock at time $t+n$ and the actual capital stock at time $t+n-1$, which is known as of time t. Similarly, replacement investment orders at time t are equal to θK_{t+n-1}. The expected desired capital stock at time $t+n$ in equation (2) depends in turn on the sequence of sales from time $t+n$ on, expected as of time t; given the delivery lags, sales expected between t and $t+n-1$ have no effect on current investment decisions. Equation (3) is the modified accumulation equation. Equation (4) gives expenditures as a distributed lag on orders. The implicit assumption is that payment for capital goods is made partly on order, partly before delivery, with the remainder paid at delivery. Delivery lags introduce therefore a more complex dynamic relation both between orders and sales and between expenditures and orders.

To summarize, the dynamic relation between investment and sales depends on the characteristics of the sales process through expectations, on costs of adjustment through λ and σ, on delivery lags through n and on order-expenditure lags through $\{\omega_i\}$, $i = 0, ..., n$. To see how they interact, we now consider a simple example.

1.1   *Persistence of sales, costs of adjustments, and delivery lags*

Consider the case in which sales follow a stationary first-order process. Ignoring constant terms for notational simplicity, let S follow

$$S_t = \rho_s S_{t-1} + \epsilon_{st}, \quad 0 \le \rho_s \le 1, \quad E(\epsilon_{st} \mid \Omega_{t-1}) = 0.$$

Solving for expectations in (2) and replacing in (1) gives

$$I_t = \alpha[\lambda \rho_s^n (1-\sigma)/(1-\sigma\rho_s)]S_t + (\theta - \lambda)K_{t+n-1} + \xi_t.$$

Thus, five coefficients affect the size of the effect of S on I: α, λ, σ, ρ_s, and n. The first is the capital–sales ratio and is nondynamic. The next two, λ and σ, are functions of costs of adjustment. More convex costs of adjustment decrease λ, reducing the effect of any change in S. They also increase σ, leading firms to look over a longer horizon; as $\rho_s < 1$, this will also decrease the effect of S. Delivery lags are responsible for the term ρ_s^n. As $\rho_s < 1$, this also decreases the effect of S on I.

If the effect of adjustment costs, delivery lags, and persistence on the size of the effect of sales on investment is relatively straightforward, their

---

[5] Jorgenson and Stephenson (1967) also assume that n periods elapse between the ordering of capital and the first arrival of capital. An extension would be to allow for different delivery lags. However, doing so is interesting only if capital is heterogeneous. See Lucas (1965) for a discussion. This leads to too complex an empirical specification.

effect on the dynamic, distributed lag relation is much less obvious. Indeed, in the preceding example, only current sales affect current orders. Only if sales follow a higher order process will investment orders depend on a distributed lag of sales. In that case, the lag of investment expenditures on sales will be a convolution of this lag and the order–expenditure lag. Little can be said in general about this convolution; if forecasts of future sales depend on a distributed lag of past sales with both positive and negative coefficients, some coefficients on lagged sales may well be negative.

2 Basic characteristics of data

We have selected all two- or three-digit manufacturing sectors for which we had quarterly data on orders, shipments, and investment expenditures as well as associated price deflators. The result was the choice of 13 sectors, 11 two-digit sectors, and 2 three-digit sectors (motor vehicles and aircraft). Their names and mnemonics are given in the first two columns of Table 1. Orders, shipments, and expenditures are directly available. Capital stock series, which are needed for estimation, are constructed by accumulation of investment expenditures. Appendix A gives sources, methods of construction, and other information on the data. One data problem must be mentioned in the text: Shipments are collected on an establishment basis, whereas investment expenditures are collected on a company basis. This is not a major problem for most sectors except for petroleum, in which a large proportion of investment expenditures by companies classified in petroleum takes place in activities largely unrelated to petroleum (see Appendix A for details). The sample period is 1958, quarter 1, to 1979, quarter 3.

In examining the data, both informally here and using econometric techniques later, we assume that investment and shipments have both a deterministic and a stochastic component. We assume the deterministic component to be the sum of an exponential time trend and seasonal dummies. Examining the data using the alternative assumption that there is no deterministic time trend would be useful, but we have not done so here.

The first six columns of numbers in Table 1 give the estimated growth rates and the means and standard deviations of the deviations from trend and seasonal for investment and shipments for each sector. Although we shall not focus on these deterministic components in what follows, it must be noted that there is wide variation of growth rates both among sectors and between investment and shipments in a given sector; this last fact is evidence of long-run movements in the capital–shipments ratio.

A reason why investment may move more or less compared to shipments across sectors is simply the difference in their capital–shipments

Table 1. *Investment expenditures and shipments: 1958, quarter 1, to 1979, quarter 3*

	Mnemonics	Growth rates (%)		Means (billions of 1972 dollars)		Standard deviations (billions of 1972 dollars)		α (K/S)	R $(\sigma_x/X)/(\sigma_s/S)$
		g_x	g_s	X	S	σ_x	σ_s		
Food	FO	3.5	2.3	2.9	85.2	0.3	1.6	0.24	5.0
Textiles	TX	1.5	4.0	0.8	20.4	0.2	1.6	0.31	2.8
Paper	PA	6.0	3.6	1.8	21.6	0.3	1.2	0.50	3.0
Chemicals	CH	5.3	5.0	4.0	45.2	0.6	3.6	0.56	1.7
Petroleum	PET	3.7	3.0	5.8	22.8	0.8	1.2	2.10	2.8
Rubber	RU	3.3	6.1	0.9	15.6	0.2	1.2	0.40	2.5
Stone, clay, and glass	SCG	3.1	2.4	1.3	14.8	0.2	0.8	0.63	2.8
Primary metals	PM	2.4	1.9	3.2	43.2	0.7	4.8	0.58	1.6
Fabricated metals	FM	3.0	2.8	1.3	36.8	0.2	3.6	0.24	1.7
Nonelectrical machinery	NEM	6.2	5.0	3.6	49.6	0.6	4.0	0.41	2.1
Electrical machinery	EM	5.4	4.5	2.9	41.2	0.7	4.0	0.45	2.9
Motor vehicles	MV	3.5	4.4	3.2	46.4	0.6	6.0	0.45	1.5
Aircraft	AC	10.3	0.3	1.3	19.6	0.5	3.2	0.30	2.4

Note: See appendix for definitions and construction. All variables are at annual rates.

ratios α. The next column gives mean capital–shipments ratios. For reasons explained earlier in this section, the main outlier, petroleum, overestimates the true capital–shipments ratio, probably by a factor of 2. Otherwise, the capital–shipments ratio varies between 0.24 and 0.63.

Two sectors that are similar in all respects except in their mean capital–shipments ratio will have the same ratio of coefficient of variation of investment to coefficient of variation of shipments. This ratio, denoted R, is given in the last column. Except for food, where it is equal to 5, this ratio varies across sectors from 1.5 to 3.0.

Table 2 gives further evidence on the relation between investment and shipments by giving, for each sector, estimates of the relation

$$X_t = bK_{t-1} + \sum_{i=0}^{6} c_i S_{t-i} + u_t, \quad u_t = \rho u_{t-1} + \epsilon_t. \tag{5}$$

We shall see in Section 5 that this equation is, under specific assumptions about the information set, the approximate reduced form of the structural model described in equations (1)–(4).[6] Equation (5) gives investment expenditures as depending on capital at the end of the previous quarter, current and lagged values of shipments up to six lags, and a first-order disturbance term. In addition to these variables, regressions include a constant, a deterministic exponential time trend, and seasonal dummies.

The coefficients on $K(-1)$ and S to $S(-6)$ are reported in the first seven columns. The next two columns give the sum of coefficients on shipments, Σ, and the sum divided by the mean capital–shipments ratio (Σ/α). If all sectors were the same, except for their mean ratio, Σ/α would be the same across sectors. The next column reports the value of the likelihood ratio test statistic, L, associated with the hypothesis that shipments play no role in explaining investment expenditures. The last two columns give the coefficient of serial correlation of the disturbance and the R^2 on the ρ-transformed variables after taking out the deterministic trend and the seasonal component.

For five of the sectors (FO, TX, CH, PET, and PM) shipments have no significant effect on investment, and the cumulative effect (measured by Σ/α) is quantitatively small. For eight of the sectors and for most of durable manufacturing (PA, RU, and SCG in nondurable manufacturing and FM, NEM, EM, MV, and AC in durable manufacturing), shipments have a very significant effect, with an average cumulative effect of 0.31. To get

---

[6] The use of "approximate" is due to the fact that, in going from the structural model to (5), two approximations are made. One is the use of K_{t-1} as an empirical counterpart to the variable implied by (1)–(4), which is unobservable. The other is in the approximation by an AR(1) of the process followed by the disturbance term. This is further discussed in Section 5.

Table 2. *Reduced form: investment and shipments: 1959, quarter 2, to 1979, quarter 3*

Sector	K(-1)	S	S(-1)	S(-2)	S(-3)	S(-4)	S(-5)	S(-6)	Σ	Σ/α	L	ρ	$\bar{R}^2$
FO	0.03	0.2	-1.1	0.3	-0.2	-0.3	1.9	-0.4	0.00	0.02	4	0.87	-0.04
TX	-0.18	1.7	2.2	0.1	-0.2	1.3	2.7	-0.2	0.07	0.24	12	0.94	0.05
PA	-0.18	3.0	4.7	5.1[a]	1.3	6.7	1.3	0.1	0.22	0.44	24[a]	0.89	0.24
CH	-0.21	-0.1	-2.2	5.3[a]	-0.6	0.4	2.8	-2.0	0.04	0.07	10	0.94	0.18
PET	-0.11	0.5	-1.7	11.6	-8.6	0.7	7.0	-3.2	0.06	0.03	12	0.89	0.05
RU	-0.00	3.0[a]	3.6[a]	2.9[a]	1.5	-0.7	0.1	-0.3	0.10	0.25	44[a]	0.79	0.41
SCG	-0.08	4.5[a]	4.1	3.0	5.1[a]	1.3	1.4	-0.0	0.19	0.31	16[a]	0.91	0.10
PM	-0.06	0.0	0.9	1.1	1.7[a]	1.6[a]	1.7[a]	0.8	0.08	0.13	12	0.90	0.05
FM	-0.12	1.5	0.5	1.4	1.2	1.6	-0.7	-0.5	0.05	0.20	24[a]	0.53	0.36
NEM	0.03	5.5[a]	3.6	2.0	5.6[a]	-3.5	-0.2	0.6	0.13	0.33	38[a]	0.77	0.36
EM	-0.03	1.5	2.9	2.3	1.7	2.9	0.7	-0.8	0.11	0.25	26[a]	0.93	0.21
MV	-0.03	0.8[a]	1.2[a]	2.5[a]	2.4[a]	1.9[a]	1.6[a]	0.6	0.11	0.24	54[a]	0.83	0.51
AC	-0.36	-0.1	2.5	4.1	1.2	0.3	2.5	2.6	0.13	0.43	14[a]	0.99	0.07

Note: S, all coefficients on shipments are multiplied by 10^{-2}; Σ, sum of coefficients on shipments; Σ/α, sum of coefficients on shipments divided by capital-shipment ratio; *L*, value of likelihood ratio test statistic associated with hypothesis that shipments do not affect investment; R^2 on ρ-transformed variables after detrending and deseasonalization.

[a] Significant at the 5% level.

a feel for the size of this coefficient, suppose that shipments followed a random walk; the cumulative effect of shipments as measured by Σ/α would then be equal to λ. A coefficient of 4 would then mean full adjustment of investment to the anticipated gap between desired capital and actual capital.[7]

As we do not impose constraints on the distributed-lag structure, multicollinearity implies that the shape of the lag structure is not estimated very tightly. The lag structure shows no definite pattern and, in particular, no sign of smooth decay as the lag length increases; in many sectors, coefficients on $S(-1)$ to $S(-3)$ are larger and more significant than the others.

In the rest of this chapter, we try to explain the characteristics of these distributed-lag structures and why they differ across sectors. But before we turn to this task, we must mention another characteristic of these reduced forms. For all sectors, even those where shipments are quantitatively and statistically significant, the disturbance term, which measures the effects of variables other than sales, is highly serially correlated and explains a good part of the movement in investment. The adjusted R^2 is in most cases not very high; its average value for the sectors in which shipments are significant is on the order of 0.29.[8] A large part of movements in investment is thus not due to shipments [this is true also when shipments are replaced by orders in (5)]. Even if we were successful in explaining the effects of shipments on investment, there would be a lot left to be explained.

3   Direct evidence on delivery lags

In this section, we construct direct estimates of delivery lags facing each of the sectors. We proceed in four steps. We first derive the capital composition of each sector and then calculate the delivery lag associated with each type of equipment and structure. Next, we combine the information on capital composition and delivery lag by type of good to get average delivery lags by sector. Finally, we study whether the delivery lag associated with each type of good is approximately constant or, instead, varies cyclically with the output of the sector producing the type of capital good.

---

[7] Because α denotes the ratio of capital to annual shipments, λ is also expressed at annual rates. That is, for a given value λ, investment will close during a quarter ($\lambda/4$) of the difference between desired and actual capital. This is why the number 4 rather than 1 appears in the text.

[8] This result, which initially surprised us, is in fact consistent with previous studies at the sectoral level [see, e.g., references in the surveys by Jorgenson (1971) and Uri (1982)]. These studies usually report the R^2 on the original variables, which is obviously much higher. In our case, e.g., it always exceeds 0.9.

Table 3. *Composition of capital stock by sector*

Sector of destination	Sector of origin				
	FM	NEM	EM	MV	Structures
FO	0.04	0.34	0.02	0.06	0.52
TX	0.00	0.51	0.03	0.03	0.43
PA	0.11	0.41	0.08	0.03	0.37
CH	0.18	0.27	0.05	0.03	0.46
PET	0.06	0.08	0.02	0.02	0.83
RU	0.01	0.55	0.02	0.02	0.40
SCG	0.01	0.35	0.04	0.06	0.53
PM	0.06	0.32	0.09	0.02	0.50
FM	0.00	0.43	0.05	0.07	0.46
NEM	0.01	0.44	0.07	0.04	0.44
EM	0.00	0.36	0.18	0.03	0.44
MV	0.00	0.53	0.04	0.03	0.41
AC	0.00	0.40	0.11	0.05	0.44

3.1   *Sectoral composition of capital*

We construct a capital stock decomposition for each sector. We start from the capital flow tables, which give the amount of investment of each type for each sector for both 1967 and 1972. We then go from these flows to stocks by using information about depreciation and growth rates for each type of good and each sector. The details of the computation are given in Appendix B. The results are given in Table 3.

Capital equipment comes nearly entirely from four sectors, mainly from nonelectrical machinery, with smaller amounts coming from fabricated metals, electrical machinery, and motor vehicles. The ratio of capital equipment to structures is similar across sectors and close to unity, except for petroleum, which has a much larger proportion of structures.

3.2   *Delivery lags by type of capital good*

We use different approaches for the construction of delivery lags for structures and equipment.

Data on time to completion for different types of structures are directly available; we therefore use them.

No such data exist on equipment, and more work is needed. Of the four sectors producing equipment, only three have delivery lags; motor vehicles may be assumed to be sold from stock. We have data on unfilled

Table 4. *Delivery/construction lags*

Type of good	Average lag, in quarters
Fabricated metals	2
Nonelectrical machinery	2
Electrical machinery	3
Motor vehicles	0
Industrial structures	3–5
Commercial structures	3–6
Other structures	4–8

and new orders as well as on shipments for the remaining three sectors. If these sectors produced only capital goods and if all goods were produced to order, the ratio of unfilled orders to shipments would give a good estimate of the average delivery lag associated with these goods. These two assumptions are, however, strongly violated: The proportion in total sales of goods sold as capital goods is only 4 percent for fabricated metals, 20 percent for electrical machinery, and 43 percent for nonelectrical machinery. We therefore use the following approach. We assume that all capital goods are produced to order and that all sales by the producing sector to wholesalers and retailers, and only these sales, are from stock. We then estimate the mean delivery lag by

$$V_i/(1-b_i)S_i,$$

where V_i, S_i, and b_i are mean unfilled orders, mean shipments, and the proportion of shipments sold to wholesalers and retailers for sector i, respectively. (Details of construction are given in Appendix B; b_i varies between 42 and 46 percent.) The results are given in Table 4. Delivery lags appear similar across the different types of equipment; this uniformity no doubt hides differences at a more disaggregated level. Not surprisingly, delivery lags are longer for structures than for equipment. It takes on average a year to build an industrial structure, whereas it takes approximately 6 months to receive equipment.

3.3   Delivery lags by sector

All that is left to do is to combine results about sectoral composition with those about delivery lags by type of capital. Implied average delivery lags by sector of destination are given in Table 5. For our purposes, the main

Table 5. *Average delivery lag*

Sector of destination	Average lag, in quarters
FO	3.4
TX	3.2
PA	3.2
CH	3.3
PET	5.3
RU	3.2
SCG	3.5
PM	3.5
FM	3.3
NEM	3.3
EM	3.5
MV	3.2
AC	3.3

result is that, except for petroleum, all sectors face very similar delivery lag structures; the mean delivery lag varies between 3.2 and 3.5 quarters.[9] This is therefore not the source of the difference of the response of investment to shipments across sectors.

3.4   *Cyclical behavior of delivery lags*

Before leaving delivery lags, we return to a maintained assumption of our model, and indeed of all models that assume a fixed distributed-lag relation between demand and investment, namely, that of constancy of delivery lags. We can use the time series on orders and shipments for the capital-producing sectors to examine the validity of this assumption. If we assume that the proportion of production to order in total production is constant over the cycle, then if delivery lags are constant, the relation between orders and shipments should be constant through time. We therefore run the following regression:

$$S_t = f \sum_{i=0}^{\infty} w_{it} O_{t-i} + e_t, \quad w_{it} = (1-d_t)^2 (i+1) d_t^i,$$

where

$$d_t = d + c(O_t - \bar{O}_t).$$

[9] If we recognized explicitly the heterogeneity of capital in our model of investment and assumed, e.g., the technology to be Leontief in the various types of capital, the longest delivery lag would be more relevant than the mean lag. Sectors would still look fairly similar.

Under the null hypothesis of constant delivery lags, $c = 0$ so that d_t is constant and equal to d. The distributed lag of orders on shipments is taken to be a Pascal distribution, a parameterization that is convenient under both the null and the alternative hypotheses. The coefficient f is allowed to differ from 1 to reflect that some orders are canceled and not all shipments are in response to orders. The mean lag is given by $2d/(1-d)$.

Under the alternative hypothesis, c is positive, and the mean lag is an increasing function of the level of demand measured by the deviation of orders from an exponential deterministic trend and seasonals.

The relation between shipments and orders can be rewritten as

$$S_t = 2d_t S_{t-1} - d_t^2 S_{t-2} + f(1 - d_t)^2 O_t + e_t'.$$

In the absence of good reasons to the contrary, we assume that e_t', the disturbance term after transformation, is white and thus estimate the preceding equation. Results are reported in Table 6. In addition to the estimates of d and c, we give estimates of the mean lag when deviations of orders from trend are respectively equal to plus and minus one standard deviation.

The results are quite clear and show delivery lags to be procyclical.[10] Having duly registered this result, we nevertheless proceed to estimate our model, which is based on constant lags; but these results make clear that the linear relation between investment and shipments is at best a rough approximation and that further research might uncover nonlinearities.

4   Dynamic behavior of sales

We have seen that whether or not an increase in current sales is expected to persist is an important determinant of the relation between investment expenditures and shipments, and that differences in processes for shipments across sectors have the potential to explain differences in the dynamic response of investment to shipments. In this section, we examine the characteristics of the univariate representation of shipments across sectors.

Table 7 presents the results of estimation of AR(4) processes for shipments. As discussed earlier, we maintain the assumption of a deterministic time trend and deterministic seasonality. Thus, we also include an exponential time trend and seasonal dummies; their coefficients are not reported. An AR(4) representation is sufficient to capture the dynamics of the stochastic component of shipments (Q statistics are given in the

---

[10] Because we do not make any explicit correction for the fact that production is partly to stock, or equivalently that some of the orders are satisfied without lag from the shelf, the estimated mean lag is much shorter than the estimated delivery lag constructed earlier.

Table 6. *Cyclical behavior of delivery lags*

Sector of origin	d	c	$O = \bar{O} - \sigma_o$		$O = \bar{O}$		$O = \bar{O} + \sigma_o$	
			d(O)	ML	d(O)	ML	d(O)	ML
Fabricated metals	0.29 (7.4)	0.38×10^{-4} (4.7)	0.11	0.25	0.29	0.81	0.47	1.77
Nonelectrical machinery	0.30 (9.2)	0.12×10^{-4} (2.9)	0.23	0.60	0.30	0.85	0.37	1.17
Electrical machinery	0.33	0.16×10^{-4}	0.25	0.66	0.33	1.00	0.41	1.38

Note: Period of estimation: 1958, quarter 3, to 1979, quarter 3. Numbers in parentheses are t statistics. Abbreviation: ML, mean lag defined as $2d(O)/(1 - d(O))$.

Table 7. *Univariate representations of shipments*

Sector	a_1	a_2	a_3	a_4	R^2	$Q(27)^a$	Sum^b	Cycle length^c	$(\Sigma/\alpha)^d$
FO	0.82	−0.45	0.20	−0.07	0.42	21.4	0.50	6.6	0.02
TX	1.22	−0.14	−0.38	0.25	0.90	21.0	0.95	16.5	0.24
PA	1.17	−0.36	0.07	−0.07	0.79	11.2	0.81	12.0	0.44^e
CH	1.41	−0.65	0.09	0.01	0.86	18.9	0.86	14.0	0.07
PET	0.91	−0.21	0.23	−0.14	0.64	7.6	0.79	9.9	0.03
RU	0.94	0.11	−0.04	−0.15	0.82	14.2	0.86	13.2	0.25^e
SCG	0.88	−0.30	0.27	−0.02	0.63	33.4	0.83	9.2	0.31^e
PM	0.66	−0.06	0.25	−0.08	0.52	10.7	0.77	7.8	0.13
FM	1.15	−0.26	0.21	−0.20	0.89	9.6	0.90	16.3	0.20^e
NEM	1.21	−0.31	0.03	−0.04	0.86	24.6	0.89	15.4	0.33^e
EM	1.35	−0.46	0.01	0.02	0.91	10.6	0.92	17.1	0.25^e
MV	0.59	0.11	0.02	−0.06	0.81	9.1	0.66	7.3	0.24^e
AC	0.82	0.35	−0.14	−0.09	0.89	7.9	0.94	17.9	0.43^e

Note: Period of estimation is 1958, quarter 4, to 1979, quarter 3.

^{a} The Q statistic associated with hypothesis that residuals are white. It is distributed as $\chi^2(27)$; $\chi^2(27) = 40.1$ at 0.05.

^{b} Sum of coefficients on lagged shipments.

^{c} Cycle length, defined as $360/\cos^{-1}(\rho)$, where ρ is the correlation between S and $S(-1)$.

^{d} Normalized sum of coefficients on shipments in investment equation, from Table 2.

^{e} Set of coefficients on lagged sales (from Table 2) is significant at the 5% level.

table). In addition to the coefficients and their sum, Table 7 presents the expected time between two successive downcrossings of the mean, which provides a measure of the length of the cycle in shipments.

Table 7 shows large variations in persistence across sectors. Food exhibits low persistence; at the other end, textiles, fabricated metals, electrical and nonelectrical machinery, and aircraft exhibit high persistence. In two of these sectors (TX and AC), the hypothesis of nonstationarity cannot be rejected (using the distribution appropriate under the assumption of a unit root and the presence of a deterministic time trend in the regression). In many sectors, the degree of persistence is such that, even with delivery lags of up to a year, we would expect substantial effects of current shipments on investment orders.

To see whether these differences in processes may help explain variations in the investment–shipments relation, the last column reports the normalized sum of coefficients on shipments in the investment equation (from Table 2). One expects, ceteris paribus, a positive relation between persistence and the normalized sum of coefficients. There is indeed some relation between the two: The rank correlation between cycle length and the normalized sum is 0.42, which is significant at the 10 percent level. The relation is, however, not tight; motor vehicles, for example, has low persistence of shipments but a strong effect of shipments on investment. The next section provides a more formal assessment by estimating the structural investment equation implied by (1)–(4) given the sales process.

5   Structural estimation

5.1   *Derivation of reduced form implied by equations (1)–(4)*

The first step is to eliminate unobservable expectations. We assume that the information set includes only current and lagged investment expenditures and shipments and that shipments are uncorrelated at all leads and lags with the disturbance ξ. This implies that expectations of shipments conditional on the information set are the same as forecasts of shipments using a univariate representation. This joint assumption is stronger than is needed for estimation but allows a more intuitive interpretation of the relation between the characteristics of the shipment process presented in Section 4 and the characteristics of the relation between investment and shipments.[11] Let the AR(4) process for shipments be given by

[11] This joint assumption implies that investment should not help predict sales given past sales and is thus testable. It is rejected in 3 sectors at the 5 percent level and in 2 (petroleum and aircraft) at the 1 percent level. Thus, for these 2 sectors, the results that follow are biased. For the other 10 sectors, the assumption in the text is an acceptable first approximation.

$$S_t = a_1 S_{t-1} + a_2 S_{t-2} + a_3 S_{t-3} + a_4 S_{t-4} + \epsilon_{st}.$$

Rewriting it in companion form gives

$$Z_t = AZ_{t-1} + \Psi_t, \quad Z_t' = [S_t, S_{t-1}, S_{t-2}, S_{t-3}], \quad \Psi_t' = [\epsilon_{st}, 0, 0, 0]. \quad (6)$$

From the definition of Z_t, S_t is given by

$$S_t = \beta Z_t, \quad \text{where } \beta = [1, 0, 0, 0].$$

The desired capital stock in equation (2) is then given by

$$K_{t+n}^* = \alpha(1 - \sigma)\beta A^n (I - \sigma A)^{-1} Z_t.$$

Investment orders are given, from equation (1), by

$$I_t = \lambda \alpha(1 - \sigma)\beta A^n (I - \sigma A)^{-1} Z_t + (\theta - \lambda)K_{t+n-1} + \xi_t.$$

Investment expenditures are given, from equation (4), by

$$X_t = \lambda \alpha(1 - \sigma)\beta A^n (I - \sigma A)^{-1} \sum_{i=0}^{n} \omega_i Z_{t-i}$$

$$+ (\theta - \lambda) \sum_{i=0}^{n} \omega_i K_{t+n-i-1} + \sum_{i=0}^{n} \omega_i \xi_{t-i}. \quad (7)$$

Investment expenditures depend on three sets of terms. The first is a distributed lag of sales; the second depends on capital from K_{t-1} to K_{t+n-1}, which determine past and current orders and thus current expenditures; the third depends on current and past disturbances.

Equation (7) is the equation to be estimated. Before we do so, we make two approximations. The first follows from the fact that K_t is unobservable. We only observe expenditures, not deliveries of capital. Thus, the K series constructed by accumulation using expenditures includes capital paid for but not yet delivered. If capital goods were paid fully on order, our constructed K_t would measure the true K_{t-n}, and we could use our constructed $K_{t-n-1}, ..., K_{t-1}$ in equation (7); if capital goods were instead paid fully on delivery, our constructed K_t would correctly measure the true K_t, and we should use our constructed $K_t, ..., K_{t+n-1}$ in equation (7). Rather than attempt to construct a two-sided moving average of K to capture the second term in (7), we simply proxy $\sum \omega_i K_{t+n-i-1}$ by our constructed K_{t-1}. Given the slow movement of K compared to X, this is unlikely to be a source of major problems. It may however bias the coefficient on capital, an issue to which we shall return.

The second approximation is in the specification of the process followed by the disturbance term in (7). If ξ_t followed an AR(1), the disturbance term would follow an ARMA(1, n). In general, the disturbance term in (7) is likely to have an MA component at least of order n. For computational convenience, we ignore this MA component and assume that the disturbance term follows an AR process. We have found that an AR(1) appears sufficient to yield white-noise residuals.

With these two approximations, equation (7) becomes

$$X_t = \lambda\alpha(1-\sigma)\beta A^n(I-\sigma A)^{-1} \sum_{i=0}^{n} \omega_i Z_{t-i} + (\theta-\lambda)K_{t-1} + u_t, \quad (8)$$

where

$$u_t = \rho u_{t-1} + \epsilon_t.$$

5.2   *Prior restrictions and identification*

The structural parameters in equation (7) are λ, σ, n, θ, α, $\{\omega_i\}_i$, ρ, and the nontrivial elements of A (β is a vector of 1 and 0's). From the previous section, we have information on some of these elements, which we now use.

From Section 3, we know that n, the average delivery lag, is (for all sectors except petroleum) approximately equal to 3. Thus, we use $n=3$ in what follows.[12]

In Section 4, we have estimated the univariate representations of shipments. We use these estimated coefficients to construct the matrix A for each sector.[13] The combination of the assumption that $n=3$ and that S follows an AR(4) implies the presence of S to $S(-6)$ in the investment equation.

This leaves the parameters λ, σ, α, θ, ρ, and $\{\omega_i\}$, $i=0,\ldots,3$.

If the order–expenditure structure is left unconstrained, there are enough structural parameters to fit the reduced form exactly. Even if we impose that the ω_i be nonnegative, the model is in practice overparameterized, and we are likely to end up explaining the reduced-form distribution lag by a pseudo-structural order–expenditure lag structure. We therefore constrain the lag structure $\{\omega_i\}$ to obey

$$\omega_0 \text{ free}$$
$$\omega_1 = (1-\omega_0)(1+\omega+\omega^2)^{-1}\omega^{i-1} \text{ for } i=1,2,3.$$

Weights are exponentially declining if ω is less than unity and exponentially increasing if ω is greater than unity.

Under the preceding assumptions, all remaining structural parameters are identified. We have found however that our estimates of $\lambda\alpha$ and σ

---

[12] We have also done estimation assuming $n=4$ and $n=5$ for petroleum. The differences are not substantial.

[13] Thus, rather than estimating (6) and (8) simultaneously, we first estimate (6) and replace A in (8) by its estimated counterpart. This procedure is much cheaper as the first estimation is linear but is less asymptotically efficient.

were highly correlated. Thus, it is impossible to estimate precisely the discount parameter σ,[14] and we are forced to assume rather than estimate the value of σ. This is unfortunate as σ, which measures the degree to which firms discount the future, is one of the most interesting parameters of the model. We choose a value of σ of 0.9 (values between 0.85 and 0.95 make little difference to the fit).

Finally, returning to equation (8), we see that we can estimate separately $\lambda\alpha$ and $\lambda-\theta$. Using the values of α and θ derived in Sections 2 and 3 imposes an overidentifying restriction on λ; using either α or θ just identifies λ. We decided to estimate $\lambda\alpha$ and $\lambda-\theta$ unconstrained. Given these estimates, we can, by using the values of α and θ from the previous sections, construct two estimates of λ, one from the reaction of investment to sales and one from the effect of the past capital stock on investment.

5.3 Implied constrained reduced forms and estimated structural parameters

Equation (8) is estimated by maximum likelihood.[15] The results of estimation of equation (8) are reported in Tables 8 and 9. Table 8 reports the coefficients of the constrained reduced form and repeats for comparison the coefficients of the unconstrained reduced form already reported in Table 2. Table 9 gives the values of the structural parameters.

We start with Table 8. In addition to the coefficients, it gives the values of two test statistics. The first one, L1, tests the constrained model against a model where all coefficients on shipments are equal to zero; it shows therefore whether shipments play an important role in explaining investment in the structural model. The second one, L2, tests the constrained model, equation (8), against the unconstrained form, equation (5); it shows therefore whether the constraints imposed by the structural model on the distributed lag on shipments are rejected by the data. Other things being equal, high values of L1 and low values of L2 are good news for the structural model.

Examining first the values of L1 and L2 suggests the following conclusions. Overall the structural model performs well in approximately two-thirds of the sectors. Looking at L1, the constrained model significantly outperforms (at the 5 percent level) a model with no role for shipments in 9 of the 13 sectors. In 4 sectors (FO, PA, CH, and AC), the constrained

---

[14] The difficulty of estimating precisely the discount rate in this type of estimation has often been documented.

[15] The likelihood function is maximized using Davidon–Fletcher–Powell until convergence. Newton–Raphson is then used to obtain an estimate of the covariance matrix of the estimated parameters.

Table 8. *Constrained and unconstrained reduced forms*

Sector		$K(-1)$	S	$S(-1)$	$S(-2)$	$S(-3)$	$S(-4)$	$S(-5)$	$S(-6)$	ρ	L1	L2
FO	u	0.03	0.2	-1.1	0.3	-0.2	-0.3	1.9	-0.4	0.87	0.5	3.4
	c	-0.03	-0.6	-1.0	-0.5	-0.9	-0.2	0.2	-0.1	0.89		
TX	u	-0.18	1.7	2.2	0.1	-0.2	1.3	2.7	-0.2	0.94	7.5[a]	4.9
	c	-0.15	1.8	2.3	-0.1	0.2	0.6	0.2	0.1	0.95		
PA	u	-0.18	3.0	4.7	5.1[a]	1.3	6.7	1.3	0.1	0.89	1.3	24.0[b]
	c	-0.31	-0.4	3.3	1.2	1.1	-1.8	-0.4	0.3	0.89		
CH	u	-0.21	-0.1	-2.2	5.3[a]	-0.6	0.4	2.8	-2.0	0.94	0.2	10.5[a]
	c	-0.26	-0.1	0.4	0.6	1.7	-1.4	0.3	0.0	0.95		
PET	u	-0.11	0.5	-1.7	11.6	-8.6	0.7	7.0	-3.2	0.89	7.2[a]	5.2
	c	-0.11	-0.2	-8.4	10.1	-10.9	3.5	-2.0	1.6	0.90		
RU	u	-0.00	3.0[a]	3.6[a]	2.9[a]	1.5	-0.7	0.1	-0.3	0.79	34.6[b]	8.1
	c	0.11	2.7	3.6	2.6	1.7	-2.2	-1.6	-0.7	0.82		
SCG	u	-0.08	4.5[a]	4.1	3.0	5.1[a]	1.3	1.4	-0.0	0.91	14.8[b]	1.4
	c	-0.04	4.0	3.9	4.7	4.3	0.9	0.8	-0.1	0.92		
PM	u	-0.06	0.0	0.9	1.1	1.7[a]	1.6[a]	1.7[a]	0.8	0.90	12.0[b]	1.5
	c	-0.06	0.0	1.5	1.2	1.2	0.1	0.0	0.1	0.94		
FM	u	-0.12	1.5	0.5	1.4	1.2	1.6	-0.7	-0.5	0.53	13.0[b]	9.9[a]
	c	-0.00	1.5	0.8	1.5	1.9	-1.1	-0.5	-0.6	0.55		
NEM	u	0.03	5.5[a]	3.6	2.0	5.6[a]	-3.5	-0.2	0.6	0.77	32.0[b]	3.2
	c	0.04	5.2	2.8	4.0	4.6	-3.1	-0.4	-0.3	0.79		
EM	u	-0.03	1.5	2.9	2.3	1.7	2.9	0.7	-0.8	0.93	12.5[b]	13.6[b]
	c	-0.02	1.7	2.9	1.9	2.0	-1.5	0.2	0.1	0.95		
MV	u	-0.03	0.8[a]	1.2[a]	2.5[a]	2.4[a]	1.9[a]	1.6[a]	0.6	0.83	13.1[b]	40.3[b]
	c	-0.06	0.3	1.1	1.3	1.6	-0.2	-0.3	-0.2	0.94		
AC	u	-0.36	-0.1	2.5	4.1	1.2	0.3	2.5	2.6	0.99	3.7	11.1[a]
	c	-0.12	0.0	2.9	2.5	1.1	-0.6	-0.6	-0.2	0.98		

Note: Period of estimation: 1959, quarter 2, to 1979, quarter 3. Coefficients on shipments are multiplied by 10^{-2}; L1 is distributed $\chi^2(3)$; L2 is distributed $\chi^2(4)$; u, unconstrained, from Table 2; c, constrained.
[a]Significant at the 5% level.   [b]Significant at the 1% level.

Table 9. *Structural parameters*

Sector	$\hat{\lambda\alpha}$	$\theta\hat{}-\lambda$	ω_0	ω	α	θ	λ_1	λ_2
FO	0.072	−0.007	0.07	−0.42	0.24	0.110	0.300	0.117
TX	0.023	−0.037	0.30[a]	0.35[b]	0.31	0.112	0.074	0.149
PA	0.105	−0.077	−0.05	0.93[b]	0.50	0.110	0.210	0.187
CH	0.028	−0.065	−0.04	2.83[b]	0.56	0.106	0.050	0.171
PET	−0.125	−0.027	0.03	−1.03[a]	2.10	0.084	−0.059	0.111
RU	0.103[a]	0.027	0.19[a]	0.96[a]	0.40	0.114	0.257	0.087
SCG	0.172[b]	−0.010	0.27[a]	0.93[a]	0.63	0.110	0.273	0.120
PM	0.040[b]	−0.015	−0.33	0.68[b]	0.58	0.104	0.068	0.119
FM	0.037	−0.001	0.20	1.53	0.24	0.119	0.154	0.120
NEM	0.141[b]	0.010	0.22[a]	1.22[a]	0.41	0.115	0.343	0.105
EM	0.058[a]	−0.005	0.13	0.99[a]	0.45	0.115	0.123	0.120
MV	0.141[a]	−0.015	0.08	1.27[a]	0.45	0.117	0.313	0.105
AC	0.027	−0.003	0.00	0.74[a]	0.30	0.116	0.090	0.119

Note: α, capital–shipment ratio from Table 1; θ, depreciation rate from Table A in appendix; $\lambda_1 = (\hat{\lambda}\alpha/\alpha)$, $\lambda_2 = \theta - (\theta\hat{} - \lambda)$; FO, Newton–Raphson not converged, Davidon–Fletcher–Powell results (no standard deviations reported).
[a] Significant at the 1% level.
[b] Significant at the 5% level.

distributed lag on shipments does not help predict investment. Looking at L2, the restrictions imposed by the structural model are significantly rejected in 6 of the sectors at the 5 percent level and in 3 of them (PA, EM, and MV) at the 1 percent level.

Turning to the coefficients, the structural model is often successful at replicating the unconstrained distributed-lag structure (SCG and NEM in particular). The model is able in most sectors to generate a flat, or slightly hump-shaped, distributed-lag structure.

Being able to replicate approximately the reduced form is only good news if the underlying estimated structural parameters make sense. These are given in Table 9.

Consider first the *order–expenditure* lag structure implied by the estimates of ω_0 and ω. Apart from a few outliers, the results imply a relatively flat order–expenditure structure, which corresponds well to the available qualitative evidence.

From the estimates of $\lambda\alpha$ and $\theta - \lambda$ and the values of α from Table 1 and θ from Table A, we construct two estimates of *the gap parameter* λ. The first one, λ_1, is obtained by dividing the estimated $\lambda\alpha$ by α and is therefore derived from the response of investment to movements in shipments. The second one, λ_2, is obtained by subtracting from θ the estimated $\theta - \lambda$ and is therefore obtained from the effect of the lagged capital stock on investment. The gap parameters λ_1 and λ_2 are reported in the last two columns of Table 9 (they are measured at annual rates). Thus, an estimated value for the gap parameter implies that investment responds within a quarter to close a proportion $\lambda/4$ of the gap between desired and actual capital.

The estimated value of λ_1 varies between -0.06 and 0.35. The estimated value of λ_2 varies between 0.08 and 0.18. The average value of λ_1 is equal to 0.19 (so that approximately 5 percent of the gap is closed within the quarter) and is higher than the average value of λ_2, 0.12. This result is interesting. One interpretation is that it captures the notion that investment overreacts to sales. Consider, for example, the case of motor vehicles: We have seen that the sales process is not very persistent but that the effect of shipments on investment is large. The structural model estimates, therefore, a large value of λ_1, consistent with low costs of adjustment. But if costs of adjustment were low, the effect of the lagged capital stock on investment should be strongly negative, and λ_2 should be large. Such is not the case; in this sense investment appears to overreact to sales. But the result that λ_1 exceeds λ_2 can also be due to the use of a proxy for the correct capital stock series, which leads to a bias toward zero in its coefficient. If the true coefficient is negative, then there will be a downward bias in λ_2.

6   Conclusion

We set out to give a structural interpretation to the distributed-lag relation between investment and shipments at the two-digit level. We have learned the following:

1. Examination of the reduced form in Section 2 reveals that there is no standard and robust accelerator relation between investment and shipments at that level of disaggregation. The relation between investment and shipments varies substantially across sectors. In all sectors, a good part of investment is not explained by shipments; indeed, in a few cases, there is no significant effect of shipments on investment.

When shipments affect investment, they do so through a long and rather flat, or hump-shaped, distributed lag.

2. Because the composition of capital is very similar across sectors, delivery lag structures facing each sector are also very similar. All industries except petroleum face a mean delivery lag of approximately three quarters. Differences in delivery lags are therefore unlikely candidates to explain differences in the effects of shipments on investment across sectors.

A by-product of our work on delivery lags shows that they appear procyclical. This suggests a nonlinear specification of the effect of shipments on investment that we do not pursue further here.

3. Shipments follow very different processes across sectors. The processes differ significantly in their degree of persistence. There is a relation, although not a tight one, between the degree of persistence of shipments and the size of the effect of shipments on investment. This suggests that the distributed lag in the investment equation depends on the characteristics of the sales process in a way that is at least qualitatively consistent with the theory.

4. The results of estimation of the structural model in Section 5 suggest that the following model can generate roughly the distributed-lag structure found in the data. Firms face delivery lags of three quarters. They also face adjustment costs, which imply that (1) they take all future expected sales, with discount factor 0.9, into consideration when constructing the desired capital stock, and (2) they close 5 percent of the gap between desired and actual capital stock each quarter. They pay for orders at a constant rate between the time of order and the time of delivery.

5. Whereas this model can generate the long, flat, or hump-shaped distributed lag found in the data, the ability of the structural model to fit each sector and to give plausible explanations to differences across sectors is limited. The model performs poorly in some sectors. It does not attribute differences in distributed lags across sectors to any single main

cause, such as differences in sales processes. In particular, it attributes these differences in part to differences in both costs of adjustment and in order-expenditure lags. Although we do not have direct evidence on these costs of adjustment, it is not clear why – especially given that capital composition and delivery lags are so similar across sectors – costs of adjustment or order-expenditure lags should differ substantially across sectors. It would be interesting to examine formally how much of the differences across sectors could be explained by differences in any one element, for example, differences in shipment processes with identical technologies (up to a capital–shipments ratio) across sectors. We have not yet done so.

6. We set up estimation of the structural model so as to get two separate estimates of the gap parameter. A comparison of these estimates shows the estimate obtained from the response to shipments often exceeds the one obtained from the response of investment to the lagged capital stock. The result may be explained by bias from the presence of errors in variables; if not, it may indicate an overreaction of investment to shipments. Although this result is suggestive, our model is too crude and ignores too many factors, and the difference between the two estimates is often too small for us to push it too strongly.

Appendix A

1   *Data sources*

For the construction of investment, orders, and shipments time series:

[1]   Plant and equipment expenditures, seasonally adjusted, quarterly, for manufacturing industries, constant 1972 dollars, 1947 (quarter 1) to 1982 (quarter 1), from the Bureau of Economic Analysis (tape).

[2]   Manufacturers' shipments, inventories, and orders, monthly, for manufacturing industries, current dollars, 1958 (January) to 1980 (December), from the Bureau of the Census M3-1-10 (tape).

[3]   Implicit price deflators for shipments, monthly, three-digit manufacturing, 1972 = 100, 1958 (January) to 1980 (December), from the Bureau of Labor Statistics (tape).

For the construction of delivery lag structures:

[4]   New structures and equipment by using industries, 1972, detailed estimates and methodology, Bureau of Economic Analysis publication 035, September 1980.

[5]   Capital flow tables for 1967 and 1972, Survey of Current Business, September 1975 and July 1980.

[6]   Capital stock estimates for I/O industries: methods and data, Department of Labor, Bulletin 2034, 1979.

[7]   Census of Manufacturers, 1977, Volumes II and III, Industry Statistics.

[8]   Construction Reports, Department of Commerce, various issues (1-70, 12-70, 3-75, 12-78, 8-79, 8-80, 8-81).

2   Data construction

SIC and I/O codes of sectors

	SIC code	I/O code
Food (FO)	20	14
Textiles (TX)	22	16, 17, 19
Paper (PA)	26	24, 25
Chemicals (CH)	28	27–30
Petroleum (PET)	29	31
Rubber (RU)	30	32
Stone, clay, glass (SCG)	32	35, 36
Primary metals (PM)	33	37, 38
Fabricated metals (FM)	34	39–42
Nonelectrical machinery (NEM)	35	43–52
Electrical machinery (EM)	36	53–58
Motor vehicles (MV)	371	59
Aircraft (AC)	372	60

Discrepancies between establishment and company-based data

Investment expenditures are collected on a company basis; shipments and orders are collected on an establishment basis. A company may operate in sectors other than its main sector of activity. Information about activities of companies classified in a given sector can be obtained by computing the ratio of employees of these companies working in the sector to the total number of employees of these companies, using the Enterprise Statistics from the Department of Commerce and aggregating to the two-digit level. This ratio is over 75 percent in all sectors except petroleum (67 percent) and motor vehicles (59 percent). Employees in motor vehicles companies not working in the sector work, however, in sectors closely related to motor vehicles. Such is not the case for petroleum.

Construction of investment, shipments, and orders
Investment series are directly obtained from [1]. Real shipments and orders series are obtained by deflation of series in [2], by price deflators constructed by aggregation of three-digit deflators in [3], and by time aggregation from monthly to quarterly and transformation to annual rates.

Construction of capital stock series
Time series for sectoral capital stocks are constructed using the following accumulation equation:

$$K_{it} = (1 - \theta_i)K_{it-1} + X_{it},$$

where θ_i is the depreciation rate for capital of sector i. The construction of θ_i is described in Appendix B.

The series is benchmarked so that the mean level of the capital stock is equal to the mean level of investment expenditures divided by the rate of growth of investment plus the rate of depreciation. This mean capital stock value is used in Table 1 to compute the mean capital–shipments ratio as the ratio of mean capital to mean shipments.

This crude computation of the mean level of capital can be compared to ratios using alternative establishment-based measures of capital, such as those given in [6]. Columns 4 and 5 of Table A give, respectively, our estimated mean capital–shipments ratio and the mean capital–shipments ratio implied by [6]. (The two definitions of capital differ slightly, and the results are not strictly comparable.) The main discrepancy is for petroleum, due to the establishment/company discrepancy discussed previously.

Appendix B: Delivery lags

1   *Construction of capital composition*

Let i denote the sector and j denote the type of capital good, which may be either a type of equipment or a structure. Let θ_{ij}, g_{ij}, I_{ij}, and K_{ij} be depreciation rate, rate of growth of capital, rate of investment, and level of capital of type j in sector i, respectively. For a given year, the following two identities hold:

$$I_{ij} = K_{ij} - (1 - \theta_{ij})K_{ij}(-1),$$

$$K_{ij} = (1 + g_{ij})K_{ij}(-1).$$

These identities imply

Table A. *Average lives and depreciation*

Sector	Average life of equipment by sector of origin (1)	Average life of structure by sector of destination (2)	Annual depreciation rate by sector of destination (3)	Constructed K/S (4)	Alternative K/S (5)
FO	[a]	29	0.110	0.24	0.28
TX	10	30	0.112	0.31	0.41
PA	[a]	29	0.110	0.50	0.80
CH	[a]	29	0.106	0.56	0.79
PET	[a]	28	0.084	2.10	0.80
RU	10	28	0.114	0.40	0.50
SCG	[a]	29	0.110	0.63	0.45
PM	14	28	0.104	0.58	0.84
FM	18	29	0.119	0.24	0.34
NEM	14	27	0.115	0.41	0.40
EM	14	30	0.115	0.41	0.39
MV	7	30	0.117	0.45	0.27
AC	9	31	0.116	0.30	0.40

[a] Sector does not produce capital goods.

$$K_{ij}/K_i = [(1+g_{ij})/(g_{ij}+\theta_{ij})]I_{ij} \bigg/ \left\{ \sum_j [(1+g_{ij})/(g_{ij}+\theta_{ij})]I_{ij} \right\}.$$

This is the formula we use to compute capital composition. We compute the composition for two different years, 1967 and 1972, and then take the average.

Data for I_{ij} are obtained by aggregation of capital flow tables from [5].

Rates of growth g_{ij} are assumed, for a given sector, to be the same across all types of equipment. Thus, for each sector i, only two values of g_{ij} are computed, one for equipment and one for structures. These are computed using net capital measures from [6].

Rates of depreciation θ_{ij} for each type of equipment are assumed to be independent of the sector in which the equipment is used. Thus, for equipment, $\theta_{ij} = \theta_j$ for all i. Depreciation rates for each type of capital equipment are obtained from average lives, L_j, from IRS Bulletin F lives (Table 3 in [6]). These average lives are given in column 1 of Table A. Depreciation rates θ_j are then constructed as $2/L_j$.

Rates of depreciation of structures are allowed to differ across sectors of destination. Average lives of structures for each sector, L_i, are computed using structure composition from [4] and lives by type of structure from Table 3 in [6]. These average lives are given in column 2 of Table A. Depreciation rates are computed as $2/L_i$.

The implied sectoral capital compositions are reported in Table 3 in the text.

Finally, the sector-specific depreciation rates used to compute the time series for capital in each sector, θ_i, are computed as

$$\theta_i = \sum_j \frac{K_{ij}}{K_i} \theta_{ij}.$$

The constructed depreciation rates are given in column 3 of Table A.

2   Construction of delivery lags by type of good

Delivery lags are computed using the formula $V_i/(1-b_i)S_i$, where V_i, S_i, and b_i are unfilled orders, shipments, and proportion of shipment sold to wholesalers and retailers, respectively. V_i and S_i are obtained from [7] for 1977, and b_i is obtained from Table 13a in [7]. The values of b_i are 46 percent for FM, 42 percent for NEM, and 46 percent for EM. The implied delivery lags can be compared to estimates by the Department of Commerce (Survey of Current Business, July 1975) using a different approach; they are very similar.

REFERENCES

Blanchard, O. 1986. Comment on Matthew Shapiro, "Investment, Output and the Cost of Capital." *Brookings Papers on Economic Activity,* pp. 153–8.
Jorgenson, D. 1971. "Econometric Studies of Investment Behavior: A Survey." *Journal of Economic Literature* 9(4): 1111–47.
Jorgenson, D. and J. Stephenson. 1967. "The Time Structure of Investment Behavior in United States Manufacturing, 1947–1960." *Review of Economics and Statistics* 49(1): 16–27.
Lucas, R. 1965. "Distributed Lags and Optimal Investment Policy." In *Rational Expectations and Economic Policy,* Vol. 1, R. Lucas and T. Sargent, Eds. Minneapolis: University of Minnesota Press.
Uri, N. 1982. "Testing for Stability of the Investment Function." *Review of Economics and Statistics* 64(1): 117–25.

CHAPTER 14

Me and my shadow: estimating the size of the U.S. hidden economy from time series data

Dennis J. Aigner, Friedrich Schneider, and Damayanti Ghosh

1   Introduction

In the last few years a growing concern over the phenomenon of the shadow (or hidden) economy has arisen, and as a consequence this topic has received increased attention among public officials, politicians, and social scientists. For the United States, like many other industrial countries, there are several important reasons why politicians and the public in general should be concerned about the growth and size of the shadow economy. Among the most important of these are:

If an increase in the size of the shadow economy is mainly caused by a rise in the tax burden, an increased tax rate may lead to a decrease in tax receipts and thus further increase the budget deficit.

If economic policy measures are based on mistaken "officially measured" indicators (such as unemployment), these measures may be at least of a wrong magnitude. In such a situation a prospering shadow economy may cause a severe problem for political decision makers because it leads to quite unreliable officially measured indicators, so that even the direction of intended policy measures may be questionable.

The rise of the shadow economy can be seen as a reaction of individuals to their overburdening by state activities (such as high taxes and an increasing number of state regulations).

Prepared in part under the auspices of National Science Foundation Grant No. SES-8319129. We wish to thank Joseph G. Hirschberg for help with the design and programming of the DYMIMIC estimation algorithm.

Table 1. *Size and development of shadow economy as percentage of GNP for United States (1970s)*

Approach	Size of shadow economy in percentage of GNP					Author(s)
	1970	1974	1976	1979		
Unobserved variable approach: cross-sectional study of OECD countries	–	–	–	8.3[a]		Frey and Weck-Hannemann, 1984
Tax auditing	–	–	4.4–5.9	–		IRS, 1979[b]
Initial discrepancy: national income level	5.0	4.3	3.6	4.0		Park, 1979[b]
Initial discrepancy: labor force participation rates	3.0–7.9[c]	–	–	5.2–11.8[d]		O'Neill, 1983
Fixed currency demand deposit ratio	6.2	6.2	11.0	13.5		Gutmann, 1979[b]
Simple and modified transaction method	–	–	13.2–22.0	25.7–33.0[a]		Feige, 1979, 1982
Currency demand approach: one cause, different tax variables	2.6–4.6	3.4–4.9	3.6–5.5	3.7–5.4		Tanzi, 1983
Currency demand approach: multiple causes: tax burden, regulation, tax morality	9.8–11.0	10.6–12.1	10.9–12.4	11.8–13.1		Schneider and Pommerehne, 1985

[a] Year 1978.
[b] Taken from Frey and Pommerehne (1984, Table 1, p. 13).
[c] Interpolated figure (by the authors).
[d] Year 1981.

This growing concern is reflected in many attempts by economists to measure the size of the shadow economy. In Table 1 the main findings of the studies known to the authors measuring the size and development of the U.S. shadow economy for the seventies are shown.[1] The general impression of Table 1 is that the shadow economy is sizeable for the United States. Averaged over the years 1976-9, for which estimates are available for all approaches, the size is 8-11 percent of GNP.

But what can also be observed from Table 1 is the rather large variation in the estimates. If one considers only estimates that rely on the monetary approach, the size of the shadow economy in 1976 ranges from 3.4 to 28.0 percent of GNP. Hence, the question arises of how reliable these results are, even if one takes into consideration that with the different methods different aspects of the shadow economy are being measured.[2] Each of the approaches shown in Table 1 has been criticized due to the following:

(i)   They use only one indicator (e.g., money) for measuring the shadow economy.[3]

(ii)   Some studies *do not* take into account possible causes (e.g., a rising tax burden, increased regulation, declining tax morality) that determine the size of the shadow economy or others – such as the monetary approaches – use only one cause, the tax burden.

(iii) They are burdened with a lot of statistical/econometric difficulties (large errors in the variables, extreme autocorrelation of the residuals, multicollinearity of the independent variables, etc.).

The present study tries to overcome these criticisms by using several indicators for the shadow economy and by considering several causes for determining the size of the shadow economy over an extended period (1939-82) for the United States.[4] The statistical method applied here is a

[1] As various surveys have already been published that give a detailed description of the various approaches and undertake a comparison between the different methods (e.g., Blades 1982; Boeschoten and Fase 1984; Frey and Pommerehne 1982, 1984; Gaertner and Wenig 1985; Kirchgaessner 1984; Weck 1983), only a very short description of some approaches is given in Section 2.

[2] Due to this variation in estimates of the size of the shadow economy, some economists like Porter and Bayer (1984, p. 187) conclude that the analysis of underground activities has not progressed enough to permit a reliable estimate. Or, Denison (1982) claims that the huge size of the hidden economy found by some studies could *not* be corroborated by his research of the necessary consequence in the labor market.

[3] The weaknesses of the currency demand approach are discussed in detail in Blades (1982) and Schneider (1986); those of the transactions approach are discussed in Boeschoten and Fase (1984), Frey and Pommerehne (1984), and Kirchgaessner (1984).

[4] These two aspects have already been taken into account in a pioneering study by Frey and Weck-Hannemann (1984) and Weck (1983), but their analysis was for cross-sectional data from the 17 OECD countries and not for a single country over time.

dynamic version of the MIMIC (multiple-indicators multiple-causes model), which recently has been applied in another context by Engle et al. (1985). In Section 2 a short description and criticism of the various previous approaches is given. Section 3 contains empirical results derived from our approach and a discussion of the robustness of the results. In Section 4 some conclusions are drawn.

2   Methods to estimate size of shadow economy

To measure the size and the development of the shadow economy, three types of methods arc most commonly distinguished.

2.1   *Direct approaches*

In these approaches either well-designed surveys and samples based on voluntary replies[5] or tax auditing and other compliance methods are employed.[6] These approaches operate at the microlevel, and samples are used. However, in most cases these approaches only lead to point estimates, and it is unlikely that they capture all "black" activities, so they can be seen as providing lower bound estimates. Moreover, they are not able (at least at the current stage) to provide estimates of the development of the shadow economy over time. But they have at least one considerable advantage – they can provide detailed information about the structure and composition of the labor force in the shadow economy.

2.2   *Indirect approaches*

The indirect approaches use various economic indicators from which conclusions can be derived about the development of the shadow economy over time. All of them operate at the macrolevel, and there are at least four macroeconomic indicators whose trajectories leave some "traces" about the development of the shadow economy:

(a)   *Discrepancy between national expenditure and income statistics*
In most OECD countries the size of GNP is computed from both the expenditure and income sides of the national accounts. Quite often in na-

---

[5] The direct method of voluntary sample surveys has been extensively used for Norway by Isachsen, Kloveland, and Strøm (1982), and Isachsen and Strøm (1980). An attempt for Denmark to use this method is made by Mogensen (1985), who reports an "estimate" of the shadow economy of 5.5 percent (of GNP) for the year 1984 as a minimum figure.

[6] Compare, for the United States, IRS (1979), Simon and Witte (1982), and Clotefelter (1983).

tional account statistics, it is revealed that the expenditure side is larger than the income side. This "initial discrepancy" between expenditures and income can be seen as a part of hidden economic activities.[7] The weakness of this "fiscal" method is that the differences may arise not only due to shadow economy activities but also due to well-known measurement errors in the national account statistics. Hence, these estimates may be very crude and of little reliability.

(b)   *Discrepancy between officially measured and actual labor force participation rates*

A decline in labor force participation in the official economy can be seen as an indication of increased activities in the shadow economy. Here it is assumed to be constant over time; thus, a decreasing (officially measured) participation rate can be seen as an indicator of shadow economy activities (ceteris paribus).[8] Again, the weakness of this method is that differences in the participation rate may have other causes and, moreover, that people can work in the shadow economy *and* have a job in the "official" economy. Again, such estimates may be viewed as weak indicators of the size of the shadow economy.

(c)   *Transactions approach*

In the transactions approach, which was developed by Feige,[9] it is assumed that according to the quantity theory of money, there is a constant relation over time between the transactions volume and official GNP. Relating total nominal GNP to total transactions, the shadow economy's share of GNP can be derived residually by subtracting the officially measured GNP from the total nominal GNP. In order to derive figures for the shadow economy, Fiege must assume a base year wherein the ratio of nominal transactions to total nominal (official and total) GNP was "normal" and would have been constant over time if there were no shadow economy. This method has several weaknesses, for instance, the assumption of a base year with no shadow economy and the assumption of a "normal" and constant (over time) ratio of transactions. Moreover, to obtain reliable estimates, quite precise figures of the total volume of transactions should be available. This might be especially difficult for transactions undertaken by cash because they depend, among other factors, on

---

[7] Compare, e.g., Macafee (1980) for Great Britain, Petersen (1982) for Germany, and Park (1979) for the United States.

[8] Such studies have been made for Italy (see, e.g., Contini 1981; Del Boca 1981) and for the United States (cf. O'Neill 1983).

[9] For an extended description of this approach and a discussion of the results for the United States, see Feige (1979, 1982). Further applications were made for the Netherlands by Boeschoten and Fase (1984) and for Germany by Langfeldt (1984).

the quality of the paper used in the currency.[10] In general, although this approach is theoretically quite attractive, the empirical requirements that are necessary to obtain reliable estimates are so difficult to fulfil that its application may lead to doubtful results.

(d)   *Currency demand approach*

This approach assumes that shadow transactions are undertaken in form of cash payments in order to leave no observable traces for the state authorities,[11] and therefore an increase in the shadow economy will increase the demand for currency. In order to isolate this "excess" demand for currency due to the shadow economy, a currency demand equation is econometrically estimated over time, controlling for all conventional possible factors like income, payment habits, interest rates, and so on. Additionally, variables such as the tax burden, which are assumed to be one of the major reasons people work in the shadow economy, are included in the estimation equation. The "excess" increase in currency, that is, the amount not explained by the conventional or normal factors already mentioned, is then attributed to the rising tax burden. Figures for the size and development of the shadow economy can be calculated by a comparison of the difference between the development of currency when the tax burden is held at its lowest value and the development of currency with the actual burden of taxation. One of the problems with this approach is the difficulty in estimating a "normal" currency demand equation for a country over an extended period of time, and another problem goes back to the fact that shadow economy activities can be undertaken in the form of barter or payment by check.[12] Therefore, the figures derived by this method may underestimate the "true" size. Such an underestimation may additionally come from the fact that in most studies only one cause (a rising tax burden) for the increase of a shadow economy is taken into account.[13]

---

[10] For a detailed criticism see Frey and Pommerehne (1984) and Kirchgaessner (1984).

[11] The currency demand approach was first used by Cagan (1958), who correlated the variable "demand for currency" with the variable "tax pressure" for the United States over the period 1919–55. Twenty years later Gutmann (1979) used the same approach, but he "only" looked at the ratio between currency and demand deposits over the years 1937–76. Cagan's approach was further developed by Tanzi (1980, 1983), who estimated a currency demand function for the United States for the period 1929–80.

[12] Further weaknesses of this approach are discussed by Garcia and Pack (1979), who point out that increases in currency demand deposits are largely due to a slowdown in demand deposits rather than to an increase in currency caused by shadow economy activities. Blades (1982) criticizes Tanzi's approach due to the fact that the U.S. dollar is used as an international currency, so that Tanzi should consider (and control for) the amount of U.S. dollars in cash held abroad. Also, the assumption that the velocity of currency is the same in the official and shadow economy is questionable (Frey and Pommerehne 1984).

[13] Schneider and Pommerehne (1985) include more than one cause for the size of the shadow economy in the currency demand equation for the United States. Besides the tax

2.3   *Model approach*

All methods described so far that are designed to estimate the size and development of the shadow economy consider just *one* indicator that must capture all effects of the shadow economy. However, it is obvious that its effects show up simultaneously in the production, labor, and money markets. An even more important critique is that the *causes* that determine the size of the hidden economy are taken into account only in some of the monetary approach studies that consider one cause, the burden of taxation.

Our approach explicitly considers *multiple causes* leading to the existence and growth as well as the *multiple effects* of the shadow economy over time. The empirical method used is quite different from those used heretofore. It is based on the statistical theory of *unobserved variables,* which considers multiple causes *and* multiple indicators of the phenomenon to be measured. For the estimation, a factor-analytic approach is used to measure the hidden economy as an unobserved variable over time. The unknown coefficients are estimated in a set of structural equations within which the "unobserved" variable cannot be measured directly. The DYMIMIC (dynamic multiple-indicators multiple-causes) model consists in general of two parts, the measurement model and the structural equations model. The measurement model links the unobserved variables to observed indicators. The structural equations model specifies causal relationships among the unobserved variables. In our case, we have one unobserved variable, the size of the shadow economy. It is assumed to be influenced by a set of exogenous causes. Another set of variables is assumed to serve as the set of *indicators* for the shadow economy's size, thus capturing the structural dependence of the shadow economy on variables that may be useful in predicting its movement and size in the future. The interaction over time between the causes Z_{it} ($i = 1, 2, ..., k$), the size of the shadow economy X_t, and the indicators Y_{jt} ($j = 1, 2, ..., p$) is shown in Figure 1. Today there is a large literature[14] on the possible causes and indicators of the shadow economy in which the following three types of causes are distinguished:

(i)   The burden of taxation, which consists of the *actual* burden of taxation and of the *perceived* tax burden. It is hypothesized that increases in the "actual" and the "perceived" tax burdens provide a strong incentive to work in the shadow economy, although it

---

burden, only the regulation measure yields a statistically significant and quantitatively important influence in the currency demand equation.

[14] Compare, e.g., the recent published books by Weck (1983) and Gaertner and Wenig (1985).

Causes $\qquad$ X_{t-1} $\qquad$ Indicators

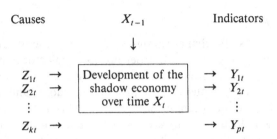

Figure 1. Development of the shadow economy over time.

should be mentioned that there are situations leading to the opposite hypothesis. For example, in Italy the burden of taxation is low, but the *underground economy* (economic activity that should be in official GNP but that eludes measurement) flourishes because the scope for evasion is great. Sweden, on the other hand, has high taxes and a low scope for evasion, and the *informal economy* (economic activity excluded from GNP by definition) is therefore important.

(ii) The burden of regulation as proxy for all other state activities. A rise in the burden of regulation gives a strong incentive to enter the shadow economy.

(iii) *Tax morality* (citizens' attitudes toward the state), which captures the readiness of individuals (at least partly) to leave their official occupations and enter the illegitimate shadow economy. As a proxy for this variable, which has *not* been directly measured over time, a set of survey questions is taken. They relate to the population's attitude toward taxes and government, and they are available for the period 1955–82.[15] The questions chosen for our use herein are: "Do you consider the amount of federal income tax you have to pay too high?" "Do you think that governments waste a lot of money?" "Do you think that government is untrustworthy?" "Do you think that government does not care much what people like you think?" It is hypothesized that a declining tax morality tends to increase the size of the hidden economy.

A change in the size of the shadow economy over time may be reflected in the following indicators:

(i) Development of *monetary* indicators. If shadow economy activities rise over time, additional monetary transactions are demand-

---

[15] There were 18 missing values that were interpolated using a cubic spline function.

ed. As monetary indicators, we will use Feige's figures for the shadow economy, Tanzi's figures for the shadow economy, or currency divided by M2.

(ii) Development of the *labor* market. An increasing participation of workers in the hidden sector results in a decrease in participation in the official economy, as measured by the participation rate. Similarly, increased activity in the hidden sector may be expected to be reflected in shorter working hours in the official economy. As our labor market indicator, we will use the official "male of working age" nonparticipation rate.[16]

(iii) Development of the *production* market. An increase in the shadow economy over time means that inputs (especially labor) move out of the official economy (at least partly); this might have a depressing effect on the officially measured growth rate of the economy. (On the other hand, the growth rate in GNP may be positively related to X_t under the notion that the official and underground economies act as complements.) As the production market indicator, we use the growth rate in real gross national product (total or per capita).

The sources for and other details on all variables used in the study are contained in the Appendix.

3 Econometric model and empirical results

3.1 *Econometric model*

In order to operationalize the structure suggested by Figure 1, we consider estimating the following econometric model. It is a generalization of what Watson and Engle (1983) have called the dynamic MIMIC, or DYMIMIC, model.

Using the notation just introduced, our model structure is written as

$$X_t = \phi X_{t-1} + \underset{1\times K \ \ K\times 1}{\gamma' \ \ \mathbf{Z}} + u_t, \quad t = 1, \dots, T, \tag{3.1a}$$

$$\underset{p\times 1}{\mathbf{Y}_t} = \underset{p\times 1}{\alpha} \ X_t + \underset{p\times K \ \ K\times 1}{B \ \ \mathbf{Z}} + \underset{p\times 1}{\epsilon_t}, \tag{3.1b}$$

where

$$\begin{pmatrix} u_t \\ \epsilon_t \end{pmatrix} \sim \text{IIDN}\left(0, \begin{pmatrix} \sigma_{uu} & 0 \\ 0 & R \end{pmatrix}\right),$$

---

[16] As the participation rate of women in the United States is increasing due to factors not related to the hidden economy (e.g., the general emancipation of women), "official" participation is restricted to males of working age.

R being $E(\epsilon_t \epsilon_t')$, $|\phi| < 1$, and IIDN means i.i.d. normal. Here X_t is an unobserved latent variable, $\mathbf{Y}_t$ is a vector of "indicators" for X_t, and $\mathbf{Z}_t$ is a vector of exogenous explanatory variables. Equation (3.1a) is called the process or transition equation describing the process of the state variable X_t. Equation (3.1b) consists of measurement equations providing measures for the latent variable X_t. Note also the additional generality provided by (3.1b), which allows the indicators to be dependent on the causes. Here R need not be a diagonal matrix, allowing for correlated measurement errors.

This model is a special case of the so-called state space model in the engineering literature with direct physical interpretation. There X_t can be a signal that is not directly observable, being subject to systematic distortion as well as contaminated by "noise." The model there is used mainly for "filtering" purposes, that is, to get the (best) estimate of the state from the given measurements. In many situations the parameters are assumed to be known (see Jazwinski 1970). Mehra (1974) shows the similarity between this model and some econometric models and gives a maximum-likelihood estimation technique (assuming the parameters to be unknown) based on one-period-ahead prediction errors or on "innovations" derived from the Kalman filter (Kalman 1960) built on the model. In fact, as early as 1965, Scheweppe (1965) showed how the state space specification can help in writing the likelihood function in terms of prediction errors, which in turn are obtainable from the Kalman filter based on the model specification.[17] Watson and Engle (1983) link this state space model to several econometric models. The DYMIMIC model is one of these.

Given the fact that the likelihood function of the DYMIMIC model admits to a prediction error decomposition, Engle and Watson (1983) try two methods to maximize the likelihood, namely, the maximum-score algorithm and the EM algorithm. Because of difficulty in applying the score algorithm (as discussed in their work), we here elaborate on the EM algorithm.

All our discussion on estimation presumes *identifiability*.[18] It should also be noted that the EM algorithm does not produce an estimate of the variance–covariance matrix of estimators. For that, we can use the estimator of the information matrix developed by Watson and Engle (1983).

---

[17] The technique is also described in Harvey (1981).

[18] Identification of a DYMIMIC model is discussed by Lehman (1981). In general, $\sigma_{uu} = 1$ is required. It is apparent that identification will be a problem unless B is suitably *sparse*. In all of our models identification is confirmed by checking the relevant moment equations. It should be noted that, in general, the independence of u_t and ϵ_t is not required for identification; we impose it to reflect common practice.

Since we have an unobserved variable in our model corresponding to which there is a set of measures, we can view the whole issue as an incomplete data problem. Naturally, therefore, the algorithm for estimation that comes to mind is the EM algorithm developed by Dempster, Laird, and Rubin (1977), which is, in their words, "a general approach to iterative computation of maximum likelihood estimates when the observations can be viewed as incomplete data." In our problem, we can interpret $(\mathbf{Y}, Z)$ as "incomplete" data and $(\mathbf{Y}, Z, \mathbf{X})$ as "complete" data. Here $\mathbf{Y}$ is $PT \times 1$, Z is $T \times K$, and $\mathbf{X}$ is $T \times 1$.

The EM algorithm consists of two steps at each iteration:

Step 1. Form

$$Q(\theta \mid \hat{\theta}^{(h)}) = E[L(\theta \mid \mathbf{Y}, Z, \mathbf{X}) \mid \mathbf{Y}, Z, \hat{\theta}^{(h)}],$$

where θ is the parameter (column) vector in the r-dimensional space Ω, L stands for the log-likelihood function, and the superscript (h) indicates a value obtained in the hth iteration.

Step 2. Maximize $Q(\theta \mid \hat{\theta}^{(h)})$ with respect to (w.r.t.) θ to obtain $\hat{\theta}^{(h+1)}$. The intuitive reasoning is that one would like to maximize

$$L(\theta \mid \mathbf{X}, \mathbf{Y}, Z) = \ln f(\mathbf{Y}, \mathbf{X} \mid \theta, Z),$$

the complete data log-likelihood function. However, since we do not have observations on $\mathbf{X}$, we maximize the expectation of the complete data likelihood function conditional on observed data (and current parameter values).[19] Dempster et al. show that this algorithm will converge to the maximum-likelihood estimator $\hat{\theta}$ under general conditions.

The necessary conditional expectations of $\mathbf{X}$, $\mathbf{X}'\mathbf{X}$, and $\mathbf{X}'\mathbf{Y}$ can be obtained via the Kalman filtering and smoothing techniques, leading to implementation of the E-step of the EM algorithm in this dynamic latent variables setting. In the M-step, then, we maximize the expected value of the likelihood function. In the present context this is very similar to obtaining the iterative Aitken estimator.

If we have a higher order AR process in the transition equation and/or AR(1) measurement errors, we can accommodate that in our estimation technique by suitably augmenting the state vector and transforming the measurement equation variable in order to apply the Cochrane–Orcutt iterative technique. For example, consider an AR(2) process in X_t and AR(1) measurement errors; that is,

$$X_t = \phi_1 X_{t-1} + \phi_2 X_{t-2} + \gamma' \mathbf{Z}_t + u_t, \tag{3.2a}$$

[19] We note here that since $\mathbf{Z}$ is exogenous, the whole analysis is carried out conditional on $\mathbf{Z}$.

$$\mathbf{Y}_t = \alpha X_t + B\mathbf{Z}_t + \boldsymbol{\epsilon}_t, \tag{3.2b}$$

where

$$\epsilon_{it} = \rho_i \epsilon_{it-1} + e_{it}, \quad |\rho_i| < 1 \;\; \forall i = 1, \dots, p$$

and

$$\binom{u_t}{\mathbf{e}_t} \sim \text{IIDN}\left[0, \begin{pmatrix} \sigma_{uu} & 0 \\ 0 & \Sigma_{ee} \end{pmatrix}\right].$$

Rewriting (3.2a) yields

$$\binom{X_t}{X_{t-1}} = \begin{pmatrix} \phi_1 & \phi_2 \\ 1 & 0 \end{pmatrix}\binom{X_{t-1}}{X_{t-2}} + \binom{\gamma'}{0'}\mathbf{Z}_t + \binom{1}{0}u_t \tag{3.3a}$$

and rewriting (3.2b) yields

$$\underset{p \times 1}{\mathbf{YT}_t} = \underset{p \times 2}{ALFN}\underset{}{\binom{X_t}{X_{t-1}}} + \underset{p \times pk}{BT} \cdot \underset{pk \times 1}{\mathbf{ZT}_t} + \underset{p \times 1}{\mathbf{e}_t}, \quad t = 2, \dots, T, \tag{3.3b}$$

where

$$\mathbf{YT}_t = \begin{bmatrix} Y_{1t} - \rho_1 Y_{1,t-1} \\ Y_{2t} - \rho_2 Y_{2,t-1} \\ \vdots \\ Y_{pt} - \rho_p Y_{p,t-1} \end{bmatrix}, \qquad ALFN = (\alpha \;\; \tilde{\alpha}), \qquad \tilde{\alpha} = \begin{bmatrix} -\rho_1 \alpha_1 \\ -\rho_2 \alpha_2 \\ \vdots \\ -\rho_p \alpha_p \end{bmatrix},$$

$$B = \begin{bmatrix} \beta_1' \\ \beta_2' \\ \vdots \\ \beta_p' \end{bmatrix}, \qquad BT = \begin{bmatrix} \beta_1' & 0 & 0 & \cdots & 0 \\ 0 & \beta_2' & \cdots & \cdots & 0 \\ \vdots & \vdots & \cdots & \cdots & \vdots \\ 0 & 0 & \cdots & \cdots & \beta_p' \end{bmatrix},$$

$$\mathbf{ZT}_t = \begin{bmatrix} \mathbf{Z}_t - \rho_1 \mathbf{Z}_{t-1} \\ \mathbf{Z}_t - \rho_2 \mathbf{Z}_{t-2} \\ \vdots \\ \mathbf{Z}_t - \rho_p \mathbf{Z}_{t-p} \end{bmatrix}, \qquad \mathbf{e}_t = \begin{bmatrix} e_{1t} \\ \vdots \\ e_{pt} \end{bmatrix}.$$

Equations (3.3a) and (3.3b) are in state space form, $(X_t \;\; X_{t-1})'$ being the state vector. Hence, the required conditional moment matrices in the E-step can be obtained via Kalman filtering and smoothing on the basis of (3.3a) and (3.3b).

We can rewrite (3.3a) and (3.3b) also as

$$X_t = \phi_1 X_{t-1} + \phi_2 X_{t-2} + \gamma' \mathbf{Z}_t + u_t, \tag{3.4a}$$

$$\underset{p \times 1}{\mathbf{YT}_t} = \underset{p \times p}{\alpha T} \cdot \underset{p \times 1}{\mathbf{XT}_t} + \underset{p \times kp}{BT} \cdot \underset{kp \times 1}{\mathbf{ZT}_t} + \underset{p \times 1}{\mathbf{e}_t}, \quad t = 2, \dots, T, \tag{3.4b}$$

where

$$\alpha T = \begin{pmatrix} \alpha_1 & 0 & 0 & \cdots & 0 \\ 0 & \alpha_2 & 0 & \cdots & 0 \\ \vdots & \vdots & \vdots & \cdots & \vdots \\ 0 & \cdots & \cdots & \cdots & \alpha_p \end{pmatrix} \quad \text{and} \quad \underset{p \times 1}{\mathbf{XT}_t} = \begin{pmatrix} X_t - \rho_1 X_{t-1} \\ X_t - \rho_2 X_{t-1} \\ \vdots \\ X_t - \rho_p X_{t-1} \end{pmatrix}.$$

The transformed model (3.4a) and (3.4b) is now suitable for application of the iterative Aitken estimation technique in the M-step. Given the auto-regressive nature of the measurement errors, this amounts to the familiar Cochrane–Orcutt iterative procedure.[20]

3.2 Preliminaries

We have experimented with a wide variety of models involving the variables summarized in the Appendix. For convenience they are also briefly presented in Table 2.

As a sensible jumping-off point, we consider "naive" regression models whereby each of the indicators is regressed on itself lagged one year and variables representing the three main causal factors, the degree of government regulation of business, "tax morality," and personal income tax rates. Not to be too naive, we have also estimated these benchmark models to account for serial correlation in their error terms.[21] The results are displayed in Table 3 for the indicators of primary interest using variants of the causes we found to be most reliable in the subsequent DYMIMIC models.

What is especially striking about these results is the very different actual behavior and estimated dependence on the causes of each of the main proxies for the relative size of the shadow economy. Feige's original measure, SEMTA, shows a fairly consistent and significant dependence only on the regulation variable, with the anticipated positive sign. The "refined" transactions method embodied in SERTA depends significantly on tax morality in the log-linear ordinary least-squares (OLS) results and on regulation (with a negative sign) and the tax rate in the linear form, but all statistical significance with regard to the causes disappears once serial correlation in the error term is accounted for. In both cases, internal dynamics and/or the serially correlated residual tend to dominate in importance.

[20] See Ghosh (1985) for details.
[21] Since a lagged value of the dependent variable appears as an explanatory variable, OLS will not do in this event. We have used an instrumental variables approach, substituting a consistent predictor of the lagged dependent variable prior to applying the Cochrane–Orcutt procedure.

Table 2. *Variables used in study*

Mnemonic	Variable description	Anticipated sign: naive hypothesis
Indicators		
SEMTA	Feige's indicator, modified transactions method, in percentage of GNP	+
SERTA	Feige's indicator, refined transactions method, in percentage of GNP	+
SETAS	Tanzi's measure, in percentage of GNP	+
GPR72	Annual rate of growth in gross domestic product in 1972 dollars	±
NLFPR	Nonlabor force participation rate for males 25–64 years of age	+
C/M2	Currency divided by M2, %	+
Causes		
EREG1	Measure of intensity of economic regulation (regulation variant 1)	+
EREG2	Measure of intensity of economic regulation (regulation variant 2)	+
EREG3	Measure of intensity of economic regulation (regulation variant 3)	+
TTH1	Percent saying "taxes are too high" (tax morality variant 1)	+
TTH2	Percent saying "taxes are too high" (tax morality variant 2)	+
TW	Percent saying "taxes are wasted" (tax morality variant 3)	+
TXAM1	Average marginal tax rate on personal (adjusted gross) income (tax rate variant 1)	+
TXAM2	Adjusted marginal tax rate on personal income (tax rate variant 2)	+
TXAM3	Overall average marginal tax rate on personal income (tax rate variant 3)	+
TXAM4	Overall average marginal tax rate on labor's marginal product (tax rate variant 4)	+
TXAVW	Weighted average tax rate on interest income (tax rate variant 5)	+
TXRGI	Ratio of total income tax payments after credit to adjusted gross income (tax rate variant 6)	+

Note: See Appendix for details and sources.

Table 3. *"Naive" regressions results: coefficients and absolute t-ratios (in parentheses) based on annual data, 1939–82*

Indicator/ estimation method	Intercept	Indicator lag	Regulation (EREG1)	Tax morality (TTH1)	Tax rate (TXAM1)	$\hat{\rho}$	R^2
SERTA/OLS							
Log-linear	−3.06 (2.16)	0.88 (14.49)	−0.23 (1.51)	0.89 (2.10)	0.24 (1.10)	—	0.89
Linear	−17.80 (2.34)	0.84 (13.64)	−0.25 (2.02)	0.15 (0.97)	1.12 (3.39)	—	0.89
SERTA/IV							
Log-linear	1.68 (0.78)	0.29 (1.92)	−0.14 (0.29)	−0.03 (0.07)	0.31 (0.90)	0.69 (5.85)	0.84
Linear	9.22 (0.74)	0.31 (1.75)	−0.06 (0.19)	−0.08 (0.56)	0.68 (1.14)	0.75 (6.84)	0.86
SEMTA/OLS							
Log-linear	−4.99 (3.04)	0.84 (13.88)	0.02 (0.13)	1.12 (2.58)	0.39 (1.70)	—	0.94
Linear	−141.97 (1.96)	0.97 (15.89)	2.24 (1.97)	0.82 (0.66)	2.65 (1.02)	—	0.96
SEMTA/IV							
Log-linear	−4.14 (1.66)	0.32 (2.18)	1.64 (2.97)	−0.01 (0.01)	0.60 (1.67)	0.72 (6.28)	0.93
Linear	−338.12 (2.10)	0.26 (1.29)	14.94 (3.82)	0.23 (0.15)	0.42 (0.08)	0.69 (5.74)	0.93
SETAS/OLS							
Log-linear	−1.31 (1.83)	0.23 (1.61)	−0.09 (0.91)	0.38 (1.55)	0.43 (2.80)	—	0.46
Linear	−0.09 (0.08)	0.31 (1.99)	−0.01 (0.46)	0.03 (1.32)	0.10 (1.80)	—	0.40
SETAS/IV							
Log-linear	−0.04 (0.03)	0.91 (1.52)	0.01 (0.09)	0.00 (0.01)	0.05 (0.13)	0.22 (1.40)	0.49
Linear	0.21 (0.16)	1.00 (2.03)	0.00 (0.20)	−0.02 (0.07)	−0.01 (0.11)	0.19 (1.15)	0.43

continued

Table 3 *(cont.)*

Indicator/estimation method	Intercept	Indicator lag	Regulation (EREG1)	Tax morality (TTHI)	Tax rate (TXAMI)	$\hat{\rho}$	R^2
C/M2/OLS							
Log-linear	0.91 (3.52)	0.72 (15.05)	−0.24 (7.12)	0.05 (0.95)	0.15 (5.02)	—	0.98
Linear	2.16 (1.93)	0.77 (16.03)	−0.10 (5.64)	0.01 (0.67)	0.18 (5.08)	—	0.97
C/M2/IV							
Log-linear	1.63 (2.84)	0.57 (4.77)	−0.19 (2.01)	−0.03 (0.62)	−0.07 (1.64)	0.74 (6.72)	0.96
Linear	7.47 (2.87)	0.55 (4.26)	−0.05 (1.09)	−0.01 (0.88)	0.06 (0.98)	0.81 (8.35)	0.96
GPR72/OLS							
Log-linear[a]	16.70 (0.90)	0.28 (1.90)	−1.06 (0.47)	0.91 (0.17)	−4.93 (1.75)	—	0.22
Linear	8.71 (1.71)	0.30 (2.08)	−0.03 (0.37)	0.03 (0.30)	−0.39 (1.86)	—	0.23
GPR72/IV							
Log-linear[a]	−0.42 (0.03)	1.01 (5.04)	0.05 (0.03)	−0.02 (0.00)	0.09 (0.04)	−0.06 (0.37)	0.48
Linear	−0.46 (0.10)	1.03 (4.89)	0.00 (0.04)	−0.00 (0.02)	0.02 (0.10)	−0.10 (0.61)	0.45

[a] Since there are instances of negative values for GPR72, the dependent variable is not logged.

On the other hand, the SETAS equations are almost totally benign, the only exception coming with the significance of the tax rate variable in the OLS results, which is not surprising since SETAS is, in fact, constructed from a regression with the tax rate as an explanatory variable (Tanzi 1983).

The C/M2 OLS results are quite good, with the tax rate and regulation variables statistically significant (though, again, the sign on EREG1 is negative). Compensating for a first-order autocorrelated error destroys any dependence on the causes, however. The GPR72 results, on the other hand, are totally uninteresting (with the exception, perhaps, of the explosive models estimated using the IV correction), reflecting the more or less random pattern of GPR72 over time (see the Appendix).

What is to be concluded from such results? There seems not only to be a big difference in them across the three main indicators as regards their dependence on the causes (which is tenuous, in any event), but there are also substantial problems within each equation pair in sorting out the underlying dynamics. Clearly, a better econometric approach is needed.

3.3   DYMIMIC results

There are, of course, a myriad of different indicator sets, measures of the causes, and model structures that might be considered in the context of the DYMIMIC specification. The most illustrative of these (not just the best!) are presented in Tables 4 and 5. In all the results we have constrained the coefficient on X_t in the SERTA measurement equation to equal 1 *instead* of putting $\sigma_{uu} = 1$ as a theoretically more attractive normalization rule. This is equivalent to adopting a specific rotation in factor analysis. The estimated α-coefficients reflect, accordingly, the importance of each indicator relative to SERTA, but it should be noted that the results are quite robust, whichever indicator is taken as the numeraire in this way.

Table 4 summarizes our findings for the two-indicator model involving SETAS and SERTA and C/M2 and SERTA. The indicator side of the model and its internal dynamics are robust to changes in the way the causal factors are measured in the few log-linear models reported. SERTA has by far the largest direct connection to X_t, with an estimated weight of 0.13 for SETAS in all of the models. The coefficient on X_{t-1} is quite stable at approximately 0.84. The evolution of X_t is therefore dominated by its past, with only the tax rate variable modifying this tendency in any consistent and statistically significant way. We note that the regulation variable(s) always has the wrong sign, being significant in only one case. Tax morality appears to be at least marginally significant in all three models.

Table 4. *DYMIMIC results, U.S. annual data, 1939–82, two indicator models*

Indicators	AR structure in X_t	Causes	
		Regulation	Tax morality
Log-linear models			
1. SETAS, 0.13 (4.81) SERTA, 1.00 (constraint)	AR(1), $\hat{\phi}=0.84$ (13.23) intercept, $\hat{\gamma}_0 = -3.78$ (2.52)	EREG1, -0.32 (1.70)	TTH1, 0.82 (1.86)
2. SETAS, 0.13 (4.81) SERTA, 1.00 (constraint)	AR(1), $\hat{\phi}=0.83$ (12.68) intercept, $\hat{\gamma}_0 = -3.79$ (2.52)	EREG1, -0.38 (1.80)	TTH2, 0.87 (1.87)
3. SETAS, 0.13 (4.88) SERTA, 1.00 (constraint)	AR(1), $\hat{\phi}=0.84$ (15.53) intercept, $\hat{\gamma}_0 = -4.65$ (3.89)	EREG3, -0.36 (2.56)	TW, 1.09 (3.19)
Linear models			
4. SETAS, 0.03 (3.56) SERTA, 1.00 (constraint)	AR(1), $\hat{\phi}=0.84$ (14.48) intercept, $\hat{\gamma}_0 = -18.41$ (2.59)	EREG1, -0.24 (2.09)	TTH1, 0.15 (1.04)
5. SETAS, 0.03 (3.63) SERTA, 1.00 (constraint)	AR(1), $\hat{\phi}=0.82$ (18.16) intercept, $\hat{\gamma}_0 = -32.25$ (6.30)	EREG1, -0.37 (3.49)	TTH1, 0.18 (1.98)
6. C/M2, 0.55 (12.26) SERTA, 1.00 (constraint)	AR(1), $\hat{\phi}=0.83$ (12.26) intercept, $\hat{\gamma}_0 = -10.33$ (1.99)	EREG1, -0.23 (2.61)	TTH1, 0.12 (1.25)
7. C/M2, 0.19 (5.05) SERTA, 1.00 (constraint)	AR(1), $\hat{\phi}=0.67$ (8.09) intercept, $\hat{\gamma}_0 = 6.43$ (1.29)	EREG1, -0.30 (1.90)	TTH1, -0.06 (0.89)

Note: Numbers in parentheses are absolute *t*-ratios.
[a]Abbreviation: i.i.d., independent and identically distributed.

These log-linear models have the unfortunate consequence that the actual "size" of the shadow economy cannot be calculated. For this reason, we present results for four linear models, two of them being offshoots of model 1 in Table 4. They appear as models 4 and 5. The AR dynamics in X_t are essentially the same as in the log-linear models. EREG1, the regulation variable, is significant now but still has the pervasive negative influence. In model 5, where an apparent AR(1) process in the error term in the SERTA measurement equation is accounted for, all coefficients are judged to be significantly different from zero at the (asymptotic) 5 percent level.

Models 6 and 7 use C/M2 along with SERTA instead of SETAS. Qualitatively, the results are similar to those of model 5, with TXAM1 and

Tax rate	Error structure[a]	Correlated measurement errors?	Remarks
TXAM1, 0.68 (3.77) $\hat{\beta} = 0.41$ (15.25)	i.i.d.	yes	β is coefficient on tax rate variable in measurement equation for SETAS
TXAM1, 0.69 (3.85) $\hat{\beta} = 0.41$ (15.23)	i.i.d	yes	compare to 1; change only in tax morality variable
TXAM1, 0.57 (3.77) $\hat{\beta} = 0.41$ (15.37)	i.i.d.	yes	compare to 1; change in regulation and tax morality variables
TXAM1, 1.14 (4.38) $\hat{\beta} = 0.23$ (20.55)	i.i.d.	yes	β is coefficient on tax rate variable in measurement equation for SETAS
TXAM1, 1.96 (5.94) $\hat{\beta} = 0.23$ (20.82)	AR(1) in measurement equation for SERTA; $\hat{\rho}_2 = 0.38$ (3.24)	yes	compare to 4; change only in error structure
TXAM1, 0.76 (4.04)	i.i.d.	yes	
TXAM1, 1.01 (4.14)	AR(1), $\hat{\rho}_1 = 0.99$ (89.95) $\hat{\rho}_2 = 0.97$ (27.35)	yes	compare to 6; change only in error structure; also compare to 5

EREG1 being statistically significant. The pervasive negative sign on the regulation variable(s) in all of these models suggests that EREG1 is perhaps too crude a measure of regulatory "intensity." In particular, it may be that some of the more recently created regulatory agencies are, in fact, devoted to regulating underground activities – hence, the prospect of a negative influence on X_t.

Prediction of the size of the shadow economy is, of course, of particular interest to us, and this is illustrated in Figure 2 for model 5 in Table 4.[22] The figure suggests a pattern of evolution over time with a peak around 1943–4 and a trough in 1967–8. The predicted values of X_t in 1967–8 from the linear model are, respectively, 4.17 percent and 4.01 percent. By 1982,

[22] All the plots are of the smoothed estimates of the unobserved variable, i.e., these are $E(X_t \mid$ all data and MLE of the parameters), where X_t is the unobserved/latent variable.

Table 5. *DYMIMIC results, U.S. annual data, 1939–82, three indicator models*

		Causes	
Indicators	AR structure in X_t	Regulation	Tax morality
Log-linear models			
1. SETAS, 0.13 (4.54)	AR(1), $\hat{\phi} = 0.88$ (14.30)	EREG1, -0.24 (1.40)	TTH1, 0.76 (1.98)
GPR72[a], 1.20 (6.07)			
SERTA, 1.00	intercept,		
(constrained)	$\hat{\gamma}_0 = -3.00$ (2.35)		
2. SETAS, 0.14 (4.65)	AR(1), $\hat{\phi} = 0.91$ (15.63)	EREG1, -0.25 (1.55)	TTH1, 0.98 (2.56)
GPR72[a], 1.21 (3.71)			
SERTA, 1.00	intercept,		
(constrained)	$\hat{\gamma}_0 = -2.99$ (2.33)		
3. SETAS, 0.11 (3.53)	AR(2), $\hat{\phi}_1 = 1.62$ (21.10)	EREG1, -0.13 (1.76)	TTH1, 0.56 (2.57)
GPR72[a], 1.12 (3.64)	$\hat{\phi}_2 = -0.68$ (9.38)		
SERTA, 1.00	intercept,		
(constrained)	$\hat{\gamma}_0 = -2.29$ (2.07)		
Linear models			
4. SETAS, 0.04 (4.42)	AR(1), $\hat{\phi} = 0.84$ (13.40)	EREG1, -0.20 (0.11)	TTH1, 0.11 (14.61)
SERTA, 1.00	intercept,		
(constrained)	$\hat{\gamma}_0 = -15.61$ (2.43)		
GPR72, 0.12 (4.07)			
5. SETAS, 0.04 (3.27)	AR(1), $\hat{\phi} = 0.85$ (15.44)	EREG1, -0.34 (2.87)	TTH1, 0.29 (2.92)
SERTA, 1.00	intercept,		
(constrained)	$\hat{\gamma}_0 = -17.90$ (3.59)		
GPR72, 0.11 (2.38)			

Note: Numbers in parentheses are absolute t-ratios.

[a] Since there are instances of negative values for GPR72, it is not logged in these models.

the predicted value of X_t had grown to 29.15 percent of GNP. The predicted path of X_t is dominated by SERTA. It is to be stressed that the scale of X_t is inherently ambiguous in our model, and so while a comparison of the 29.15 percent figure in 1982 to the value 4.17 percent in 1967 is meaningful, the 29.15 percent and 4.17 percent *levels* are not. Nevertheless, something can be said: Setting the low point of the graph at 0, one still gets a healthy 25 percent estimate for the size of the underground economy (as a percentage of official GNP) in 1982. From another point of view, if tax evasion was roughly 5 percent of GNP in 1976 (our only "hard" piece of evidence), is the fixing of our predicted path for X_t at approximately 4 percent in 1967–8 really so contentious?

The three-indicator models of Table 5 are introduced in order of increasing complexity, beginning with a model directly comparable to mod-

Tax rate	Error structure	Correlated measurement errors?	Remarks
TXAM1, 0.36 (2.36) $\hat{\beta} = 0.41$ (15.08)	i.i.d.	yes	$\hat{\beta}$ is coefficient on tax rate variable in measurement equation for SETAS
TXAM1, 0.05 (1.26) $\hat{\beta} = 0.41$ (14.18)	AR(1) with $\rho_1 = 0$, $\hat{\rho}_2 = 0.31$ (4.73), $\hat{\rho}_3 = 0.41$ (3.01)	yes, except $R_{12} = 0$, $R_{13} = 0$	compare to 1; restrictions on measurement error covariance structure
TXAM1, 0.21 (1.37) $\hat{\beta} = 0.43$ (14.06)	AR(1) with $\rho_1 = 0$, $\hat{\rho}_2 = 0.74$ (5.70), $\hat{\rho}_3 = 0.38$ (2.48)	yes, except $R_{12} = 0$, $R_{13} = 0$	compare to 2
TXAM1, 1.02 (4.32) $\hat{\beta} = 0.22$ (17.92)	i.i.d.	yes	$\hat{\beta}$ is coefficient on tax rate variable in measurement equation for SETAS
TXAM1, 0.74 (2.74) $\hat{\beta} = 0.22$ (15.00)	AR(1) with $\rho_1 = 0$, $\hat{\rho}_2 = 0.70$ (4.51) $\hat{\rho}_3 = 0.49$ (3.74)	yes	compare to 6; change only in structure of measurement errors

el 1 of Table 4. All the indicators are significant in the first model, with GPR72 now being most important (and with a *positive* sign). Tax morality and the tax rate have significant coefficients in the structural equation. Model 2 incorporates AR(1) measurement errors and covariance restrictions suggested by results obtained in a previous (unreported) model. In model 2 the qualitative conclusions of model 1 are preserved, except that TXAM1 becomes insignificant. GPR72 and SERTA have similar weights attached to them. Jumping down to model 5 in Table 5, the only change is to allow for an AR(2) process in X_t. The ϕ_2 coefficient is significantly different from zero, with the rest of the qualitative and quantitative features of model 2 being preserved.

Figure 3 is derived from model 5 of Table 5, one of two linear models presented. The qualitative conclusions are similar to those of the comparable log-linear models, but the error dynamics are different. Using an

SMOOTHED ESTIMATES OF SHADOW ECONOMY OVER TIME

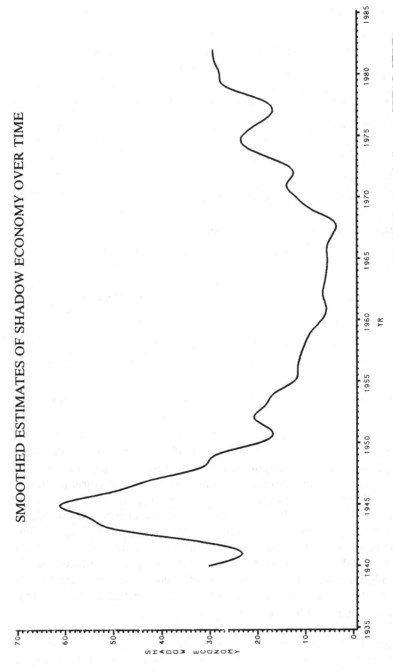

Figure 2. Predicted evolution of shadow economy, 1939–82, from model 5 of Table 4 (two indicators: SETAS, SERTA, with AR(1) measurement error in SERTA).

SMOOTHED ESTIMATES OF SHADOW ECONOMY OVER TIME

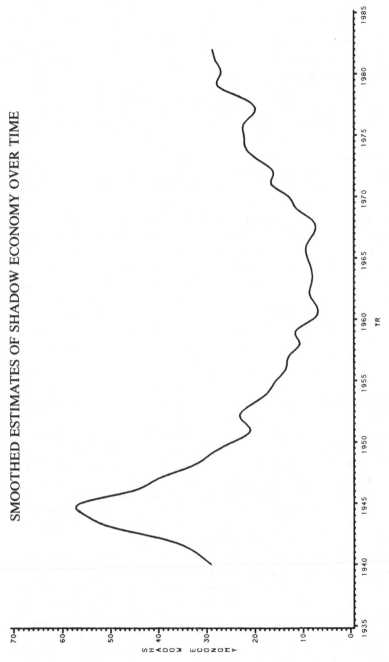

Figure 3. Predicted evolution of shadow economy, 1939–82, from model 5 of Table 5 (three indicators: SETAS, SERTA, GPR72, with AR(1) measurement error in SERTA and GPR72).

asymptotic 5 percent test, all the coefficients in model 7 would be judged to be statistically significant.[23] The predictions displayed in Figure 3 for model 5 show a fairly sustained trough in the 1960s with a low point in 1961 of 6.98 percent (7.68 percent in 1967) and a value for 1982 of 28.63 percent, roughly the same forecast as obtained before.

In the interest of space we do not present results for the few four-indicator models we have tried so far (adding NLFPR). This work is ongoing. Four-indicator models with all the complexities we allow are expensive to estimate, and so something other than an "experimental" approach to model building is called for. More thought also needs to go into the question of proper model specification when using indicators like GPR72 and NLFPR, though the presence of additional indicators in general ought to help determine X_t.

The matter of very large estimates of X_t during the World War II years is, of course, an obvious criticism of our results. Most people would be shocked to learn that 60 percent of GNP was "unofficial" then. SETAS and SERTA (and C/M2) both display this trait – hence the outcome we observe. There are reasons the underground economy might be his large during the war years, but the indicators and causes may mean different things for those years than for the postwar era (cf. Romer 1986). When the models are fitted on postwar data only (1947–82), however, *the same evolutionary path emerges,* though the statistical significance of the causes deteriorates.[24]

4   Summary and conclusions

In this chapter we have explored in some detail the adaptation of the DYMIMIC model to a natural application, that of estimating the size of the U.S. shadow economy from annual time series data. Certainly, this is an attractive approach in principle, since it captures most of the salient features of the underlying phenomenon: measured causes and measured indicators feeding into and out of a single latent variable that is dependent as well on its past history, which is not accounted for by the causal variables. A complicated error structure is allowed.

The relationships of the indicators to the latent variable and the internal dynamics of the structural model appear to be quite robust. The importance of some of the causal factors is as well, with the subjective "tax

---

[23] That the calculated t-statistic should be compared to critical points obtained from the standard normal distribution is only correct asymptotically. We do not know, even for the simplest dynamic models, whether this is an error in the conservative direction or otherwise in small samples.

[24] This could be due entirely to a lack of degrees of freedom with the smaller data set.

morality" variable(s) emerging as a significant positive influence in most of the variants we have tried so far and the tax "burden" in many of them. Of course, the regulation, tax morality, and tax rate factors are properly viewed as latent in their own right, with the several alternative variables available as proxies for them being merely "indicators" themselves. There is some previous research to draw on in the standard errors-in-variables literature to aid in dealing with this complication,[25] but as yet we have not attempted to incorporate it into our DYMIMIC structure. Nor have we exhausted the set of potential indicators and causes. Of particular interest in this regard are various crime statistics (e.g., arrest rates) and the unemployment rate.

One other thing could be done by way of validating our specification. A natural specification test suggests itself, namely, to test the restrictions that emerge from the exact moment equations for any particular model with the "unrestricted" reduced-form covariance structure suggested by the Kalman filter/EM approach to its estimation. No direct goodness-of-fit statistic is available when comparing a prediction to its *unobservable* true value, of course, so some sort of specification test is the only available source of validation evidence. In this regard, Engle and Watson (1981) suggest that a likelihood ratio test within the DYMIMIC framework may also be available.

Appendix: data and sources

C/M2: Currency holdings as proportion of money stock.
> *Source:* Tanzi 1983.
> *Datenote:* Data for 1930–82. Provisional figures for year 1981 on.

EREG1: Economic regulations: general business, stock accumulated (i.e., number of agencies).
> *Source:* Penoyer 1981.
> *Datenote:* Data for 1929–82. Provisional figures from the year 1980 on.

EREG2: Economic regulations: industry-specific agencies, stock accumulated.
> *Source:* Same as that of EREG1.
> *Datenote:* Data for 1929–82. Provisional figures from the year 1980 on.

EREG3: Economic regulation: finance and banking, stock accumulated.
> *Source:* Same as that of EREG1.
> *Datenote:* Data for 1929–82. Provisional figures from the year 1980 on.

[25] See Ghosh (1985) and references cited therein.

GPR72: Growth rate in gross private product in billions of 1972 dollars.
> *Source:* Darby 1984.
> *Datenote:* Data for 1929–82. Provisional figures from the year 1981 on.

NLFPR: Non-labor-force participation rate. For U.S. male population, 25–64 years of age.
> *Source:* For total residential population data: U.S. Bureau of the Census, Current Population Reports, Population Estimates Series P-25, Nos. 98, 310, 519, 721, 870. For labor force data: U.S. Department of Labor Statistics, Handbook of Labor Statistics 1980 and Current Employment and Earnings Publication.
> *Datenote:* Data for 1947–82.

SEMTA: Hidden sector measured by modified transaction method in "biopercent."
> *Source:* Feige 1980.
> *Datenote:* Data for 1939–82. Provisional figures to year 1980.

SERTA: Hidden sector measured by refined transaction method in percentage of official GNP.
> *Source:* Same as that of SEMTA.
> *Datenote:* Same as that of SEMTA.

SETAS: Estimated underground economy as percentage of GNP.
> *Source:* Tanzi 1983.
> *Datenote:* Data for 1930–82. Provisional figures for year 1981 on.

TTH1: Percent saying "Taxes are too high."
> *Source:* Hansen 1983.
> *Datenote:* Data for 1939–82.

TTH2: Percent saying "Taxes are too high," Harris Poll.
> *Source:* Same as that of TTH1.
> *Datenote:* Same as that of TTH1.

TW: Percent saying "Taxes are wasted."
> *Source:* Based on an election survey conducted by Center for Political Studies, Survey Research Center, University of Michigan and published in *Public Opinion,* various numbers.
> *Datenote:* Data for 1939–82.

TXAM1: Average marginal federal personal income tax rate on adjusted gross income.
> *Source:* Seater 1985.
> *Datenote:* Data for 1929–82. Provisional figures from 1981 on.

TXAM2: TXAM1 multiplied by ratio of total adjusted gross income to gross national product to adjust for the fraction of GNP subject to personal income tax.
> *Source:* Same as that of TXAM1.
> *Datenote:* Same as that of TXAM1.

TXAM3: Overall average marginal tax rates on personal income.
Source: Same as that of TXAM1.
Datenote: Same as that of TXAM1.
TXAM4: Overall marginal tax rates on labor's marginal product.
Source: Same as that of TXAM1.
Datenote: Same as that of TXAM1.
TXAVW: Weighted average tax rate on interest income.
Source: Tanzi 1983.
Datenote: Same as that of SETAS.
TXRGI: Ratio of total income tax payments after credit to adjusted gross income.
Source: Same as that of TXAVW.
Datenote: Same as that of TXAVW.

Plots of the main variables used in the study are shown in Figures 4 to 12.

REFERENCES

Blades, D. 1982. *The Hidden Economy and the National Accounts.* Paris: OECD (Occasional Studies), pp. 28–44.
Boeschoten, W. C. and M. M. G. Fase. 1984. *The Volume of Payments and the Informal Economy in the Netherlands 1965–1982.* Dordrecht: Nijhoff.
Cagan, P. 1958. "The Demand for Currency Relative to the Total Money Supply." *Journal of Political Economy* 66(3): 302–28.
Carter, M. 1984. "Issues in the Hidden Economy – A Survey." *The Economic Record* 60: 209–21.
Clotefelter, C. T. 1983. "Tax Evasion and Tax Rates: An Analysis of Individual Return." *Review of Economics and Statistics* 65(3): 363–73.
Contini, B. 1981. "Labor Market Segmentation and the Development of the Parallel Economy – The Italian Experience." *Oxford Economic Papers* 33(4): 401–12.
Darby, M. R. 1984. "Labor Force Employment and Productivity in Historical Perspective." Table A-20.
Del Boca, D. 1981. "Parallel Economy and Allocation of Time." *Micros (Quarterly Journal of Microeconomics)* 4(2): 13–18.
Dempster, A. P., N. M. Laird, and D. B. Rubin. 1977. "Maximum Likelihood from Incomplete Data Via the EM Algorithm." *Journal of the Royal Statistical Society, Series B* 39: 1–38.
Denison, E. F. 1982. "Is U.S. Growth Understated Because of the Underground Economy: Employment Ratios Suggest Not." *Review of Income and Wealth* 28(1): 1–43.
Engle, R. F., D. M. Lilien, and M. Watson. 1985. "A DYMIMIC Model of Housing Price Determination." *Journal of Econometrics* 28: 307–26.
Engle, R. F. and M. Watson. 1981. "A One-Factor Multivariate Time Series Model of Metropolitan Wage Rates." *Journal of the American Statistical Association* 76: 774–81.
Feige, E. L. 1979. "How Big is the Irregular Economy?" *Challenge* 22(1): 5–13.
1980. "A New Perspective on Macroeconomic Phenomena." Discussion Paper, Wassenar, Netherlands Institute for Advanced Studies.

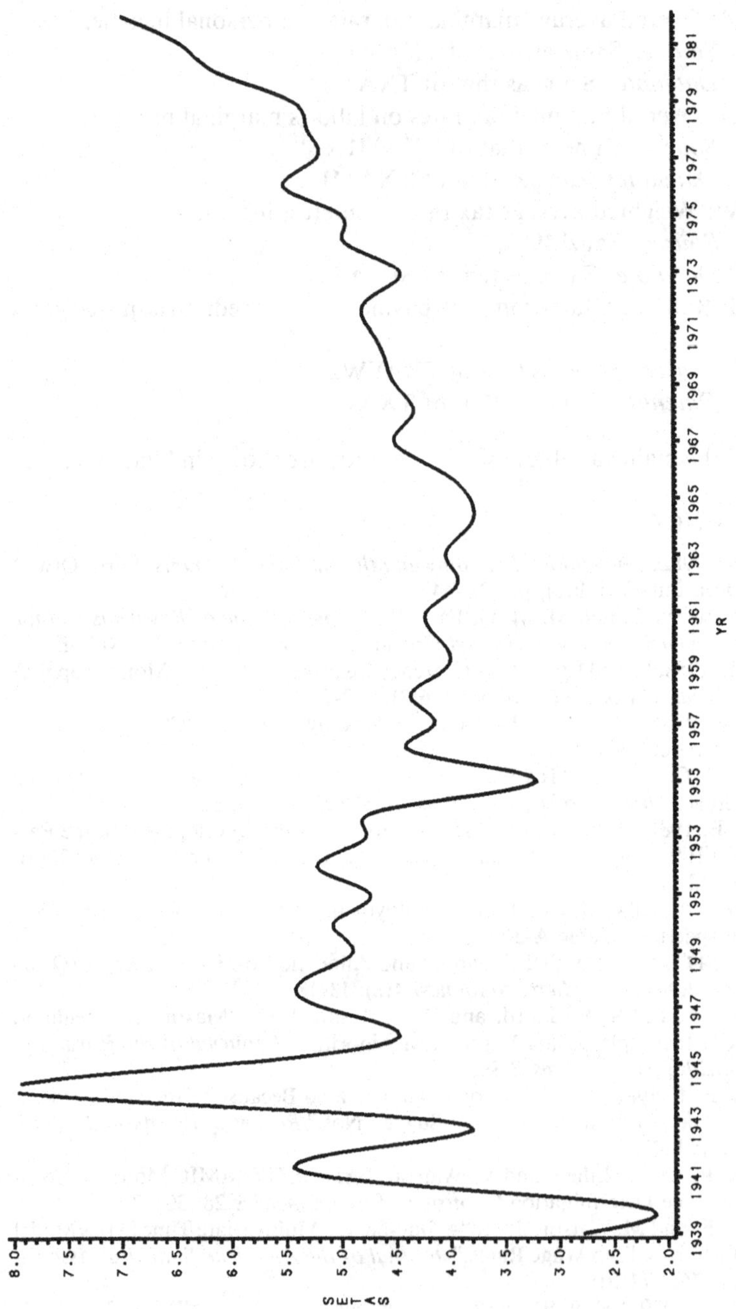

Figure 4. SETAS, 1939–82.

324

325

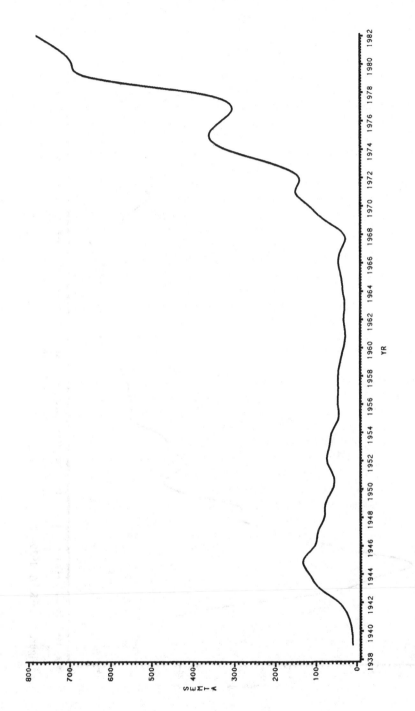

Figure 5. SEMTA, 1939–82.

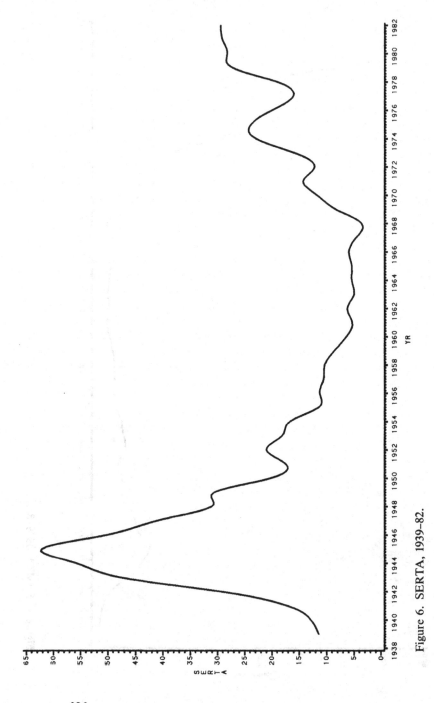

Figure 6. SERTA, 1939–82.

326

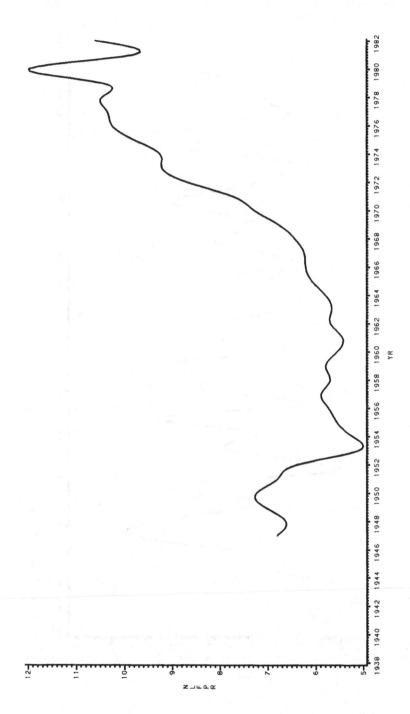

Figure 7. NLFPR, 1939–82.

327

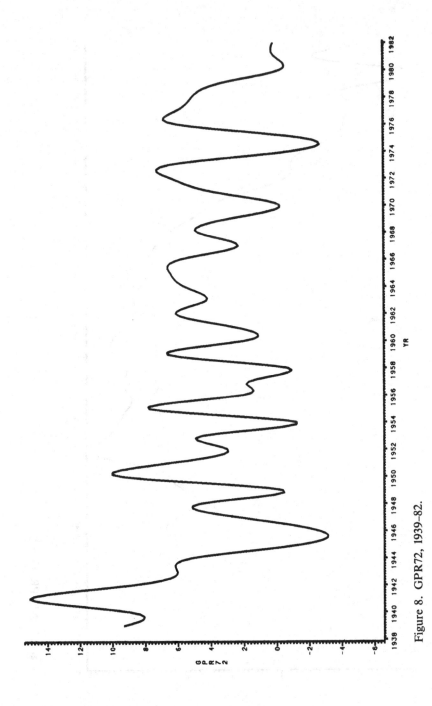

Figure 8. GPR72, 1939–82.

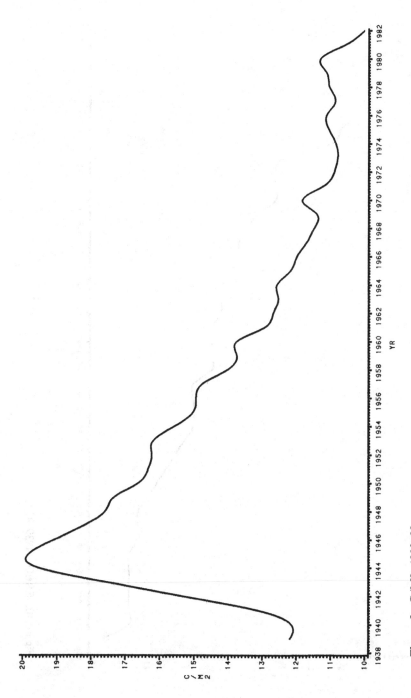

Figure 9. C/M2, 1939–82.

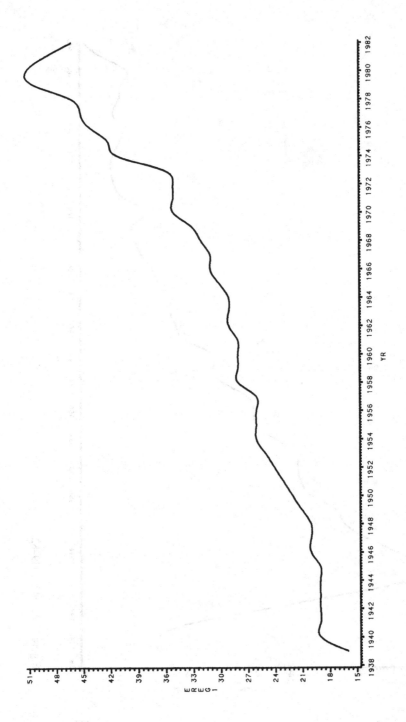

Figure 10. EREG1, 1939–82.

330

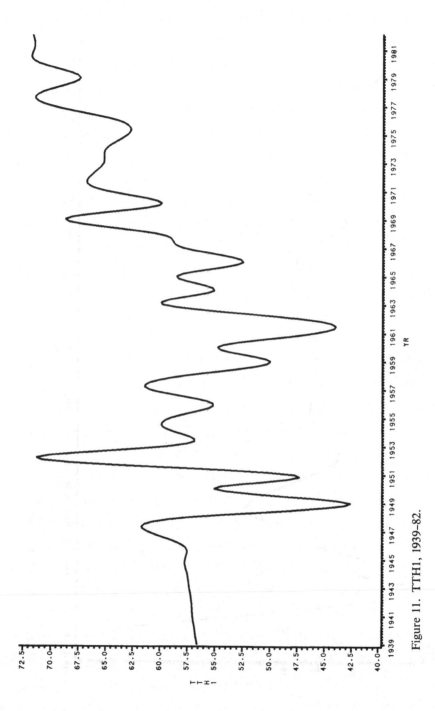

Figure 11. TTH1, 1939–82.

331

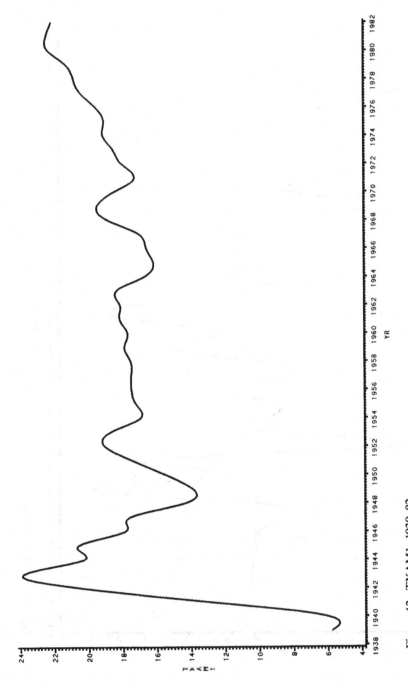

Figure 12. TXAM1, 1939–82.

1982. "A New Perspective on Macroeconomic Phenomena: The Theory and Measurement of the Unobserved Economy of the United States: Causes, Consequences, and Implications." In *International Burden of Government,* M. Walker, Ed. Vancouver, pp. 112-36.

Frey, B. S. and W. W. Pommerehne. 1982. "Measuring the Hidden Economy: Though There Be Madness, Yet Is There Method in It?" In *The Underground Economy in the United States and Abroad,* V. Tanzi, Ed. Lexington: Heath, pp. 3-27.

1984. "The Hidden Economy: State and Prospects for Measurement." *Review of Income and Wealth* 30(1): 1-23.

Frey, B. S. and H. Weck-Hannemann. 1984. "The Hidden Economy as an 'Unobserved' Variable." *European Economic Review* 26(1): 33-53.

Gaertner, W. and A. Wenig. Eds. 1985. *The Economics of the Shadow Economy.* Heidelberg: Springer-Verlag.

Garcia, G. and S. Pack. 1979. "The Ratio of Currency to Demand Deposits in the United States." *Journal of Finance* 34(4): 703-15.

Ghosh, D. 1985. "Maximum Likelihood Estimation of the Dynamic Shock-Error Model." MRG Working Paper No. M8522, University of Southern California, October. To appear in *Dynamic Latent Variable Models,* D. Aigner and M. Deistler, Eds., *Journal of Econometrics (Annals, 1988),* North-Holland.

Gutman, P. M. 1979. "Statistical Illusions, Mistaken Policies." *Challenge* 22(6): 14-17.

Hansen, S. B. 1983. *The Politics of Taxation.* New York: Praeger.

Harvey, A. C. 1981. *Time Series Models.* New York: Halsted.

Internal Revenue Service (IRS). 1979. *Estimates of Income Unreported on Individual Income Tax Returns.* Washington, DC: U.S. Government Printing Office.

Isachsen, A. J., J. Kloveland, and S. Strøm. 1982. "The Hidden Economy in Norway." In *The Underground Economy in the United States and Abroad,* V. Tanzi, Ed. Lexington: Heath, pp. 209-31.

Isachsen, A. J. and S. Strøm. 1980. "The Hidden Economy: The Labor Market and Tax Evasion." *Scandinavian Journal of Economics* 82(4): 304-11.

Jazwinski, A. H. 1970. *Stochastic Processes and Filtering Theory.* New York: Academic.

Kalman, R. E. 1960. "A New Approach to Linear Filtering and Prediction Problems." *Transactions of the American Society of Mechanical Engineers, Journal of Basic Engineering* (Series C) 82: 35-45.

Kirchgaessner, G. 1984. "Verfahren zur Erfassung des in der Schattenwirtschaft erarbeiteten Sozial produkts." *Allgemeines Statistisches Archiv* 68(4): 378-405.

Langfeldt, E. 1984. "The Unobserved Economy in the Federal Republic of Germany." In *The Unobserved Economy,* E. L. Feige, Ed. Cambridge: Cambridge University Press, pp. 236-60.

Lehman, B. 1981. "What Happens During Business Cycles?" Ph.D. dissertation, Department of Economics, University of Chicago, Chicago, IL.

Macafee, Kerrik. 1980. "A Glimpse of the Hidden Economy in the National Accounts." *Economic Trends* 316: 81-7.

Mehra, R. K. 1974. "Identification in Control and Economics: Similarities and Differences." *Annals of Economic and Social Measurement* 3: 21-47.

Mogensen, G. V. 1985. *Sort Arbejde i Danmark*. Kopenhagen: Nyt Nordisk Forlag.

O'Neill, D. M. 1983. "Growth of the Underground Economy 1950–81: Some Evidence from the Current Population Survey." *Study for the Joint Economic Committee*. Congress of the United States, Joint Committee print 98-122. Washington, DC: U.S. Government Printing Office.

Park, T. 1979. "Reconciliation Between Personal Income and Taxable Income, 1947–1977." Mimeo, Bureau of Economic Analysis, Washington, DC.

Penoyer, R. J. 1981. "Directory of Federal Regulatory Agencies." St. Louis, Washington University, Center for the Study of American Business.

Petersen, H.-G. 1982. "Size of the Public Sector, Economic Growth and the Informal Economy: Development Trends in the Federal Republic of Germany." *Review of Income and Wealth* 28(2): 191–215.

Porter, R. D. and A. S. Bayer. 1984. "A Monetary Perspective on Underground Economic Activity in the United States." *Federal Reserve Bulletin* 70(3): 177–89.

Romer, C. D. 1986. "Is the Stabilization of the Postwar Economy a Figment of the Data?" *American Economic Review* 76(3): 314–34.

Schneider, F. 1986. "Estimating the Size of the Danish Shadow Economy Using the Currency Demand Approach." *Scandinavian Journal of Economics* 88(4): 643–68.

Schneider, F. and W. W. Pommerehne. 1985. "The Decline of Productivity Growth and the Rise of the Shadow Economy in the U.S." Unpublished manuscript, University of Århus, Århus.

Schweppe, F. 1965. "Evaluation on Likelihood Functions for Gaussian Signals." *IEEE Transactions on Information Theory* 11: 61–70.

Seater, J. J. 1985. "On the Construction of Marginal Tax Rates." *Journal of Monetary Economics* 15(1): 121–35.

Simon, C. P. and A. D. Witte. 1982. *Beating the System: The Underground Economy*. Boston: Auburn House.

Tanzi, V. 1980. "The Underground Economy in the United States: Estimates and Implications." *Banca Nazionale del Lavoro* 135(4): 427–53.

1983. "The Underground Economy in the United States: Annual Estimates, 1930–1980." *IMF-Staff Papers* 30(2): 283–305.

Watson, M. W. and R. F. Engle. 1983. "Alternative Algorithms for the Estimation of Dynamic Factor, MIMIC and Varying Coefficient Regression Models." *Journal of Econometrics* 23(3): 385–400.

Weck, H. 1983. *Schattenwirtschaft: Eine Möglichkeit zur Einschränkung der Öffentlichen Verwaltung?* Bern: Peter Lang Verlag.

CHAPTER 15

Estimating structural models of unemployment and job duration

Dale T. Mortensen and George R. Neumann

Available theoretical models of unemployment and job duration are based on a dynamic formulation of an individual worker's job search and job-matching problems. In general versions of the theory, the individual anticipates future arrival of an uncertain sequence of employment opportunities, whether currently employed or not. The worker controls the transition process between employment states and jobs by choosing search and acceptance strategies that maximize expected wealth given current information. In other words, the strategy is the solution to a well-defined dynamic programming problem.

Given a model of this type, the properties of the probability distributions of both the length of time spent looking for an acceptable job while unemployed and, once employed, the length of the specific job spell are endogenously determined by the optimal strategy and the structure of the decision problem. Hence, observations on the completed unemployment and job spell lengths experienced by a sample of workers provide information about the problem's structure. The purpose of this chapter is to develop methods suggested by the theory that an econometrician might find useful for the purpose of estimating structural parameters from available observations on realized unemployment and job spell lengths and to test their potential usefulness using Monte Carlo techniques.

Although structural models of unemployment and job spell duration have been available for some time, there are few attempts to estimate them in the literature. Instead, ad hoc specifications of the duration hazards borrowed from the statistical literature on survival and reliability analysis are estimated.[1] This state of affairs is not surprising given the problems

The research reported in this chapter was funded by a collaborative National Science Foundation grant.

[1] The empirical literature on unemployment duration that apply a search-theoretic framework include Ehrenberg and Oaxaca (1976), Kiefer and Neumann (1979a, 1981), Flinn and

335

posed by any dynamic optimization theory. The stumbling block is a consequence of the "forward-looking" nature of the solution to any intertemporal optimization problem. Given this nature, no general method for representing the optimal decision rules as closed-form functions of the structural parameters and regressors of the model is available. Hence, one does not know the form of the likelihood function or any other criterion for estimation.

In this chapter, the model considered is a generalization of Burdett's (1978) job search model.[2] Workers choose to search, whether employed or not, at endogenous intensities in the model studied. Hence, the worker is presumed to determine both an offer acceptance strategy and a search intensity strategy that maximize expected wealth. The optimal search strategy, given the structure of the decision problem, determines the hazard rates associated with the implied probability distribution over the length of both an unemployment spell and the subsequent job spell. Given a particular parameterization of the structure of the worker's decision problem, these spell length distributions and appropriate data on unemployment and job spells experienced by a sample of workers allow one to define a sample likelihood function of the parameters.

However, one cannot derive the likelihood function associated with any reasonable parameterization of the structure, at least not in closed form. In this chapter, several related methods for computing the value function are suggested that permit a numerical representation of the optimal search strategies and the associated spell duration hazard rates that appear in the likelihood function.

The principal method is based on the mathematical structure of discounted dynamic programming, the fact that the value function is the unique fixed point of a contraction map. The contraction map itself provides an algorithm for computing its own fixed point. However, in the

Footnote 1 (cont.)
Heckman (1983), Nickell (1979), Lancaster and Nickell (1980), and Burdett et al. (1984). Theoretical and empirical studies of job spell duration that emphasize job search and matching include Burdett (1978), Jovanovic (1979a, b, 1984), Mincer and Jovanovic (1981), Flinn (1986), Miller (1984), Mortensen (1984), and Topel and Ward (1985). Econometric methodology is discussed in many of these papers and in Flinn and Heckman (1982) and Heckman and Singer (1982). Among the empirical papers in this collection, only Miller attempts to estimate the structure of the underlying decision problem.
2 The original theoretical formulation of the search on the job problem can be found in Burdett (1978) although the model abstracts from the search effort choice. Burdett and Mortensen (1978) consider a generalization which allows for search intensity choice as well as search while employed. Benhabib and Bull (1983) represents a more recent contribution to the theory of search intensity choice. Finally, Jovanovic (1984) and Mortensen (1984) study generalizations of the model that allow for learning about match specific quality.

case under study, the modulus of the contraction is close to unity for reasonable parameter values. Consequently, a sufficiently close approximation can be expected to require considerable computing time as well as a special programming effort. The second method suggested is based on the fact that the optimal search and acceptance strategies can be represented as solutions to ordinary first-order differential equations. In this case, a numerical solution to the equation can be computed relatively easily using generally available software. Finally, for the model under study, the closed-form optimal strategy and the associated likelihood function can be derived for the limiting case in which the modulus of the contraction converges to unity. The estimates obtained using the functional form associated with this limiting case are of interest in their own right but also provide natural starting values for an iterative estimation procedure that uses either of the other two methods.[3]

The suggested computation methods are used here to estimate a special case of the model, that of constant search intensities, using synthetic data generated with the true model. That the computations are feasible and that the method of locating maximum-likelihood estimates (MLE) using them has satisfactory properties is established using Monte Carlo techniques.

The text that follows is composed of four principal sections. In the first, the formal optimization problem that a worker faces is formulated and the optimal search strategy is characterized. The computation methods are developed in the second section. The third section reports on Monte Carlo estimation experiments applying the methods. This effort and directions for future research are summarized in the final section.

1 Theoretical model of unemployment and job duration

A job is characterized by a stationary wage which generally differs across employers for a given worker. Whether the worker is employed or not, the arrival of wage offers to the worker is generated by a Poisson process. The arrival rate depends on the worker's search intensity which is chosen subject to a cost that may depend on the worker's employment status.

---

[3] The only related literature on the estimation problem other than Miller (1984) of which we are aware are papers by Rust (1984) and Pakes (1986). The optimization problem that Rust considers does not include the model studied here as a special case; consequently, his theorems and method do not apply. Pakes, on the other hand, does estimate an optimal stopping model similar to ours using a maximum-likelihood procedure augmented by a computational algorithm that computes the optimal stopping rule at each iteration of the procedure. However, his data, duration distributions of patent lives, have a quite different structure than that available for job and unemployment spells. Hence, the specifics of his procedure are not applicable.

Let $c_i(s)$, $s \in \mathbb{R}_+$, denote search cost per period at intensity s, where $i = 0$ and $i = 1$ denote not employed and employed respectively. A wage offer, $w \in W$, that is a random draw from the offer distribution $F: W \to [0, 1]$ is accepted or rejected on arrival. The worker is assumed to know the wage offer distribution and to make each acceptance decision and search intensity choice so as to maximize the expected present value of future income, expected wealth. The discount rate, denoted as r, is stationary and the working life is of indefinite length. When not employed, the worker receives a benefit b that is foregone once employed. Hence, the structure of the decision model is a specification of the interest rate, the unemployment benefit, the wage offer distribution, and the two cost-of-search functions.

Let $V_0(b)$ represent maximal expected wealth when unemployed and the benefit received is b, and let $V_1(w)$ denote expected wealth when employed at wage w. By applying Bellman's dynamic optimization principle, one can represent the two value functions as the solutions to the two functional equations represented in what follows. Because (1) the time required for the arrival of an alternative offer when unemployment, denoted as T, is exponentially distributed with hazard rate equal to the offer arrival rate as a consequence of the Poisson arrival assumption, (2) the offer arrival rate can be regarded as the worker's search intensity s without loss of generality, (3) the worker can choose between the wealth associated with continued unemployment and that offered by employment at the realized wage X given an arrival, and (4) the worker's income per period is b until the arrival of an offer, maximal expected wealth when unemployed, $V_0(b)$, solves the equation

$$V_0(b) = \max_{s \geq 0} E\left\{ \int_0^T [b - c_0(s)] e^{-rt}\, dt + e^{-rT} \max[V_0(b), V_1(X)] \right\}$$

$$= \max_{s \geq 0} \left[\frac{b - c_0(s)}{r + s} + \frac{s}{r + s} \int \max[V_0(b), V_1(x)]\, dF(x) \right]. \qquad (1.a)$$

The first term on the right is the expected present value of benefits received net of the cost of search paid during the waiting time required until the next offer, and the second term is the present value of the worker's best choice at the time an offer arrives. Analogous reasoning for the case of employment at wage w implies that

$$V_1(w) = \max_{s \geq 0} E\left\{ \int_0^T [w - c_1(s)] e^{-rt}\, dt + e^{-rT} \max[V_1(w), V_1(X)] \right\}$$

$$= \max_{s \geq 0} \left[\frac{w - c_1(s)}{r + s} + \frac{s}{r + s} \int \max[V_1(w), V_1(x)]\, dF(x) \right]. \qquad (1.b)$$

Define the "permanent income" associated with unemployed and employed, respectively, as

$$v_0(b) \equiv rV_0(b) \quad \text{and} \quad v_1(w) \equiv rV_1(w). \tag{2}$$

Given (2), equations (1) can be rewritten as

$$v_0(b) = \max_{s \geq 0} \Bigg[[1 - \beta(s)][b - c_0(s)]$$
$$+ \beta(s) \int \max[v_0(b), v_1(x)] \, dF(x) \Bigg] \tag{3.a}$$

and

$$v_1(w) = \max_{s \geq 0} \Bigg[[1 - \beta(s)][w - c_1(s)]$$
$$+ \beta(s) \int \max[v_1(w), v_1(x)] \, dF(x) \Bigg], \tag{3.b}$$

where

$$\beta(s) \equiv s/(r+s). \tag{4}$$

The following series of results establish the existence of unique solutions to equations (3) and characterize the optimal search strategy associated with them. Three reasonable economic conditions are sufficient for existence:

Assumption 1. The set of possible wage offers W and the set of unemployment benefits B are both bounded.

Assumption 2. The interest of discount rate r is positive.

Assumption 3. The cost-of-search function $c_i(s)$ is twice differentiable, $c_i(0) = c_i'(0) = 0$, and $c_i''(s) > 0$ for $i = 0, 1$.

In stating the results, which are formally proved in the appendix, we use the fact that W can be regarded as a subset of B by virtue of Assumption 1 without loss of generality. Let

$$\bar{w} = \sup W \quad \text{and} \quad \underline{w} = \inf W \tag{5}$$

represent the largest and smallest wage offer, respectively.

Lemma 1. *Any solution $v_0 : B \to \mathbb{R}$ to (3.a) or $v_1 : W \to \mathbb{R}$ to (3.b) is continuous and strictly increasing.*

Lemma 1 implies that the employment acceptance decision satisfies the *reservation property*, that is, a unique reservation wage, denoted as $R(b)$, generally exists for every b such that a wage offer is acceptable if and only if it is no less than the reservation wage. Given the unemployment benefit, the reservation wage equates the values of employment and unemployment:

$$v_0(b) = v_1(R(b)). \tag{6}$$

Because both functions are increasing and continuous, the reservation wage increases continuously with the unemployment benefit. Finally, the optimal acceptance decision when employed is trivial since the indifference condition $v_1(w) = v_1(x)$ and the fact that $v_1(x)$ is continuous and increasing in x implies that any offer greater than or equal to the worker's current wage w yields a higher expected wealth.

Given any solution (v_0, v_1) to equations (3), Assumption 3 implies that a unique search-intensity strategy exists both when employed and not. Let $\lambda_0(R(b))$ and $\lambda_1(w)$ represent these optimal search intensity choices (the offer arrival rates) contingent on the worker's reservation wage when not employed and the wage when employed. These are the solutions to the maximization problems defined on the right sides of equations (3.a) and (3.b), respectively. Consequently, the optimal intensity equates the marginal cost and expected marginal return-to-search effort:

$$rc_0'(\lambda_0(R(b))) = \int_{R(b)}^{\bar{w}} [v_1(x) - v_1(R(b))]\, dF(x) \tag{7.a}$$

in the case of unemployment and

$$rc_1'(\lambda_1(w)) = \int_{w}^{\bar{w}} [v_1(x) - v_1(w)]\, dF(x) \tag{7.b}$$

in the case of employment by virtue of equations (2)–(4). Under Assumption 3, one can show that the first-order condition is sufficient. Hence, equations (7) imply that the optimal offer arrival rate is continuous and decreasing in the unemployment benefit when not employed and the wage when employed.

Note that equations (3), (4), and (7) imply that

$$v_0(b) = b + \lambda_0(R(b))c_0(\lambda_0(R(b))) - c_0(\lambda_0(R(b))) \tag{8.a}$$

and

$$v_1(w) = b + \lambda_1(w)c_1(\lambda_1(w)) - c_1(\lambda_1(w)). \tag{8.b}$$

Hence, given the optimal intensity functions, the reservation wage function $R(b)$ can be obtained using equation (6) after appropriate substitution from equations (8).

To complete the existence argument, we need the following.

Lemma 2. *If the solution to* (3.b), $v_1: W \to \mathbb{R}$, *is unique, continuous, and bounded, then* (3.a) *has a unique solution,* $v_0: B \to \mathbb{R}$.

Note that any solution to equation (3.b) is a fixed point of the transformation T defined by the right side of the equation:

$$(Tv)(w) = \max_{s \in \mathbb{R}_+} \left[[1 - \beta(s)][b - c_0(s)] \right.$$
$$\left. + \beta(s) \int \max[v_0(b), v_1(x)]\, dF(x) \right]$$
$$= [1 - \beta(\lambda_1(w))][w - c_1(\lambda_1(w))]$$
$$+ \beta(\lambda_1(w)) \int \max[v_1(w), v_1(x)]\, dF(x). \qquad (9)$$

By virtue of Lemma 1, the fixed point must be an element of the space of continuous and increasing real-valued functions. Furthermore, for any function in this space, equations (9) and (7.b) imply

$$w \le v_1(w) \le (Tv_1)(\bar{w}) = \bar{w} \quad \text{because } \lambda_1(\bar{w}) = 0. \qquad (10)$$

Let $\mathfrak{F}$ represent the set of functions with these properties, that is,

$$\mathfrak{F} = \{v: W \to \mathbb{R} \mid v(w) \text{ is continuous and increasing and } w \le v(w) \le \bar{w}\}. \qquad (11)$$

Lemma 3. *The transformation T* (a) *maps the function space $\mathfrak{F}$ into itself and* (b) *is a contraction on $\mathfrak{F}$.*

Because $\mathfrak{F}$ is a complete metric space under the supremum norm, Lemma 3 implies that T has a unique fixed point. [See Ross (1970, p. 192) for a proof.] Consequently, the three lemmas together imply existence and uniqueness of an optimal search strategy:

Theorem. *Unique, continuous, and strictly increasing value functions exist.*

As an implication of the model, a completed spell of unemployment given the unemployment benefit b is an exponentially distributed random variable with hazard rate equal to

$$\eta_0(R(b)) = \lambda_0(R(b))[1 - F(R(b))]. \qquad (12)$$

Similarly, the completed length of any subsequent job-paying wage w is exponentially distributed with hazard

$$\eta_1(w) = \lambda_1(w)[1 - F(w)]. \tag{13}$$

These facts provide the means for estimating the structure of the model: interest rate, cost-of-search functions, and wage offer distribution. Specifically, given a parameterization of the cost-of-search and wage offer distribution functions, one can use equations (12) and (13) to construct the likelihood function for a sample of unemployment and job spell durations experienced by identical workers. Ideal data for the purpose would include observations on the completed length of an unemployment spell and the unemployment benefit received during the spell together with the length of the subsequent postunemployment job spell (complete or not) and the wage earned for each worker in the sample. However, in order to characterize the likelihood function and compute its value for any point in the parameter space, one needs to solve the model for the optimal search intensity strategies and the reservation wage expressed as functions of both the "regressors" b or w and the model's structural parameters.

2 Computing optimal search strategy functions

In order to estimate the model's structure, one must solve for the optimal search strategy functions given specific parameterizations of the cost-of-search and the wage offer distribution functions. Closed-form solutions cannot be obtained in general even for very simple specifications. The problem is the forward-looking nature of the worker's dynamic decision problem. As a consequence of this nature, the current decision depends on the structure not only through its effect on the current decision criterion, the right sides of equations (3) given the value function. A given structural parameter also affects the criteria for future search intensity choices, and these effects feed back as determinants of the value function that enters the criterion for the current choice.

All the effects on future decisions of any one of the problem's structural parameters are embedded in the value function. Although closed-form solutions for the value of the problem and the associated optimal strategy cannot be obtained, both can be computed. Because the value-of-employment function is the unique fixed point of a contraction map defined on a known function space, strategy can be computed to any degree of accuracy desired.

Specifically, consider the sequence of functions generated by iterating the contraction T defined in equation (9):

$$
\begin{aligned}
v_1^{n+1} &= Tv_1^n \\
&\equiv \max_{s \geq 0} \Bigg[[1 - \beta(s)][w - c_1(s)] \\
&\quad + \beta(s) \int \max[v_1^n(w), v_1^n(x)] \, dF(x) \Bigg].
\end{aligned}
\tag{14}
$$

Because T is a contraction on $\mathcal{F}$, any sequence of value functions that initiates in $\mathcal{F}$ converges uniformly (in the supremum norm) to the unique fixed point of T. Hence, the computed function is an approximation of the true function for sufficiently large n. Given this approximation, one can compute the associated optimal search intensity functions and the reservation wage function using equations (6)–(8).

Although the algorithm suggested by (14) is technically feasible, it can be very computer time intensive. An important factor determining the computer time required by the algorithm to find a sufficiently close approximate value function is the speed with which the contraction T converges. The slower the rate of convergence, the greater is the number of iterations required to obtain any allowable approximation error. Specifically, the fact that

$$\|v_1^{n+1} - v_1^n\| \leq \beta \|v_1^n - v_1^{n-1}\|, \tag{15.a}$$

where $\|\cdot\|$ represents the supremum norm,

$$\beta = \hat{\lambda}/(r + \hat{\lambda}) \quad [\hat{\lambda} \text{ solves } (r + \hat{\lambda})c_1'(\hat{\lambda}) - c_1(\hat{\lambda}) = \bar{w} - \underline{w}], \tag{15.b}$$

is established in the proof to Lemma 3. Bounds on the number of iterations of the contraction required to guarantee a given approximation error can be determined using either of the following inequalities:

$$\|v_1 - v_1^n\| \leq [\beta/(1-\beta)] \|v_1^n - v_1^{n-1}\| \leq [\beta^n/(1-\beta)] |\bar{w} - \underline{w}|, \tag{15.c}$$

where the first inequality is an implication of (15.a) and the second is an implication of (15.a) and the fact that $\underline{w} \leq v(w) \leq \bar{w}$ for all $v \in \mathcal{F}$.[4]

Later we will argue that β is likely to be close to unity in practice because available evidence suggests that the offer arrival rate when employed at the reservation wage is large relative to the interest rate. If so, equations (15) imply that the number of iterations required to guarantee a reasonable bound on approximation error is large. Consequently, alternative computation methods may prove useful as a means of significantly reducing computation costs. The remainder of the section considers a general and several special alternative approaches.

In some cases of interest, one does not need the value of employment function. For example, in the limiting case of costless search up to some upper bound on intensity, that is, $c_i(s) = 0$ for $s \leq \lambda_i$ and $c_i(s) = \infty$ otherwise, equation (6) together with (3) and (4) imply

---

[4] The second inequality can be used to compute an absolute upper bound on the number of iterations of the contraction required to attain a given approximation error ex ante. The first inequality provides a stopping rule that guarantees a given approximation error. In practice, the actual number of iterations that are required by the stopping rule, the first inequality, should be significantly smaller than the absolute upper bound implied by the second. We thank Nicholas Kiefer for pointing out the first of these two inequalities.

$$v_1(R(b)) = R(b) + \frac{\lambda_1}{r} \int_{R(b)}^{\bar{w}} [v_1(x) - v_1(R(b))] \, dF(x)$$

$$= b + \frac{\lambda_0}{r} \int_{R(b)}^{\bar{w}} [v_1(x) - v_1(R(b))] \, dF(x)$$

since $s_i = \lambda_i$ is optimal.[5] If $F(x)$ is continuous, the value of employment is differentiable. Indeed,

$$v_1'(w) = \frac{r}{r + \lambda_1[1 - F(w)]}$$

by virtue of equations (3.b) and (4). Finally, because integration by parts implies

$$\int_{R(b)}^{\bar{w}} [v_1(x) - v_1(R(b))] \, dF(x) = \int_{R(b)}^{\bar{w}} v'(x)[1 - F(x)] \, dx,$$

$R(b)$ can be numerically computed as the unique solution to

$$R(b) = b + (\lambda_0 - \lambda_1) \int_{R(b)}^{\bar{w}} \frac{1 - F(x)}{r + \lambda_1[1 - F(x)]} \, dx. \tag{16}$$

Note that the reservation wage is greater than the unemployment benefit in this case if and only if the offer arrival rate when unemployed, λ_0, exceeds the offer arrival rate when employed, λ_1. This implication is a reflection of the fact that employment is less desirable in the short run to the extent that the waiting time required for the arrival of the next offer is greater when employed than when not.

Computing the value function by iterating the contraction can be avoided for the more general model as well because the optimal search intensity strategy when employed can be represented as the solution to an ordinary first-order differential equation, provided that the wage offer distribution is continuous and the cost-of-search function is twice differentiable. To establish this claim, note that equation (3.b) and the fact that the value-of-employment function is increasing in w imply

$$v_1'(w) = \frac{r}{r + \lambda_1(w)[1 - F(w)]} \tag{17}$$

by virtue of the envelope theorem. Consequently, by differentiating both sides of equation (7.b) and then substituting from equation (17), one obtains the ordinary first-order differential equation

$$\lambda_1'(w)c_1''(\lambda_1(w)) = \frac{-[1 - F(w)]}{r + \lambda_1(w)[1 - F(w)]}, \quad \text{where } \lambda_1(\bar{w}) = 0, \tag{18}$$

---

[5] Although, strictly speaking, this cost function violates Assumption 3, it lies at the boundary of the set of functions defined by the assumption.

is the needed boundary condition. Readily available numerical methods exist that yield approximate solutions to such an equation.

After solving (18) for the optimal offer arrival rate when employed, the associated offer arrival rate when not employed and the reservation wage can be obtained by using the following facts:

$$c_0'(\lambda_0(R(b))) = c_1'(\lambda_1(R(b))),\tag{19}$$

and

$$b + \lambda_0(R(b))c_0'(\lambda_0(R(b))) - c_0(\lambda_0(R(b)))$$
$$= R(b) + \lambda_1(R(b))c_1'(\lambda_1(R(b))) - c_1(\lambda_1(R(b))),\tag{20}$$

where equation (19) is an implication of equations (7) and equation (20) is a consequence of (6)–(8).

The marginal response of the reservation wage to an increase in the unemployment benefit reflects the relative magnitude of the job spell and unemployment spell hazard rates in the general model. Specifically, differentiating (20) with respect to b yields

$$1 + \lambda_0(R)c_0''(\lambda_0(R))\lambda_0'(R)R'(b) = R'(b) + \lambda_1(R)c_1''(\lambda_1(R))\lambda_1'(R)R'(b).$$

Consequently, equations (18) and (19) and equations (12) and (13), respectively, imply that $R(b)$ is the solution to the following differential equation:

$$R'(b) = \frac{r + \lambda_1(R)[1 - F(R)]}{r + \lambda_0(R)[1 - F(R)]} = \frac{r + \eta_1(R)}{r + \eta_0(R)}, \quad \text{where } R(\bar{w}) = \bar{w}.\tag{21}$$

Empirical evidence on the magnitudes of $R'(b)$ and the unemployment spell hazard rate $\eta_0(R)$ provides a means of obtaining an estimated lower bound on the size of β, the modulus of the contraction T. A range of 8–16 weeks easily incorporates most estimates of the average completed unemployment spell found in the empirical literature. Since expected unemployment duration is $1/\eta_0(R)$, the implied unemployment hazard estimate is 0.33 per month at the midpoint of this range. Feldstein and Poterba (1984) report estimates of the responsiveness of reservation wage rate to unemployment insurance (UI) benefits received, $R'(b)$, that range around 0.33. These numbers, equation (21), and an interest rate of 1 percent per month imply the following estimate of the job duration hazard per month when employed at the reservation wage:

$$\eta_1(R) = [r + \eta_0(R)]R'(b) - r = (0.01 + 0.33)(0.33 - 0.01) = 0.102.$$

Hence, the argument used in the proof to Lemma 3 (see the appendix) and the fact that

$$\lambda_1(R) \geq \lambda_1(R)[1 - F(R)] = \eta_1(R)$$

imply

$$\beta \geq \lambda_1(R)/[r+\lambda_1(R)] \geq \eta_1(R)/[r+\eta_1(R)] = 0.102/0.112 = 0.91.$$

In short, the contraction T can be expected to converge quite slowly. Hence, the alternative computational procedure implicit in equations (18)–(20) may well be much faster than that associated with iterating the contraction map.

The evidence that the job duration hazard rate is large relative to the interest rate suggests another approach to estimation. Namely, the offer arrival rate when employed can be approximated by its zero interest rate limit when the latter is sufficiently large relative to the former. Formally, as $r \to 0$, the limiting optimal offer arrival rate function converges to the solution

$$c_1''(\lambda_1)\lambda_1'(w) = -1/\lambda_1, \quad \text{where } \lambda_1(\bar{w}) = \bar{w}.$$

Since $\lambda c''(\lambda)$ is the derivative of $\lambda c'(\lambda) - c(\lambda)$ with respect to λ, the limiting solution for the offer arrival rate solves

$$\lambda_1(w)c_1'(\lambda_1(w)) - c_1(\lambda_1(w)) = \bar{w} - w \quad \text{when } r = 0. \tag{22}$$

Since the left side is strictly increasing in λ_1 given $c_1''(s) > 0$, the optimal offer arrival rate converges to an increasing function of the difference between the largest wage offer and the current wage earned as the interest rate becomes small.

The limiting solution for $\lambda_1(w)$ together with the associated limiting solutions for $\lambda_0(R)$ and $R(b)$ can be computed directly using equations (19), (20), and (22). Indeed, closed-form limiting solutions can be obtained in interesting cases. For example, in the case of a quadratic cost of search of the form

$$c_i(s) = \gamma_i s^2, \quad i = 0, 1, \tag{23}$$

one obtains square-root representations of the optimal offer arrival rates,

$$\lambda_1(w) = [(\bar{w} - w)/\gamma_1]^{1/2}, \tag{24.a}$$

$$\lambda_0(R(b)) = (\gamma_1/\gamma_0)\lambda_1(R(b)) = [(\bar{w} - b)/\gamma_0]^{1/2}, \tag{24.b}$$

and a linear reservation wage function of the form

$$R(b) = (\gamma_0/\gamma_1)b + (1 - \gamma_0/\gamma_1)\bar{w}. \tag{24.c}$$

3   Monte Carlo evidence on estimating structural duration models

In this section, a series of estimation experiments using Monte-Carlo-generated data are conducted. The experiments are designed to check the performance of the estimation procedures outlined previously in the constant search intensity case. The series include experiments that study the accuracy of the estimates obtained when the limiting zero interest rate solution is used as an approximation to the true reservation wage. For this purpose, we assume that the wage offer distribution is known. The other experiments deal with the problem of estimating the other structural parameters of the job search model jointly with the parameters of the offer distribution using the true optimal job search strategy.

The question of the quality of the estimates obtained when the zero interest rate approximation is used is of interest for three related reasons. First, the limiting solution can be expressed as closed-form differentiable functions of the structural parameters. Consequently, maximum-likelihood estimates of the parameters can be obtained using standard methods, for example, Newton's. Second, the available empirical evidence suggests that the limiting solution may be an adequate approximation. Third, estimation using the true model requires the computation of the search strategy function for each trial structural parameter vector. The number of iterations required in the search for the maximum-likelihood estimates may be significantly reduced by using the estimates initially obtained for the limiting solution as starting values.

How well does the approximate model recover the true parameter values? We attempt to answer the question for sample sizes of the sort that are likely to be encountered in practice. For simplicity, only the case of a constant search intensity is considered, which corresponds to the special case of zero search costs up to some bound on search intensity. Offer arrival rates when employed or not are λ_1 and λ_0, respectively, and the offer distribution is the cumulative density function (c.d.f.) $F(x)$. The optimal job acceptance strategy for an unemployed worker receiving unemployment benefit b is to accept all offers equal to or greater than the unique reservation wage $R(b)$ that solve equation (16), restated here as

$$R(b) = b + (\lambda_0 - \lambda_1) \int_{R(b)}^{\bar{w}} \frac{1 - F(x)}{r + \lambda_1[1 - F(x)]} \, dx. \tag{25}$$

Obviously,

$$R(b) \to (\lambda_1/\lambda_0)b + (1 - \lambda_1/\lambda_0)\bar{w} \quad \text{as } r/\lambda_1 \to 0. \tag{26}$$

In other words, when the interest rate is small relative to the offer arrival rate, the approximate reservation wage is a weighted average of the unemployment benefit and the highest wage offer, where the weights reflect the relative offer arrival rates when employed and when not employed.

Each Monte Carlo data sample is generated using the true reservation wage, the solution to (25). For each individual, denoted by $i = 1, \ldots, N$, the realized completed length of an unemployment spell, T_0, and the unemployment benefit received is observed together with the completed length of the subsequent employment spell, T_1, and the wage earned during the spell. By assumption, the individuals in the sample are drawn independently from an identical population. Since T_0 and T_1 are exponential variables with hazards $\lambda_0[1 - F(R(b))]$ and $\lambda_1[1 - F(w)]$, respectively, the log likelihood of the sample of observed spell length pairs (T_{0i}, T_{1i}) conditional on the observed benefit–wage pairs (b_i, w_i), $i = 1, ..., N$, is

$$\ln L = \sum_i [\ln\{\lambda_0[1 - F(R(b_i))]\} - \lambda_0[1 - F(R(b_i))]T_{0i}]$$

$$+ \sum_i [\ln\{\lambda_1[1 - F(w_i)]\} - \lambda_1[1 - F(w_i)]T_{1i}]. \tag{27}$$

The estimates reported for each experiment are maximum likelihood in the sense that they maximize this function.

In all experiments conducted, the true offer arrival rates are $\lambda_0 = 3$ and $\lambda_1 = 1$ and the interest rate is either 0.01 or 0.04. The unemployment benefit received by an individual in the sample is either 2 or 4. To generate the data for each individual in a sample, equation (25) was first solved for the true reservation wage $R(b_i)$, where $b_i = 2$ and $b_i = 4$ depending on the individual, given the true parameter values stated above. With this reservation wage, the unemployment hazard rate $\lambda_0[1 - F(R(b_i))]$ was computed, and an exponentially distributed completed unemployment spell length was generated for the individual. (All computations were performed using the program GAUSS running on an IBM personal computer.) An acceptable wage $w_i \geq R(b_i)$ was then generated for the individual by drawings from a truncated binomial distribution, with the truncation point equal to the reservation wage. Given this acceptable wage, a new exponentially distributed random variable (length of the worker's subsequent job spell) was generated using $\lambda_1[1 - F(w_i)]$ as the hazard. This procedure was then repeated for each individual in the sample.

The sample size was fixed at 500 observations for each replication of each estimation experiment, on the belief that this was close to the best that could be expected in practical situations. One thousand samples were generated and estimates were computed for each sample in each experiment. Tables 1 and 2 report the mean and standard deviation of the simulated distribution of maximum-likelihood estimates. To avoid problems of discontinuity in the likelihood function, which complicate the computation of estimates as well as the proof of consistency of the estimators, we treat the discrete binomial distribution as an approximation to a true continuous distribution. Finally, in all experiments the interest rate and the largest wage offer are treated as known. Hence, the structural parameters to be estimated include the two offer arrival rates λ_0 and λ_1 and the offer distribution parameter p.

Table 1. *Monte Carlo results: approximate reservation wage model means of MLE estimates*

	λ_0 (true value 3.0)	λ_1 (true value 1.0)	Percentage outside (95% normal confidence interval)	
			λ_0	λ_1
$r = 0.01$	2.9714 (0.1389)	1.0237 (0.0924)	0.059	0.055
$r = 0.04$	2.9434 (0.1887)	1.1107 (0.1256)	0.069	0.063

Note: Standard errors (in parentheses) are computed from frequency distribution of computed estimates.

Table 2. *Monte Carlo results: true reservation wage model means of MLE estimates*

	λ_0 (true value 3.0)	λ_1 (true value 1.0)	p (true value 0.5)
Case 1: wage distribution known	3.0152 (0.1056)	1.0100 (0.1009)	–
Case 2: wage distribution estimated	2.9537 (0.2108)	1.1201 (0.1737)	0.5351 (0.0456)

Notes: $r = 0.01$ in both cases. Standard errors (in parentheses) are computed from frequency distribution of computed estimates.

In Table 1, the estimation procedure utilizes the approximate reservation wage given in equation (26). In this case, the approximate reservation wage is a twice-differentiable function of the arrival rates and the largest wage offer. Consequently, the likelihood function is also twice differentiable given a twice-differentiable form for F that fits the binomial distribution c.d.f. To focus on the essential aspect of estimating the structure of the job search model using the approximation, we treat the wage distribution, form, and parameters as known. Two cases are considered: an interest rate of 0.01 and of 0.04.

The estimates of the offer arrival parameters obtained seem satisfactory in both cases. The estimators are centered near their true values; the mean of the 1,000 estimates is less than one standard deviation away from the true value. There is a noticeable increase in variability and some change in the distribution of the estimates in the higher interest rate case, but the effects are not large. Column 3 of Table 1 shows the fraction of times that the estimated coefficients would lie outside a 95 percent confidence interval around the true value. For 1,000 replications a 95 percent confidence interval around the 5 percent critical level would cover 3.6–6.4 percent. Thus, there is some evidence that the empirical distribution of the estimates becomes more fat-tailed as the interest rate gets larger.

The results in Table 1 suggest that the use of the zero interest rate approximation need not cause a significant loss in accuracy, at least in the estimation of the arrival rates of wage offers. There is some evidence that the method overestimates the reservation wage and hence underestimates the arrival rate of offers while unemployed (cf. column 1, Table 1). An interesting question is whether the alternative method using the true reservation wage for each parameter configuration yields significantly better results. It is also of interest to see how well these methods work when the parameters of the wage distribution are jointly estimated.

The first panel in Table 2 provides results comparable to the first panel in Table 1. The only difference is that the Table 1 procedure uses the approximate reservation wage at each parameter configuration while the procedure used to generate Table 2 uses the true reservation wage, the solution to equation (25). Computationally, this change in procedure was not difficult because there are only two values of b to consider. However, analytical derivatives of the reservation wage function are no longer available. Without them, we employed numerical first and second derivatives in maximizing the likelihood function. As case 1 in Table 2 indicates, there is only slight gain in precision attributable to using the true rather than the approximate reservation wage.

One important aspect of the use of an approximate solution for the reservation wage is the computation time saved. In the cases considered in panel 1 of Table 2 and in Table 1, a typical estimation problem with 500 observations required 3 minutes of CPU time on an IBM personal computer using the approximate solution, whereas the corresponding time required is 14.5 minutes using the true reservation wage.

The second panel in Table 2 reports the results of estimating the parameter p of the wage distribution jointly with the arrival rates. As in the first panel, the true reservation wage function is computed for each parameter configuration. There is a noticeable decrease in precision of the estimates of the arrival rates, and the parameter p is, on average, too high. Since the hazard rates out of unemployment and employment, respectively, are $\lambda_0[1 - F(R)]$ and $\lambda_1[1 - F(w)]$, overestimation of p should result in an underestimate of λ_0 and an underestimate of λ_1. Both patterns are seen in the second panel of Table 2.

4 Summary

Although both job search and job turnover models based on intertemporal optimization theory and appropriate data for estimating their structure have been available for some time, there are few attempts to do so in the literature. The principal reason for the dearth of activity on the topic is the fact that the behavioral strategies implied by any realistic parameterization of the structure of the underlying dynamic programming problem cannot be represented as closed-form functions of the regressors and parameters. In this chapter, the nature of the optimal search strategy implied by a general job search model is studied in more detail. The purpose of the study is to find solutions to the representation problem that may prove useful as part of an estimation procedure.

Three approaches are suggested. The first is based on the fact that the optimal search and reservation wage functions can be computed given the value function and the fact that the value function can be computed as a fixed point of a known contraction map. The second approach is derivative of the fact that the optimal search intensity is the solution to a known first-order differential equation that can be solved numerically. Finally, the model considered has a limiting solution for the optimal strategy that can be characterized in closed form for realistic parameterizations of the structure. This solution is an approximation to the optimal strategy when the interest rate is small relative to the frequency with which the worker receives wage offers, a condition which is consistent with available empirical evidence.

For a special case of the model, that of fixed search intensities, the properties of the approaches are studied using Monte Carlo techniques. In this case, the results imply that a procedure that uses the limiting solution as an approximation of the optimal strategy recovers estimates of the structural parameters that are quite close to their true values for a wide range of the critical parameter, the interest rate. Although using the true optimal strategy for each parameter candidate in an iterative computation procedure is shown to be computationally feasible on a standard IBM personal computer, in this special case there is little gain in accuracy relative to the alternative computationally cheaper procedure in the experiment considered.

In many ways, the paper is just a first step. Realistic search and matching models are much richer than that considered in Monte Carlo studies reported in this paper. Further Monte Carlo testing of the approaches using a variable search intensity version of this model is in progress. In the future, studies that incorporate matching phenomena along the lines of that developed in Jovanovic (1984) and Mortensen (1984) are planned. Nevertheless, we feel that the results obtained in this initial effort are encouraging and we look forward to the successful application of the techniques using real data.

Appendix

Proof of Lemma 1:   Either equation (3.a) or (3.b) can be written as

$$v(y) = \max_{s \in \mathbb{R}_+} \Big[[1 - \beta(s)][y - c(s)]$$
$$+ \beta(s) \int \max[v_1(x), v(y)] \, dF(x) \Big], \qquad \text{(A.1)}$$

where $y = b$ and $c(s) = c_0(s)$ in the case of (3.a) and $y = w$ and $c(s) = c_1(s)$ in the case of (3.b). Given the definition of $\beta(s)$ in (4), equation (A.1) is equivalent to

$$rv(y) = \max_{s \in \mathbb{R}_+} \Big[r[y - c(s)] + s \int \max[v_1(x) - v(y), 0] \, dF(x) \Big]. \qquad \text{(A.2)}$$

The continuity of $v(y)$ follows by virtue of the continuity of the maximum function and the implicit function theorem. Finally, were $v(y)$ nonincreasing in y, the right side of (A.2) would be strictly increasing in y, which is a contradiction.   Q.E.D.

Proof of Lemma 2:   It is sufficient to show that (A.2) has a unique solution for $v(y)$ for all $y \in B$. In other words, given the function

$$f(z) \equiv \max_{s \in \mathbb{R}_+} \Big[r[y - z - c(s)] + s \int \max[v_1(x) - z, 0] \, dF(x) \Big], \qquad \text{(A.3)}$$

we need only show that $f(z) = 0$ has a unique solution. First, note that the optimization problem is well defined for all finite values of z given Assumption 3. Hence, $f : \mathbb{R} \to \mathbb{R}$ exists. Second, the fact that the maximum function is strictly increasing and continuous implies that $f(z)$ is strictly decreasing and continuous. Consequently, $f(z) = 0$ has no more than one root.

Because the support of the wage offer distribution W is bounded by Assumption 1 and $c(s)$ is nonnegative and $c(0) = 0$ by Assumption 3, $f(y) < 0$ for sufficiently large but finite values of z and $f(y) > 0$ for sufficiently small values of z. Indeed,

$$f(z) = r(y - z) < 0 \quad \forall z > \max_{w \in W}[v_1(w), y]$$

and

$$f(z) = r(y - z) + \max_{s \in \mathbb{R}_+} \Big[s \int \max[v_1(x) - z, 0] \, dF(x) - c(s) \Big]$$
$$\geq r(y - z) > 0 \quad \forall z < \min_{w \in W}[v_1(w), -y].$$

Finally, these facts and the continuity of $f(v)$ implies that $f(z) = 0$ has a solution. Q.E.D.

Proof of Lemma 3: The transformation T is defined by

$$(Tv)(w) = \max_{s \geq 0} \left[[1 - \beta(s)][w - c(s)] \right.$$
$$\left. + \beta(s) \int \max[v(w), v(x)] \, dF(x) \right], \quad (A.4)$$

where

$$\beta(s) \equiv s/(r+s). \quad (A.5)$$

Under Assumption 3, the optimal search intensity function given v, $\lambda(w; v)$, is the unique solution to the first-order condition to the optimization problem on the right side of (A.4), that is,

$$(r + \lambda(w; v))c'(\lambda(w; v)) - c(\lambda(w; v))$$
$$= \int \max[v(x), v(w)] \, dF(x) - w. \quad (A.6)$$

Claim (a) is an immediate implication of (A.4)–(A.6). Here, Tv is increasing and continuous given that v has those properties by virtue of the fact that the maximum function is continuous and increasing. If $v(\bar{w}) = \bar{w}$ then $\lambda(\bar{w}, v) = 0$, which implies $(Tv)(\bar{w}) = \bar{w}$ given the assumption that $c(0) = c'(0) = 0$ and the fact that $\beta(0) = 0$. Finally, $c(0) = \beta(0) = 0$ implies $(Tv)(w) \geq w$.

Claim (b) holds if a number $0 \leq \beta < 1$ exists such that $\|Tv - Tu\| \leq \beta \|v - u\|$, where v and u are any two elements of $\mathcal{F}$ and $\|\cdot\|$ represents the supremum norm. Note that (A.6) implies $\lambda(w; v) \leq \lambda(w; \bar{w})$ for all v such that $w \leq v(w) \leq \bar{w}$, where $\lambda(w; \bar{w})$ is the continuous increasing function defined by

$$(r + \lambda(w; \bar{w}))c_1'(\lambda(w; \bar{w})) - c_1(\lambda(w; \bar{w})) = \bar{w} - w. \quad (A.7)$$

In what follows we establish the required inequality for

$$\beta \equiv \sup_{w \in W} [\beta(\lambda(w; \bar{w}))] = \beta(\lambda(\underline{w}; \bar{w})) \equiv \frac{\lambda(\underline{w}; \bar{w})}{r + \lambda(\underline{w}; \bar{w})}, \quad (A.8)$$

which is both nonnegative and strictly less than 1 given W bounded. The equality in (A.8) is an implication of the fact that $\lambda(w; v)$ is strictly decreasing in w by virtue of (A.7) and Assumption 3. Because (A.4) implies

$$(Tu)(w) \geq [1 - \beta(s(w, v))][w - c(s(w, v))]$$
$$+ \beta(s(w, v)) \int \max[u(w), u(x)] \, dF(x),$$

v and u both increasing respectively yield

$(Tv)(w) - (Tu)(w)$

$$\leq \beta(s(w, v)) \left[\int \max[v(w), v(x)] \, dF(x) - \int \max[u(w), u(x)] \, dF(x) \right]$$

$$= \beta(s(w, v)) \left[[v(w) - u(w)] F(w) + \int_w^{\bar{w}} [v(x) - u(x)] \, dF(x) \right].$$

Finally, because the first term in the final product satisfies $0 \leq \beta(s(w, v)) \leq \beta$ and because the absolute value of the second term is less than or equal to $\sup |v(w) - u(w)|$,

$$\|Tv - Tu\| \equiv \sup_{w \in W} |(Tv)(w) - (Tu)(w)| \leq |\beta| \sup_{x \in W} |v(x) - u(x)|$$

$$\equiv \beta \|v - u\|. \qquad \text{Q.E.D.}$$

REFERENCES

Benhabib, J. and C. Bull. 1983. "Job Search: The Choice of Intensity." *Journal of Political Economy* 91: 747–64.

Burdett, K. 1978. "Employee Search and Quits." *American Economic Review* 68: 212–20.

Burdett, K. and D. T. Mortensen. 1978. "Labor Supply under Uncertainty." In *Research in Labor Economics*, Vol. 2, R. G. Ehrenberg, Ed. Greenwich, CT: JAI, pp. 109–58.

Burdett, K., N. Kiefer, D. T. Mortensen, and G. Neumann. 1984. "Earnings, Unemployment, and the Allocation of Time Over Time." *Review of Economic Studies* LI: 559–78.

Ehrenberg, R. G. and R. L. Oaxaca. 1976. "Unemployment Insurance, Duration of Unemployment, and Subsequent Wage Gain." *American Economic Review* 66: 754–66.

Feldstein, M. and J. Poterba. 1984. "Unemployment Insurance and Reservation Wages." *Journal of Public Economics* 23: 141–67.

Flinn, C. J. 1986. "Wages and Job Mobility of Young Workers." *Journal of Political Economy* 94: S88–S110.

Flinn, C. and J. J. Heckman. 1982. "New Methods for Analyzing Structural Models of Labor Force Dynamics." *Journal of Econometrics* 18: 115–68.

1983. "Are Unemployment and Out of the Labor Force Behaviorally Distinct Labor Force States?" *Journal of Labor Economics* 1: 28–42.

Heckman, J. J. and B. Singer. 1982. "The Identification Problem in Econometric Models for Duration Data." In *Advances in Econometrics*, W. Hildenbrand, Ed. Cambridge: Cambridge University Press, pp. 39–77.

Jovanovic, B. 1979a. "Job Matching and the Theory of Turnover." *Journal of Political Economy* 87: 972–90.

1979b. "Firm-Specific Capital and Turnover." *Journal of Political Economy* 87: 1246–60.

1984. "Matching, Turnover and Unemployment." *Journal of Political Economy* 92: 108–22.

Kiefer, N. and G. Neumann. 1979a. "An Empirical Job Search Model with a Test of the Contest Reservation Wage Hypothesis." *Journal of Political Economy* 87: 69–82.

1979b. "Estimation of Wage Offer Distributions and Reservation Wages." In *Studies in the Economics of Search,* S. A. Lippman and J. J. McCall, Eds. New York: North-Holland, pp. 171–89.

1981. "Individual Effects in a Nonlinear Model: Explicit Treatment of Heterogeneity in the Empirical Job Search Model." *Econometrica* 49: 965–80.

Lancaster, T. and S. Nickell. 1980. "The Analysis of Reemployment Probabilities for the Unemployed." *Journal of the Royal Statistical Society (Series A)* 135: 257–71.

Miller, R. A. 1984. "Job Matching and Occupational Choice." *Journal of Political Economy* 92: 1086–1120.

Mincer, J. and B. Jovanovic. 1981. "Labor Mobility and Wages." In *Studies in Labor Markets,* S. Rosen, Ed. NBER Conference Report, Chicago: University of Chicago Press, pp. 21–64.

Mortensen, D. T. 1984. "Quit Probabilities and Job Tenure: On the Job Training or Matching?" Center for Mathematical Studies Discussion Paper No. 630, Northwestern University.

Nickell, S. 1979. "Estimating the Probability of Leaving Unemployment." *Econometrica* 47: 39–57.

Pakes, A. 1986. "Patents as Options: Some Estimates of the Value of Holding European Patent Stocks." *Econometrica* 54: 755–84.

Ross, S. M. 1970. *Applied Probability Models with Optimization Applications.* San Francisco: Holden-Day.

Rust, J. 1984. "Maximum Likelihood Estimation of Controlled Discrete Choice Processes." Social Systems Research Institute, University of Wisconsin.

Topel, R. and M. P. Ward. 1985. "Job Mobility and the Careers of Young Men." Mimeo, University of Chicago and University of California at Los Angeles.

CHAPTER 16

Comparison of dynamic factor demand models

Peter E. Rossi

1   Introduction

In order to explain the cyclical behavior of investment, the single-period neoclassical model of the firm has been revised to include nonlinear and time-dependent investment good production technologies. It has been observed that the shadow price of capital varies considerably over the business cycle and that the price of investment goods differs substantially from measures of the shadow price of capital. These macroeconomic phenomena have prompted modification of the model of the firm to include costs of adjustment of the capital stock and capital stock vintage effects. Both the cost-of-adjustment approach as proposed by Lucas (1967) and the vintage model [the "time-to-build" approach of Kydland and Prescott (1982)] give rise to a system of dynamic factor demands that allow for a richer class of investment behavior than static models. The object of this chapter is to examine the competing vintage and cost-of-adjustment models using U.S. production data. A new statistical methodology for choosing among nonnested models of optimizing behavior is developed and applied to this critical investment problem.

Empirical work on the derived demand for capital and other factors of production has focused on one-period models of the firm. A wide variety of functional forms have been proposed for production and cost functions. The translog form [see Berndt and Wood (1975) for production applications], the miniflex Laurent form proposed by Barnett (1983), and the Fourier flexible form proposed by Gallant (1982) have all been applied within the context of static models of the firm. The work on flexible functional forms has concentrated on obtaining functional approximations that can allow for arbitrary substitution and complementarity between factors of production. Extensions of the flexible form literature to the

Support of National Science Foundation Grant No. SES-8510193 is gratefully acknowledged.

dynamic factor demand problem have been limited [Epstein (1981) is an exception].

Compared to the vast literature on flexible functional forms, little attention has been given to dynamic models of firm behavior. In part, this is due to inadequate production data (most authors use U.S. annual aggregate manufacturing data) and the lack of appropriate econometric techniques for the nonlinear stochastic difference equations that arise as first-order conditions for dynamic models. The econometrician no longer has recourse to the simple duality theory useful for the one-period certainty case. Modeling expectations and imposition of the rational expectations hypothesis on systems of factor demand equations presents further econometric problems.

For the most part, linear-quadratic approximations have been used to develop the econometric specification for dynamic models of factor demand. Sargent (1978) set down the basic model and econometric specification of a system of dynamic factor demands with rational expectation imposed. In order to permit closed-form solutions for the dynamic factor demand functions, a quadratic production technology and linear time series models for factor prices are assumed. Berndt et al. (1979), Kennan (1979), Meese (1980), Pindyck and Rotemberg (1983), and Epstein and Yatchew (1985) have followed the basic Sargent approach with some variations in the methods of estimation and the manner in which the rational expectations hypothesis is imposed. This work assumes a first-order adjustment cost model in which a "penalty" term consisting of a quadratic form in the first difference of the factor vector is added to the objective function. Taken as a whole, these linear-quadratic versions of the adjustment cost models have been only moderately successful. Frequently, the restrictions generated by the rational expectations hypothesis are rejected, and there appears to be evidence of higher order adjustment cost terms.

Empirical work on the "time-to-build" model of Kydland and Prescott has been of a much more preliminary nature. Kydland and Prescott aim to convince the reader that their model is consistent with "summary" statistics of aggregate output and price data. However, since the Kydland and Prescott model is an equilibrium model, it is very difficult to separate the importance of the time-to-build feature of the investment good technology from the introduction of nontime-separable utility functions. The problem of disentangling the labor supply from capital demand is compounded by the use of aggregate data. Altug (1985) uses formal statistical techniques to fit a variant of the Kydland and Prescott model and pays careful attention to the restrictions the model imposes on the time series properties of macrodata series. Her work provides a step toward a better understanding of the empirical weaknesses of alternative production technologies.

The statistical problem associated with comparison of alternative dynamic factor demand models is the problem of choice between two nonnested economic hypotheses. It is fundamentally impossible to nest the cost of the adjustment model within the time-to-build framework. This same problem arises in the choice between alternative functional forms for production–cost functions (see Rossi 1985). This chapter aims to extend the statistical methodology proposed in Rossi (1985) to handle comparison of nonnested dynamic models.

2   Time series properties of input and factor price series

A natural starting point for any analysis of dynamic factor demand models is the time series representation of the factor and factor price time series. In this chapter, we restrict attention to the linear dynamic factor models derived from the firm decision problem with quadratic objective function and linear forecasting rules. The hypothesis of rational expectations coupled with a linear time series representation of the factor price series generates an econometric specification that amounts to a restricted vector autoregression model for the vector of factors and factor prices:

$$\begin{bmatrix} x_t \\ p_t \end{bmatrix} = \Phi_1 \begin{bmatrix} x_{t-1} \\ p_{t-1} \end{bmatrix} + \cdots + \Phi_p \begin{bmatrix} x_{t-p} \\ p_{t-p} \end{bmatrix} + \epsilon_t, \tag{1}$$

where x_t is the vector of factor demands and p_t is the vector of factor prices.

The optimal control solution imposes restrictions that relate the parameters of the time series process to the underlying technology parameters. The hypothesis of rational expectations imposes cross-equation restrictions between parameters of the price process and parameters of the factor demand process. For example, in an adjustment cost model with first-order adjustment cost terms and a factor price process that is VAR(q), the factor demand process is an ARMAX process (see, e.g., Hansen and Sargent 1980). One lagged vector of factor demands corresponds to the linear feedback rule, whereas the current and $q-1$ lagged values of factor prices are introduced from the optimal future forecasts of factor prices:

$$x_t = \Theta_1 x_{t-1} + \Gamma_1 p_t + \Gamma_2 p_{t-1} + \cdots + \Gamma_{q-1} p_{t-q+1} + \epsilon_t. \tag{2}$$

The parameters of the x_t process ($\Theta_1, \Gamma_1, \ldots, \Gamma_{q-1}$) are linked through a complicated set of restrictions to the production technology and the marginal process on p_t. In addition, it is frequently assumed that the factor price processes follow a *stationary* autoregressive process that is *exogenous* to the factor demands.

Before making detailed comparisons between alternative dynamic models, the time series properties of factor demand data should be examined to determine if observed processes have the appropriate order and linear form implied by the solutions to the control problems. Identification of the time series process governing factor prices seems a natural place to start. Correct identification of the factor price process is critical since the restrictions imposed by the rational expectations hypothesis are imposed conditional on the factor price model. Virtually all authors (see Sargent 1978; Meese 1980; Epstein and Yatchew 1985) "detrend" the factor price data by regressing factor prices on a constant, linear, and possibly quadratic time trend. This detrending operation is designed to induce stationarity in the data.

To evaluate the effect of detrending and to investigate the time series properties of factor demands, we examine two of the most widely used data sets on U.S. aggregate manufacturing. The first data set (hereafter referred to as the Berndt and Wood, or BW, data) is obtained from Morrison (1982) and reprinted in Epstein and Yatchew (1985). The BW data consist of measures of output, output price, labor, capital, and factor price indices for the period 1947–77. Morrison created this data set by extending the work of Berndt and Wood. All factor prices are normalized by dividing by the output price index. Data obtained from Berndt and Christensen's (1973) work on the separability of equipment and structures from labor in the aggregate production function are also examined. This data on U.S. manufacturing from 1929 to 1968 provides indices of two capital stock inputs: equipment and structures. Price indices are constructed by dividing the cost data given in Berndt and Christensen by the quantity index and renormalizing so that the price series is in index form and the quantity indices are now in current-dollar amounts. The Berndt and Christensen (BC) data allows for more detailed modeling of the investment good production technology by separating out structures from equipment. It may well be the case that a time-to-build model is more appropriate for the structures series than the equipment series, and certainly the gestation lag should be different for the two types of capital.

Cursory examination of the time series plots of the price of labor and price of capital series from the BW data set reveal pronounced random-walkish behavior. A random-walk model with a drift parameter would seem appropriate for these series. Of course, a trend regression will have a very significant trend term, but the residuals from the trend regression will again exhibit random-walkish behavior. Linear trend models are rarely appropriate for economic time series. The residuals from the "detrended" price series showed pronounced random-walk behavior. Clearly, detrending is not useful in inducing stationarity in these economic time series.

The conditions for existence of solutions to the linear-quadratic control problem do not require the exogenous price series to be stationary. As Sargent (1978) and others have noted, the only requirement is that the price series grow at a mean exponential rate lower than the discount rate. As long as this condition on mean growth rates is met, the transversality conditions necessary for existence are also satisfied. Typically, stationarity imposed on the price series allows for the routine application of Wiener–Kolmogorov prediction rules [see Hansen and Sargent (1980) for the details of this approach]. The Wiener–Kolmogorov formulas rely on moving-average representations of the time series, which are available only for stationary series. Random walks with drift admit very simple prediction formulas and satisfy the mean growth conditions. If a process follows a random walk with drift $y_t = \delta + y_{t-1} + \epsilon_t$, then $E[y_{t+s} \mid y_t, y_{t-1}, \ldots] = \delta s$. The conditional mean grows linearly and is dominated by any function of the form $(1-r)^s$, $r > 0$.

Recognizing the fundamental random-walk behavior in both the factor price and factor demand series is also important in the identification of time series processes. In applications of the linear-quadratic control framework, many authors model the detrended price series as a VAR(1) process. A VAR(1) fitted to random-walk data will show very significant coefficients and mislead the investigator into believing that the firm faces a nontrivial forecasting problem. In addition, the identification of the joint factor demand–factor price process is hampered by the random-walk behavior. As Granger and Newbold (1974) have pointed out, spurious relationships can be detected between even independent random walks. In our analysis, the data is first differenced before vector time series models are identified.

If the factor price series follow a random walk, the forecasting problem faced by the firm is trivial. The problem of estimating the factor demand system with rational expectations imposed degenerates to the simple static expectations model. In order to test formally the random-walk hypothesis, we embed the random walk in a richer class of VAR models and compute approximate posterior probabilities using an expression due to Schwartz (1978). We start with a VAR model for the differences of the factor price series. We approximate the posterior probability of the VAR(p) model using the Schwartz approximation:

$$\log(P_j = \text{probability of } j\text{th order model}) \approx \log \ell \mid_{\theta = \hat{\theta}_{\text{MLE}}} - \tfrac{1}{2} k_j \log \nu,$$

(3)

where k_j is the number of parameters in the model,

$$\theta' = (\text{vec}(\phi_1)', \ldots, \text{vec}(\phi_p)'),$$

and ν is the number of degrees of freedom. The conditional likelihood function for the VAR(p) model is the same as the multivariate regression model, and $\log \ell$ evaluated at the maximum-likelihood estimate reduces to the determinant of the residual variance–covariance matrix.

Table 1. *Values of Schwartz criterion*

	$\log\|\hat{\Sigma}\|$	S
Berndt and Wood data[a]		
Random walk	−14.31	214.7
Vector ARIMA(1, 1, 0)	−14.58	203.4
Vector ARIMA(2, 1, 0)	−14.90	179.1
Berndt and Christensen data[b]		
Random walk	−11.08	216.0
Vector ARIMA(1, 1, 0)	−11.78	202.9
Vector ARIMA(2, 1, 0)	−12.19	184.7

Note: $S = \log \ell(\theta = \hat{\theta}_{\text{MLE}}) - \frac{1}{2}k_j \log \nu$.
[a] U.S. manufacturing, 1947–77; capital and labor inputs.
[b] U.S. manufacturing, 1928–68; equipment, structures, and labor inputs.

The Schwartz criterion captures an explicit trade-off between goodness of fit and the complexity of the model. Schwartz has shown that this criterion is consistent in model selection, unlike the Akaike information criterion. The Schwartz adjustment for model complexity and sample size is particularly important in applications with a large number of parameters relative to the sample size.

Table 1 presents the values of the Schwartz criterion for both the BW and BC data. The random-walk model has the highest posterior probability in both the BW and BC data sets. Examination of residuals from the random-walk model fit to the BW data confirm the random-walk hypothesis. If factor prices follow a random walk and factor prices can be viewed as exogenous to the factor demand system, the forecasting problem faced by the firm and the imposition of the rational expectations hypothesis are radically simplified. In the comparison of models discussed in what follows, we will assume that the factor price vector follows a random walk with drift. Several studies of dynamic factor demand [see Epstein and Yatchew 1985 and Meese 1980 (quarterly data)] have used the BW data and use VAR models of one kind or another fit to the raw data. Incorrect identification of the time series process of factor prices leads to erroneous results when the rational expectations hypothesis is imposed.

In many studies of factor demand, the factor price series are assumed to be exogenous to the factor demand system. Before proceeding to compare alternative dynamic factor models, the hypothesis of exogeneity should be investigated. Without imposing exogeneity, the system of factor demands is not identified unless a supply-side model is appended, as in Kydland and Prescott (1982). Comparison of alternative equilibrium models is difficult since it is not possible to trace particular model inadequacies to differences in specification of preferences or technology. Exogeneity is a restriction on the joint factor demand–factor price time series process. To identify a time series model for both input and price series, a sequence of autoregressive models were fit to the data with careful examination of the model residuals. Evidence from the cross-correlation matrices of the residuals and from univariate diagnostics ruled out mixed models.

For the BW data set, a VAR(1) model on the differences was tentatively identified:

$$\begin{bmatrix} \Delta x_t \\ \Delta p_t \end{bmatrix} = \alpha + \begin{bmatrix} \phi_{11} & \phi_{12} \\ \phi_{21} & \phi_{22} \end{bmatrix} \begin{bmatrix} \Delta x_{t-1} \\ \Delta p_{t-1} \end{bmatrix} + \epsilon_t. \tag{4}$$

The hypothesis of exogeneity amounts to the restriction that $\phi_{21} = 0$. The posterior odds ratio for the hypothesis of exogeneity can be approximated by using the Schwartz criterion. The posterior odds ratio is the ratio of the posterior probabilities of each hypothesis [see the section on Bayesian approaches to hypothesis testing and Rossi (1984) for an exact approach to computing the posterior odds ratio for linear hypotheses in the multivariate regression model]:

$$-2 \log K \approx \chi_q^2 - q \log \nu, \tag{5}$$

where χ_q^2 is the likelihood ratio statistic, q is the number of restrictions, and $K = \Pr(H_0)/\Pr(H_1)$. In Table 2, approximate odds ratios are calculated for the hypothesis of exogeneity conditional on identification of the multiple time series model. For the BW data, the hypothesis of exogeneity is overwhelmingly favored. This finding is consistent with tests of exogeneity performed by Epstein and Yatchew. For the BC data, a VAR(2) model was identified, and the exogeneity restrictions are imposed on both autoregressive parameter matrices. In the BC case, the odds ratio is approximately 4:1 against the hypothesis of exogeneity. Although there is moderately strong evidence that exogeneity is unreasonable to assume for the BC data, the restricted model tracks the factor demand and price series with virtually the same residual properties as the unrestricted model. For the purposes of the testing of alternative models, exogeneity is retained as an assumption.

Finally, under the assumption of exogeneity, time series models were identified for the input process conditional on factor prices. The orders of the identified models can shed some light on the nature of the control problem that faces the firm. In the standard linear-quadratic set-up, the linear decision rule has an error term whose stochastic process is determined by the nature of the process governing technology shocks [see Hansen and Sargent 1980, equation (10)]. Although it is difficult to draw any

Table 2. *Posterior odds ratios for hypothesis of exogeneity*

	$\log\|\hat{\Sigma}\|$	S
Berndt and Wood data[a]		
Restricted VAR(1)	-10.37	122.5
Unrestricted VAR(1)	-10.39	113.8
Odds ratio:	$K = 6000$	
$H_0: \phi_{21} = 0$ (exogeneity restriction)		
$H_1: \phi_{21} \neq 0$		
Likelihood ratio test:		
LR = 0.58 ($\sim \chi^2$ with 4 degrees of freedom under null)		
Berndt and Christensen data[b]		
Restricted VAR(2)	-20.43	239.6
Unrestricted VAR(2)	-22.28	241.0
Odds ratio:	$K = 0.25$	
$H_0: \phi_{21}^1 = \phi_{21}^2 = 0$ (exogeneity)		
$H_a: \phi_{21}^1 \neq 0, \ \phi_{21}^2 \neq 0$		
Likelihood ratio test:		
LR = 68.45 ($\sim \chi^2$ with 18 degrees of freedom under null)		

Note: See equation (5) for approximation used in calculating odds ratio.
[a] U.S. manufacturing, 1947–77; capital and labor inputs.
[b] U.S. manufacturing, 1928–68; equipment, structures, and labor inputs.

conclusion in a general case, if the technology shocks are independent and identically distributed (i.i.d.), we would expect to find a first-order autoregressive process linking up the current values of labor and capital inputs to the first lag of inputs and a distributed lag of factor prices. Table 3 presents summary information on the posterior distribution of VAR parameters. The fact that a first-order process links the *differences* of inputs and input prices suggests that higher order mechanisms other than a simple adjustment model may be at work.

3   Model solutions and control rules

The essential challenge in the formulation of dynamic investment models is to formulate a model that will explain the procyclical nature of investment and the comovement of the shadow price of capital and the level of investment. The cost-of-adjustment approach first put forth by Lucas (1967) allows the shadow price of capital (q_t) and investment to move together over the business cycle. The standard neoclassical production function is modified by the addition of a cost-of-adjustment term:

Table 3. *Model parameter estimates*

Model: $\Delta x_t = \alpha_1 + \phi \Delta x_{t-1} + B_1 \Delta p_{t-1} + \epsilon_{1t}$

$\Delta p_t = \alpha_2 + B_2 \Delta p_{t-1} + \epsilon_{2t}$

Berndt and Wood data [a]

$$\hat{\phi} = \begin{bmatrix} L & K \\ \cdot & - \\ + & + \end{bmatrix} \qquad \hat{B}_1 = \begin{bmatrix} PL & PK \\ \cdot & \cdot \\ + & \cdot \end{bmatrix}$$

Berndt and Christensen data [b]

$$\hat{\phi} = \begin{bmatrix} L & E & S \\ \cdot & + & - \\ + & + & - \\ \cdot & + & \cdot \end{bmatrix} \qquad \hat{B}_1 = \begin{bmatrix} PL & PE & PS \\ + & + & \cdot \\ \cdot & \cdot & \cdot \\ \cdot & + & \cdot \end{bmatrix} \qquad \hat{B}_2 = \begin{bmatrix} PL & PE & PS \\ \cdot & + & \cdot \\ \cdot & \cdot & - \\ + & + & \cdot \end{bmatrix}$$

Note: +, posterior probability that parameter greater than 0 exceeds 0.75; −, posterior probability that parameter less than 0 exceeds 0.75. Posterior probabilities computed using a diffuse prior.
[a] U.S. manufacturing, 1947–77; capital and labor inputs.
[b] U.S. manufacturing, 1928–68; equipment, structures, and labor inputs.

$$y_t = f(k_t) - c(k_t - k_{t-1}) \quad \text{with} \quad c', c'' > 0,$$
$$k_t = (1 - \delta)k_{t-1} + i_t.$$

The linear-quadratic version of the cost-of-adjustment approach popularized by Sargent combines a quadratic production function with a quadratic adjustment cost term and a linear time series model for factor prices.
Firm problem:

$$\max_{\{x_t\}} E_0 \left\{ \sum_{t=0}^{\infty} \beta^t [y_t - w_t L_t - q_t(k_t - (1 - \delta)k_{t-1})] \right\} \tag{6}$$

subject to

$$y_t = x_t' A x_t + (k_t - k_{t-1})' D(k_t + k_{t-1}),$$
$$x_t' = (L_t, k_t),$$
$$D = \text{diag}(d),$$
$$p_t = \alpha + p_{t-1} + u_t, \qquad p_t' = (w_t, q_t').$$

Note that we do not include labor in the adjustment term. Many authors find that estimated adjustment costs are not convex in the change in labor input. Solution of this problem separates into the solution of the quadratic control problem coupled with solution of the linear prediction problem.
Linear decision rule:

$$x_t = \Theta x_{t-1} + \Gamma p_t + \epsilon_t. \tag{7}$$

In general, the parameters in the linear decision rule are complicated functions of the production technology parameters and the VAR parameters for the price process (see Chow 1975, e.g., for the derivation of matrix Ricatti equations). Of course, if the input price process follows a random walk, imposition of the rational expectations hypothesis amounts to imposing a static expectations hypothesis in which $E_t[p_{t+s}] = \alpha s + p_t$ (here α is a vector of drift parameters). The implication of optimizing behavior on the part of the firm is then only that the adjustment matrix Θ be symmetric.

Several empirical tests of the parametric restrictions implied by the cost-of-adjustment model coupled with rational expectations strongly reject the model. As Kydland and Prescott have noted, the simple first-order adjustment cost model is not consistent with the observed relationship between investment and lagged values of q_t. Higher order investment behavior can arise in a model in which the duration of investment projects is long relative to the length of the business cycle. If firms must precommit to capital projects several years before productive capital comes on-line, a complicated lagged relationship will exist between current investment and the history of previous investment projects. A linear-quadratic version of this time-to-build model can be easily postulated and solved for the decision rules. If the gestation lag of firm's capital is J periods (some studies indicate an average of 2 years may be appropriate), then the firm must decide how much to invest in new capital projects each time period. The firm's decision rule will depend on the current stock of productive capital, the distribution of completion times of current investment projects, and the firm's expectations of the future price of capital.

Firm problem:

$$\max_{\{s_{J,t}\}} E_0 \left\{ \sum_{t=0}^{\infty} \beta^t \left[y_t - w_t L_t - q_t \left(\sum_{1}^{J} \phi_i s_{i,t} \right) \right] \right\} \tag{8}$$

subject to

$$y_t = x_t' A x_t,$$
$$k_t = (1-\delta) k_{t-1} + s_{1,t-1},$$
$$s_{j,t} = s_{j+1,t-1}, \quad j = 1, \ldots, J-1.$$

In the time-to-build model, the investment good production technology is described by the sequence of ϕ weights and the length of gestation, J. Each period, the firm decides how many investment projects to start (or how much resources to devote to starting new projects expressed in terms of the output good). Here $s_{j,t}$ denotes amount of capital stock j periods from completion at time t. Once an investment project is started, the firm commits to devoting ϕ_j in resources in each of J periods before a unit of productive capital is produced. Total investment in any one period is $i_t = \sum \phi_j s_{j,t}$. The laws of motion of the system in (8) are linear and can be expressed as a first-order linear system by using an augmented state vector (see, e.g., Chow 1975). If we couple the control problem in (8) with some assumptions about the input price process, a linear decision rule can easily be derived.

Linear decision rule: Assuming as before that $p_t = \alpha + p_{t-1} + u_t$,

$$s_{J,t} = \Delta_1 k_t + \Delta_2 s_{1,t} + \cdots + \Delta_J s_{J-1,t} + \Gamma p_t. \tag{9}$$

To express this in terms of the observable capital stock measures, we recognize that

$$s_{j,t} = s_{1,t+j-1} = k_{t+j} - (1-\delta)k_{t+j-1} \equiv \dot{k}_{t+j}.$$

Substituting into the decision rule, we obtain

$$\dot{k}_t = \Delta_1 k_{t-J} + \Delta_2 \dot{k}_{t-J+1} + \cdots + \Delta_J \dot{k}_{t-1} + \Gamma p_t. \tag{10}$$

In the case studied here, $J = 2$, and we can rewrite (10) as

$$k_t = (I + \Delta_2)k_{t-1} + (\Delta_1 - I)k_{t-2} + \Gamma p_t.$$

The relationship between the unrestricted parameters of the linear decision rules given in (7) and (10) and the underlying parameters of the production technology and the price process involves a set of complicated nonlinear functional relationships. A strategy for comparison of the adjustment cost and time-to-build models must involve more than merely a test of these parametric restrictions against some vague, unrestricted alternative.

4 Bayesian approaches to comparison of nonnested dynamic models

The linear-quadratic version of the adjustment cost and time-to-build models should be regarded as approximations to the underlying production technology. The decision rules in (7) and (10) are two nonnested models of dynamic factor demand. One possible approach would be to nest the models by allowing for both costly adjustment and gestation lags in the investment process (see, e.g., Park 1983). In order to more clearly distinguish between the features of the two different approaches, we will not nest the models. Comparisons between these models should be based on the relative performance of the two models, recognizing that both models are only approximations to the underlying technology. The econometric problems involved in comparing nonnested hypotheses are further complicated by the complex nonlinear restrictions imposed on the linear decision rule by the rational expectations hypothesis. Furthermore, small sample sizes make it difficult to routinely apply large-sample approximations to the distribution of test statistics.

Work on nonnested hypothesis testing in econometrics has centered on the likelihood ratio approach suggested by Cox (1961). Aguirre-Torres and Gallant (1982) consider the distribution of the generalized likelihood ratio test for comparison of alternative multivariate nonlinear regression models. Singleton (1984) considers a testing procedure very similar to the likelihood ratio procedure for comparison of nonnested models.

The central problem with the classical approaches to nonnested hypothesis testing is the assumption that one of the models under scrutiny is the true population model that generates the data. In production modeling, the linear-quadratic model is only an approximation to the underlying technology. We are interested in which form provides a better approximation to the dynamic behavior of factor demand. The Bayesian procedures are specifically designed to address the approximation issue. The Bayesian approach is very much in the spirit of Efron's (1984) comparison of mean-squared errors for competing linear regression models. Other key problems with the classical approach stem from the artificial designation of models as the maintained, or "null," and the alternative models. The assignment of models to the null and alternative hypotheses dramatically influences the outcomes of nonnested hypothesis testing procedures. This sensitivity is due to the asymmetry of the Neyman–Pearson approach to hypothesis testing. Type I and type II errors should be regarded symmetrically in the comparison of nonnested hypotheses. The "accept–reject" philosophy of classical sampling procedures is also difficult to adapt to hypothesis-testing problems in economics. Very rarely do we have enough sample evidence to either conclusively affirm or reject any particular model or restriction. Instead, we accumulate a body of evidence from many different studies as to the adequacy of any particular model. The testing procedures should provide a method of aggregating information across many diverse studies.

In the Bayesian approach to hypothesis evaluation, the posterior probabilities of alternative hypotheses are compared. The posterior probabilities represent the weight of prior belief and sample evidence for or against a particular hypothesis. The posterior probabilities of hypotheses can be conveniently summarized in the posterior odds ratio. The posterior odds ratio for the comparison of two hypotheses H_1 and H_2 can be written as

$$K_{12} = \frac{p(H_1 \mid D)}{p(H_2 \mid D)} = \frac{p(D \mid H_1)}{p(D \mid H_2)} \cdot \frac{p(H_1)}{p(H_2)}, \tag{11}$$

where D stands for the data. The quantity $p(H_1)/p(H_2)$ is called the prior odds ratio and may be taken to be one-to-one for a "reference" prior. For parametric models, the posterior odds ratio can be expressed as the ratio of the predictive densities of the data for each of the two models:

$$K_{12} = \frac{\int p_1(D, \phi_1) \, d\phi_1}{\int p_2(D, \phi_2) \, d\phi_2} \cdot \Pi_{12}$$

$$= \frac{\int p_1(D \mid \phi_1) p_1(\phi_1) \, d\phi_1}{\int p_2(D \mid \phi_2) p_2(\phi_2) \, d\phi_2} \cdot \Pi_{12}, \tag{12}$$

where $p_1(D \mid \phi_1)$ is the data density under H_1 and $p_2(D \mid \phi_2)$ is the data density under H_2. The term Π_{12} is the prior odds ratio. By integrating out the parameters from the joint distribution of the data and the parameters, we obtain the predictive density of the data for each of the two models. The posterior odds ratio is the ratio of the predictive densities evaluated at the observed data point. The predictive densities can be used as diagnostic tools by comparing the properties of the predictive density with the data distribution. Note that the Bayesian approach extends without modification to the choice between nonnested alternatives.

The Bayesian approach to nonnested hypothesis testing has three distinct advantages over the classical approach:

1. No approximations are required; inference is exact.
2. An accept–reject philosophy is avoided, and information from different studies can be aggregated.
3. The asymmetric treatment of the null, or "maintained," model and the alternative model is avoided.

The key ingredients for the successful application of the posterior odds ratio are the formulation of a reasonable prior that does not unwittingly favor either of the models and a method for evaluating the appropriate integrals.

In Rossi (1985), solutions are offered for each of these problems in the context of the comparison of two multivariate linear regressions. Priors on the regression coefficient matrices and the share covariance matrix are constructed to relatively diffuse and centered over a Cobb–Douglas specification. The prior covariance matrices of the regression coefficients are assessed using the g-prior idea of Zellner (1980). The g-priors are chosen so that the prior specification is locally uniform. Klein and Brown (1984) utilize limiting arguments to construct "uninformative" priors. Unfortunately, the odds ratios derived by Klein and Brown are sensitive to the way in which the limits are taken.

The results given in Rossi (1985) cannot be directly applied to the problem choice between alternative dynamic models. The nonlinear restrictions imposed by the rational expectations hypothesis make the process of prior assessment and integration required to compute the posterior odds ratio difficult. To isolate the central features of the econometric problem and facilitate reference to the literature, let us introduce a new notation for decision rules (7) and (10). To compare two linear decision rules, two restricted multivariate regressions are compared:

$$
\left.\begin{aligned}
\mathbf{y}'_{1t} &= \mathbf{x}'_{1t} B_1 + \mathbf{u}'_{1t} \\
\mathbf{y}'_{2t} &= \mathbf{x}'_{2t} B_2 + \mathbf{u}'_{2t}
\end{aligned}\right\} \quad \mathbf{u}'_{it} \sim \mathrm{MVN}(0, \Sigma),
$$

$$
\mathbf{y}'_{1t} = (L_t, \mathbf{k}'_t, \mathbf{p}'_t), \quad \mathbf{x}'_{1t} = (\mathbf{k}'_{t-1}, \mathbf{p}'_{t-1}),
$$

$$
\mathbf{y}'_{2t} = (L_t, \mathbf{k}'_t, \mathbf{p}'_t), \quad \mathbf{x}'_{2t} = (\mathbf{k}'_{t-1}, \mathbf{k}'_{t-2}, \mathbf{p}'_{t-1}).
$$

$$(13)$$

In (13), the Y matrix consists of observations on factor demand and factor prices, and the X matrix is made up of lagged factor demand and factor price variables. We will use conditional likelihood functions for the time series processes throughout the analysis. We do not allow for productivity shocks, which would introduce a moving-average error component into the multivariate system. The matrix of coefficients, B, is linked with the parameters of the production process and the factor price process through a set of nonlinear restrictions:

$$
\mathrm{vec}(B_i) = f_i(\theta_i), \quad i = 1, 2, \tag{14}
$$

where θ_i is typically of much lower dimension than the parameter space of the vector autoregression due to the overidentifying restrictions of the rational expectations hypothesis.

Simple and reasonable assessment of priors for key system parameters is critical in the formulation of practical Bayesian hypothesis-testing procedures. The strategy we follow for assessment of priors in this problem is to split the sample into two parts and use an informative prior based on the first portion of the sample to compute the posterior odds ratio for the second half of the sample. Partition Y_i and X_i into two submatrices corresponding to the subsamples and compute the posterior distribution of θ_i given the first sample:

$$
p(\theta_i, \Sigma \mid Y_{1i}, X_{1i}) \propto p(\theta_i, \Sigma) \ell(\theta_i, \Sigma \mid Y_{1i}, X_{1i}),
$$

$$
Y_i = \begin{bmatrix} Y_{1i} \\ Y_{2i} \end{bmatrix}, \quad X_i = \begin{bmatrix} X_{1i} \\ X_{2i} \end{bmatrix}, \tag{15}
$$

$$
\ell(\theta_i, \Sigma \mid Y_{1i}, X_{1i}) \propto \|\Sigma\|^{-T/2} \exp\{-\tfrac{1}{2}(y_{1i} - Z_{1i} f(\theta_i))'(\Sigma \otimes I_T)^{-1}(\cdot)\}.
$$

Here $Z_{1i} = (I_m \otimes X_{1i})$, and $y_{1i} = \mathrm{vec}(Y_{1i})$. We employ the standard diffuse prior on (θ_i, Σ):

$$
p(\theta_i, \Sigma) \propto \|\Sigma\|^{-(m+1)/2}.
$$

The nonlinearity of the function mapping θ_i to B_i precludes analytical analysis of this posterior distribution. However, we can easily approximate this posterior distribution by a normal asymptotic approximation:

$$p(\theta_i \mid Y_{1i}, X_{1i}) \doteq \text{MVN}(\hat{\theta}_i, I(\theta_i)^{-1} \mid_{\theta_i = \hat{\theta}_i}), \tag{16}$$

where $I(\theta_i)$ is the information matrix and $\hat{\theta}_i$ is the maximum-likelihood estimator (MLE), which is the mode of the posterior distribution. This posterior distribution given in (16), which is based on the fist part of the sample, is used as an informative prior for the second part of the sample. [An alternative procedure in which the posterior mean and variance matrix given in (16) are scaled so that the predictive distribution of the first observation of the second part of the sample given the first half has approximately the same first and second moments for both models yields much the same results in this example.] The virtue of using the first sample partition to generate an approximate posterior is that this removes the problem of assessing the high-dimensional prior covariance matrix for the θ_i vector.

To compute the posterior odds ratio for the second half of the sample, we must evaluate the integrals:

$$\int p(\theta_i, \Sigma) \ell(\theta_i, \Sigma \mid Y_{2i}, X_{2i}) \, d\theta_i \, d\Sigma, \quad i = 1, 2, \tag{17}$$

where (θ_i, Σ) are taken a priori independent with θ_i distributed according to (16) and Σ diffuse. To evaluate the integrals in (17) for each of the competing models, Monte Carlo numerical integration techniques are used. The Monte Carlo integration technique views the integral as taking the expectation of the integrand with respect to a uniform distribution of the arguments. To evaluate $I = \int f(\beta) \, d\beta$, it seems reasonable to approximate I by drawing random β vectors from some bounded subset of the parameter space and simply computing the sample mean, $\hat{I} = \sum f(\beta^i)/N$. If the β^i are drawn uniformly, many sample points will be associated with very small values of the integrand. In this chapter, we use a variation of the importance sampling technique in which the points are not sampled uniformly but according to the distribution of an importance function taken equal to a multivariate student t distribution with mean equal to the posterior mode and variance–covariance matrix proportional to the inverse of the information matrix evaluated at the posterior mode. Details of this procedure and a comparison with other numerical integration techniques can be found in Zellner and Rossi (1984).

The odds ratio is computed by forming the ratio of the estimates of the integrals given in equation (17):

$$\hat{K} = \frac{\hat{I}_1}{\hat{I}_2}, \quad \text{where } I_i = \int p(\theta_i, \Sigma) \ell(\theta_i, \Sigma \mid Y_{2i}, X_{2i}) \, d\theta_i \, d\Sigma.$$

These integrals are approximated by drawing from the importance sampling distribution with density proportional to $I(\cdot)$. Estimates of the integrals are simply a sum of the weights, which are the ratio of the integrand to the importance function:

$$\hat{I}_i = \sum_j w_i(\theta_i^j, \Sigma^j), \quad w_i = p(\theta_i^j, \Sigma^j) \frac{\ell(\theta_i^j, \Sigma^j \mid Y_{2i}, X_{2i})}{I(\theta_i^j, \Sigma^j)}.$$

Regarding $\hat{I}_i$ as a sample moment, we can conclude that $\hat{I}_i$ is strongly consistent for I_i and that $\mathrm{Var}(\hat{I}_i) = \sigma^2/n$, where $\sigma^2 = \mathrm{Var}(w(\theta, \Sigma))$. A consistent estimate of the $\mathrm{Var}(w(\theta, \Sigma))$ can be obtained from the sample second moment. These importance sampling calculations are somewhat different from the standard approach [see Zellner and Rossi (1984) and Geweke (1986) for applications of importance sampling in calculating the posterior distribution of model parameters]. In the hypothesis-testing application, a normalized density function is used, and we are integrating out the parameters rather than calculating the posterior expectation of a function of the model parameters.

The standard error of the numerical approximation of K can be computed using the delta method:

$$\mathrm{Var}(\hat{K}) \approx \frac{\hat{I}_1^2\, \mathrm{Var}(\hat{I}_2) + \hat{I}_2^2\, \mathrm{Var}(\hat{I}_1)}{(\hat{I}_2)^4}. \tag{18}$$

To compare the cost-of-adjustment and time-to-build models, the techniques described are used to evaluate the integrals in (18) for both the BW and BC data. One-third of the sample is used in assessing the prior, and two-thirds is used for computation of the odds ratio. Since the time series are extremely short for these models, the prior assessed is very diffuse, and we should not expect overwhelming evidence either in favor of or against any particular model. A time-to-build model with a gestation lag of 2 years is used. Table 4 gives the posterior distribution of the technology parameters based on the entire sample.

Table 5 presents odds ratio calculations for both the BW and BC data. For the simple two-input case, the time-to-build specification is favored approximately 2:1 over a first-order cost-of-adjustment model. Similarly, in the BC data, the time-to-build specification is favored over the simple cost-of-adjustment model, although the odds are hardly overwhelming. There is some evidence that a time-to-build model should be applied to both equipment and structures. The clear impression from the results on both data sets is that the time-to-build model is useful in capturing the dynamic properties of factor demand. In addition, even with a relatively small number of draws, the importance sampling numerical integration procedure approximates the integrals and odds ratios very well. With 15,000 draws (which takes only a few hours of PC-AT time), we can achieve one significant digit of accuracy, which is sufficient for judging the relative merits of the models. Low variation in the importance sam-

Table 4. *Posterior distribution[a] of model parameters*

Cost-of-adjustment model

Berndt and Wood data (labor and capital inputs)
$a_{LL} = 0.031$ (0.012)
$a_{KK} = 0.011$ (0.0081)
$a_{LK} = -0.027$ (0.011)
$d_K = 0.035$ (0.015)

Berndt and Christensen data (labor, equipment, and structures)
$a_{LL} = 0.042$ (0.029)
$a_{EE} = 0.015$ (0.021)
$a_{SS} = 0.026$ (0.014)
$a_{LE} = -0.021$ (0.019)
$a_{LS} = -0.024$ (0.013)
$a_{SE} = 0.019$ (0.0091)
$d_S = 0.051$ (0.031)
$d_E = 0.016$ (0.025)

Gestation lag model

Berndt and Wood data (labor and capital inputs)
$a_{LL} = 0.032$ (0.014)
$a_{KK} = 0.045$ (0.0070)
$a_{LK} = -0.015$ (0.0097)
$\phi^b = 0.43$ (0.39)

Berndt and Christensen data (labor, equipment, and structures)
$a_{LL} = 0.061$ (0.021)
$a_{EE} = 0.023$ (0.013)
$a_{SS} = 0.015$ (0.0088)
$a_{LE} = -0.031$ (0.033)
$a_{LS} = -0.015$ (0.012)
$a_{SE} = 0.025$ (0.010)
$\phi_E = 0.47$ (0.21)
$\phi_S = 0.68$ (0.15)

Note: Numbers in parentheses are posterior standard deviations.
[a] Based on asymptotic approximation to posterior distribution.
[b] The gestation lag is 2 years; ϕ is portion of total investment committed for first year of project.

pling weights suggests that the multivariate student t importance function approximates the posterior very well.

5　Conclusion

We have demonstrated in this chapter that Bayesian techniques for comparison of alternative dynamic models are feasible and yield useful results

Table 5. *Odds ratios for comparison of cost-of-adjustment and time-to-build models*

Berndt and Wood data (labor and capital inputs)
H_1: first-order cost of adjustment
H_2: time to build on capital (gestation lag 2 years)
$K_{12} = 0.59$ (0.03)
Berndt and Christensen data (labor, equipment, and structures)
H_1: first-order cost of adjustment
H_2: time to build on structures only (gestation lag 2 years)
H_3: time to build on both structures and equipment
$K_{12} = 0.71$ (0.02) $K_{13} = 0.63$ (0.02)

Note: Odds ratios computed by evaluating equation (19) with importance sampling Monte Carlo numerical integration; 15,000 points samples; standard errors of numerical integration are in parentheses.

when applied to factor demand data. Bayesian approaches are very useful for the comparison of the relative performance of alternative models even when these models do not exhaust the set of plausible economic models. This new approach is made feasible by the use of numerical integration techniques that can be applied to relatively high dimensional nonlinear models in a straightforward manner.

Further research on the use of Bayesian techniques for predictive evaluation of alternative models should focus on computing the n-step-ahead predictive distributions. By simulating these distributions, the researcher can compare the implied time series properties of the model and compare these properties with the sample information. This would formalize the model calibration techniques of Kydland and Prescott. Recent work by Thompson and Miller (forthcoming) for unrestricted univariate models could be extended to the problem of restricted multivariate time series models.

REFERENCES

Altug, S. 1985. "Gestation Lags and the Business Cycle." Working paper, University of Minnesota.

Aquirre-Torres, V. and A. R. Gallant. 1982. "The Null and Non-null Asymptotic Distribution of the Cox Test for Multivariate Nonlinear Regression Alternatives and a New Distribution Free Cox Test." Working paper, North Carolina State University.

Barnett, W. 1983. "New Indices of the Money Supply and the Flexible Laurent Demand System." *Journal of Business and Economic Statistics* 1: 7–23.

Berndt, E. and L. Christensen. 1973. "The Translog Function and the Substitution of Equipment, Structures, and Labor in U.S. Manufacturing, 1929–69." *Journal of Econometrics* 1: 81–114.

Berndt, E. and D. Wood. 1975. "Technology, Prices and the Derived Demand for Energy." *Review of Economics and Statistics* 57: 259–68.

Berndt, E., M. Fuss, and L. Waverman. 1979. "A Dynamic Model of Costs of Adjustment and Interrelated Factor Demands." Working paper 7925, University of Toronto.

Chow, G. 1975. *Analysis and Control of Dynamic Economic Systems.* New York: Wiley.

Cox, D. R. 1961. "Tests of Separate Families of Distributions." In *Proceedings of the Fourth Berkeley Symposium on Mathematical Statistics and Probability,* Vol. 1. Berkeley: University of California Press.

Efron, B. 1984. "Comparing Non-nested Models." *Journal of the American Statistical Association* 79: 791–803.

Epstein, L. 1981. "Duality Theory and Functional Forms for Dynamic Factor Demands." *Review of Economics Studies* 48: 81–95.

Epstein, L. and A. Yatchew. 1985. "The Empirical Determination of Technology and Expectations: A Simplified Procedure." *Journal of Econometrics* 27: 235–58.

Gallant, A. R. 1982. "Unbiased Determination of Production Technologies." *Journal of Econometrics* 20: 285–324.

Geweke, J. 1986. "Bayesian Inference in Econometric Models Using Monte Carlo Integration." Working paper, Duke University.

Granger, C. and P. Newbold. 1974. "Spurious Regressions in Econometrics." *Journal of Econometrics* 2: 111–20.

Hansen, L. and T. Sargent. 1980. "Formulating and Estimating Dynamic Linear Rational Expectations Models." *Journal of Economic Dynamics and Control* 2: 7–46.

Kennan, J. 1979. "The Estimation of Partial Adjustment Models with Rational Expectations." *Econometrica* 47: 1441–56.

Kydland, F. and E. Prescott. 1982. "Time to Build and Aggregate Fluctuations." *Econometrica* 50: 1345–71.

Lucas, R. E. 1967. "Adjustment Costs and the Theory of Supply." *Journal of Political Economy* 75: 321–34.

Meese, R. 1980. "Dynamic Factor Demand Schedules for Labor and Capital under Rational Expectations." *Journal of Econometrics* 14: 141–58.

Morrison, C. J. 1982. "Three Essays on the Dynamic Analysis of Demand for Factors of Production." Ph.D. dissertation, University of British Columbia.

Park, J. 1983. "Gestation Lags with Variable Plans: An Empirical Study of Aggregate Investment." Ph.D. dissertation, Carnegie-Mellon University.

Pindyck, R. and T. Rotemberg. 1983. "Dynamic Factor Demands and the Effects of Energy Price Shocks." *American Economic Review* 73: 1066–79.

Rossi, P. 1984. "Specification and Analysis of Econometric Production Models." Ph.D. dissertation, University of Chicago.

   1985. "Comparison of Alternative Functional Forms in Production." *Journal of Econometrics* 30: 345–61.

Sargent, T. 1978. "Estimation of Dynamic Labour Demand Schedules under Rational Expectations." *Journal of Political Economy* 86: 1009–44.

Schwartz, G. 1978. "Estimating the Dimension of a Model." *Annals of Statistics* 6: 461–4.

Singleton, K. 1984. "Testing Specifications of Economic Agents' Intertemporal Optimum Problems Against Non-nested Alternatives." Working paper, Carnegie-Mellon University.

Thompson, P. and R. Miller. Forthcoming. "Simulating the Future." *Journal of Business and Economic Statistics.*

Zellner, A. 1980. "On Bayesian Regression Analysis with g-Prior Distributions." Working paper, University of Chicago.

Zellner, A. and P. Rossi. 1984. "Bayesian Analysis of Dichotomous Quantal Response Models." *Journal of Econometrics* 25: 365–93.